Creating Portland

Revisiting New England: The New Regionalism

SERIES EDITORS

Siobhan Senier, University of New Hampshire
Darren Ranco, Dartmouth College
Adam Sweeting, Boston University
David H. Watters, University of New Hampshire

This series presents fresh discussions of the distinctiveness of New England culture. The editors seek manuscripts examining the history of New England regionalism; the way its culture came to represent American national culture as a whole; the interaction between that "official" New England culture and the people who lived in the region; and local, subregional, or even biographical subjects as microcosms that explicitly open up and consider larger issues. The series welcomes new theoretical and historical perspectives and is designed to cross disciplinary boundaries and appeal to a wide audience.

Richard Archer, *Fissures in the Rock: New England in the Seventeenth Century*
Judith Bookbinder, *Boston Modern: Figurative Expressionism as Alternative Modernism*
Donna M. Cassidy, *Marsden Hartley: Race, Region, and Nation*
Joseph A. Conforti, editor, *Creating Portland: History and Place in Northern New England*
Nancy L. Gallagher, *Breeding Better Vermonters: The Eugenics Project in Vermont*
Sidney V. James, *The Colonial Metamorphoses in Rhode Island: A Study of Institutions in Change*
Maureen Elgersman Lee, *Black Bangor: African Americans in a Maine Community, 1880–1950*
Christopher J. Lenney, *Sightseeking: Clues to the Landscape History of New England*
Donald W. Linebaugh, *The Man Who Found Thoreau: Roland W. Robbins and the Rise of Historical Archaeology in America*
Pauleena MacDougall, *The Penobscot Dance of Resistance: Tradition in the History of a People*
T. A. Milford, *The Gardiners of Massachusetts: Provincial Ambition and British-American Career*
Diana Muir, *Reflections in Bullough's Pond: Economy and Ecosystem in New England*
James C. O'Connell, *Becoming Cape Cod: Creating a Seaside Resort*
Priscilla Paton, *Abandoned New England: Landscape in the Works of Homer, Frost, Hopper, Wyeth, and Bishop*
Jennifer C. Post, *Music in Rural New England Family and Community Life, 1870–1940*
David L. Richards, *Poland Spring: A Tale of the Gilded Age, 1860–1900*
Mark J. Sammons and Valerie Cunningham, *Black Portsmouth: Three Centuries of African American Heritage*
Adam Sweeting, *Beneath the Second Sun: A Cultural History of Indian Summer*

Creating PORTLAND

History and Place
in Northern
New England

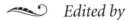 *Edited by*

Joseph A. Conforti

University of New Hampshire Press
Durham, New Hampshire

PUBLISHED BY
UNIVERSITY PRESS OF NEW ENGLAND
HANOVER AND LONDON

University of New Hampshire Press
Published by University Press of New England,
One Court Street, Lebanon, NH 03766
www.upne.com
© 2005 by University of New Hampshire Press
Printed in the United States of America

5 4 3 2 1

LIBRARY OF CONGRESS CATALOGING-IN-PUBLICATION DATA

Creating Portland : history and place in northern New England / edited by Joseph
   A. Conforti.
      p.   cm. — (Revisiting New England)
   Includes index.
   ISBN-13: 978–1–58465–521–3 (cloth : alk. paper)
   ISBN-10: 1–58465–521–6 (cloth : alk. paper)
   1. Portland (Me.)—History. 2. Portland (Me.)—Intellectual life. 3. Portland
   (Me.)—Economic conditions. 4. Portland (Me.)—Social conditions.
   I. Conforti, Joseph A. II. Series.
   F29.P9C73 2005
   974.1'91—dc22   2005020243

*For the University of Southern Maine community,
and especially for the students and alumni of the graduate
program in American and New England Studies*

Contents

Acknowledgments

This book is a study of Portland as a New England community rather than a detailed local history. The idea for the volume originated with Robert Gormley, former Editor-in-Chief at Northeastern University Press. Bob invited us to submit a proposal on Portland as a New England place and then offered us a contract. Before the manuscript was finalized, the Northeastern administration decided to close the press as an independent publisher. Bob remained committed to the project and contacted other presses on its behalf. We are much indebted to him. We are also very pleased that the University Press of New England saw the value of the book and offered us a new contract. At UPNE, we have benefited from the encouragement and sound advice of our editor, Phyllis Deutsch. It has been a pleasure to work with her.

Others have had a hand in the completion of this book. Readers of our proposal and of the final manuscript made numerous suggestions, many of which we followed, that have improved the book. At the University of Southern Maine, Provost Joseph Wood, himself a distinguished historical geographer of New England, strongly supported this project from the start. His office provided funding for the preparation of maps and illustrations and the completion of the index. The University also granted me a sabbatical leave to finish this book and another volume. Without the contribution of Madeleine Winterfalcon, administrative assistant par excellence, this book would not have been completed in a timely fashion, if at all. We are all grateful for her patience, efficiency, and technological skill. I would also like to thank Robin O'Sullivan, my former graduate assistant, for all of her help gathering material for parts of this book.

Finally, this book is dedicated to the community of people who make USM such an interesting place and to the students and alumni of the American and New England Studies program who, over nearly two decades, have explored with us the issues and approaches that inform this book and have made teaching at USM enjoyable.

Introduction

Placing Portland

Joseph A. Conforti

Like the brick and granite architecture that defines its historic maritime core, Portland is a blend of often complementary elements. The city is a composite of natives and newcomers, of Maine unpretentiousness and urban sophistication, of Downeast individualism and New England civic-mindedness, of Old Port boutiques and a working waterfront, of dense city wards on a narrow peninsula and "suburban" neighborhoods shaped first by streetcar lines and then by automobiles. Rising westward above island-studded Casco Bay, Portland endures as one of New England's most attractive cities. It has also been recognized as one of the region's most livable places. A financial and cultural center for northern New England, Portland boasts many of the amenities of a city much larger than its population of approximately 64,000. Twenty years ago, after the revival of the Old Port maritime district, *New England Monthly* magazine devoted a cover story to Portland as the "best" city in New England. "Imagine a city with a rich cultural life, a spectacular physical setting, an enormous wealth of old buildings, [and] a host of fine restaurants . . . ," the magazine enthused. "Imagine a city 'Too Good to be True.'"[1]

Of course Portland is no city upon a hill. *New England Monthly*'s influential portrait of the city, geared to the magazine's upscale readers, slighted urban problems. Portland is not plagued by a high crime rate or rush-hour traffic jams, but the handsome city by the sea has continued to grapple with stubborn urban ills: poverty, homelessness, high rents, escalating property values, and hefty property taxes.

Yet Portland remains among New England's most attractive cities, and a recent national report underscores its appeal. Between 1995 and

2000, the city ranked among the top ten places in the country in the rate of growth among newcomers who were young college graduates.[2] Portland has continued to draw mid-career professionals, gay people, and retirees in search of Maine's often invoked quality of life. In recent years such transplants have been joined in Portland by immigrants from Africa, Central America, and Southeast Asia. At the same time, as a destination in its own right and a gateway to Maine's fabled rockbound coast, Portland is sought out each year by tourists from across the region, nation, and world.

Despite the city's historic importance and abiding prominence in New England as well as its continuing appeal to newcomers and tourists, we have no up-to-date study of how Portland became Portland. That is, we have no broad understanding of Portland's layered past and how history, geography, and public policy have created one of New England's most habitable places. The original essays in this volume stretch across four centuries, but they do not pretend to offer a comprehensive history of the city. Rather, the essays focus on the physical, social, and cultural landscapes that have structured Portland as a real and imagined place. Historians know that the past never repeats itself in exactly the same way. They also realize that the "history of one place is never quite that of another place."[3]

As residential and commercial landscapes throughout the nation grow increasingly interchangeable, the study of place has become a burgeoning field of interdisciplinary analysis. On one level the sense of place is personal and experiential. It is the product of accumulated lived experience in a particular locale, an often "unreflective immersion in or movement through" a familiar landscape.[4] Even Henry David Thoreau, who was deeply reflective about place, acknowledged how quickly he beat a well-worn path from his hut to Walden Pond. Through family life, work, and recreation we habitually inscribe our experience into place.

Still, the sense of place involves far more than personal associations on a particular landscape. Physical geography and the built environment shape our relationship to a place, as do the stories that are told about a locale's history. In other words, place is shared, public, communal space—a terrain distinguished by nature's bestowals and layers of human activity. The essays that follow examine how geography, history, and public policy have shaped Portland on the ground and how writers and artists have represented the city as a place of the imagination.

Whatever distinctiveness Portland acquired and retains, the city is, like all places, a patchwork of material and mental landscapes that have changed over time.

Place: From Geography to Public Memory

Studies of place often begin with physical geography. Nature sets "boundaries" to and creates "possibilities" for human activity.[5] Consider Portland. The modern city was originally part of colonial Falmouth, which included present-day Cape Elizabeth, South Portland, Westbrook, and Falmouth. Portland was incorporated as a town in 1786. What became Portland was known for most of the eighteenth century as "the Neck," an apt description of the geography of colonial Falmouth's maritime center. The Neck identified a peninsula that was three miles long and of varying width, averaging about three-quarters of a mile. Two hills, later named Munjoy and Bramhall, presided over the eastern and western ends of the peninsula (Figure I-1).

Geography created the possibilities for a successful maritime economy. Portland is only three and a half miles from open ocean. It has a deep channel that usually does not freeze over in winter and a protected harbor along the Fore River, which borders the southern side of the peninsula. Other natural advantages underpinned the rise of Falmouth Neck and then Portland as an entrepot—a place where goods are exchanged. The location of the port linked it to a hinterland that eventually included Canada. Merchants on the peninsula were amply supplied with farm products which they shipped to markets throughout the Atlantic world. They also imported and produced goods that were distributed to markets in a backcountry that extended to Canada.

Geography bestowed other natural advantages on the peninsula that laid a foundation for commercial prosperity. The port's proximity to Maine's extensive forests not only made lumber an important commodity of trade. Forests supplied abundant masts and inexpensive timber for shipbuilding; they furnished the raw material for the peninsula's wooden maritime infrastructure of wharves, warehouses, and ropewalks; and they provided the material for the crates and barrels in which goods were shipped.[6] Fish was one of those trade goods. The retreat of the last glacier over 15,000 years ago sculpted the New England coast and left behind fishing banks from the Gulf of Maine to Cape Cod. Glacial

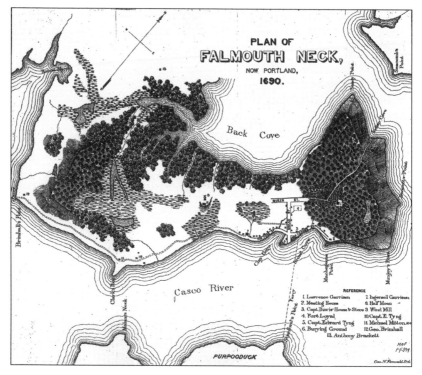

Figure I-1. "Plan of Falmouth Neck, Now Portland, 1690." Collections of Maine Historical Society, Map FF 394.

deposits and a rising sea created relatively shallow water in places. At these banks light penetrated to the ocean floor creating abundant plant life on which fish thrived.

Geography and natural endowments do not make a place. They set physical limits and define the prospects for human habitation in a locale. People transform space into place. A landscape embroidered by generations of human activity, place is an historical artifact. It is a terrain that bears the imprint of the past and present—a layered record of a people's history that is revealed in the built environment.

Portland's rise as a maritime entrepot in the nineteenth century, for example, was not simply a consequence of geography and natural resources. The city's prosperity hinged on the willingness of commercial developers and civic leaders to alter the peninsula's topography. Throughout nineteenth-century New England, coastal communities

relied on tons of fill to expand waterfronts, reshape shorelines, and promote the maritime economy. Portlanders significantly modified all four
sides of the peninsula, reconfiguring nature's endowment and creating
the contour of today's city core.

In 1847, led by John Poor, a railroad promoter and former lawyer,
Portland won the competition to become the winter port for Canada,
whose St. Lawrence River froze for five months of the year. With the
backing of the city and the financial support of local businessmen the
Atlantic and St. Lawrence Railroad connecting Portland and Montreal
was completed in 1853. The 292 miles of track with a terminus on the
Portland waterfront was leased to the Grand Trunk Railway of Canada.
Construction of this railroad transformed Portland's waterfront and
the city's position as an entrepot. Even before the railroad was completed, local leaders used fill to extend the shore and lay out a new
thoroughfare that all but obliterated coves where shipbuilding had been
located for a century. Commercial Street—more than a mile long, one
hundred feet wide, with tracks running down its middle—linked the
Grand Trunk line with the Maine Central and Boston and Maine railways further west on the peninsula.

The construction of Commercial Street facilitated the handling and
shipment by rail of an increased volume of goods. In particular, Portland became an outlet for Canadian grain, and the Grand Trunk Railway built the first of its three towering grain elevators on the waterfront
in 1875. The new wharves, warehouses, and businesses that crowded
Commercial Street reflected Portland's emergence as a railroad center, a
land and water transportation-distribution node for a regional hinterland that crossed national borders.[7]

On the northern side of the peninsula, opposite from Commercial
Street and the city's protected harbor, mid-nineteenth-century Portlanders redrew the shoreline of the saltwater inlet known as Back Cove.
In the eighteenth century, tapered Falmouth Neck accommodated only
three major streets that ran east to west on the peninsula parallel to the
harbor and tidal Back Cove: Fore, Middle, and Back (Congress)
streets. Two more streets (Cumberland and Oxford) were added in the
early nineteenth century, but the narrow neck left little land for expansion. In 1857, five years after the construction of Commercial Street,
the city broadened the back side of what had been Falmouth Neck.
Back Cove mud flats were filled in and two new streets were built.
Manufacturing and processing industries clustered around the tidal

inlet and the Portland and Rochester Railroad ran near the new shore-line to its depot on land that had been under water. Tons of rock and soil continued to be poured into Back Cove, reducing its original size by at least half and giving birth to a drab industrial district.[8] Civic efforts begun in the late nineteenth century to reclaim Back Cove from industrial blight persist today with plans for redevelopment of the area known as Bayside.

From nature's endowments nineteenth-century Portlanders also fashioned new civic and residential landscapes that continue to define the city. On Munjoy and Bramhall hills, which bracketed the peninsula, the city initiated Eastern and Western Promenades in 1836. They laid out roads that gave Portlanders access to scenic vistas of Casco Bay and the rolling countryside that stretched west to New Hampshire. Eventually, well-designed public parks graced both promenades. In 1879 the city acquired the Deering family estate between the Western Promenade and Back Cove that embraced one of the original farms of colonial Falmouth. For tax considerations, the Deering family gave the city acres of wooded and cleared land for a public park. Within a decade the shaded paths, duck pond, swan boat, and band concerts of "Deering Oaks" drew increasing numbers of residents from the peninsula's growing neighborhoods. By the end of the nineteenth century, with the enlargement of the Promenades and Deering Oaks and the creation of Lincoln Park between the mercantile district and Munjoy Hill, the compact peninsula acquired a distinctive combination of dense commercial and residential development and impressive open public spaces.[9]

As some of the essays in this volume document, both working-class neighborhoods with clear racial and ethnic profiles and upper-class enclaves spread across the peninsula, from the Eastern to the Western promenades in the second half of the nineteenth century. Sugar baron John Bundy Brown spearheaded both commercial development in the port and residential settlement of Bramhall Hill, which came to be known as the West End. In the 1840s, Brown expanded his Portland Sugar Works on the waterfront into an eight-story refinery that employed a thousand workers. The former New Hampshire farmboy opened what was described as "the finest hotel in Maine" in 1868.[10] The elegant six-story Victorian Falmouth Hotel, built of stone and brick, rose on Middle Street, the heart of the city's mercantile "exchange." Brown's financial empire and impact on the Portland peninsula included real estate development. He acquired vast acreage on the West

End, built a lavish villa, which he called "Bramhall," and developed into a fashionable residential neighborhood what had been a rural patch of the peninsula that ended at the Western Promenade.

When Portland began constructing the Promenade in 1836, some taxpayers complained that it was a waste of money because the site was too far removed from the homes of most inhabitants of the peninsula. The introduction of the horse-drawn streetcar in 1863 made residence in outlying parts of the peninsula more attractive to people who worked in the center of the city. The extension of streetcar lines and the shift from horsepower to electricity in the 1890s encouraged the growth of residential neighborhoods off the peninsula. The adjacent city of Deering became a streetcar suburb of Portland. The Town of Deering, with a population of four thousand, separated from Westbrook in 1871. Over the next decades, Deering grew as a residential community for people who worked in Portland. Adapting the motto "Deering, a City of Homes," the suburb was incorporated as a city in 1892. Portland annexed Deering in 1899. The Maine Legislature approved annexation despite the fact that Deering voters had rejected becoming part of Portland. Deering's annexation added 7,500 people to the city. [11] It also attached thousands of acres to a community that for two centuries had been bounded by a peninsula (and offshore islands) whose acreage was counted in the hundreds. Deering provided Portland with the room for residential expansion in the twentieth century, especially during post–WWII suburban development and the real estate booms of the last twenty-five years.

Nevertheless, even with such twentieth-century suburban growth, at its core Portland remains a nineteenth-century maritime city whose identity has become fixed on the Old Port. Why does the waterfront district feel like a distinctive place? For starters, it has a human scale. The Old Port was not built to accommodate cars; it preserves the qualities of the small, nineteenth-century walking city that grew out from a pinched central location on the Neck. The streets are narrow and often paved with stones; the buildings "give" something to public space because they are of appropriate height, with eclectic architecture that is mostly brick and granite. In spite of its modern commercialism and tourism, the Old Port is a palpable historical place. It has a pedestrian-friendly streetscape and a village scale that is enhanced by the smell of saltwater, the screeching of seagulls, and the sightlines of a maritime community built around access to the ocean.

Yet, for all of its seeming authenticity, the Old Port is a burnished place. It is a landscape of consumption—a spiffed up postindustrial place very different from the peninsula's historic prominence as a regional distribution, processing, and manufacturing center. Sugar refineries, distilleries, canning factories, foundries, tanneries, grain elevators, shipyards, railyards, coalyards, and steamboats once dominated the peninsula's "sensory landscape." The history of the senses is one of the frontiers in the study of place. The sights, sounds, and smells of a locale shift over time altering the texture of a place as lived experience.[12] In the Portland area and throughout Maine, to cite one example, the decline of papermills as well as new pulp production technology have changed the place-defining scent of the air.

One hundred years ago the peninsula was a much dirtier, smellier, and noisier place than it is today. After decades of defilement, for instance, Back Cove endured as a brackish basin. It reeked from a combination of industrial pollution, sewage, and the natural stench of mud flats at low tide. Noxious Back Cove, Mayor James Phinney Baxter complained in 1895, remained "a slimy and ill-odored waste not only offensive to the nostril and eye, but a menace to the health of the city."[13]

As a transportation center, Portland was the home of multiple railways whose tracks marked miles across different parts of the peninsula. Large railyards contributed to the grittiness of the working landscape. Moreover, before the rise of the automobile, the railroad transformed the "acoustic landscape," as Thoreau bemoaned in *Walden*'s discussion of the locomotive's grating sounds. As the pioneering local historian Joseph Amato has noted, "Train sounds were many: shrill signaling whistles, grinding engines, hissing and sighing steam valves. Setting those tons of steel in motion required a lot of creaking and groaning" while stopping them produced "screeching, shuddering, and scraping."[14] One freight railroad still rumbles through Portland's neighborhoods, disrupting traffic and reminding contemporaries of what had been a pervasive aspect of the city's historic soundscape.

The decline of railroads suggests another way that Portland has changed as a sensory place. Railroad stations, along with other architectural monuments to nineteenth-century progress, have perished. Before widespread ownership of the automobile, people traveled by rail. Train stations served as the introduction to a community; terminal buildings made a civic statement, often announcing a city's aspirations and faith in progress. As a transportation hub Portland boasted two el-

egant train stations. Union Station, on the western side of the peninsula, was completed in 1888. Designed by a Boston firm, the beautiful
Romanesque Revival stone structure included a one-hundred-and-
twenty-five-foot clock tower. Fifteen years later the Grand Trunk freight
railway built another imposing stone station with a tower on the eastern
end of the waterfront.

These grand structures, once testimonials to Portland's prosperity,
progress and civic pride, fell victim to a fit of urban renewal in the
1960s. Union Station was demolished in 1961, the Grand Trunk Terminal
five years later. In between those dates the grandeur of Portland's built
environment was diminished by the loss of other landmark structures.
The wrecking ball leveled John Bundy Brown's Falmouth Hotel in 1963.
Nearby, at the corner of Middle and Exchange streets, the Old Post Office stood for almost a century at what had been the peninsula's mercantile crossroads. Constructed of white Vermont marble and accented by
Corinthian columns, the refined civic building made way for a parking
lot in 1965.[15]

Other architecturally and historically significant structures in the Old
Port and across the peninsula were also flattened under the banner of
urban renewal in the 1960s and '70s. But if Portland's built environment
was diminished from what it had been, much of the nineteenth-century
landscape escaped the ravages of progress. In the first place, Portland, a
declining former entrepot, lost residents to suburbs like Falmouth,
Cumberland, Yarmouth, and Cape Elizabeth. The city shed 20 percent
of its population between 1950 (77,634) and 1980 (61,572).[16] Commercial
and residential developers found more promising investment opportunities outside of Portland, especially after the Maine Mall opened in
South Portland in 1971. Portland's status as an economic backwater preserved much of its historic built environment by default.

At the same time the destruction of Union Station galvanized the
preservation movement in the city. Greater Portland Landmarks was incorporated in 1964 and evolved into one of the most influential local
preservation organizations in New England. The founders of Landmarks have been dubbed "staid radicals."[17] Yankee women from established families formed the vanguard of organized preservation, individuals such as Mrs. Edith Sills, widow of a Bowdoin College president,
and Elizabeth Ring, a retired history teacher. The passage of the National Historic Preservation Act in 1966 aided the work of Portland's
fledgling preservation movement. Then, beginning in 1970, parts of the

city were gradually listed on the National Register of Historic Places. Still, the modernizing momentum of the era often defeated Landmarks' best efforts. Demolition and redevelopment continued to win support in a shrinking city with a decaying waterfront, a dingy, deserted Old Port, and a shabby gentility in once-elegant peninsula neighborhoods.

Beyond individual preservation victories, Landmarks brought a new consciousness to Portland about place. Through education programs and publications Landmarks helped create a community awareness of the relationship between the built environment and the sense of place. In 1972, the organization published *Portland*, an introduction to the city's past and a review of the peninsula's historic architecture. This influential local history sold five thousand copies during its first year and has been reprinted twice. At the beginning of the book, the reader encountered a stunning photograph of Union Station's clock tower as it collapsed into a pile of debris. Images of the building have circulated widely, fashioning a story of twin desecrations. The magnificent station was destroyed and replaced by one of Portland's most aesthetically impoverished places, a trite 1960s commercial strip. Images of Union Station have served as more than a memorial to past grandeur; they have been a summons to safeguard the architectural heritage that distinguishes Portland as a place.

In revising perceptions and understanding of Portland's built environment, Landmarks' efforts remind us that communities are storied places. Their identities are shaped by narratives about the past. Place is the result of geography, history, and public policy decisions like the reshaping of shorelines, the development of Deering Oaks, and the support of historic preservation. Place is also the product of representation—of the stories and images that structure how we perceive a particular locale and define its significance and distinctiveness. A community's historical works, literature, art, museums, and civic monuments create a narrative sense of place. They convey stories about the "authentic" people, events, sites, and artifacts that come to stand for a community's past.[18]

But such local narratives often rest on inclusions and exclusions that influence both historical understanding and the sense of place. For example, during the eighteenth century when New England's mostly enslaved African American population reached its height of 3 percent, Portland's population was about 2.5 percent black. The American Revolution launched a gradual emancipation movement that, over time, erased legal bondage from New England and Maine. Yet there is far more to the history of Yankee involvement in New World bondage than the familiar narrative of a "mild," small, temporary system of enslavement. From the colonial era well into the nineteenth century, New England's maritime economy was tied to major slave society markets. Slave labor in the West Indies produced the molasses that kept Portland's sugar refineries and distilleries operating. In turn, as David Carey's essay in this volume documents, Portland's commercial prosperity was bolstered by the export of Maine lumber, fish, and ice to the southern hemisphere, including to slave societies. This exchange also generated a Latino influence and presence in nineteenth-century Portland—a forgotten historical backdrop to the recent renewal of the city's Hispanic community.

Other essays in *Creating Portland* analyze how artists and writers have often selectively represented Portland's landscape and people. Still others, like those by Maureen Elgersman Lee and Eileen Eagan, examine the residential patterns that defined black and Irish neighborhoods. We know much about the great men of Portland and the enduring imprint of their activities on the cityscape. Portland's three eminent Johns, for instance, have deservedly received much historical attention: John Poor, John Bundy Brown, and noted architect John Calvin Stevens. But ordinary people also participate in the making of a place. From the days of Falmouth Neck to the twenty-first century, working class and ethnic neighborhoods have been part of Portland's character as an entrepot and urban place. We do not know enough about those neighborhoods, some of which were perceived as slums long before they were reduced to rubble during urban renewal. In his fictional autobiography *The Boys of Thirty Five: A Story of a Seaport Town* (1884), Portland writer-journalist Edward H. Elwell recalled with disdain the temper of Gorham's Corner, a working-class area near the waterfront that became heavily Irish: "an unsavory locality of the town, in bad repute because of the turbulent character of its inhabitants, the center of sailor boarding houses, and the scene of street brawls and drunken rows."[19]

Increased immigration and the growth of working class neighborhoods around the turn of the twentieth century distressed some Portland civic leaders, including James Phinney Baxter, the city's wealthiest citizen and renowned philanthropist. Baxter's numerous public benefactions and powerful impact on the city are widely recognized and appropriately commemorated. First elected mayor in 1893, the wealthy businessman drew on the ideas of the City Beautiful movement, which was inspired by the Columbian Exposition in Chicago held during the year Baxter took office. The movement influenced the urban vision for Portland that Earle Shettleworth's essay discusses. Baxter advocated aesthetic and cultural improvements in Portland that would draw the "right" kind of citizens to the city. Baxter oversaw the development of the Eastern and Western Promenades into attractive public parks and the enlargement of Deering Oaks. He created and publicized an ambitious plan to transform toxic Back Cove into a scenic asset for the city that would be encircled by a boulevard connecting it to the promenades and Deering Oaks. A Progressive reformer, Baxter was also a man of his time and class. Having made his fortune in the Portland Packing Company and invested some of it in railroads, Baxter wanted to halt the spread of industry in the city because it lured "ignorant and turbulent foreigners" who created neighborhoods incompatible with City Beautiful aspirations.[20]

After Baxter died in 1921, Back Cove Boulevard, which had opened four years earlier, was fittingly renamed for him. A Baxter Memorial Monument was later erected at Back Cove. Civic monuments are place markers; they help create in public space an official narrative of a locale's past. But the public memory that is enshrined in civic monuments is only a small segment of a place's history. The heroic public statuary on the Portland peninsula is dominated by memorials to: George Cleeve and Richard Tucker, early white settlers; Henry Wadsworth Longfellow; Congressman Thomas Brackett Reed; the Lobsterman; and Hollywood director John Ford, who grew up in the city. These monuments offer limited representation of Portland's history, and not only by gender.[21]

In recent years Portland has tried to broaden the story of its past. Officials have erected signposts throughout the city identifying its diverse neighborhoods and attempting to moor the contemporary cityscape to historic places and multiple stories about Portland's past. The essays in this volume seek to continue that goal by enlarging understanding of the city's richly textured history and demonstrating how elements from geography to public memory have shaped Portland as a place.

Historical Currents

The essays in this volume are related by more than their focus on Portland as a place. The contributors identify major continuities in the city's history. These recurring themes include the impact of the sea; the diverse communities that have inhabited the peninsula; the city's historic capacity to recover from repeated disasters; and Portland's emergence and persistence as an important New England cultural center.

As already noted, geography and enterprise combined to make Falmouth Neck and then Portland one of the region's major maritime entrepots. The peninsula's merchants, like those in other New England ports, were enmeshed in coastal, transatlantic, and global networks of trade by the middle of the eighteenth century. Among other commercial activities, Portlanders expanded their participation in what is sometimes referred to as the "first drug empire." The mass production and consumption of sugar, rum (from West Indian molasses), tea and coffee generated huge profits for importers and retailers.

The Portland Observatory, a wooden lighthouse-like structure at the crest of Munjoy Hill on the east end of the peninsula, has become the towering icon and official marker of the city's dynamic maritime past. By 1807, when the Observatory was constructed, the peninsula resembled an "ant-hill in the sea," to adapt Herman Melville's image of industrious nineteenth-century Nantucket. Portland harbor hummed with the departure and arrival of cargo-laden ships. A signal man stationed in the Observatory, which was equipped with a telescope, used a flag system to let merchants know as soon as a returning vessel entered outer Portland harbor.[22]

The Observatory affords a sweeping view of majestic Casco Bay, strewn with islands varied in shape and size that lead the eye from the inner harbor to the horizon. Most of the larger inhabited islands have long been part of Portland. Through fishing and lobstering they have been tied to Portland's maritime economy. In the nineteenth century steamboats and commercial tourism linked the peninsula and islands. Peaks Island, three miles off the coast, became Casco Bay's most popular destination for tourism and recreation. Its scenic vistas and ocean breezes drew day excursionists, campers, and summer boarders. The growth of summer visitors brought boarding houses, seafood establishments, and entertainment, including an amusement park. Peaks Island became a scaled-down version of Old Orchard Beach, "the Coney Island of Maine." Just to the south of Peaks lies Cushing Island, named for a Canadian who purchased it in the middle of the nineteenth century and built a large brick hotel, the Ottawa House, in 1853. Lemuel Cushing's island became a summer haven for well-to-do English Canadians.[23]

Of course Native people were the earliest inhabitants of the Portland peninsula and the islands of Casco Bay. They were the first to use the islands for seasonal encampments where they harvested the sea's bounty. As Emerson Baker's essay suggests, the Abenaki put their own imprint on the coastal landscape and possessed a strong sense of place. Throughout New England Native place names mapped the physical geography of tribal land and identified its natural resources. Individual and tribal lore fostered a Native narrative sense of place. Stories and legends endowed the spirit-imbued landscape with historical and cultural significance.

The Abenaki succumbed to disease and gunpowder. From Maine to Connecticut, colonists viewed Native depopulation as a Providential blessing. But even in the colonial era Falmouth Neck was far from an exclusive world of pious white Protestants. Over three centuries, the peninsula has harbored diverse communities, a second theme of the essays that follow.

Migrants from Puritan Massachusetts settled at the Neck in the eighteenth century. By the eve of the Revolution, worshippers were divided into Congregationalists, Anglicans, and Quakers. Falmouth Neck, like all of New England's colonial ports, was also home to people who were labeled "the profane": mariners, dockworkers, and fishermen who displayed indifference or hostility to organized religion. The profane, many of whom were transient mariners, preferred the peninsula's grog shops to its meetinghouses. African American slaves, who worked primarily as domestic servants, added to colonial Falmouth's diversity.[24]

A predominantly English place with scatterings of Scots and Scots-Irish inhabitants, Portland's ethnic diversity increased during the early nineteenth century. Two related developments precipitated change. In 1830, both the Cumberland and Oxford Canal and Portland's first Catholic church were completed. The canal connected Portland with Sebago Lake via the Fore and Presumpscot rivers and improved the shipment of goods between the coast and interior. In the 1820s, construction of the canal drew immigrant Irish laborers to the area. They worshipped at St. Dominic's Church located between the Western Promenade and the waterfront. Growing numbers of Irish immigrants soon found work building the railroads that by the 1840s made the Cumberland and Oxford Canal, and many others throughout New England, obsolete. Portland's Catholic population surged with the arrival of the famine Irish. The stately Cathedral of the Immaculate Conception rose at the foot of Munjoy Hill in 1869. Six years later America's first black Catholic bishop was installed in Portland. From the Cathedral, James Healy, the son of an Irish immigrant in Georgia and his black slave, oversaw the Maine diocese for twenty-five years (1875–1900).[25]

During those decades Portland attracted significant numbers of Canadians, many from Nova Scotia, New Brunswick, and Prince Edward Island, and others from Quebec. Neighborhoods of Italians, Greeks, Poles, Armenians, and Eastern European Jews also emerged on the peninsula. Portland served as an immigrant port of entry. On House Island in Casco Bay, federal officials quarantined immigrants suspected of carrying disease.[26]

Portland's increasing ethnic diversity played a role in the adoption of a city manager form of government in 1923, a Progressive-Era reform that altered politics in many American urban communities. As cities expanded social services and assumed more debt, city manager government offered the promise of greater efficiency and economy in the conduct of municipal affairs. Business principles would replace partisan politics as the mainspring of city government. Such a prospect appealed to many citizens in cities seemingly caught in a spoils system of partisan ward politics that divided a predominantly native-born Republican constituency from a rising Democratic Party increasingly ethnic and immigrant in its makeup.

For more than ninety years from its incorporation as a city in 1832 Portland was divided into wards, which grew from seven to nine, with a board of aldermen (which also expanded to nine), a common council of twenty-one, and an elected mayor. Republicans long dominated city government, but Democrats controlled ethnic wards on the peninsula. After voters narrowly rejected a new city manager charter in 1921, reformers mounted a second, acrimonious campaign two years later. Though leading politicians of both parties opposed reform, the election exposed cleavages in the city that went beyond Republican versus Democrat. Fissures emerged between the working-class wards of Munjoy Hill and the upper-middle-class neighborhoods of the West End; between the peninsula and Deering; and between Catholic-Jewish voters and native-born citizens. A prominent Jewish lawyer ridiculed city manager reform in 1923, claiming that "If this plan goes through, every man of Irish descent may as well pack up his trunk and leave the city as far as representation on the city government is concerned."[27] A revitalized Ku Klux Klan organized rallies in support of the new charter and encouraged voters to purge municipal government of Catholics and Jews.

Voters approved the new charter; it created a city manager government with five councilors elected at large rather than from wards. The reformers' candidates, all Protestants, won the five council seats. Voting plummeted in subsequent elections. A mix of progressive and reactionary elements, the city manager charter has continued to shape Portland politics. Its Progressive aspirations endure on a council that has become diverse and dominated by Democrats, who, in the eyes of some observers, do not always adhere to the nonpartisanship that the charter reformers claimed they were institutionalizing.[28]

The year 1923 marked another turning point for Portland, as Joel Eastman's essay documents. The Canadian government nationalized the Grand Trunk Railroad and through tariff policy redirected commerce away from Portland to St. John, New Brunswick, and Halifax, Nova Scotia, where public funds were invested in new port facilities. The collapse of Canadian trade eroded Portland's status as a rail and coastal entrepot. The Depression accelerated the city's economic decline. World War II defense spending, especially shipbuilding, helped lift Greater Portland out of the Depression. Geography played a role in the city's economic revival. Portland's deep water harbor was 116 miles closer to Europe than any other significant American port. Casco Bay provided anchorage and base support for the Navy's North Atlantic Fleet.

The war effort did produce some lasting economic consequences for the region. The construction of a petroleum pipeline between Portland and Montreal in 1941 transformed Casco Bay into one of the largest oil ports on the Atlantic coast. But economic decline and population loss stalked the city for three decades after the war. Prosperity returned only after Portland's emergence as a postindustrial city: a center of finance, health and social services, tourism, and the arts.

Portland's twentieth-century decline and recovery highlights a third theme in its history. For good reason, the city's historic municipal seal bears the motto *Resurgam*, "I will rise." Native people destroyed colonial Falmouth twice, once in 1676 and again fourteen years later. In the 1690 assault, Abenaki and French allies launched their attack from Peaks Island, burned homes on the peninsula, and forced survivors to flee Falmouth Neck. It took nearly a generation for the town to be resettled.[29] In its first major recovery, the Neck developed into the thriving mid-eighteenth-century port that is examined in Charles Outwin's essay.

The American Revolution visited a new disaster on the peninsula. James Leamon's contribution recreates the events surrounding the British bombing and burning of the Neck in 1775 and analyzes its causes and consequences. In 1786, when the recovering town changed its name to Portland, the community adopted the Phoenix as a symbol of civic resolve. It would not be the last time that Portlanders had reason to invoke this emblem of rebirth and hope.

On 4 July 1866, Portland's great fire, probably the worst in the country's history up to that time, started in a boat shop on Commercial Street, perhaps from a tossed firecracker. The fire spread to an adjacent lumberyard and then engulfed much of the peninsula, sparing the West End. Fanned by a stiff wind and blowing embers, the flames swept northeastward from the waterfront toward Back Cove, consuming wood, brick, and stone structures from the mercantile core of the city to Munjoy Hill. The conflagration raged all night. It destroyed eighteen hundred buildings and left almost ten thousand people without homes. Many found shelter in the tent city that sprawled over Munjoy Hill.[30]

Portland's recovery was impressive, both for the speed of reconstruction and the character of the new built environment. John Bundy Brown lost his Sugar House to the great fire, but he erected the Falmouth Hotel as part of the commercial district's rise from the ashes. Grand public buildings such as the old Post Office and the granite Customs House were also part of the city's renaissance. Massive reconstruction following the fire created the Old Port's eclectic Victorian-era built environment. The history of Portland's earlier recoveries from disaster seemed to inspire civic leaders. They established open space between the commercial district and Munjoy Hill as a firebreak, naming the city's first public park Phoenix Square (later changed to Lincoln, in honor of the assassinated President).[31]

Thus, Portland's late-twentieth-century postindustrial economic rebirth represents one chapter in a long history of civic resilience. In this most recent resurgence, a cultural revival has been intertwined with the city's economic renewal. Several essays in this volume address a fourth current in the city's history. They show how culture, as well as commerce, has long defined Portland as a place.

The peninsula's first artists were colonial craftspeople. Tinsmiths, silversmiths, furniture makers, carvers of ship figureheads, and women who embroidered samplers, for example, produced practical items that a century later would come to be valued as finely wrought antiques. By the middle of the nineteenth century, as Donna Cassidy's essay shows, the visual arts were a vital part of Portland's cultural life. From seascapes to

Depression-era public murals, artists have represented Portland's natural and social landscapes in particular ways. Historic institutions have supported the arts in the city. Founded in 1882, the Portland Society of Art sponsored a school that evolved into the Maine College of Art. The roots of the city's attractive brick art museum, which now anchors a thriving cultural district, go back nearly a century to the Portland Society of Art.

Portland's literary culture flourished alongside its rise as a nineteenth-century entrepot and art center. Harvard literary historian Lawrence Buell has described how antebellum Portland "bred an impressive array of literary entrepreneurs, including some of the most popular fiction and poetry writers of their day. . . ." In his magisterial *New England Literary Culture: From Revolution to Renaissance*, Buell goes on to say, "one could even argue that the Portland contribution to antebellum New England letters came close to rivaling that of Cambridge and Concord."[32]

Longfellow is Portland's most celebrated luminary, and Charles Calhoun's essay examines the poet's personal attachment to and imaginative investment in his native city. Portland's literary constellation contained many other bright lights. Seba Smith, John Neal, and Ann Stephens were major contributors to the fashioning of New England's Yankee identity. Smith created Major Jack Downing, a popular mouthpiece of Yankee folk wisdom. Stephens invented Jonathan Slick. Novelist Neal, one of America's first art critics, launched a weekly newspaper called the *Yankee* in 1829. Two other nineteenth-century Portlanders, Madame Sally Wood and "Fanny Fern" (Sarah Payson Willis), were among the most popular writers of their day.

Kent Ryden's essay discusses the work of Portland writers and raises important questions about the literary construction of place. John Preston is one recent writer whose representation of the city as a distinctive, tolerant New England community has had important consequences. Howard Solomon's contribution to this volume shows how Preston's writings publicized the image of Portland as a gay-friendly place. Preston's activism helped a growing gay community establish its voice in the city.

This volume is designed as a crossdisciplinary study of place rather than as a comprehensive local history. Contributors examine Portland as a place on the ground and a territory of the imagination, as lived experience and mental landscape. Some essays are thematic with broad chronologies while others focus on discrete periods. As a contribution to the study of place, *Creating Portland* should deepen readers' understanding of an important, Maine, New England, and American community.

Notes

1. Jonathan Harr, "Imagine a City too Good to Be True," *New England Monthly*, vol. 2 (March 1985): 33.

2. For a recent account of Portland's growth and demographic data, see Kelley Bouchard, "In Transition: Can Portland Afford to Pay Price of Growth?" *Maine Sunday Telegram* (8 Feb. 2004): 1, 4–5.

3. Joseph Amato, *Rethinking Home: A Case for Writing Local History* (Berkeley: Univ. of California Press, 2002), p. 7.

4. Wayne Franklin and Michael Steiner, "Taking Place: Toward the Regrounding of American Studies," in *Mapping American Culture*, Franklin and Steiner, eds. (Iowa City: Univ. of Iowa Press), p. 5. Other helpful studies of place include two books by Kent Ryden. See *Landscape with Figures: Nature and Culture in New England* (Iowa City: University of Iowa Press, 1993), and *Mapping the Invisible Landscape: Folklore, Writing, and the Sense of Place* (Iowa City: Univ. of Iowa Pres, 1993). For a study of another New England community similar to *Creating Portland*, see Dane Anthony Morrison and Nancy Lusignan Schultz, *Salem: Place, Myth, and Memory* (Boston: Northeastern Univ. Press, 2004).

5. Franklin and Steiner, "Taking Place," p. 5.

6. For an excellent discussion of New England's maritime origins, see Stephen Innes, *Creating the Commonwealth: The Economic Culture of Puritan New England* (New York: Norton, 1995), ch. 7.

7. For an excellent description of the new, thriving waterfront see, Edward H. Elwell, *Portland and Vicinity* (1876; Reprint, Portland: Greater Portland Landmarks, 1975), p. 84.

8. For an evocative description of one part of this district, see Herbert Adams,"Deering Oaks," in Theo H. B. M. Holtwijk and Earle G. Shettleworth, Jr., *Bold Vision: The Development of the Parks of Portland, Maine* (Portland: Greater Portland Landmarks, 1999), p. 81.

9. Martin Dibner, ed., *Portland* (1972; Reprint, Portland: Greater Portland Landmarks, 1986), p. 203.

10. Quoted in Mark McCain, "From Country Boy to Empire Builder," in Albert F. Barnes, ed., *Greater Portland Celebration 350* (Portland: Guy Gannett, 1984), p. 76.

11. Albert F. Barnes, "Deering's Status as a Shortlived City," Barnes, ed., *Greater Portland Celebration 350*, pp. 124–25. Also, see Greater Portland Landmarks forthcoming volume on Deering.

12. See the discussion in Amato, *Rethinking Home*, ch. 4. He uses the term sensory landscape (p. 66). On recovering sensory history, see Peter C. Hoffer, *Sensory Worlds of Early America* (Baltimore: Johns Hopkins Univ. Press, 2003), and Richard C. Rath, *How Early America Sounded* (Ithaca: Cornell Univ. Press, 2003).

13. Baxter quoted in Eleanor G. Ames, "Back Cove and Baxter Boulevard," in Holtwijk and Shettleworth, eds., *Bold Vision*, p. 94.

14. Amato, *Rethinking Home*, p. 66, where he also uses the term *acoustic landscape*.

15. Good descriptions of these historic structures may be found in the WPA *Portland City Guide* (Portland, Maine: Forest City Printing, 1940).

16. John Ferland, "Economy Changes Population Mix," in Barnes, ed., *Greater Portland Celebration 350*, p. 210.

17. Virgina Wright, "The Formative Years: 1964–1971," *Landmarks Observer* 28 (Winter 2003). 3. Beginning with this issue Landmarks ran a year-long, four-part series on the history of preservation in Portland. The series informs my discussion.

18. On historical narratives and the way the past is deployed to create place identities, see Joseph A. Conforti, *Imagining New England: Regional Identity from the Pilgrims to the Mid-Twentieth Century* (Chapel Hill: Univ. of North Carolina Press, 2001).

19. Elwell, *The Boys of Thirty-Five: A Story of a Seaport Town* (Boston: Lee and Shepard, 1884), p. 116.

20. Baxter quoted in Deborah Tracy Krichels, "James Phinney Baxter and the Portland Park System," in Holtwijk and Shettleworth, eds., *Bold Vision*, p. 111.

21. On the role of historical commemoration in one New England city, see Martha Norkunas, *Monuments and Memory: History and Representation in Lowell, Massachusetts* (Washington, D.C.: Smithsonian Institution Press, 2002). For Portland's Lobsterman Memorial and other maritime monuments in Maine and New England, see Nova Seals, "New England and the Sea: Representations of Maritime Identity and Heritage" (American and New England Studies M.A. Thesis, Univ. of Southern Maine, 2004).

22. Melville, *Moby Dick* (1851; Reprint, New York: Bantam Books, 1981), p. 67. Dibner, ed., *Portland*, p. 18.

23. Elwell, *Portland and Vicinity*, pp. 86–104, offers a late-nineteenth-century guide to the islands. See also Kimberly Erico MacIsaac, "The Golden Age of Peaks, 1880–1920," (American and New England Studies M.A. Thesis, Univ. of Southern Maine, 1994).

24. Charles F. Clark, *The Eastern Frontier: The Settlement of Northern New England* (1970, Reprint, Hanover, N.H.: University Press of New England, 1983), esp. 349–50.

25. Bob Niss, "Ethnic Groups Prosper in the Area," in Barnes, ed., *Greater Portland Celebration 350,* pp. 112–13; Daniel Murphy, "Creation of Ethnic Identity: St. Dominic's Parish Life in Portland's Antebellum Years, 1828–1861" (American and New England Studies M.A. Thesis, Univ. of Southern Maine, 2004); James O'Toole, *Passing for White: Race, Religion, and the Healy Family, 1820–1920* (Amherst, Mass.: Univ. of Massachusetts Press, 2002), ch. 7.

26. See the account in *Portland City Guide,* pp. 59–62.

27. Quoted in Kendall Holmes, "Klan Plays Part in Local Changes," in Barnes, ed., *Greater Portland Celebration 350,* p. 146. A helpful study of the political reform is Edward F. Dow, *City Manager Government in Portland, Maine* (Orono: Univ. of Maine Press, 1940). Dow ignores the ethnic dimensions of the controversy.

28. See Dow, *City Manager Government* for voting statistics. Kelley Bouchard, "Democrats' Dominance Seen in City Election," *Portland Press Herald* (12 Feb. 2004): 120.

29. Clark, *The Eastern Frontier,* ch. 5.

30. For an excellent description of the fire and its aftermath, see Augustus F. Moulton, *Portland by the Sea* (Augusta, Maine: Katahdin Publishing, 1926), ch. 24.

31. *Portland City Guide,* p. 244.

32. Buell, *New England Literary Culture: From Revolution Through Renaissance* (New York: Cambridge Univ. Press, 1986), pp. 29–30.

Creating Portland

1

Formerly Machegonne, Dartmouth, York, Stogummor, Casco, and Falmouth

Portland as a Contested Frontier in the Seventeenth Century

Emerson W. Baker

There have been many Portlands. The native peoples who occupied Casco Bay for thousands of years called it "Machegonne" or "Machegony." In the seventeenth century English explorers and settlers would rename the place Dartmouth, York, Stogummor, Casco, and Falmouth. Indeed, residents would not adopt the name Portland until the Neck separated from the rest of Falmouth in 1786.

Portland's numerous appellations reflect its history as a contested frontier. Throughout the seventeenth century the locale would have a succession of occupants and rulers, as it was rocked by both internal and external conflict. Competing groups of Englishmen claimed ownership over the territory in the 1630s and their bitter disputes continued until 1658 when the community submitted to the Massachusetts Bay Colony. Uncertainly over governance would continue until 1678 when Massachusetts bought the Province of Maine from its proprietary owners, the Gorges family. By this time, another claimant, the Wabanaki, had reasserted their ancient right of occupation. Was the location of Portland destined to remain a Native American homeland, become a Puritan city upon a hill, or something else?

Historians of early Portland have long recognized the conflicts between its various claimants, and of the community's phoenix-like ability to repeatedly rise from the ashes. Residents have pointed with pride to the city's ability to rebuild after its bombardment by the Royal Navy during the American Revolution and after the great fire of 1866. Yet, long before these tragedies, the location had been the focus of both political and military struggles. An examination of the many names given the location in its first century of European settlement reveals the conflicting visions of community, the transitory nature of place, and the many Portlands that came and went long before the British opened fire in 1775.[1]

Machegonne

Native Americans occupied Casco Bay for thousands of years before the arrival of Europeans. Several archaeological sites in southern Maine date back as far as twelve thousand years ago. As the glaciers retreated, the peoples archaeologists refer to as paleoindians moved north into the then-tundra landscape, following migrating big game like caribou and moose. No sites this early have been found on Casco Bay, though enough have been found in surrounding areas to know that paleoindians must have camped here as well. Over the ensuing millennia, a number of Native cultures would call the region home. Presumably, over time various Native peoples speaking different languages had their own names for the area. Those names are lost to time. The only terms that survive are Machegonne and Aucocisco, the names used by the Wabanaki peoples when they met European explorers at the dawn of the seventeenth century. Linguists debate the meanings of both words. Machegonne (or Machegony) appears to be a reference to the great, high, peninsula that dominates the landscape and is the heart of present-day Portland. Casco is quite possibly a clipped form of Auco-cisco, which means "muddy bay" a specific reference to Portland's Back Bay. Alternatively, Casco is the Wabanaki Indian word for the great blue heron. So, the name could also be a reference to this majestic waterfowl that frequented the extensive mud flats of the bay.[2]

Regardless of the specific meanings, the pattern of Wabanaki place names is clear. They used descriptive names that reflected local topography and natural resources. Sebago means "the big lake"; Owascoag or "place of much grass" was the name appropriately given to a stream along the Scarborough marshes. Many place names refer to locations to catch fish, or to dangerous spots for canoe travel. Wabanaki names demonstrated that Native people knew the region's details well and depended upon the land and its resources for their very existence. They knew where the best stands of birch trees were to build their canoes and wigwams. They knew the best spots and the right time to gather blueberries or catch migrating salmon. They considered themselves to be the rightful owners of the land, and their oral history holds many stories that say they had occupied the land since the beginning of time.[3]

In the early years of the seventeenth century, a series of English and French explorers would venture along the coast of Maine, in the process providing the earliest surviving written descriptions of Casco Bay and its Wabanaki inhabitants. Relatively little is known about these Native Americans, for the exploration accounts only give passing references to them. We do not even know what they called themselves, so one is reduced to using "Wabanaki" meaning "dawnlanders" in the Algonquian languages of the region. The term generally describes the Native peoples of northern New England and the Maritime Provinces who shared similar languages, belief systems, and lifeways. Before he achieved fame as the founder of New France, Samuel de Champlain was one of the first Europeans to navigate the coast of eastern New England. He referred to all the Native Peoples on the coast from the Kennebec southward into Massachusetts as the "Almouchiquois," clearly differentiating them from their fellow Wabanaki, the Etchemin (from the Kennebec to St. John region) and the Souriquois (or Micmac) who occupied the lands east of the St. John River and in present-day Nova Scotia.[4]

These European explorers found a substantial Native population in Casco Bay. Its principle town, called Ashamahaga, sat on the Presumptscot River, and its two chiefs had "240 men." Presumably this is a reference to warriors, meaning the town and surrounding villages of Casco Bay had a total population of a thousand people or more. This was a substantial settlement, occupied by farmers who grew the traditional Native trilogy of corn, beans, and squash. Though their agriculture allowed them to live a fairly sedentary life, they would have moved around the land at times to harvest its seasonal bounty, from clams and cod to duck and deer.[5]

Champlain noted that a sachem named Marchin led the Natives of the Casco Bay. Champlain's companion Marc Lescarbot even labeled Casco Bay "Bay of Marchin" on his map of the region. Unfortunately, the Frenchmen and other explorers would soon witness the death of Marchin and many of his followers. In 1607 the Almouchiquois and

their allies in Eastern Maine entered a violent war with the eastern Etchemin and the Micmac. Marchin was one of the first of many Almouchiquois casualties in a war that lasted close to a decade. Even then, the vic-
torious Micmac would carry out occasional raids on their weakened
southern neighbors until the early 1630s. Modern-day observers often
make the mistake of assuming that Native Americans lived in peace and
harmony before the arrival of Europeans. Although the Wabanaki's
close understanding of and relationship to their land is truly admirable,
the so-called Micmac War demonstrates that they too lived in an imper-
fect world.[6]

This conflict signaled just the beginning of trouble for the Almoui-
quois. From 1616 to 1619 a series of epidemics devastated the Native peoples from the coast of Maine to Cape Cod. Known as "virgin soil epidemics," these were caused by the introduction of European diseases
into a Native population with no previous exposure or immunity. In
some communities the death rate was as high as 90 percent. Not surprisingly, Lescarbot's map is the only one to include "Bay of Marchin." In
the future, when Englishmen would name the region, they would
choose instead to honor their countrymen and their hometowns.[7]

Dartmouth and York

Captain John Smith reconnoitered the coast of Maine in 1614 just before
the outbreak of the Great Plague. The region so impressed the former
leader of Jamestown that upon his return to England he began to actively promote Maine for settlement. To aid his cause, he wrote a book
and published a map of his explorations. In marked contrast to Samuel
de Champlain and Marc Lescarbot, Smith's map employed English
place names rather than Native ones. He drew names from the English
royal family and leading nobles, hoping to entice these people into in-
vesting in his enterprise. In the process Smith also bolstered English
claims to ownership. Not a single Native place name remained on the
map. Smith renamed Casco Bay as Harrington's Bay, and Dartmouth
approximates present-day Portland. As such, Smith's new name for the
region, New England, was all too appropriate. This imperialism of the
map would be short-lived. Just a few of Smith's numerous names would
stick—most notably New England and Cape Ann. Interestingly, Smith
did use the name Cape Elizabeth, but he placed it on the northeast side

of Casco Bay—the opposite side from what is now known as Cape Elizabeth. Although he left Native Americans off his map, Smith did not forget them. In fact, they played a key role in his vision of colonization. Smith envisioned an entirely different type of English settlement—modeled on the Spanish in Mexico. He wanted to use military force to enslave the local populations and put them to work in the fishing industry and other projects. Luckily for the Wabanaki, a series of misfortunes kept Smith from ever returning, despite repeated efforts.[8]

Smith's ventures had been made jointly with Sir Ferdinando Gorges, a long-time promoter of New England who had supported exploration and settlement efforts since the first years of the seventeenth century. In 1620 the wealthy English knight would secure a royal charter for the Council for New England. It had responsibility for "the planting, ruling, ordering and governing" the territory between Virginia and New France. Although given the authority to establish a government, the council restricted its activities to granting lands. Gorges and his associates dominated the Council, guaranteeing that they would receive the lion's share of the patents.[9]

In 1623 the Council for New England granted a patent of six thousand acres to Christopher Levett, to be laid out in a place of his choosing. Later that year, after considerable exploration he settled in Casco Bay. As Levett sailed the coast he observed the devastation caused by the Micmac War and European epidemics. At Casco Bay a relict band of Wabanaki, eager for trade, warmly greeted him. Levett and a small crew of men in his employment established themselves on an island in Casco Bay—quite possibly House Island. He received permission to do so from the "Queen" of the land. Unlike most English settlers, he insisted on gaining Native permission, for he considered them to be the owners of the land. Still, he would give his own name to the territory, calling his settlement York, in honor of his hometown in England. Before he left for New England, Levett had desperately sought to enlist investors and raise cash. To gain the support of his neighbors, he promised "to build a city and call it by the name of York."[10]

Relations between the English and the Wabanaki of Maine reached a high point during Levett's stay. Although he did not completely trust the Natives, he insisted on treating them fairly. When other Englishmen stole furs from the Indians or cheated them in trade, Levett tried to rectify the situation. The Wabanaki admired Levett as much as he liked them. He seems to have gotten along well with Skitterygusset, the sachem of

Casco Bay, and Natives from throughout the region frequently visited Levett's homestead, bringing gifts and furs to trade. Samoset, the Pemaquid, Maine, sachem who befriended the Plymouth colonists, called Levett his "cousin" and hoped that his son and Levett's would go through life as great companions. When Levett announced to his Native friends that he must return to England, they expressed their distress and hope for his speedy return. Unfortunately, Levett was unable to return to Maine to foster the continued growth of solid relations between the two groups. Instead, others with less understanding and concern for the Wabanaki would lead the settling of Casco Bay and Maine.11

Stogummor and Casco

Christopher Levett's activites led a wave of English settlement efforts in northern New England in the 1620s and 1630s. During its fifteen-year existence the Council for New England granted a dizzying flurry of patents. Many of these were made to Sir Ferdinando Gorges. In 1622 the council granted all lands from the Merrimac River to the Kennebec River to Gorges and his partner John Mason. A few years and several grants later, Gorges and Mason would divide their interests, with Mason organizing the southern end of the territory into New Hampshire while Gorges focused his efforts north of the Piscataqua River, in the area he called "New Somersetshire" after his home shire in the West Country of England. Finally in 1639, King Charles I formally granted Gorges a proprietary grant to what was then called the Province of Maine. Unfortunately, these and other grants made by the Council for New England and Gorges himself were authorized from distant England, for a New England that was poorly mapped. Boundaries of the patents were confusing and often overlapping, which would soon lead to conflict.12

To add to the confusion, some men who sensed opportunity but lacked the influence to receive a patent simply squatted on lands. In 1628 Englishman Walter Bagnall illegally occupied Richmond Island—named after the Duke of Richmond who held a patent for the area. Bagnall quickly established a profitable fur trading post and soon applied for his own patent to the island from the Council for New England. Most likely he assumed it would revoke the Duke of Richmond's patent, as the nobleman had failed to make any effort to colonize the lands. Bagnall's unfair trading practices soon brought down the wrath of his Native clients. In an early example of frontier justice, a group of Casco

Bay Natives, led by sachem Skitterygusset, killed Bagnall. News traveled slowly across the Atlantic, so two months later, the council approved his patent—not realizing they had granted land to a dead man.[13]

Soon Richmond Island had more occupants as the Council for New England would re-grant it and the mainland opposite it (in present-day Cape Elizabeth) to English merchants, Robert Trelawney and Moses Goodyear. In the spring of 1632, John Winter arrived on the island to establish a fishing station and trading post for Trelawney. The station would bring many workers from England and soon be a hub of activity in the region. Although cod fishing was always the primary activity at the Trelawney post, the settlement came to include such diverse ventures as raising livestock and shipbuilding.[14]

The development of the Trelawney post led indirectly to the first settlement of Machigonne (present-day Portland). When John Winter arrived on Richmond Island he found that he had neighbors. George Cleeve and Richard Tucker had established a small plantation at the mouth of the Spurwink River. The men believed they held good title from another patent issued by Sir Ferdinando Gorges. Winter disagreed, so in the fall of 1633 he and his men forcibly evicted Cleeve and Tucker. The duo immediately moved to the north, planting a new site at Machegonne. But they would not forget the dispute with Winter, which would fester and grow over the next several decades.[15]

When Cleeve and Tucker arrived at Machegonne, they already had at least one neighbor. Arthur Mackworth had occupied the neck on the east bank of the Presumpscot River since 1630. In 1635 Mackworth secured title to the island, which still bears his name, and the nearby point of land from Ferdinando Gorges. In his grant, Mackworth called the land Newton, the name of his home village in Shropshire, England. Mackworth's success may have reminded Cleeve and Tucker that they had no patent for their land, and indeed could face another eviction. So both went to England and met personally with Sir Ferdinando Gorges, who granted the duo the lands immediately south of Mackworth, between the Presumpscot Rivers and Fore Rivers, "now and forever from henceforth to be called or known by the name of Stogummor."[16] Thus Gorges named the community in honor of Stogummor (or Stogumber) Somersetshire, the home of the Cleeve and Tucker families. Like Dartmouth and York before it, Stogummor and Newton would be virtually ignored as names. Not even Cleeve, Tucker, or Mackworth seem to have bothered to use them. Instead, people continued to call the place Casco.[17]

During the 1630s, a community began to evolve around Casco Bay. By 1642, seven families with fourteen children had taken up residence at Casco—the name generally used to refer to these settlements. This small community attests to the diversity of early Casco Bay, for the settlers came from all parts of England, bringing with them differing skills. Some settlers came from the West Country, while others hailed from London or Shropshire. The group included farmers, fishermen, and traders. They lived alongside a rapidly dwindling Wabanaki population. Writing a year after the 1633 smallpox epidemic killed many Native people, John Winter observed that aside from the Natives at the mouth of the Saco River, there were no Indians within forty or fifty miles of his post at Richmond Island. He exaggerated, but it does appear that by this time the Native population of Casco Bay had all but disappeared. Certainly at least Skitterygusset and his family remained, but they had few followers left. Skitterygusset had apparently died by 1659 when his sister, the squaw sachem Warrabita (called Jane or Joan by the English) deeded land in Scarborough. Warrabita sold the land on the condition that she receive an annual rent of corn, and that she and her mother be allowed to live on the land the rest of their lives. These women were apparently the last surviving members of their band, so they traded their land in return for their care in their old age.[18]

As the Native population withered, the English settlement expanded during the 1640s and 1650s, despite a recurring conflict between the owners of competing claims to the area. Heated accusations and lawsuits flew back and forth between the claimants. Cleeve soon fell out of favor with the Gorges family and found the title to his Maine lands under threat. He went to England and, through a series of political and legal maneuverings, was able to establish his own claim to Casco Bay. A political ally of Cleeve's purchased the patent to the Province of Lygonia and appointed Cleeve as its governor. Issued in 1630, this patent whose lands overlapped with the Province of Maine had been almost forgotten. Ironically, a province once named in honor of Sir Ferdinando Gorges's mother, Cecily Lygon, would now be used as an instrument to strip the aged knight of much of his Maine lands. The dispute became so heated that in 1647 the Earl of Warwick and the Commissioners of Foreign Plantations stepped into the conflict and ruled for Cleeve and Tucker, delineating the region between the Kennebec River and the Saco River as the Province of Lygonia. That same year Sir Ferdinando Gorges had died, and Robert Trelawney had passed away in

1643. So, by 1647 Cleeve must have believed his long bitter struggle for Casco Bay had been won. He would soon find that he had to deal with much more formidable opponents than the Gorges faction, for Massachusetts Bay had set its sights on control of the English settlements in Maine—including Casco.[19]

Falmouth

During the 1650s, Massachusetts took advantage of the political squabbling and uncertainty in Maine to extend the Bay Colony's boundary northward. Using a very liberal interpretation of their charter, Massachusetts officials argued that all of Maine from Casco Bay and southward was within the colony's bounds. The end of the English Civil Wars, the execution of Charles I, and the rule of Parliament emboldened Massachusetts to act on these claims, for the colony was allied to Parliament, and there was no one left in England to defend the Provinces of Maine or Lygonia. Beginning in 1652, Massachusetts officials visited the region to negotiate with Maine settlements to become a part of Massachusetts. Although these were peaceful negotiations, they took place with the thinly veiled threat of the sizable Massachusetts militia. So, after initial reluctance, Kittery and Georgeana (soon renamed York) joined in 1652 and Wells, Cape Porpoise, and Saco became part of the Bay Colony the following year. George Cleeve strongly opposed these actions and fought for Lygonia to remain independent, but he too finally yielded in 1658. The articles of agreement between the freemen of the region and Massachusetts specified that Black Point, Blue Point, and Stratton's Islands would be organized as the town of Scarborough. Meanwhile, Spurwink and the Casco Bay settlements would be brought together in one town that would be named Falmouth.[20]

Why did the authorities choose the name Falmouth? Most contemporary Massachusetts towns were named in honor of the home of some of its settlers, for a leader of the colony, or in respect to some English supporter of the venture. One might expect that some Casco Bay settlers had ties to Falmouth and the surrounding area of Cornwall in southwestern England. Yet, only a handful of early settlers in all of New England hailed from Cornwall. In his *Topographical Dictionary of English Immigrants*, Charles Banks lists only fifteen early English migrants who definitely came to New England from Cornwall. Only one of these came from Falmouth—Peter Nowell. He settled in Salem, Massachusetts, and led a fairly unremarkable life—certainly not the man to have a town named after him. The most prominent Cornish family to migrate to New England were the Bonythons, the proprietors of Saco. As staunch opponents of Massachusetts, it is highly unlikely that Falmouth would have been chosen as a name in their honor.[21]

Sometimes geographical similarity inspires a name. Biddeford's name clearly originated with Biddeford Pool, that unusual round tidal inlet near the mouth of the Saco River. There is a very similar feature, "Appledore Pool," at the mouth of the Torridge River near Bideford, Devon. There certainly is a geographical similarity between Falmouth Bay in Cornwall, and Casco Bay. Both are substantial in size, harbor important ports, and are sited along rugged, rocky coastline with strong tidal currents. Both bays have several rivers running into them, with one river to the south and the other to the north of a substantial neck and headland. The Cornish town of Falmouth sits on this neck, with Pendennis Castle perched on the headland at its end. South of the neck lies the Helford River. Immediately north of the neck is the inner harbor—the outlet of the Penyrn River, and beyond that to the north lies the River Fal. Casco Bay has similar landmarks, with Portland Neck defined by the Fore River and Back Cove, and the Presumpscot River to the north.

Although these geographical similarities may have helped inspire the name, there is powerful symbolism in the choice of the names "Falmouth" and "Scarborough" for Maine towns. In many ways, the peaceful conquest of Maine by Massachusetts mirrored events in England. Like its Puritan allies in Parliament, Massachusetts conquered its Royalist opposition in Maine. Falmouth, Cornwall, and Scarborough, Yorkshire, were important Royalist strongholds, among the last castles to submit to Parliament. Pendennis Castle was so safe that it provided sanctuary for Queen Henrietta Maria and the Prince of Wales (the future Charles II), and would later fall only after a dramatic five-month siege. Likewise, Scarborough, Yorkshire, was a hotly contested site in the English Civil Wars, ultimately surrendering only a month before the execution of Charles I. Hence, the Puritans of Massachusetts must have considered "Falmouth" and "Scarborough" as appropriate names for the last Royalist strongholds in Maine to fall to Puritan Massachusetts.[22]

The Puritans of Massachusetts imposed the names Falmouth and Scarborough in conquest, a reminder to the population of their fate and of their new overlords. They were not the first towns to be named in this manner. In 1652 when Massachusetts usurped Gorgeana, they renamed Gorges's former capital and would-be cathedral city of the Province of Maine "York"—after the northern Royalist cathedral city that had fallen to Parliament after a bitter struggle. Clearly these names did not sit well with many long-standing residents, and some chose to continue to use the former names. Take the example of John Josselyn who resided in Black Point in 1638 and again from 1663 to 1671, and then returned to England to publish his "Two Voyages to New-England," a detailed account of the region. Josselyn rejects the Puritan names, preferring instead Black Point, Casco, and Gorgeana. His choice of terms is not surprising, considering he stayed in Black Point with his brother Henry, a former high officer of the Province of Maine and one of the leading Royalists in the region. These men understood the power of names to bolster Massachusetts's imperial claims, and fought them as best they could.[23]

John Josselyn was not alone in his preference for the name Casco over Falmouth. Residents used the term Casco repeatedly in property deeds of the 1660s and even the 1670s. When Francis Small sold land in 1663, he styled himself of "Cascoe sometyms Called Falmouth."[24] Indeed, from 1665 to 1668, Casco reappeared as the official name, as Massachusetts temporarily lost control of Maine. In 1665 a royal commission visited Maine and heard complaints from the residents about both the rule of the Gorges family and of Massachusetts. The commission temporarily put Maine directly under royal authority—to be administered by eleven prominent residents who were appointed as justices. The court proceedings for the next three years specify that court was held "at Cascoe" not Falmouth.[25] It should come as no surprise that the lead justice for these courts was Henry Josselyn. Unfortunately, the crown took no action to provide a permanent government to Maine, and in 1668 Massachusetts quietly re-established authority in the region. This time it would not relinquish Maine until it achieved statehood in 1820. These changing governments and names caused confusion, as can be seen in 1667 when Arthur Mackworth's widow, Jane, of "Casco alias Falmouth in the Province of Mayn, alias County of Yorke," gave land to her daughter and son-in-law.[26] As late as June 1675, George Munjoy stubbornly refused to accept the name change or recognize the authority of Massachusetts, when in a deed he said he was "of Casco also Falmouth in New England."[27]

Even as George Munjoy made his silent protest against the authority of the Bay Colony, others were preparing for more direct action. In June

1675, King Philip's War broke out in southern New England as a coalition of Native Americans rose up in an effort to drive the English from the land. By September, war had spread to Maine, specifically to Falmouth, where Wabanaki warriors killed several people and burned two homesteads. After these initial hostilities, an uneasy peace prevailed along the northern frontier, as the English and Wabanaki residents watched while the devastating war raged to the south. A year later, in August 1676, when the war was apparently winding down, it broke out in full force in Maine as the Wabanaki took to the warpath. In Casco Bay alone, over thirty people were killed or taken captive in a swift series of raids and attacks. This and other raids forced the abandonment of all English settlements east of the Saco. Falmouth residents initially sought refuge on Andrew's Island and Jewel's Island in Casco Bay. From this vantage point, they could see the fire and smoke as the Wabanaki burned Falmouth. Even the islands proved vulnerable and soon the Wabanaki attacked them, resulting in more English losses. At the end of September, the surviving residents of Falmouth had abandoned both islands and sought refuge in southern New England. By the end of the summer of 1676 the true irony of naming Falmouth and Scarborough after defeated forts was all too clear, for both towns had again fallen to the enemy. For several years, Casco Bay remained abandoned.[28]

A Second Falmouth

After the Treaty of Casco was signed on 12 April 1678, peace returned to the northern frontier. Some people may have gained further confidence to resettle later that year when they learned that Massachusetts had purchased the Gorges's family's title to Maine. Finally, it appeared all disputes over ownership of Maine might be at an end. Many refugees returned home and Falmouth arose from the ashes—the first of many rebuildings in the city's history. As the English made a cautious return to Falmouth and the rest of Maine they deliberately chose a different pattern of settlement. Prior to King Phillip's War, most settlers in Casco Bay and elsewhere in Maine lived in dispersed settlements, generally scattered along the bays and rivers. John Josselyn noted that "Black Point consisted of about fifty dwelling houses . . . scatteringly built." East of Black Point lay "scatteringly the Town of Casco upon a large bay."[29] King Philip's War changed that. Now people sought safety in compact settlements, with most families building their homes in close proximity to new forts that guarded settlements and provided refuge during attack. In September 1680 Thomas Danforth, the Massachusetts magistrate who had been given authority over Maine, held a court in Falmouth, specifically to create a new compact resettlement. Danforth appropriated all the land on Falmouth Neck, divided it into several dozen house lots, and distributed it to former settlers and newcomers. The focal point of these lots was Fort Loyal, constructed on a small rise on the waterfront near the foot of present-day India Street. In addition to the fort, the homes of four residents were established as stout garrison houses, where people could seek shelter should they not be able to make it to Fort Loyal during a surprise Wabanaki attack.[30]

Authorities established other formerly dispersed towns in the region in a similar fashion. Kennebec settlers gathered in a new location, appropriately called Newtown, on the southern end of Arrowsic Island. A few miles to the east, Sheepscot settlers formed a compact village renamed New Dartmouth. The former residents of Pemaquid returned, with most choosing to settle in a compact village, now called Jamestown, in honor of James the Duke of York, who had established a new government in the Kennebec-Pemaquid region. In all of these locations, the principle feature of the new communities was a substantial fort, standing on high ground to protect the nearby homesteads. The re-establishment of these settlements in such a fashion was a physical demonstration of the changed relationship between the English and Wabanaki residents of the region. In the wake of King Philip's War, English settlers expected more trouble. They were prepared to fight for their homes the next time and not abandon them.[31]

Symbolic of this political reality was the renaming of the settlements. Although many native American place names, such as Casco, had disappeared in Massachusetts' imperialism in the 1650s, most townships that still had Native names lost them with resettlement in the late 1670s. The native Names of Arrowsic, Sheepscot, and Pemaquid yielded to Newtown, New Dartmouth, and Jamestown. The principle holdout was Saco, a Native name that would not be replaced by Biddeford until the town was re-established at the end of Queen Anne's War in 1713. The English may have been driven from Maine once, but they re-established their claim with forts, compact settlements, and, in the tradition of John Smith, new English names. The choice of names reflected not just English claims of ownership, but also the West Country ties of many settlers of Maine. Kittery, Wells, Biddeford, Falmouth, and Dartmouth are all West Country place names, as is the County of Cornwall, the name chosen for the Duke of York's holdings in Maine.

However, as John Smith surely learned, naming a place does not guarantee your ownership and continued occupation of a land. In 1688 the fragile peace collapsed, and the English and Wabanaki found themselves engaged in a new struggle dubbed King William's War. This conflict soon became part of a larger war between England and France. This time, Falmouth faced attack from the Wabanaki and their French Canadian allies. Although initially successful in fending off attacks, in May 1690 Fort Loyal surrendered to a combined Wabanaki and French force after five days of bitter fighting. The inhabitants of Fort Loyal had negotiated an agreement of safe passage to other English settlements upon the surrender of the fort. Unfortunately, when they marched out under a flag of truce, the French were unable to control their Native allies, who set upon the unarmed garrison, killing most of them and taking the rest in captivity to Canada. Fort Loyal had been the key remaining stronghold in Maine. Its fall triggered the rapid abandonment of virtually all settlements in the region. Soon, only Kittery, York, and Wells remained, and these beleaguered communities faced repeated attacks and raids. Thus, the destruction of Falmouth and Fort Loyal signaled another end to English aspirations in Maine.[32]

A New Casco?

Treaties between the English and French in 1697, and Massachusetts and the Wabanaki in 1699, brought peace and a return of the inhabitants of Casco Bay. By this time, the indigenous population of Casco Bay had entirely disappeared. Those few who had not been killed off by disease or warfare had probably migrated to Wabanaki settlements up the Presumpscot River and on Sebago Lake, or to the large village at Pejepscot Falls on the Androscoggin River. Even English settlers were few. There is no evidence to suggest that anyone returned to Falmouth Neck. Perhaps the tragedy at Fort Loyal was too much for the returnees to consider. In 1700, Massachusetts established a new fort off the peninsula, on a point of land about a mile and a half east of the mouth of the Presumpscot River. The Wabanaki had requested the establishment of Fort New

Casco, a convenient and reliable place of trade, since their survival depended increasingly on English goods. The post even included a blacksmith, who could repair broken Native firearms. Authorities meant for Fort New Casco to be a place of accommodation that could rebuild friendship between the English and the Wabanaki. Perhaps the choice of name and location symbolized an effort at a new beginning for all the war-weary residents of Maine. Casco was after all, a Native place name, a term also used for the emerging English settlements in Casco Bay in the early years of English settlement. It harkened back to the peaceful relationship between Samoset, Skitterygusset, and Christopher Levett. Would New Casco be a second chance for the Native and English residents of Maine to live in peace?[33]

The establishment of Fort New Casco as a place for trade recognized Casco Bay's continued role as a "middle ground" where Englishman and Wabanaki might meet in peace. Treaties ending King Philip's War and King William's War were signed at Casco Bay, and more negotiations would occur by the Bay in the future. In June 1701 Massachusetts commissioners met with Wabanaki sachems at Casco to reaffirm an admittedly shaky peace. The negotiations concluded with the raising of two stone cairns, to be called the Two Brothers, which symbolized the peaceful relations between these two peoples. Presumably, two nearby islands still called "The Brothers" received their names at this time.[34]

Unfortunately, the peace was all too brief. In 1702 England and France renewed hostilities. In June 1703 a grand council was held between the Wabanaki and the Massachusetts Governor Joseph Dudley at Fort New Casco to renew the peace. Gifts were exchanged, and both parties added new rocks to the Two Brothers. Two months later, a combined Wabanaki and French force of five hundred men swept through Maine, killing and capturing dozens of settlers and destroying homesteads. Queen Anne's War had come to Maine. The English quickly abandoned their Casco Bay homesteads, which were soon destroyed by the Wabanaki. Fort New Casco remained as a lone English outpost in the region until peace finally returned in 1713. Though it survived the war, in 1716 the Massachusetts Legislature ordered the demolition of Fort New Casco and the removal of its stores to Falmouth Neck, where the resettlement of Falmouth was just beginning. The demolition merely confirmed what everyone knew: the dream of a New Casco had long evaporated.[35]

Portland

In 1783, at the end of the American Revolution, an effort was begun to separate the Neck from the rest of Falmouth. Eventually the Massachusetts General Court gave its assent, and, symbolically, on the United States' tenth birthday, 4 July 1786, the law took effect. Several names for the new town were considered, including Falmouthport and Casco, before the name Portland was selected. This name had previously been applied to what is now known as Bang's Island, and the nearby headland, in Cape Elizabeth. This area was named after Portland Island, on the coast of Dorset in southwestern England. Naming a town after a landmark in a neighboring community seems to be a somewhat curious choice, and unfortunately, the reasoning for it is lost. Perhaps like those before them, the people who were rebuilding Falmouth Neck after the British bombardment wanted a fresh start with a new name. As they celebrated their national independence as well as their new local autonomy, the residents of Portland must have believed that they would be the last people to choose a name and form a government for the neck of land the Wabanaki had once called Machegonne. If the ghosts of Skitterygusset and George Cleeve were looking on, surely they would have had a different view. They might have even speculated on what Portland would be, after it was Portland.[36]

Notes

1. The two most detailed histories of Portland in the seventeenth century are Edwin A. Churchill, "Too Great the Challenge: The Birth and Death of Falmouth, Maine, 1624–1676" (Ph.D. dissertation, University of Maine, 1979) and William Willis, *The History of Portland* (Portland: Bailey and Noyes, 1865). Both are excellent resources that were relied on extensively in this essay.

2. Fannie Hardy Eckstorm, *Indian Place Names of the Penobscot Valley and the Maine Coast* (Orono: University of Maine, 1941), 163–69. The best general survey of Maine prehistory can be found in Bruce J. Bourque, *Twelve Thousand Years: American Indians in Maine* (Lincoln: University of Nebraska Press, 2001).

3. Eckstorm, *Indian Place Names*, 161–62, 170–71. Harald Prins, "Children of Gluskap: Wabanaki Indians on the Eve of the European Invasion" in Emerson W. Baker, et al., eds., *American Beginnings: Exploration, Culture and Cartography in the Land of Norumbega* (Lincoln: University of Nebraska Press, 1994),

95–117; William Cronon, *Changes in the Land: Indians, Colonists, and the Ecology of New England* (New York: Hill and Wang, 1983), 55–71.

4. Emerson W. Baker, "Finding the Almouchiquois: Native American Families, Territories and Land Sales in Southern Maine," in *Ethnohistory* 51, no. 1 (2004): 73–100; Bourque, *Twelve Thousand Years*, 105–08, 142–44.

5. Samuel Purchas, "The Description of the Country of Mawooshen Discovered by the English in the Yeere 1602 3. 5. 6. 7. 8. and 9," in *Hakluytus Posthumus or Purchas His Pilgrimes*, vol. 19, Samuel Purchas, ed. (Glasgow, 1902), 400–05.

6. Emerson W. Baker, "Finding the Almouchiquois," 78–82.

7. W. L. Grant, ed., *Voyages of Samuel de Champlain, 1604–1618* (New York: Charles Scribner's Sons, 1970), 58–59, 76, 89–91. Marc Lescarbot, *Nova Francia: A Description of Acadia, 1606* (London: George Routledge and Sons, 1928), 52; Baker, "Finding the Almouchiquois," 80; Bourque, *Twelve Thousand Years in Maine*, 113, 118–19.

8. John Smith, "A Description of New England," in *Sailors' Narratives along the New England Coast*, George Parker Winship, ed. (New York: Burt Frankin, 1968), 213–47; Neal Salisbury, *Manitou and Providence: Indians, Europeans, and the Making of New England, 1500–1643* (New York: Oxford University Press, 1982), 96–102. J. B. Harley, "New England Cartography and the Native Americans," in Baker, et al., eds., *American*, 296–304.

9. The quote is from the Great Patent for New England, 3 November 1620, in Mary F. Farnham, ed., The Farnham Papers, Vol. 7 of *The Documentary History of the State of Maine* (Portland: Maine Historical Society, 1901), 26; John G. Reid, "Political Definitions: Creating Maine and Acadia," in Baker et al., *American Beginnings*, 179–80.

10. The quote is from Secretary Conway to the Lord President of York, 26 June 1623, in James P. Baxter, *Christopher Levett of York, The Pioneer Colonist in Casco Bay* (Portland, Maine, 1893), 14; Christopher Levett, "A Voyage Into New England Begun in 1623 and Ended in 1624," Roger Howell, Jr., ed., in Maine Historical Society, *Maine in the Age of Discovery: Christopher Levett's Voyage 1623, 1624 and A Guide to Sources* (Portland: Maine Historical Society, 1988), 39, 45–46.

11. Levett, "A Voyage Into New England," 44–50.

12. Reid, "Political Definitions: Creating Maine and Acadia," 173–74, 179–81; Henry Burrage, *The Beginnings of Colonial Maine, 1602–1658* (Portland, Maine: Marks Printing House, 1914), 197–213; The origins of the name "Maine" are unknown. It may have been named in honor of Queen Henrietta Maria, the wife of Charles I of England, for she was the feudal proprietor of the French Province of Maine. It may have been named after the village of Broadmayne, which was near the ancesteral home of the Gorges family. Or, it may have evolved out of sailors' references to "the main" or the mainland, as opposed to the many islands off the coast of Maine.

13. Edwin A. Churchill, "A Most Ordinary Lot of Men: The Fishermen at Richmond Island, Maine in the Early Seventeenth Century," *New England Quarterly* 57, mo. 2 (1984): 184–204; Churchill, "Too Great the Challenge," 30–31; Wilbur Spencer, *Pioneers on Maine Rivers* (Baltimore: Genealogical Publishing Company, 1973), 199–201; Richard Dunn, James Savage, and Laetitia Yeandle, eds., *The Journal of John Winthrop* (Cambridge, Mass.: Harvard University Press, 1996), 59.

14. Edwin A. Churchill, "A Most Ordinary Lot of Men,"201–04.

15. Churchill, "Too Great the Challenge," 33–39, 166–67; Churchill is the most authoritative history of early Portland and also provides the most detailed account of the Winter-Cleeve affair and related disputes. The following pages rely heavily on his interpretation of the conflict. Willis, *History of Portland*, 36–39.

16. The quote is from Sir Ferdinando Gorges to George Cleeve and Richard Tucker, 27 January 1636, *York Deeds,* Vol. 1 (Portland: Maine Historical Society, 1887), 95–96; Willis, *History of Portland*, 49; Sybil Noyes, Charles T. Libby, and Walter G. Davis, *Genealogical Dictionary of Maine and New Hampshire* (Baltimore: Genealogical Publishing Company, 1979), 451.

17. Noyes et al., *Genealogical Dictionary of Maine and New Hampshire*, 149–50, 698.

18. Churchill, "Too Great the Challenge," 107–08; James P. Baxter, ed., *The Trelawney Papers*, Vol. 3 of *The Documentary History of the State of Maine* (Portland, Maine, 1884), 461; Baker, "Finding the Almouchiquois," 82–86.

19. The best treatment of the complex proprietary struggle between Cleeve and Gorges and their allies is in Churchill, "Too Great the Challenge," 166–70, 178–96; Farnham, ed., *Farnham Papers*, 133–36; Noyes et al., *Genealogical Dictionary of Maine and New Hampshire*, 274.

20. Willis, *History of Portland*, 88–90; John G. Reid, *Acadia, Maine, and New Scotland: Marginal Colonies in the Seventeenth Century* (Toronto: University of Toronto Press, 1981), 127–35.

21. Charles Banks, *Topographical Dictionary of English Immigrants* (Baltimore: Genealogical Publishing Company, 1963), 15; Noyes et al., *Genealogical Dictionary of Maine and New Hampshire*, 98–99.

22. Almost a thousand Royalist troops defended against a five-month assault of Pendennis Castle, one of the longest and most dramatic sieges of the war. The garrison was reduced to eating horse and dog meat before yielding, and upon surrender fully half of the starved soldiers were so weak that they could not walk out of the castle. Samuel R. Gardiner, *History of the Great Civil War, 1642–1649* (New York: Longmans, Green and Co., 1897), I: 105–06; II: 284; III: 67, 92, 139; IV: 173; Ronald Hutton and Wylie Reeves, "Sieges and Fortifications," in John Kenyon and Lane Ohlmeyer, *The Civil Wars: A Military History of England, Scotland, and Ireland, 1638–1660* (New York: Oxford University Press,

1998), 225–26. Robert Ashton, *Counter-Revolution: The Second Civil War and Its Origins*, 1646–1648 (New Haven: Yale University Press, 1994), 403–05. Several strongholds in Wales did hold out after all Royalists in England surrendered.

23. Paul J. Lindholt, ed., *John Josselyn, Colonial Traveler: A Critical Edition of Two Voyages to New England* (Hanover: University Press of New England, 1988), 19, 135, 138; Noyes et al., *Genealogical Dictionary of Maine and New Hampshire*, 380–81; Emerson Baker, "The World of Thomas Gorges," in Baker et al., eds., *American Beginnings*, 281–82.

24. *York Deeds*, 2: 116.

25. Charles T. Libby, ed., *Province and Court Records of Maine*, Vol. 1 (Portland: Maine Historical Society, 1928), 317, 325: Reid, *Acadia, Maine and New Scotland*, 149–52;

26. *York Deeds*, 2: 27; Reid, *Acadia, Maine and New Scotland*, 151–52.

27. *York Deeds*, 6: 164.

28. William Hubbard, "A Narrative of the Troubles with the Indians in New England from Piscataqua to Pemaquid," in *The Indian Wars in New England*, Samuel Drake, ed. (New York, 1971, orig. publ. 1677), 50–51, 138–39; Churchill, "Too Great the Challenge," 336–38; Reid, "Political Definitions: Creating Maine and Acadia," 184.

29. Lindholdt, ed., *Two Voyages to New England*, 138–39.

30. Willis, *History of Portland*, 225–36.

31. Emerson W. Baker, "English Settlement Patterns and Site Characteristics in Seventeenth-Century Maine." Paper presented at the Council for Northeast Historical Archaeology annual meeting, Portsmouth, New Hampshire, 1993, October; William A. Baker, *A Maritime History of Bath, Maine and the Kennebec Region* (Bath, Maine: Marine Research Society of Bath, 1973), 41; David Cushman, The History of Ancient Sheepscot and Newcastle (Bath, Maine: E. Upton and Son Printers, 1882), 63–68; Franklin B. Hough, ed., "Papers Relating to Pemaquid," Maine Historical Society *Collections* Vol. 5 (1857), 79.

32. Willis, *History of Portland*, 276–88.

33. Kenneth Morrison, *The Embattled Northeast: The Elusive Ideal of Alliance in Abenaki-Euramerican Relations* (Berkeley: University of California Press, 1984), 141–50; Willis, *History of Portland*, 309–11.

34. Emerson Baker and John Reid. "Amerindian Power in the Early Modern Northeast: A Reappraisal," *William and Mary Quarterly* 61, no. 1 (2004): 102–03; Morrison, *The Embattled Northeast*, 150–53.

35. Willis, *History of Portland*, 310–13.

36. Willis, History of Portland, 579–82. In 1677, the Reverend William Hubbard described a military expedition in February 1677 that "set sayl with our Vessels from Black Point for Portland." This is the earliest surviving reference to Portland that this author has been able to find. William Hubbard, "A Narrative of the Troubles," 212.

2

Thriving and Elegant Town

Eighteenth-Century Portland as Commercial Center

Charles P. M. Outwin

To anyone standing in the driving rain at the top of Middle Street on 21 October 1775, looking northeastward and downhill toward the waterfront, the view would have been dismal. Where only a week earlier there had been a flourishing, populous and attractive seaport, teeming with business activity, full of craftsmen's shops, stores, shipyards and many homes, large and elegant to small and modest, there was now only a horrid morass of mud, wet ash and debris, with thinly scattered, blackened chimney stumps, charred and leafless trees, and a few scorched and deserted buildings. The port of Falmouth in Casco Bay, shiretown and commercial center for Cumberland County, and perhaps the most important forest products supplier in the entire British Empire at that time, had been burned by His Majesty's vengeful naval forces in one awful day of punishment. The livelihoods of thousands of people were destroyed, as was, ironically enough, the Royal Navy's principal source of masts, booms, and spars.

The seaport had become great due to its favorable location, abundant resources, and, most particularly, the determination, mercantile expertise, and manufacturing skill of its inhabitants. Its products were shipped everywhere, and its leading inhabitants were known and esteemed throughout His Majesty's realm. But Falmouth, whose very success presented an affront to British home-county mercantile domination, was to be overwhelmed at last by sociopolitical circumstances its business community had long sought to avoid or deny. In attempting to remain aloof from the noncommercial issues that so disturbed the late 1760s and early 1770s, the trade-oriented inhabitants of Falmouth failed

to legitimate themselves politically either to suspicious British authorities, or the newly and radically empowered rural folk of Cumberland
County. However, the catastrophe of 18 October 1775 would not mark
the end of trade on the Fore River. The new American city of Portland,
which was to overlay the ruins of British Falmouth's seaport, would in
time benefit from the same geographic, physical, and demographic advantages as those of the old colonial town.

Place: Environs, Resources, and the Rise of the Seaport

With the end of Queen Anne's War in 1713, the attention of merchants
and politicians in Boston had once again turned to Massachusetts' vast
if vaguely defined territories north of New Hampshire's brief shore.
Although Maine at the beginning of the 1700s remained a raw, dangerous frontier, the site of Falmouth itself had great potential. It offered
easy defensibility, because of the physical disposition of the peninsula
called "the Neck," between three substantial bodies of water: Back
Cove, southern Casco Bay, and the broad Fore River. In addition, it
possessed a large, well-protected harbor, safe from damaging winds
and usually ice-free, even in those years not long after the end of the
Little Ice Age. The Fore River bottom consisted of light gravel and
sand, eroded from the ancient metamorphic bedrock of the immediate
area, covered with a thin layer of silt, providing good anchorage everywhere. The waterway was relatively easy to negotiate, too, being well
aligned to New England's prevailing winds, with a broad, deep ship
channel that was never subject to a current of more than one or two
knots. Another attraction was the huge reserve of wood that lay readily
available and relatively close-by, providing an immediate source of employment and a highly marketable commodity. Moreover, the provincial government in Boston soon found a settlement at Falmouth convenient and safe as a headquarters for the defense of the northern
frontier, as well as a suitable venue for elaborate negotiations with leaders of the Wabanaki, Penobscot, and Passamaquoddy nations.[1]

   With this same eye for business enterprise, the conditions on land for
settlement were also determined to be fortunate. The well-watered port
area alone had at least three streams and a couple of ponds, as well as a
large public spring on the northeastern shoulder of Bramhall's Hill. The

soil on the Neck was good enough to permit the planting of kitchen gardens and orchards, and to provide sufficient pasture for livestock. A meandering natural causeway, at outer Back (now Congress) Street between Stroudwater and the place where that road was to intersect with the King's Highway (Stevens Avenue) in the late 1760s, afforded protected access to the hinterland, while a shallow ford across Wear Creek at the southern end of Back Cove led to what became that inlet's western waterside farms and mills (Figure 2-1).

As the town grew, so did demands placed on its food supply. Terrain around Falmouth was gradually cleared of trees and converted to agriculture. The best farmland in the region, indeed the finest in all of Maine until the interior of the state was opened up in the early nineteenth century, was in Gorham. This was for a simple but crucial reason: the soil (glacial marine outwash) though somewhat sandy, was nearly free of large stones. After a few years' improvement with wood ash, mulch, and manure, the extensive farms of Gorham became very productive. In 1765, a Farmers' Market was instituted on Falmouth Neck at the newly designated Haymarket (now Monument Square) as a venue for the farm owners to distribute their products. There was plenty of meat available, too, as suggested by the presence of a large and productive tannery, cobblers, saddlers, and other leather workers.

The climate in southern Maine, however, was not good for raising wheat. Farmers found that, because of the frequent damp and cold during the short growing season, ripe wheat was attacked by "black smut," (*ustilago nigra*), a form of the mildew fungus, destroying first the top of the stem and then the grains themselves from the inside out before the seedhead could be harvested. This was a problem, because when supplies of "corn" (as wheat was commonly called then) were low, the public tended to become fearful of famine, because of belief in the absolute, biblically validated necessity of bread. The merchants of Falmouth found it highly profitable, as well as a worthwhile public cause, to import great shiploads of wheat and other grains to lower Casco Bay, primarily from ports in the northern Chesapeake and Delaware Bay regions. "Indian corn," or maize, on the other hand, grew reasonably well in Cumberland County and became a staple crop on the farms of the hinterlands, if not in town.[2]

Imported wheat was stored in granaries in the port area itself, such as that belonging to the Scots immigrant Alexander Ross, Falmouth's foremost merchant in the 1760s. A large windmill was built on the southeast

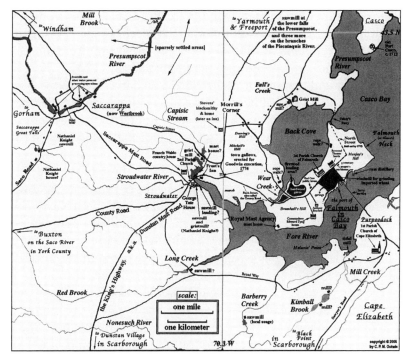

Figure 2-1. Falmouth in Casco Bay (Portland) and lower Cumberland County, c. 1775. Map by the author. Copyright © 2005 by C. P. M. Outwin.

side of Back Street, in the saddle between the port's two hills open to the prevailing winds from northwest and southwest, apparently devoted to the grinding of wheat flour. The consequential limitation of supply, though, caused the price of wheat and flour to vary widely, and some-times wildly, affecting not only the availability of bread, "the staff of life," but of beer as well, the "working man's friend" of that age. Both were used copiously at most meals throughout the colonies. The people of the hinterlands, also in need of wheat but never rich, grudgingly en-dured these price fluctuations. In time, they would conceive an ill-concealed dislike of the port's people in general and merchants in par-ticular, whom they suspected of intentionally manipulating wheat, flour, and other prices.

Beer was not the only drink available, though perhaps the safest. A number of merchants, traders, and innkeepers had licenses to sell an excellent variety of tea, including the hard-to-get Chinese green teas.

For the wealthier households, wines were also available for sipping or punch making. A distillery on the wharf at Machegonne Point, under the southeastern flank of Munjoy's Hill, produced rum from molasses brought back from the Windward Islands by traders.

Casco Bay and the Gulf of Maine bore great harvests of seafood, and most of Falmouth's inhabitants enjoyed recreational fishing. The large numbers of shell middens found at sites around Casco Bay indicate great quantities of oysters, mussels, clams, and scallops consumed over the centuries before 1760. There are also tales of merry chowdering parties that would go out for the day to the Casco Bay islands. While there is no indication of the existence of a local fishing fleet, per se, the town's merchants sent regular and frequent expeditions to eastern Nova Scotia and Newfoundland for salt fish. It is therefore unlikely that many in Falmouth's port were ever wanting for sufficient food.[3]

Nevertheless, what made Falmouth in Casco Bay so truly outstanding in the British realm was its extensive trade in forest products. In the last years before the industrial revolution, wood was still the most important strategic material in the world, and hundreds of thousands of acres of easily accessible primeval forest lay within a few miles of the Fore River. Tree trunks had not only to be collected quickly, and economically, but processed into all manner of products as well, including structural timber, implements of all types, and conveyances necessary for the support of every aspect of eighteenth-century British society. The white pine (*pinus strobus*) in particular was the central pillar of Falmouth's economy, the source of the masts and spars that drove His Majesty's fighting ships and, through its merchant vessels, the realm's commerce.[4]

Still more woodland, extending to the very feet of the White Mountains some fifty miles away, could be accessed via the Sebago Lake and Long Lake systems. Logs could not be transported farther than that by water because, except for the Fore River itself, most of the streams in lower Cumberland County are either minimally or not at all navigable. Instead, both finished lumber from inland mills and raw trunks from the forest were transported by ox-wain over excellent "mast roads" which by the mid-eighteenth century crisscrossed the relatively level countryside east and southeast of Sebago. Further, the moderate but definite slope from the White Mountain piedmont to the nearby coastal plain permitted damming and the operation of many automated "sash"-type sawmills near the narrow channels, steep banks, and gentle falls of the Stroudwater, Presumpscot, and Pisquataquis rivers of lower Cumberland County.[5]

The Royal Navy, in particular, had come to rely heavily on American sources of wood by 1760, and Falmouth was at the very center of this supply. The Admiralty had been seeking to develop and exploit Britain's New World wood resources for over a century. Before the lumbering of forests in New England and the middle Appalachian piedmont began, Britain was dependent on expensive timber from eastern Prussia, Riga, Finland, Sweden, and northern Poland, especially from this last-named source for a sufficient supply of long main masts for frigates and ships of the line. Costs for such materials when so procured could be astronomic, and were often subject to arbitrary, politically motivated interruption. Wood from America was the answer. Imperial and provincial control over the supply began to be exerted in the late 1680s, and by 1726 the Royal Mast Agency had been permanently moved to Falmouth.

Maine's forest products were shipped all over the empire, as far as Barbados and Surinam in the south and, through factors in England and Scotland, as far east as the British East India Company's holdings in wood-poor South Asia. Britain, in other words, had by the eve of the War for Independence become almost entirely dependent on American wood, especially that supplied by Falmouth in Casco Bay.[6]

People: The Size, Composition, and Character of the Seaport Population

Before 1760, the whole amorphous region called Maine had been encompassed by York County. Falmouth had by the end of the Seven Years' (French and Indian) War (1756–63) surpassed the older regional hubs at York and Saco as a "central place," due to both an exploding population and to the booming economic activity of the port, and was thought to require a jurisdiction of its own. A network of small towns north of Saco, reaching as far inland as the hills southwest of Sebago Lake and as far north as the Androscoggin River, had sprung up between the 1720s and the 1760s that were in one way or another dependent on Falmouth for supplies and services, both basic and specialized. These communities, in turn, supplied the seaport not only with food but also with the considerable raw and processed materials necessary for carrying on business. Thus, the commercial center on Falmouth Neck became the region's legal center, too, the *defacto* capital of the district of Maine. By the advent of the War for Independence, due to the demand for labor to support Falmouth's many enterprises, and the anticipation of wealth, the seaport boomtown of Falmouth in Casco Bay had also become one of the larger settlements in British North America, and far richer than most. Landless immigrants from other colonial territories, prevented from spreading west by restrictions imposed by the Proclamation of 1763, flooded into York, Lincoln, and especially, Cumberland counties.[7]

The town's business community, engaging in transactions with places very far removed from Casco Bay, had also become the biggest population group in Falmouth for which there is substantial documentation. Merchants, traders, master craftsmen (then called "mechanics") and shopkeepers, those whose primary concern *was* commerce, composed the members of Falmouth's upper and middling classes involving approximately half of the people living in the port area itself. So, in terms of both numbers and power, people occupied principally in commerce dominated life in the port area.

The next largest group of persons in the port of Falmouth may have been its poor menial laborers, perhaps as many as a thousand at the height of employment during the early 1770s. However, there is no way of establishing accurate figures for this group, because it appears that it was mostly transient. Slaves, though better documented, constituted a modest work force in Falmouth, never numbering more than 2.5 percent of the town's total population, and usually less. Nearly all of these were employed as skilled domestic servants. Unlike other colonial ports in North America at the time, almost no note is made of any slaves working on the waterfront. Instead, numerous cashiered seamen, poor landless immigrants, and members of such seasonally transient groups as "the Sumac Gatherers" provided, on a *per diem* basis, any unskilled or semiskilled labor needed along the Fore River bank and in the seaport.[8]

"Master mariners" (the period's term for sea captains) and seafarers, augmented by ship and boat builders, and shipwrights rounded out the core of the town's leading persons, along with church ministers, physicians, surgeons and apothecaries, customs officials, town and county officers, school teachers, and various draftsmen and migrant artists, some thirty-four professionals. At perhaps 60 percent, the total number of all leading commercial, professional, and shipping persons in Falmouth made up a much higher proportion of the town's population than that found in most other British North American ports. Prominent families intermarried, and relatives assisted one another in the creation and maintenance of business enterprise. Many of the men were Freemasons, members of the Falmouth Lodge, first chartered in 1764, or of another fraternal organization, the Friendly Society. Such strong relationships served to further bind the community together.[9]

But this was no rigid, hidebound upper class. Many who, by 1770, were prominent men of affairs had begun as mere craftsmen, and thus were not much removed in their origins from any town and country smallholders who later came to resent them. The way remained open throughout the period for newcomers to rise through the town's higher social circles, a phenomenon repeated in later boomtowns of the nineteenth and twentieth centuries. Even some small shopkeepers, taverners, and innkeepers came to be counted among Falmouth's respectable persons.

Thus, the seaport, in spite of the tremendous increase in immigration and political upheavals prompted by the misconduct of too many imperial officials during the 1760s and early 1770s, was in itself a remarkably well-knit and yet open community. This was because the activities of so many of its inhabitants were more keenly focused on prosperity than on the reinforcement of immutable privilege. Nevertheless, some persons with wealth or family standing were never fully accepted by "polite society." Benjamin Mussey, though good at his craft as a brick maker and moderately wealthy, never mixed in polite circles because of crude manners and generally hostile attitude. Some, like Jonathan "Pithy" Webb, though "well-born," lacked initiative, while others, such as the prosperous Winslow family of Quakers at Presumpscot village, belonged to a group that intentionally set itself off from the rest of society.

Commerce: Enterprise by Land and Sea

The merchants of Falmouth were canny, having been trained by the best not only at home but also in Boston, New York, and Britain itself. They had a solid command of double-entry bookkeeping and other sound business practices, and this knowledge extended to many who were counted mere traders, among whom barter still occurred. Further, during the boom, Falmouth was able to take advantage of reforms in currency regulation (instituted between 1749 and 1751, but whose implementation was delayed by the Seven Years' War) that brought on a tremendous expansion of trade between the British New World colonies, and with the mother country. Commercial activity generated much needed currency, so much so that projects in town developed by subscription, such as a public library opened in 1766, or the purchase of a fire engine, could be subsidized with hard cash.10

The business community of Falmouth was fortunate in this, because British supply-side merchants, called "factors," demanded payment in silver or gold specie. The leading merchants and shop owners of Falmouth, as well as the innkeepers and tavern owners, dealt mainly in coined money. This remained the rule, except where entire large cargo lots were concerned, or where unwieldy sums might be involved. In that case, the use of bills-of-credit between merchants was still the common practice, as it was all along the eastern seaboard. The issue of credit may have contributed to an increase in ill will toward the people of the port of Falmouth among Cumberland County's rural folk. For although the merchants were more than happy to extend credit to one another, knowing (or hoping) each other to be "honest men," they remained cautious of their inland clients, as the number of writs for the collection of debt still in existence indicate. Traders filled some of the country folks' needs through barter, of course, but in the case of store-bought items, a cash and carry rule still applied, even if some merchants also did, on occasion, permit small credit arrangements for their best customers.11

The extraordinary quantities of masts and spars required by the Royal Navy alone at mid-century played a critical role in Falmouth's prosperity. A "first-rate" ship of the line, with a displacement of some three thousand tons, required mainmasts that could reach over two hundred feet in length, and fore and mizzen masts of between 150 and 185 feet long. Even with segmented masts, the lengths required for each piece were quite long and, necessarily, thick. Trees of such immensity could only be found in the few remaining untouched old-growth forests of Maine and New Hampshire. Furthermore, each ship had to carry enough extra spars not only to replace yards and booms carried away in action or bad weather, but also to jury-rig masts if the regular ones were lost overboard or broken. Add to this the needs of an ever-expanding commercial fleet, and one realizes that (regular trade in lumber aside) many thousands of tons of masts and spars alone had to pass through Falmouth each year, both for local use and for the world at large. All these goods had to be loaded safely and shipped where they were most needed, and Falmouth's merchants and mariners rose smartly to the test.12

Even so, contrary to the inference of some historians, masts and spars were not the only important goods manufactured in quantity both for domestic use and for export from Falmouth. Cargo vessels of anywhere from one hundred to over one thousand gross tons, as well as boats of all sizes and for all uses, were built and entirely outfitted in several yards around the Fore River with items made in Falmouth. The seaport's waterfront itself had two considerable shipyards, producing as many as two or three large vessels per year each at the height of their activity and one large boatyard making everything from small skiffs to medium-sized sloops. These vessels were built primarily using oak, but also maple, birch, chestnut, beech, elm, or even fir, as any given project might call for. Bigger ships required thousands of trees per hull, representing the clearing of twenty-five acres or more of woodland per ship. Sails were made in Falmouth, too, and there may have been a ropewalk somewhere on the southwestern shore of Back Cove, and perhaps another on the northwestern side of Munjoy's Hill above that protected tidal basin (Figure 2-2).[13]

The port was vibrant with the sights and sounds of thriving maritime-related industry. The multiple blacksmithies in the port area itself, owned by such masters as the Pettingill brothers, were the high-tech engineering outfits of the day. They produced and repaired all sorts of iron domestic, commercial and ship's hardware and tools, and possibly even firearms. A large tannery belonging to the Cotton family supplied a variety of materials to both tradesman and leather workers including cobblers, saddlers, ship and boats wrights, and bosun's crews. Ephraim Broad, the greengrocer on Preble's wharves at the foot of King (now India) Street, may have acted as a ship's chandler, as well as supplying the land-based population.

All crafts associated with wood products had to be present to make the economy of Falmouth operate, although there is little evidence for the existence of some. For instance, charcoal burners appear nowhere in the colonial records of Falmouth and Cumberland County. The same applies to pine tar producers, who made more of their product than was turned out by the Carolinas at that time, and there is no record of large amounts of pitch, gum, or turpentine being brought into Falmouth. There must have been many more loggers, too, than is suggested by surviving records, not only because of the demands of the Royal Mast Agency in Stroudwater, which collected masts from as far away as the Saco and Kennebec river valleys, but because of the vast quantities of

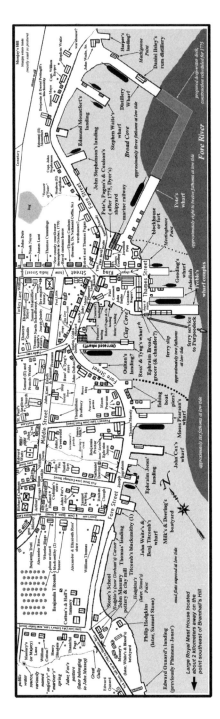

Figure 2-2. Falmouth in Casco Bay (Portland), Maine, c. 1770–1775. * Ross' and Tyng's wharf, their shop, and the businesses gathered around the Hodgkin's Corner were the only structures spared in the central commercial district during the catastrophe of 18 October 1775. Some buildings above southwestern Middle Street, and beyond Bank (Congress) Street, also survived. Chart by the author. Copyright © 2005 by Charles P. M. Outwin. All Rights Reserved. Sources: Goodue 1890; Willis 1864; Freeman 1832; Deane c. 1810; Seymour 1786; Murray 1781; Pointer 1776; Polaskowitz (at the British Museum 1770; Mowatt/DesBarres, 1760 & 1775.

privately exported lumber and ships' materials. Transport of timber and long mast segments required numerous large ox teams, but there is little or no mention of these, or their drovers, either. Although blacksmithies and brass smiths in Falmouth are well documented, it is not known if they also worked in copper, although they must have had to, at least in some measure, both because of the need for copper ships' rivets that would not "rot," and because the size of ships built there necessitated protection of hulls from sea worms by means of copper sheathing. Yet, simply because of the presence of so many active shipyards and such large, productive blacksmithies alone in the immediate vicinity of Falmouth, all these enterprises had to exist and in fact thrive.

Thus, many if not most crafts practiced around and on Falmouth Neck appear to have been geared one way or another toward ship production or maintenance, employing the now largely faceless, skilled, and semiskilled work force in addition to better-documented apprentices and journeymen. All implements made of iron, leather, wood, canvas, hemp, as well as all chandlers' materials were produced locally. The vessels built at Falmouth's yards were provisioned and equipped, fully loaded with products, and then often sold in their entirety upon reaching Britain or one of the other colonial ports, particularly the British West Indies.

Most communication with the outside world, predictably, was by water. Packet boats for Boston and other seafaring towns came and went regularly. Royal Navy ships, especially an unremarkable, medium-sized, sixteen-gun hydrographic survey sloop named the *Canceaux*, called often. Local coasting and transoceanic brigs and flutes, sloops, schooners, and barks visited with such regularity that Arthur Savage, the Royal Collector of Customs appointed in 1759, had a covered all-weather naval observatory built on top of his grand new house on Middle Street in 1763, so that newcomers could be seen arriving in the Portland ship channel at any time.[14]

He believed he had reason to be concerned. The sheer volume of trade out of Falmouth raised suspicions of importation irregularity with Royal customs officials in both Boston and at home. Smuggling, as a result, was a major issue of contention between colonial merchants and Royal customs officials. Legitimate businessmen were often accused of evading importation duties in the fifteen years preceding the outbreak of hostilities in 1775. Some of these charges were undoubtedly warranted. In spite of that, because corruption in the customs service was rampant, as it was also in appointive offices throughout the British Empire at that time, other allegations of contraband activity were angrily contested. In a suit argued on 4 July 1771 at Falmouth by John Adams himself, for example, his client Enoch Freeman decried the unjust seizure earlier in the year of a vessel belonging to him. Such reprehensible official behavior doubtlessly added to growing anger in the region; Freeman, previously an enthusiastic British partisan, would soon become chairman of the Falmouth Committee of Correspondence, and the offending official, Arthur Savage, a refugee.[15]

Falmouth's merchants were not averse to risk; just sending wooden ships across the seas involved considerable hazard. Since rum production had proven profitable elsewhere, Jedediah Preble, Enoch Ilsley and his younger brother Daniel, Simeon Mayo, and John Waite, five of the foremost merchants in Falmouth, together invested in the construction of a large distillery, on its own wharf at the far northeastern end of Fore Street. In spite of some local interference due to alcohol-related criminality, this operation, overseen by Daniel Ilsley, was producing enough rum by 1774 to meet substantial regional demand. To be sure, Fiddle Lane (now Franklin Street) that was laid out in 1756 became infamous for its "watering holes," frequented by laborers and sailors on shore leave in their brief periods of leisure. Falmouth's businessmen protected themselves against the occasional consequences of such speculation by means of modest real estate speculation. Major Samuel Waldo (the younger), Falmouth's most prominent citizen before his death in 1769, for example, made most of his money from the development and sale of parcels of his vast real estate holdings in Maine. The value of property was well known to resist changes in economic cycles, and acted as insurance against many less-than-successful mercantile and maritime ventures.[16]

Falmouth's merchants came to fill most of the town's important civic offices, both before and after 1775. Professionals immigrated to town along with the rest of the flood of émigrés in the 1760s, including private schoolmasters, physicians and surgeons, apothecaries, ministers and attorneys, expanding the available pool of talent. The number of master mariners and shipowner-traders also grew to provide for the expanding needs and wants of the port area populace. In addition, the establishment of Cumberland County in 1760 brought imperial offices and personnel. Moses Pearson and William Tyng, for instance, became county sheriff in succession, with Pearson's son-in-law Ephraim Jones briefly filling in as Sheriff *pro tem* in 1767. Theophilous Bradbury (of Newbury, Massachusetts, and a relative of William Tyng) who had first come to Falmouth as a schoolmaster in 1761, soon began law practice in the new county court. Before long, he was made King's Counsel. The highest-ranking royal official in Falmouth was Francis "Frank" Waldo, younger brother of Major Samuel. He was appointed Royal Collector of Customs and actually began work for the customs service in Falmouth in 1758. Both he and other members of Falmouth's social elite with ties to the Crown would eventually flee Massachusetts and America as proscribed Loyalists.[17]

Culture: Mixing Pleasure with Business

Falmouth's elite, whose members also generally belonged to its commercial community, dominated the town's culture. There was no formal protocol for admission to this group. Rather, as suggested previously, a flexible set of criteria included but was not exclusively dependent on tenure as resident, family background and marriage ties, education, wealth, property, military or civic achievement and service, profession or craft, perceived collective indispensability and business capacity. In other words, the boundaries of the social elite were permeable, its membership in constant, if slow, flux. With effort, accumulation of wealth, and the cultivation of civility, almost anyone could achieve good standing in the elite.

Re-examination of membership roles for the Falmouth Lodge of Freemasons, chartered in 1764, proves that members of the social elite mixed with more "humble" artisans, mariners, and farmers.[18] Master craftsmen could be welcomed into the circles of the elite, too, usually after they had branched out into other enterprises and accumulated some wealth and property. Benjamin Titcomb, for instance, came to Falmouth as the town's first blacksmith in 1746. As time went by, he bought land and ships, began sending traders to sea, opened two blacksmithies serving different needs, and served in various town and provincial offices. John Butler, who had apprenticed as a silver- and goldsmith in Boston, also branched out into trade and landownership. He built a very fine house, containing both his business office and his jeweler's shop, adjacent to Preble's Wharf complex, and was accepted by the elite as "handsome, gay, and accomplished."[19]

Unlike other colonial centers in late-eighteenth-century British North America, industriousness appears to have been the principal avenue to success and prestige in Falmouth, perhaps because of its unique status as a boomtown. This does not by any means suggest that family background and luck had no hand in social advancement, but rather that energetic endeavor in business or civic duty was regularly rewarded with recognition and celebrity in Falmouth. Moses Pearson, for example, was by 1760 one of the town's most outstanding residents, a hero of the first Louisburg campaign, a judge and justice of the peace, several times a town official, the first Cumberland County sheriff, and a very wealthy merchant with many advantageous marital connections. Yet he had come to Falmouth from Newbury, Massachusetts, a little over three decades earlier as a nearly penniless carpenter and joiner. Through hard work, land acquisition, civic and military service, and mercantile enterprise, he had made a place for himself among Maine's most distinguished personages.[20] A similar principle could be said to have applied on a humbler level to Bryce "Mac" McLellan, who, though he arrived destitute from Northern Ireland and with little in the way of marketable skills, proved himself valuable as the town's handyman. He accepted municipal positions that no one else wanted, such as coroner and hog reeve, and through application and diligence gained a reputation for reliability. He was therefore enabled to find good positions for his children, and advantageous marriages. His descendants have been among Cumberland County's leading citizens ever since.[21]

The women of Falmouth were by no means inestimable or unenterprising members of society. Many, such as Elizabeth Duguid Ross, wife of Alexander, ran their merchant or professional husband's shops for them or owned business establishments outright. Still others, like Alice Ross Greele (no relation to Alexander) and Johanna Sparhawk Frost, operated their own large taverns and inns. Certainly, such women as Ross, Frost, Sarah Jones Bradbury (diarist and wife of Theophilous, daughter of Ephraim Jones and granddaughter of Moses Pearson) and Elizabeth Foster Coffin (the cultivated wife of Falmouth's foremost surgeon, Nathaniel Coffin Jr.) inhabited the pinnacle of society in Falmouth. They influenced and enriched not only its business climate but its cultural life as well, both before and long after the War of Independence.

Prior to 1760, poorer landowners still lived among the wealthy and had not yet been marginalized. Most houses then were single-family structures. The social elite soon began building big, elegant homes on the upper reaches of King and Middle Streets and along Back Street. Many of the town's leading citizens also owned large country houses, farms, and much undeveloped land in Stroudwater, Saccarappa (now Westbrook), Windham, Gorham, Pearsontown (now Standish), and even farther afield. They eventually functioned as landlords for many of the people they employed, putting them up in multifamily dwellings and other less graceful accommodations on the Neck.

As was true elsewhere, the wealthier inhabitants of Falmouth aspired to and achieved a considerable degree of architectural grandeur, in imitation of the British aristocracy. We have clear descriptions and representations of some houses and buildings, including those belonging to Richard Codman and Arthur Savage. There they lived in comparative luxury. John Adams, in town to argue a case before the Cumberland County court, wrote on 9 July 1774,

I dined with [Richard Codman] in company with Brigadier [Jedediah] Preble, Major [Enoch] Freeman and his son [Samuel] etc., and a very genteel dinner we had. Salt fish and all its apparatus, roast chickens, bacon, peas, as fine a salad as ever was made, and a rich meat pie, tarts and custard, etc., good wine and as good a punch as you ever made. A large, spacious house, yard and garden; I thought I had got into the house of a nobleman.[22]

Codman's home was in point of fact neither the largest nor the grandest in town, nor was Savage's three-story house next door. The biggest home, at four stories excluding a full basement, belonged to Dr. Isaac Watts; the most elegant were perhaps the homes of John Greenwood, catty-cornered across Middle Street from Dr. Watts, and John Butler's, directly behind the shops on Preble's Wharf. These were built in the latest style, with brick ends and delicate architectural ornamentation. There were many more that were not quite as big or elaborate, but still estimable, such as the Reverend Samuel Deane's. The "Pointer Draft," a map of Falmouth made in 1776 to support an ultimately unsuccessful case for reparations from the Massachusetts Provincial Congress, shows that houses in the port area were painted a variety of colors: white, brown, red, yellow, green, and blue. There is also considerable evidence that English-made wallpapers could be afforded even by modest households. Perhaps the most expensive and controversial of all colonial luxuries and status symbols, domestic slaves, also ornamented the wealthiest households.[23]

Records remaining of everyday life in Falmouth indicate that many of the townspeople possessed significant disposable income. They commissioned portraits, some of which survive today in spite of the 1775 catastrophe or subsequent dispersal. There were two silversmiths in town to choose from, as well as a goldsmith *cum* jeweler, and a brass smith whose main consumer stock-in-trade seems to have been the production of buckles and buttons. Several saddlers were active, too, suggesting considerable demand for tack and horse fittings. Benjamin Mussey, the brick maker, doubled as a hatter, and there was also a clothier, Sylvanus Bramhall. The town as a whole may have sustained as many as eight blacksmithies. Further, there were three apothecary shops and six physicians (three of whom were surgeons, one of them hospital trained in London) all in the port area alone by the early 1770s. Last, but far from least, Falmouth was one of the few towns in North America during the colonial era that possessed a pump fire engine.[24]

The activities that the wealthier townsfolk enjoyed also indicate the extent of their disposable income. Many, unsurprisingly, owned their own pleasure boats, in which they enjoyed fishing and excursions to nearby islands. They gathered at one another's houses for sumptuous dinners (as John Adams's account indicates) and at local inns for feasts and, to the displeasure of some rigidly traditional and moralistic Congregationalists, dances. One of their favorite activities was the "frolic" that could last several days, in any season, and sometimes involved rather boisterous travel as well as rowdy partying. The poor laborers in Falmouth sought their own pleasures within their very modest means among the rum shops of Fiddle Lane and at Alice Greele's famous tavern on Back Street, and engaging in other, less legal amusements.[25]

Although members of Falmouth's social elite clearly enjoyed their position, wealth, and privilege, there is no indication that they intentionally oppressed the poor or rural people, beyond the conventions common to that period in British society. If truth be told, the leading citizens of Falmouth and of Cumberland County, especially such individuals as Richard King of Scarborough, Dr. Nathaniel Coffin Jr. of Falmouth, his gracious wife, Elizabeth Foster Coffin, and the much maligned Sheriff (later, Loyalist colonel) William Tyng, were well known near and far for the reach of their philanthropy and the depth of their humanitarian concern. It is ironic that, when political disturbances were reaching their climax just before the outbreak of open warfare in the mid-1770s, it was Richard King who was brutally assaulted by a mob of renegade militiamen from Gorham. He died of complications from that trauma only six and a half months before Falmouth itself was wrecked. Sheriff Tyng, too, was compelled to flee. But Colonel Edmund Phinney, his second-in-command, Captain Edward Whitmore, and their followers in the Gorham militia *believed* themselves to be monstrously oppressed, and that was all that mattered to them.[26]

A Question of Purpose: The Seaport Since 1775

The celebrations that attended the end of the Seven Years' War in America had been heartfelt. Falmouth rejoiced in the prosperity and peace that the American–British military victory promised. The rupture that occurred only thirteen years later was unimaginable in 1763. But for the policies of the British imperial government, conflict might have been avoided indefinitely. The political convulsions and violence, which subsequently shred the fabric of Falmouth's society, are addressed in this volume by James S. Leamon.

Falmouth's misfortune in 1775 is typical in one respect at least: throughout human history, not much effort has ever been required either to destroy commercial infrastructure, or to fatally disrupt business activity. The forces that bombarded and burned Falmouth in Casco Bay on 18 October 1775 were more than sufficient to demolish Falmouth's business district, including the all-important granaries where imported wheat was stored. Nearby inns filled up quickly with refugees, as did churches, but food began to run out nearly as soon. Those who could retreated to their summerhouses and farms inland or found themselves imposing on friends. Others, having no recourse, and finding too many people in Gorham and Windham hostile rather than sympathetic, shifted for themselves in the woods as best they might. The poor simply vanished; they, after all, were used to hardship, and let their tired feet carry them away to wherever they might find some refuge. Torrential rains arrived on the twenty-first of the month, resulting in killing floods on the Saco River, more misery for those stranded outdoors, and destruction of those possessions that had been saved but stored outside and had not been retrieved. Soon, hard currency ceased to flow at all, and prices skyrocketed. Famine and epidemic fed off one another over the next eight years, and the population of Falmouth in Casco Bay plunged as much as 80 percent. The Anglican priest Jacob Bailey, himself physically isolated and philosophically beset in Pownalborough and impotent to help, mourned the passing of the "thriving" and "elegant" town.[27]

In the nineteenth and twentieth centuries, the entrepot of Portland was to go through fire and prosperity as well as depression and revival. Nineteenth-century Maine farmers and craftsmen continued to bring products to the city for distribution abroad, while consumers goods were manufactured or imported for dispersal over thousands of square miles of countryside and coast.

At the beginning of the twenty-first century, the port performs many of the same functions it did when Falmouth first rose to prominence in the 1760s: by serving the immediate exportation and importation needs of producers and merchants in Cumberland, York, and Lincoln counties it acts as a conduit for commodities destined for more remote markets. Portland actually has at last achieved a measure of that ascendancy over Boston as an *entrepot* long dreamed of by its eighteenth- and nineteenth-century advocates. Because of oil shipments intended for Canada, Portland outstrips its old capital, and is ranked twenty-third in the top one hundred ports in the United States. It has more people employed on the waterfront (some three thousand) than Boston. Indeed, Portland, Maine. is now the largest gross tonnage port in the United States. It does this, furthermore, with an efficiency and care for safety that is admired by port authorities everywhere, and that continues to attract entrepreneurs in ever-increasing numbers.[28]

The waterfront itself undergoes continual improvement as a venue for new and continuing business enterprise. Jeffrey Monroe, Portland's director of transportation and waterfront, has observed that the strongest opposition to continued commercial enhancement of the waterfront comes from real estate developers who want to exploit the harbor's exquisite beauty for the purpose of selling exclusive residential properties, thereby reducing Portland's potential for increase in per capita prosperity. "More damage is done today," he says, "by people with non-maritime interests in the waterfront than could ever be done by enemy gunfire."[29]

Would the people of colonial Falmouth in Casco Bay have agreed?

Notes

Many thanks to James S. Leamon, Richard W. Judd, and, of course, to editor and project leader Joseph Conforti for their very helpful comments during the composition of this essay. My daughter Pamela Ruth also rendered invaluable assistance as a highly perceptive proofreader, and I am deeply grateful to my wife.

1. Interview with Captain Jeffrey W. Monroe, Director of the Department of Transportation and Waterfront in Portland, Maine, 26 May 2004, conducted by Charles P. M. Outwin.

2. Clarence Day, *The History of Maine Agriculture, 1604–1860* (Orono: University of Maine Press, 1954). Many varieties of wheat have since been hybridized that are resistant to this pest. The Black Smut problem did not prevent farmers from repeated efforts to grow wheat, as the journals of Steven Longfellow, a Gorham farmer late in life, show. See also *www.clemson. edu/psapublishing/pages/entom/ce13.pdf,* "Small Grain Diseases," PDF document at the Clemson University Public Service Publications web site, Clemson, South Carolina. Proof of the differentiation in terminology between wheat as "corn" and maize as "Indian corn" on the local level can be found in many places, such as this entry in the Reverend Thomas Smith's journal: "8 October 1772: There is a famine of bread in town, no Indian and no flour . . ." Samuel Freeman and William Willis, eds. *The Journals of Rev. Thomas Smith & Rev. Samuel Deane* (Portland, Maine: Joseph S. Bailey, 1849), 221. This reflected other European usage: "Other points of grammatical confusion include referring to 'corn' as 'maise' or 'maize,' and 'wheat' as 'corn'. The German word 'Korn' refers to the kernels of wheat, an ancient staple in Europe, which did not know of American 'Indian' corn until Native Americans taught explorers about it in the New World." From Bill Cross, "The Kearny Guards: Notes to a German Lexicon of the American Civil War," an essay prepared to assist Don Williams with the composition of portions of the essay, "Playing Fritz Right: Some Basics of a German-American First-Person Impression" to be published in the second edition of *The Columbia Rifles Research Compendium.* Text found at *www.kearnyguards.org/KearnySiteMedia/ NotesGerman.pdf.*

3. Mark Kurlansky, *Cod: A Biography of the Fish that Changed the World.* (New York: Walker and Co., 1997), 78–101. Lobster was generally used for bait or pig feed.

4. Richard G. Wood, *A History of Lumbering in Maine, 1820–1861* (Orono: University of Maine Press, 1935), 18 (Reprinted 10 April 1961, in *The Maine Bulletin,* Maine Studies 33); Robert G. Albion, *Forests and Sea Power, the Timber Problem of the Royal Navy 1652–1862* (Cambridge, Mass.: Harvard University Press, 1926); Charles F. Carroll, *The Timber Economy of Puritan New England* (Providence, R.I.: Brown University Press, 1973); James Eliot Defebaugh, *History of the Lumber Industry of America,* Two Volumes (Chicago: The American Lumberman, 1906–07); Joseph J. Malone, *Pine Trees and Politics: The Naval Stores and Forest Policy in Colonial New England, 1691–1775* (Seattle: University

of Washington Press, 1964); S. F. Manning, *New England Masts and the King's Broad Arrow* (Gardiner, Maine: Tilbury House, 1979); Robert Everding Pike, *Tall Trees, Tough Men* (New York: W. W. Norton, 1967).

5. Paul E. Rivard, *Maine Sawmills: A History* (Augusta, Maine: Maine State Museum, 1990). See also Richard W. Judd, *Aroostook: A Century of Logging in Northern Maine*, with research assistance by Patricia A. Judd (Orono: University of Maine Press, 1989); David C. Smith, *A History of Lumbering in Maine, 1861–1960* (Orono: University of Maine Press, 1961); John S. Springer, *Forest Life and Forest Trees* (New York: Harper and Brothers, 1851); Philip T. Coolidge, *History of the Maine Woods* (Bangor, Maine: Furbush-Roberts, 1963); Roger P. Nason, *Meritorious but Distressed Individuals*. M.A. thesis, University of New Brunswick, Fredericton (Ottawa: National Library of Canada microfiche, 1982) 17–18.

6. William Carlton, "New England Masts and the King's Navy," *New England Quarterly* 12, no. 1 (March 1939): 4–18; L. B. Chapman, "The Mast Industry of Old Falmouth," *Collections and Proceedings of the Maine Historical Society*, Second Series, vol. 7 (Portland, Maine: Maine Historical Society, 1896), 390–404; John Howard Kyan, *An Answer to the Supplemental Chapter in Lord Anson's Life (by Sir John Barrow, Bart.) in Reference to the Preservation of Timber for the Navy* (London: W. H. Cox, 5, GT. Queen Street, Lincoln's-Inn-Fields, 1839).

7. Walter Cristaller, *Die zentralen Orte in Süddeutschland* (Jena: Gustav Fischer, 1933); Walter Cristaller, "Die Hierarchie der Städte" in "Proceedings of the IGU Symposium in Urban Geography," Lund, 1960 (Knut Norborg, ed.), *Lund Studies in Geography*, Ser. B, Human Geography, no. 24, 1962, 3–11; Walter Cristaller, "Some Considerations of Tourism Location in Europe," *Papers, Regional Science Association*, vol. 12, 1964: 95–105; Walter Cristaller, "How I Discovered the Theory of Central Places: A Report about the Origin of Central Places," in P. W. English and R. C. Mayfield, eds., *Man Space and Environment* (London: Oxford University Press, 1972), 601–10. Sometimes called an "economic geographer," Cristaller (1893–1969) first proposed "central place theory" in 1933.

8. Dorothy Libbey, *Scarborough Becomes a Town* (Freeport, Maine: Bond Wheelwright, 1955), 88–93

9. Sarah Jones Bradbury (Mrs. Theophilous Bradbury) extracts from her journal, c. 1750–c. 1766, in a late-nineteenth-century typescript copy of an original, assumed lost, thought to have spanned her whole life. This fragment is on deposit at the Maine Historical Society Archives, Portland, acquisition number S-5081/MS69-6.

10. Freeman and Willis, *Journals of Rev. Thomas Smith & Rev. Samuel Deane*, 441 for "Library Society"; 335 and 338 for fire engine.

11. Leslie V. Brock, "The Colonial Currency, Prices, and Exchange Rates," Ron Michner, ed. (Charlottesville, Va.: Corcoran Department of History of the University of Virginia, 1992). Online at *etext.lib.virginia.edu/journals/EH/ EH34/brock34.htm*. See also Robert E. Wright, *Origins of Commercial Banking in America, 1750–1800* (Lanham, Md.: Rowman and Littlefield, 2001). Many writs of indebtedness, such as document #S-223 and in collections #34, 35 and 64 may be found at the Maine Historical Society Archives, Portland.

12. William Hutchinson Rowe, *The Maritime History of Maine: Three Centuries of Shipbuilding and Seafaring* (Gardiner, Maine: The Harpswell Press, 1989). First published in 1948. See also William Willis, *The History of Portland, 1632–1864* (facsimile of the 1865 ed.) (Somersworth: New Hampshire Publishing Co., 1972). This work is referred to hereafter as "*HOP.*" Willis glossed over matters that would have made British Falmouth look good in comparison to American Portland. Although he makes some note of numbers involved in the mast trade, the impression he gives of total volume is misleading. He also does not record that Robert Pagan of Falmouth, by 1775, was owner of an enormous former *East Indiaman*, the *Falmouth*, which had been hired back to the British East India Company to help carry tea to Boston in 1773, and was one of those vessels attacked during the Boston Tea Party. Willis may not have been aware of this, however, because the records that prove this are in London, Nova Scotia, and elsewhere.

13. Thomas Coulson's importation of sails and rigging materials to Falmouth in March of 1775 does not indicate that these materials were not made in Falmouth, but that the capacity of local manufacturers to meet demand had been exceeded; it is, in other words, an indication of the high level of Falmouth's ship-building activity. Locals were angry because they thought the local producers *could* meet the demand, but were being cheated by Coulson's actions.

14. See Earle G. Shettleworth, *Mr. Goodhue Remembers Portland: Scenes from the Mid-Nineteenth Century* (Augusta: Maine Historic Preservation Commission, 1981). This contains an excellent illustration of both Arthur Savage's house and Captain Richard Codman's, next door, both built in the 1760s, and which survived into Goodhue's youth. Henry Wadsworth Longfellow would also have been familiar with these buildings.

15. Enoch Freeman, *Personal Journal, 1735–1783,* especially the 1757 entry. Unpublished manuscript, Portland Room collection, Portland (Maine) Public Library.

16. See Ephraim Jones, "A Journal of a Voyage from Falmouth in Casco Bay to the Island of Bermuda," which also documents the further progress of the voyage to the Turks Islands, and Boston (Marblehead), made in 1765. In the Willis Collection, vol. K (rear), Maine Historical Society Library,

Portland. Transcribed by Charles P. M. Outwin, September 2004. Record of a voyage in 1765 in an apparent attempt to establish a Falmouth-based salt trade to Massachusetts.

17. Charles Outwin, *An Index of Persons and Institutions at Falmouth in Casco Bay, c. 1760–1775,* on deposit in the Maine Historical Society Library, Portland; Myrtle K. Lovejoy and William D. Berry, *This Was Stroudwater* (Portland: National Society of Colonial Dames of America in Maine, 1985).

18. See Edwin A. Churchill, "Merchants and Commerce in Falmouth," *Maine Historical Society Newsletter,* vol. 9, no. 4 (May 1977): 93–104, for an opposing viewpoint. See also Peter Burke, *History and Social Theory* (Oxford, U.K.: Oxford University Press, 1992), 64–66.

19. Willis, *HOP,* 792.

20. See Willis, ibid., 421, footnote.

21. Clifford K. Shipton, *Sibley's Harvard Graduates,* vol. 14, 1756–1760 (Boston: Massachusetts Historical Society, 1968).

22. L. H. Butterfield, et al., eds. *The Adams Family Correspondence,* vol. 6 (Cambridge, Mass.: Belknap Press, 1963), 362.

23. Obits for Captain Richard Codman (1730–1793), in the *Eastern Argus* (9 September 1833): 2, 3, and the *Portland Advertiser* (10 September 1833): 2–4. Willis, *HOP,* 795–96. "Lost and Found: the Pointer Draft of Falmouth in October 1775," which also appeared in *Maine History,* vol. 39, no. 2, "The Early Coast of Maine" (Portland: Maine Historical Society, Summer 2000), 133–36. Concerning slaves, see Charles Outwin, "A Company of Shadows: Slaves and Poor Free Menial Labors in Cumberland County, Maine, c. 1760–c. 1775," forthcoming in *Maine History.*

24. This was probably just a large pump on wheels, similar to that first invented in England by Joseph Jencks in 1659 and improved in 1721 by Richard Newsham, a recreation of which is on display at Colonial Williamsburg today. The only other places that certainly had fire engines at this time were Philadelphia, Boston, Williamsburg, and perhaps William and Mary College in Virginia. See *http://www.pbs.org/williamsburg/backdraft/timeline.html,* on the PBS-sponsored Web site, "Backdraft: the fire engine in the colonial community." The Falmouth engine was destroyed with the rest of the port on 18 October 1775.

25. Accounts of frolics may be found in the journals of Sarah Jones Bradbury and Rev. Thomas Smith: for example, Bradbury, *Journal,* 10–12, and Freeman and Willis, *Journals of Rev. Thomas Smith & Rev. Samuel Deane,* 321. There is some indication that prostitution may have been practiced in Falmouth; see "Fornication Charges in Cumberland County, 1759–1790, from the Cumberland County Commissioners records" (copyright July 1997 by Dana E. Edgecomb). Text at "USGenWeb Project" Web site at *http://ftp. rootsweb.com/pub/usgenweb/me/cumberland/court/adultery/file0001.txt.*

26. Willis, *HOP*, 439–40, 443; two portraits of Elizabeth Foster Coffin by Badger and Peale still exist, both showing clearly her lively character. See also Libbey, *Scarborough Becomes a Town*, 113–14

27. Jacob Bailey, "Letter Narrative of the Burning of Falmouth," *Collections of the Maine Historical Society*, ser. #1, vol. 5, 1857.

28. Monroe Outwin interview, 26 May 2004.

29. Ibid.

Falmouth, the American Revolution, and the Price of Moderation

James S. Leamon

On 18 October 1775, at precisely 9:40 on a clear, bright morning, Lieutenant Henry Mowat gave the order. His squadron of four British men o' war anchored in Casco Bay opened fire. Their target: the defenseless town of Falmouth located on the peninsula jutting into the bay. Panic engulfed the community; townspeople jammed the streets and alleys frantically evacuating families and possessions by whatever means possible. Miraculously, no one was killed in the cannonade that continued all day long, consuming 136 dwellings, along with the Anglican church, the new court house, a fire station, public library, stores, wharves, and warehouses. At least two-thirds, perhaps three-fourths, of the town was destroyed. To further the devastation, landing parties from the British vessels came ashore to torch prominent buildings that might have escaped the conflagration. Nor was that all. Thirteen merchant vessels, some still loaded with cargos from the West Indies, crowded the harbor. Mowat seized two and sank the rest.[1]

Adding to the confusion, militia from surrounding towns including Gorham, Brunswick, and Scarborough had filtered into Falmouth when the British squadron first appeared several days earlier. But rather than defend the town from the British, the militiamen from the interior used the ensuing panic and confusion as an opportunity to loot abandoned houses and stores even as they were being bombarded. An eyewitness later described with outrage that a "multitude of villains were purloining their goods and carrying them into the country beyond the reach of justice . . . [T]he country people," he con-

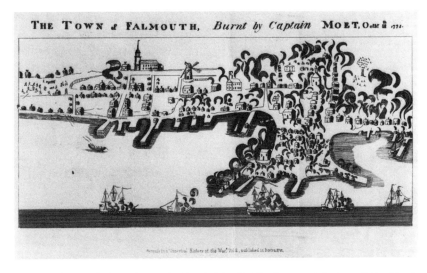

Figure 3-1. "Town of Falmouth Burnt by Captain Moet," 18 October 1775. Collections of Maine Historical Society, GA67.

tinued, "were hardly restrained from destroying those houses that escaped the general devastation."[2]

The picture could hardly be more depressing. A mere six months earlier, Massachusetts minutemen had forced British regulars to retreat from Lexington and Concord to the confines of Boston. By contrast, Falmouth, the most flourishing, populous town in the part of Massachusetts now called Maine, lay in ruins, burned by the British and pillaged by fellow Americans. Who were the real enemy, and how had it come to this?

Falmouth's sad fate resulted from several interrelated factors. One was the town's ambivalent role in the growing resistance to Parliament's new program to tax Americans directly and to regulate the colonies more strictly now that the French and Indian War was won and had to be paid for. At first Falmouth's leaders, following Boston's direction, readily participated in the early stages of colonial protest. But over time, as protest led to violence and escalated into rebellion, Falmouth's mercantile elite became increasingly aware of their town's vulnerability, first, to British retaliation by sea, and second, to social unrest from the town's "lower orders." The laborers, apprentices, sailors, and artisans who made up the mobs, or crowd actions, against local British authority just might not stop there.

Finally, as Falmouth's leaders tried to draw back from the abyss of imperial anger on the one hand and of social disorder on the other, a third factor surfaced in the emerging political radicalism of Maine's once-isolated country towns. Falmouth's neighboring communities, such as North Yarmouth, Harpswell, Brunswick, Gorham, Windham, and Scarborough, had been slow to join the protest against Parliament's arbitrary acts until sufficiently "educated" by Boston's Committee of Correspondence and by events in that town. Their increasing commitment to the cause of the American colonies contrasted with Falmouth's growing reluctance. Fueling a mix of envy, contempt, and hostility for Falmouth was the backcountry's economic dependence on Falmouth, their local entrepot. Artisans and merchants of Falmouth served the entire region with all manner of goods, made there and imported, as well as with the credit to buy them. And as the shire town for Cumberland County, Falmouth had sufficient lawyers on hand to pursue those who failed to pay their debts. The burning of Falmouth on 18 October 1775, was the culmination of all these factors.

Serious opposition to England's efforts to tax the colonists directly started in 1765. Americans throughout the colonies protested and rioted against Parliament's Stamp Act taxing legal documents, licenses, diplomas, newspapers—even playing cards. Falmouth joined in the patriotic opposition. Not only did Falmouth's town meeting instruct its representative to the provincial legislature in Boston, called the General Court, to use his "utmost efforts" to prevent the act from taking effect, but Falmouth's leaders themselves resorted to direct action to nullify the tax. In January 1766, the justices comprising the Court of Common Pleas met in Falmouth and voted to continue their judicial activities without stamped paper. Meanwhile, a crowd gathered around the customs house to force officials there to open the port without stamped clearances. Another well-organized crowd made certain there would be no stamps to distribute when it intercepted a shipment of stamped paper from Halifax and paraded "an Article so *odious* to all America" at the end of a pole to be consumed in a ceremonial bonfire. A newspaper account of the event concluded approvingly, "They then dispersed without offering the least injury to any person."[3]

The newspaper's comment reflected relief that the crowds who had threatened the customs house and destroyed the stamps had served their intended purposes with a minimum of social disorder. In the eighteenth-century Anglo-American world, mobs, or "organized crowds," could and did serve an almost semi-legitimate function to enforce community standards against those who defied them. Falmouth's disciplined opposition to the Stamp Act indicated a high degree of social control and support in the town's resistance to Parliamentary taxation. When, in mid-May 1766, news reached Falmouth that Parliament had repealed the obnoxious act, the town exploded with excitement and relief. In his diary, Falmouth's Congregational minister, the Reverend Thomas Smith, reported, "Our people are mad with drink and joy." Bells pealed, drums beat, cannon fired from the fort, and vessels in the harbor broke out their colors. Everywhere loyal toasts were drunk to the king and queen, to members of the royal family and even to members of Parliament—at least those friendly to the American cause.[4] With the Stamp Act crisis apparently resolved, not only might imperial relations return to normal, but so too might colonial society. But it was not over yet.

Several months later, patriotic violence again erupted in Falmouth on the evening of 7 August 1766, when a crowd rescued a cargo of smuggled sugar and rum belonging to merchant Enoch Ilsley. The Stamp Act already had been repealed, but patriotic violence, so successful in nullifying the Stamp Act, was now directed against unpopular customs officials trying to enforce Parliament's navigation acts regulating colonial trade. Customs Collector Francis Waldo and Comptroller Arthur Savage had seized contraband goods at Enoch Ilsley's store, located along the waterfront, on the north side of Fore Street about midway between what is now the Franklin Arterial and India Street. Having no safe keeping place, the customs officers simply assigned a local deputy sheriff as a guard until the next day when officials could properly dispose of the illegal goods. During the evening, a noisy crowd surrounded the house where the two officers were spending the night, assaulting it with sticks and stones for several hours. Only in the morning did the officials realize that while one crowd had been diverting them at their lodgings, another had been busy carrying off and hiding the illegal goods from Ilsley's store. The prime suspect in the event, merchant Ilsley, protested he had been confined to his house by illness all evening and could identify no one. The deputy sheriff was no more help; he stated the mob had forcibly carried him away from the store and even confiscated his warrant, thereby preventing him from performing his duty. When the Massachusetts royal governor heard of the affair, he grumbled that enforcement of Parliament's acts of trade "is now become a meer farce of Government; since no one dares to discover or prosecute the Offenders, if they were so disposed; & indeed the Offenders are some times, as in this Case, the greatest part of the Town."5

But to Falmouth's merchant elite, crowds were dangerous, unpredictable tools under the best of circumstances as an earlier event had proved on the night of 10 September 1765. Perhaps inspired by the recent Stamp Act rioting in Boston, a mob in Falmouth descended on the house of William Bennet, Falmouth innkeeper and creditor to numerous persons. The exact locations of Bennet's house and tavern are unclear; they might have been situated next to each other on Fiddle Lane (now the Franklin Arterial), a section of old Falmouth notorious for its places of boisterous entertainment. Armed with axes and clubs the crowd broke into Bennet's house, bound him hand and foot, gutted the interior of the house, and then departed carrying Bennet's petty cash and his account books. The lost records included notes against a number of persons, including those of a business competitor, James Bryant, with whom Bennet was entangled in a legal dispute and who appears to have stirred up Bennet's debtors into a mob intent on destroying evidence of their financial obligations. Some of the recovered notes included those of local merchants, but the blame fell on Bryant, who was sentenced to be whipped and fined. Two of his associates were later sentenced to jail; yet another mob later freed these two prisoners who apparently were never retaken.6 The Bennet riot clearly revealed the dangerous tendencies of "crowd actions" to become means of private gain and threats to social order, but with the repeal of the Stamp Act, most Americans regarded such dangers as in the past, not the future.

Then in 1767 came a new series of parliamentary measures called the Townshend Acts, designed to raise a revenue through import duties on certain goods, including tea, and strengthening the customs agency in America. Following Boston's lead, Falmouth, now along with several other Maine towns, voted to reduce dependence on British manufactures by promoting domestic industry and frugality. But as the major Downeast seaport, Falmouth's merchants found it impossible to escape the unpleasant necessity of joining a growing intercolonial movement for nonimportation of British goods. Falmouth's "Merchants, Traders,

and other Inhabitants," voted in spring of 1769 to join merchants elsewhere in refusing to import any goods from Britain except those necessary for fishing and manufacturing. At best Falmouth's was a grudging
sort of resolve since it came relatively late, included no enforcement
provisions, and would remain in effect for only six months. Actually the
embargo lasted far longer, for Falmouth's reluctant merchants were kept
in line by a public warning from Boston printed in the newspapers. Such
notoriety elicited from Falmouth a more vigorous resolve to adhere
strictly to the nonimportation agreement until, in 1770, most of the
Townshend duties were repealed and embargoes everywhere collapsed.[7]

The most serious result of the Townshend Acts was not merely the renewal and intensification of the constitutional dispute about Parliament's authority over the colonies, but the escalation of violence. The
enforcement of nonimportation, the presence of a more aggressive customs service, and the arrival in Boston of royal troops to protect the
customs agents all increased points of conflict that culminated in the
Boston Massacre of 5 March 1770.

Falmouth had no royal troops to contend with, but did have its share
of conflict with the vigorous, sometimes unscrupulous customs officers
who had developed customs racketeering into a fine art. One of their
techniques involved the use of informants who divulged information
concerning illegal cargos for a share in the profits when the confiscated
vessel and cargo were sold. One of the most tumultuous of Falmouth's
riots occurred in an effort to discover such a person. On the night of 12
November 1771, shortly after Comptroller Arthur Savage had seized a
sloop belonging to William Tyng, a crowd in disguise visited Savage's
prominent home, located at what is now the north side of Middle Street.
The crowd demanded that Savage disclose the informer's name. When
Savage refused to tell, the crowd paraded the comptroller about town,
periodically stopping to demand the informer's identity and threatening
him with his life. Savage finally gave in when the crowd leader presented
a loaded pistol to his head and swore, "That by the living God [he] must
lett them know, or take the consequence." After Savage repeatedly swore
to the truth of his information, the crowd released him with dire warn-
ings as to what would occur should he take legal action against them.[8]

Despite the threats, Savage did institute legal proceedings, but not in
Falmouth where not a single justice of the peace was willing to accept
his sworn testimony. Only in Boston could the customs officer give his
testimony under oath as a basis for warrants. Eventually three persons

were arrested and held for trial. They were not laborers, sailors, or apprentices, but masters of vessels then lying in Falmouth Harbor.[9] Their concern lay not with the plight of the sloop's owner, William Tyng, a Tory and a sheriff, but rather to expose an informer in Falmouth's mercantile community. The name and fate of the culprit is not known— mute evidence that suggests he quickly left town. The mere suspicion of being an informer was enough to lead to social and economic ostracism, and worse. One suspect complained he was "in Danger of being mobb'd and evilly entreated by sundry of the Kings disorderly subjects who have at all Times heretofore been used to mobb & otherwise evilly entreat all Persons supposed or known to be informers to any of the King's officers . . . appointed to collect the customs."[10]

Since the British navy had the task of assisting customs officers in enforcing trade regulations, it too shared in the growing tension and occasionally contributed to it. Early in 1775, four impressed crewmen tried to escape from the HMS *Gaspee* then anchored in Casco Bay. The escapees stole the ship's boat and rowed for the shore while the crew fired upon them from the vessel. Once ashore, three of the sailors fled, leaving behind one of their fellows mortally wounded. The officers aboard the *Gaspee* dared not pursue for fear of violence from an aroused crowd. The commanding officer not only refused to send medical help, but also refused to attend the inquest into the sailor's death on the excuse that the alleged offense was not within the jurisdiction of civil authority. The *Gaspee* then departed Falmouth leaving behind a growing conviction that royal authority—be it the army in Boston, the navy in Falmouth, and customs officers everywhere—were all equally disdainful of civilian government and even of human life.[11]

Such an impression was being carefully nurtured by Boston's Committee of Correspondence that skillfully educated the provincial towns about the latest threats to their liberties and co-ordinated opposition to British policy. By 1772, when a new crisis arose over whether salaries of royal governors and judges should be paid by colonial legislatures or by the British government, a veritable stream of letters and pamphlets went out from Boston to virtually every town and precinct in Massachusetts, providing an opportunity to discuss far-reaching constitutional issues in public and even to send back replies. Collectively the town responses demonstrated an expanding and deepening awareness of the imperial constitutional struggle. Whereas Falmouth alone had been alert to such issues in 1765, by 1772 the debates had energized towns all over Maine.

Parliament's notorious Tea Act one year later intensified even more the constitutional debate concerning the relationship between Britain and her American colonies, and unleashed a far more immediate crisis for the town of Falmouth. The Tea Act allowed the British East India Company the special privilege of importing tea directly to the colonies duty free—except for a small tax retained to maintain the principle of parliamentary taxation. To Americans, the Tea Act was a double threat: The East India Company's cheap tea threatened the livelihood of colonial merchants and, in addition, cunningly tempted Americans to accept the principle of parliamentary taxation by purchasing and consuming the cheaper tea. Americans thus viewed the Tea Act as nothing less than a conspiracy, and in seaports throughout the colonies, East India Company tea remained unsold or was returned to England—except in Boston. There, in mid-December 1773, a crowd thinly disguised as Indians boarded the three tea ships and dumped tea worth nine thousand pounds sterling into Boston Harbor.

Boston's Committee of Correspondence quickly set to work rallying support for the Boston Tea Party from the towns of Massachusetts. Many Maine towns joined in the response, denouncing parliamentary taxation and praising the Bostonians for their vigorous action in defense of liberty. A few of the towns demonstrated their support by voting a boycott on tea and establishing local committees of correspondence. Falmouth cogently expressed the general conviction that while colonists remained loyal to the king, neither Parliament nor any power on earth had the right to tax Americans without their consent, and that the only rightful authority to tax and to legislate for the colonies lay in their own freely elected provincial legislatures. At the same time, Falmouth's town meeting resolved to refrain from buying, selling, or even using tea. To enforce its boycott, the town chose its selectmen as a Committee of Inspection and also appointed a Committee of Correspondence to share information with other communities.[12]

But Falmouth's public support in the common cause masked deepening divisions within the community. At a town meeting in early February 1774, a paper circulated assuring the citizens of Falmouth that while there might be some reluctance in enforcing their embargo against tea, the authors promised that "no Person in this Town, Great or Small, Rich or Poor, shall dare to counteract your laudable Designs." The aliases of those signing the document suggested the means of enforcement: Thomas Tarbucket, Peter Pitch, Abraham Wildfowl, David Pilaster,

Benjamin Brush, Oliver Scarecrow and Henry Handcart, who collectively styled themselves, "Committee for Tarring and Feathering."13

The alarmed townspeople of Falmouth responded at a subsequent town meeting with a unanimous resolve to"detest and abhor" the threatening circular and to "discourage and discountenance Riots & Mobs, let their Pretence be what it will."14 Constitutional resolutions, boycotts, and even controlled "crowd actions," as against the Stamp Act or even customs informers, were acceptable forms of protest, but unregulated mobs and tarrings and featherings were a direct threat to the social order.

Indeed, there existed a group in Falmouth for whom even resolves and boycotts went too far. Only a week following the Thomas Tarbucket circular, this group sent a "Letter of Appreciation and Farewell" to the royal governor, Thomas Hutchinson, who was about to depart Boston for London. Not only did the letter wish the governor well, but apologized for Falmouth's recent resolves and begged the governor to disassociate the signers from them. Among those who attached their signatures to the letter were many of Falmouth's leading figures: Jeremiah Pote, Robert Pagan, Thomas Oxnard, Thomas Coulson; but included with this company of evolving loyalists were the names of Stephen Longfellow, Theophilus Bradbury, Benjamin Titcomb, and even Enoch Ilsley, active Whigs, the last two of whom were members of Falmouth's Committee of Inspection. When the Hutchinson letter became public knowledge, many who had originally signed it now signed a public letter of recantation, claiming they had been duped by the wiley governor and his allies.15 Thomas Tarbucket and his sticky, feathery friends well knew whereof they warned.

Events would soon overtake the efforts of Falmouth's leaders to temporize and moderate the protest movement. Parliament vented its anger over the Tea Party and its frustration with Massachusetts in a complex series of acts collectively dubbed the "Intolerables" in America and as the "Coercives" in Britain. As the terms imply, they were punitive in nature: the port of Boston was to be closed until the tea was paid for; the provincial charter of Massachusetts was revised making provincial government, from top to bottom, more dependent on the authority of the royal governor—now a military appointee. Finally, an act making it easier for British troops to be quartered in private buildings, and another measure reorganizing government in recently conquered Quebec (Canada) were not intended to penalize Massachusetts in particular, but the colonists readily interpreted them as such.

Nothing could have more thoroughly united the colonists and strengthened the conviction that a conspiracy existed in England to deprive them of their constitutional liberties as Englishmen. Parliament's attack upon the charter of Massachusetts appeared as an attack upon rights of colonial self-government everywhere. At Boston's suggestion, virtually all the American colonies sent delegates to a Continental Congress at Philadelphia in the summer of 1774 to devise means of opposing the Coercive Acts. In addition to passing the usual resolves declaring loyalty to the king while denouncing Parliament, the Continental Congress voted to nullify the Coercive Acts—by force if necessary. But first the delegates resorted to methods of economic persuasion by recommending the adoption of an intercolonial nonimportation, nonexportation, and nonconsumption agreement, called the Association, to be enforced by locally elected town committees.

Falmouth's response to the Coercives was typical of many towns throughout Massachusetts, New England, and even beyond. First came the inevitable resolves denouncing Parliament and expressing sympathy for Boston. Tangible evidence of sympathy soon followed in the form of money, food, and firewood. On the day the Port Act shutting up Boston Harbor went into effect, Falmouth's Congregational church bell tolled all day long and the town held a public fast to contemplate "the sad state of our public affairs." By contrast, the bell of the Anglican church remained silent while a small number of Tories displayed their opposition to the town's proceedings by keeping their businesses open and by holding a public celebration of their own to express their loyalist sentiments.[16]

Meanwhile, Falmouth's leading Whig merchant, Enoch Freeman, confided to a journal his thoughts on the significance of recent events. What, he asked, was the relationship between a government and its people? Freeman fully accepted the widely held Whig belief that legitimate government evolved from consent of the people, and therefore the relationship was contractual in nature. As government meets human needs, so people owed allegiance to their government. But who was to judge when the contract was broken and the connection between ruler and ruled was dissolved? After contemplating various alternatives, Freeman concluded, "The People shall be Judge." But if "the People" judge the government to be dissolved, does that lead to anarchy? No, mused Freeman, there still remains a social compact binding the people together from which they could then reform or rebuild their political compact. Freeman seemed to imply that the spokesmen for the sovereign people must be their trusted community leaders, the Enoch Freemans of Falmouth, entrusted with preserving the social compact while restoring just government with a minimum of social disruption.[17] But it would not be an easy task.

Enoch Freeman's philosophical musings assumed virtual reality as royal government crumbled throughout Massachusetts. The "sovereign people" gradually assumed power through a series of elected conventions on the provincial and county levels and by local committees in the towns. Former government officials were required to publicly repudiate their commissions under the "illegal" royal government established by Parliament's Coercive Acts. Delegates from towns in Cumberland County met in Falmouth in late September 1774 at Alice Greele's tavern, the informal headquarters of the local Whigs located on the corner of Congress and Hampshire Streets. Here the convention required from Sheriff William Tyng a solemn oath that he would exercise his commission as sheriff only with the consent of the convention. To reinforce this repudiation of imperial authority, convention delegates then accompanied the sheriff to Falmouth's nearby townhouse where he publicly repeated his declaration to a crowd of some five hundred people identified simply as "the body of the people."[18]

Just who composed this "body of the people" is not clear; many were armed and their presence added a turbulent tone to the gathering that clearly worried Falmouth's mercantile leaders. Among the convention's several resolutions decrying the Coercive Acts and supporting the boycott against Britain was one that urged the preservation of public order. All people, declared the convention, should discourage "riots, mobs, and all licentiousness," and should consider that they were always in the "presence of the great *God*, who loveth order, and not confusion."[19] Since the convention delegates included Brunswick's Samuel Thompson and Edmund Phinney from Gorham, already known for their zeal in the American cause, the convention leaders had good reason for their exhortation to preserve order.

By the summer of 1774, the towns of Gorham and Brunswick had begun to assume a more aggressive role in the reaction to the Coercive Acts. In particular, they vigorously urged the adoption of an earlier and more stringent embargo of British goods before the one later recommended by the Continental Congress. To these zealous towns, the hesitation of their more exposed neighbors was an obvious sign of moral laxity and a lack of commitment to the American cause. Falmouth's

mercantile community, however, was reluctant to make yet another sac-
rifice of business and to endure a renewed threat of violence in still another embargo. So in the summer of 1774, when Falmouth's leaders felt
obliged to support the boycott movement, a town meeting grudgingly
resolved to boycott all goods from Great Britain, and to refrain from
purchasing goods from those who continued to do so, subject to any al-
terations the Continental Congress might propose. By whom and by
what date the embargo agreement should be signed was left conveniently vague. A day after Falmouth's half-hearted resolution, the town of
Gorham challenged the shire town's leadership by authorizing its clerk
to inform the other towns of Cumberland County that "the Covenant
signed by the Inhabitants of Falmouth is not satisfactory to this town."20

Gorham did not limit its challenge to words alone. During the turbulent autumn of 1774 militia from Gorham invaded neighboring communities to humiliate Tories and enforce the embargo on towns that
could not or would not do it themselves. In similar fashion, Brunswick's
militia, led by Samuel Thompson, criss-crossed the lower Kennebec valley fulfilling a similar role. Soon Thompson and his militia would shift
their attention to Falmouth to enforce the embargo there.

A sloop from England arrived in Falmouth Harbor in early March 1775,
carrying sails, rigging, and equipment for a ship that merchant Thomas
Coulson was building. The embargo recommended by the Continental
Congress, called the Association, was now in effect, and enforcing it became a test of Falmouth's patriotic commitment to the American cause.
At first Falmouth's Committee of Inspection, chaired by the ubiquitous
Enoch Freeman, ordered Coulson to send the vessel back to England
without unloading. But the committee was not unanimous, several
members arguing that Coulson should be free to receive the goods since
he had ordered them before the embargo took effect. Coulson argued, in
addition, that the vessel was unseaworthy and needed repairs which
would necessitate first unloading the cargo—a dangerous concession.
The committee relented by giving Coulson a week to repair the sloop
without unloading or to send the cargo back on a different vessel. Coulson, instead, sought to rally support within Falmouth's maritime community and also from British officials in Boston. The new governor of
Massachusetts, General Thomas Gage, responded to Coulson's plea for
help by ordering the navy to send an armed vessel to Falmouth to deter
possible violence. Such was the tension in Falmouth that when the HMS

Canceaux arrived, Falmouth's customs officials fled aboard and eighteen "friends of government" wrote to Governor Gage expressing their relief the vessel had arrived but also their concern over what might happen to them when it left.[21]

Even Falmouth's Whigs worried over the threat of violence as the confrontation narrowed. The Committee of Inspection resolved that it would use its utmost efforts to prevent the "inhabitants of this Town from engaging in any riots, tumults, and insurrections, or attacks on the private property of any person, as pernicious to the real interests thereof, as well as injurious to the liberty of *America* in general, and that they will, as far as lies in their power, promote peace and good order, as absolutely necessary to the existence of society."[22] A short while later, another Cumberland County Convention echoed similar sentiments by resolving to discourage riots and mobs, and "to promote peace, order and decorum, as essentially necessary for the safety of the people at this critical day."[23] That Samuel Thompson was once again a convention delegate may have accentuated the fears of a violent solution to a delicate situation.

Falmouth's Committee of Inspection finally published the name of Thomas Coulson as a violator of the Continental Association. Undeterred, he kept busy transferring cargo directly from the recently arrived sloop to his new ship, protected by the *Canceaux*'s guns. At almost the same moment from the Committee of Inspection at Boston arrived a sharp reminder to their counterparts in Falmouth that "the eyes of the whole Continent" were upon them, urging "that you conform strictly and religiously to the Association of the Continental Congress in every respect, without favour or affection to any person whatever."[24] A major dilemma now confronted Falmouth's leaders: enforce the embargo at the risk of their town's destruction, or incur a reproach for failure to take that risk in the patriot cause. Had Falmouth's leaders been more bold, the American Revolution might have begun in Falmouth.

Instead, the fighting began at Lexington and Concord on 19 April 1775, with rumors reaching Falmouth by 21 April. Fearful of a violent confrontation, some cautious people began to move their possessions out of town; business came to a standstill while Coulson, aided by the *Canceaux*, continued to make a mockery of the Association and to rig his new ship—and still Falmouth refused to resort to the means necessary to stop him.[25]

Brunswick's Samuel Thompson, therefore, took it upon himself to do what Falmouth appeared incapable of doing. Although he had reassured

Falmouth's nervous Committee of Correspondence that he intended no such thing, he had a plan to end the deadlock by seizing the commanding officer of the *Canceaux*, Lieutenant Henry Mowat, and, using him as a decoy or a hostage, to seize the naval vessel itself. What was supposed to follow after that was never clear. Nonetheless, from Brunswick Thompson led a band of fifty militiamen who secretly arrived at Falmouth on 7 May 1775. They lay concealed in woods on what is still called Munjoy Hill, at that time the easterly outskirts of town. It was a Sunday, and Thompson had planned to seize Mowat and several of his officers as they were ashore attending church service. He arrived too late for that, so instead, he and his militia remained hidden until they announced their presence to the horrified town two days later by capturing Mowat and his ship's surgeon while they were strolling along the shore chatting with Falmouth's Anglican priest, the Reverend John Wiswall.[26]

Hysteria seized Falmouth; the *Canceaux*'s second in command fired off several warning shots and threatened to bombard the town unless the captives were released at once. In response, a thoroughly aroused Thompson, stuttering with excitement, vowed to sever a member from Mowat's body for every shot fired: "F-f-fire away!" he exclaimed, "Every gun you fire, I will c-c-cut off a joint."[27] Terror-stricken residents fled from the town carrying their belongings in carts, wheelbarrows, wagons, and by every means imaginable. Meanwhile, leading townsmen besieged Thompson to save the town by releasing his prisoners. Some even proposed calling up Falmouth's militia, not to attack the *Canceaux*, but to force Thompson into releasing his captives.[28] But Falmouth's militia was nowhere to be found; some undoubtedly were off to join the Continental Army besieging the British inside Boston. The remainder were probably preoccupied with saving their own possessions from the expected bombardment. In any case, throughout the entire crisis, they never appeared as an organized force.

Other militiamen did appear, however. Some six hundred fully armed, poorly led militiamen from neighboring towns poured into Falmouth, reducing civil government to a cipher. In desperation, Enoch Freeman, as Chair of the Committee of Inspection, wrote to the Provincial Congress to learn if Thompson had any authorization for his actions and pleading for some direction, "for we are in such confusion nobody seems to be rational."[29]

Samuel Thompson, the cause of all the uproar, now had to decide what to do with those he had seized. He had Mowat, but no way of capturing the *Canceaux*, and unless he released Mowat and the others, the man-o'-war in the harbor would very likely fire on the town On the other hand, if Thompson did release his captives, how could he defend seizing them in the first place? Thompson's solution was typical of the man: he finally agreed to free his prisoners for the night on the condition that Mowat promised to return the next day, and provided that two prominent Whig residents, Enoch Freeman and Jedediah Preble, stand surety for Mowat's return. Since it was doubtful that Mowat would return to so chaotic a situation, Thompson could shift the blame onto the deceitful British officer and his two sureties.

Meantime, the militia officers interrogated local Tories such as the Anglican preacher, John Wiswall, Thomas Oxnard, Robert Pagan, and Jeremiah Pote, while the troops amused themselves by plundering their homes and consuming their liquor supplies.[30] After several days of harassing local Tories, the militiamen became impatient to return home. The residents of Falmouth eagerly urged them on their way by meeting their demands for provisions and money as compensation for their time and trouble in coming to Falmouth. By 13 May 1775, Falmouth was finally free of its troublesome neighbors. The town fathers apologized to Lieutenant Mowat for the humiliation he had endured at the hands of Thompson's militia which the town had been helpless to prevent. Mowat seemed to understand the situation, and so the townspeople feared no retribution. The *Canceaux*, carrying the first of Falmouth's loyalist refugees, departed Casco Bay on 15 May in convoy with Thomas Coulson's newly completed vessel that had successfully defied the embargo. Coulson returned to Falmouth a short while later to retrieve a valuable cargo of masts, but the town's Committee of Inspection, anticipating that possibility, had moved the masts out of reach. Coulson returned to Boston empty-handed except for rescuing more loyalists eager to escape an increasingly hostile environment.[31]

Depriving Coulson of his cargo of masts was but a small triumph for the town of Falmouth. The Coulson affair, or "Thompson's War," as it has been called, clearly illustrated the town's timidity in taking the last final step to uphold the embargo. Too exposed physically and with too much to risk in position and property, Falmouth's leaders drew back when words gave way to deeds. Leadership passed into the hands of the less wealthy, more aggressive towns of the interior. Gorham and Brunswick now assumed a sense of moral superiority over their shire town. Gorham had publicly challenged Falmouth's stand on nonimportation, and it was Brunswick's Samuel Thompson and his armed crowd, followed by Edmund Phinney with his followers from Gorham, who invaded the entrepot to enforce the Association when Falmouth seemed to falter. Of course Thompson failed to prevent Coulson from sailing away in his new ship—but the blame was chiefly Falmouth's. The attitude of the interior towns is perhaps best reflected in remarks attributed to some of the departing militia who had nothing good to say of the Falmouth gentry and were heard to exclaim, "This Town ought to be laid in Ashes."[32]

Six months later that indeed was Falmouth's fate, occasioned not by radicals from neighboring towns, but by events in the Downeast town of Machias. Once again, the embargo sparked the crisis. A small British naval vessel, the HMS *Margaretta*, arrived at Machias to protect a merchant in his efforts to defy the embargo by trading with the inhabitants. The situation was similar to what had occurred in Falmouth, except that in Machias violence erupted when Whig radicals not only seized the offending trading vessels but also the *Margaretta*, killing the commanding officer in the process. In retaliation for this outrageous act, as well as for an increasing number of warlike incidents along the New England coast, Vice Admiral Samuel Graves in Boston determined to make the rebellious Americans pay for their actions. Early in October 1775, the Admiral issued orders to Lieutenant Henry Mowat to "lay waste burn and destroy" a list of nine coastal towns extending eastward from Marblehead all the way to Machias, "where the *Margueritta* was taken, the Officer commanding her killed, and the People made Prisoners . . ."[33] Among the towns listed for destruction was Falmouth. The squadron of four war vessels, including the *Canceaux* and a supply ship, sailed from Boston 8 October and proceeded downeast. But one after another, the little fleet bypassed the towns to be "chastized," either because of adverse winds or because the communities themselves were too dispersed for effective bombardment. Weather became so bad, in fact, that the squadron eventually had to take refuge in Townshend (Boothbay) Harbor. Since Mowat had by-passed all the towns on his list except one, it appears the squadron was headed for Machias, but the winds that blocked his passage there, opened the way to nearby Falmouth.[34]

The appearance of Mowat's vessels in Falmouth in the evening of 16 October caused no particular alarm among the townspeople who assumed the lieutenant's gratitude for saving him from Samuel Thompson. They were staggered, then, the following afternoon when Mowat sent an officer ashore to read a proclamation accusing the townspeople of "unpardonable rebellion" and "premeditated attacks on the legal prerogative of the best of sovereigns." Their penalty was nothing less than the destruction of the town to commence after a two-hour respite allowing the "human species" time to evacuate—provided they offered no resistance.[35] In a panic, the townspeople elected a three-person committee, representing a cross section of political opinion, to negotiate with Mowat. At length he relented to the extent that he would delay the bombardment and even seek confirmation of his orders from Admiral Graves in Boston, if the citizens would surrender all their arms and ammunition by nine o'clock the next morning. In the atmosphere of panic and confusion, Falmouth found it impossible to convene a town meeting to discuss or, if approved, carry out such a proposal. Instead, virtually everyone, including Falmouth's militia, seemed preoccupied with removing family and valuables from the doomed town.[36]

The log of the *Canceaux* as well as Mowat's letter to his superior, Admiral Graves, provide terse, laconic reports of the action that followed. Much more vivid is the eyewitness account by the Reverend Jacob Bailey of Pownalborough (Dresden). Although an Anglican and a loyalist, there is no doubting the accuracy of his dramatic description of the terror, the conflagration, the total lack of any effort to defend the town, and the looting of Falmouth by the militiamen from the interior.[37] Falmouth officials later estimated the loss in buildings, personal estate, and equipment totaled fifty-five thousand pounds. Probably 160 families were destitute not only of housing, but of livelihood since the fire destroyed the commercial as well as the residential center of the town.[38] By today's terms, the destruction encompassed the area from India Street up the hill to Congress Street, and then in a rough diagonal down to the foot of Exchange Street, then easterly back along Fore Street, which was then the waterfront, to India Street and even beyond.

The plight of at least one thousand refugee men, women, and children, as well as unnumbered transient laborers and seamen, from a population on the Neck estimated at 2,500, evoked charity from nearby towns and tax relief from the Provincial Congress—nonetheless, a strong sentiment prevailed that Falmouth had gotten what it deserved for its timidity in the face of the enemy.[39] During the remainder of the war, Falmouth never recovered from its destruction. Loyalists, refugees, and survivors of the bombardment seeking safety and a more promising environment deserted the Neck. The few remaining residents tried to rebuild their blackened site and even prepared to defend it, but the fact the British never again attacked what had once been the leading town in Maine testifies to Falmouth's wartime insignificance and poverty.

One nemesis Falmouth did not escape was Samuel Thompson, whose name had become a byword for unrestrained zeal in the patriot cause. Not only did the Provincial Congress fail to censure him for his unauthorized intrusion into Falmouth, but it actually replaced a motion of censure with one of approval. Congress then rewarded him in 1776 with a commission as Brigadier General of Cumberland County—of which Falmouth was still shire town, reduced as it may have been. Falmouth's leaders were furious that the defense of their county and town lay in the hands of one so lacking in gentlemanly qualities, balanced judgment, and military experience. But when they tried to engineer Thompson's removal on grounds of incompetence, they failed utterly owing to Thompson's powerful political support from delegates representing small interior towns of Cumberland County: Windham, Gray, Bakerstown (Poland and Minot), Harpswell, and, of course, Brunswick and Gorham. Residents of these economic and political satellites to Falmouth still retained their envy, resentment, and contempt for their commercial shire town.[40] For the backcountry, Brigadier General Thompson came to epitomize not just a political revolution, but a social revolution as well. The contest over Thompson's military appointment was part of this simmering unresolved debate over the nature of the Revolution which had worried genteel leaders from the very start. Falmouth's prominent Whig, Enoch Freeman, may have romanticized "the People" in their collective and theoretical capacity to judge of government's validity—but up close and personal, "the People" could be as unpredictable and dangerous as Samuel Thompson.

The end of the Revolutionary War and independence left unresolved just who "the People" were, and the means by which they expressed and realized their demands. On a grand scale the same questions involved the nature of the new United States: how united this new United States should really be, and how and when a revolution should stop—and who decides? For Falmouth the Revolution had carried a terrible price, but once over, independence opened the way for the revived community to build a new identity, separate from its rural backcountry with a new name, Portland. And the ambitions of Falmouth's leaders did not end there for, imbued by postwar revival and a revolutionary ideology of self-determination, they envisioned Portland as the proud capital of an autonomous state of Maine separate from its parent, Massachusetts.

Falmouth's transformation into Portland reflected an economic postwar revival that astonished the residents themselves. The bird of classical mythology called the Phoenix, rising renewed and revitalized from its own ashes, still offers an irresistible analogy. Even before the war had officially ended in 1783, refugees began returning to reconstruct their burned-out homes accompanied by optimistic newcomers. Despite a severe postwar depression that affected the entire country, Falmouth underwent a veritable building boom: forty-one new dwelling houses, ten stores, and seven shops were built in 1784, followed the next year by thirty-three new houses. "This place fills up very fast," Rev. Thomas Smith noted in his journal in 1784. "The trade of this place surprisingly increases," he continued. "Strangers (traders and others) crowd in among us surprisingly." The revival continued; by 1797 the town on the peninsula consisted of over four hundred dwellings, eighty-six mechanic shops, seventy-eight stores and shops, five offices, three rope factories, two distilleries, four meetinghouses, two schools, a court house and a jail.[41]

The rise of the McLellan clan from prewar obscurity to towering prosperity and prominence reflects the economic opportunities in Falmouth's fluid postwar society. By 1800 the McLellans owned not only the largest fleet of ships in Maine, but headed Falmouth's first bank and insurance company. This emergent elite family typically expressed its power and prestige in two of the finest residences in Falmouth, the elegant Hugh McLellan mansion on the corner of High and Spring Streets, now an annex to the Portland Museum of Art, and the equally impressive dwelling across the street, currently the Cumberland Club, built by Hugh's brother, Stephen.[42] Although much disrupted by war and depression, commerce, the lifeblood of the community, was recovering. Between 1785 and 1789, the number of vessels arriving in Portland Harbor increased from sixty to eighty-nine. Many, indeed, were British registry trading Maine's fish, lumber, and barrel staves with the West Indies, from which American vessels were now excluded. American merchants, however, soon found new markets in Europe and even in Asia, and once Britain and France resumed their longtime hostilities, American merchants profited from their status as neutral traders.[43]

The rate and degree with which the Neck recovered from its wartime destruction is difficult to determine precisely. But to local leaders at that time the signs of material progress were sufficiently encouraging for them to seek a new identity free from the envy and influence of the more rural mainland sections of what had been the original town. The Neck had long dominated the entire community, economically and administratively, so that Cape Elizabeth, Stroudwater, New Casco, Back Cove, and Purpoodock offered no opposition when on 4 July 1786, the Massachusetts General Court approved an act setting off the Neck as a separate municipality to be called Portland. Elected as moderator of Portland's first town meeting was, of course, Enoch Freeman.[44]

Even as Falmouth's leaders were transforming the ruined town into a thriving commercial center separate from its rural hinterland, yet more ambitious plans were underway to separate Maine itself from Massachusetts. The impetus came from a handful of prominent men in the Falmouth-Gorham area who had played locally important roles during the Revolution: merchants Enoch Ilsley and Stephen Hall, Enoch Freeman's son, Samuel, a merchant and professional office holder, and the two ministers of Falmouth's First Parish Church, the Reverend Thomas Smith and his associate, Samuel Deane. A newcomer to the group was a former general, Peleg Wadsworth who had settled in Falmouth after the war as a merchant. Two more advocates of separation came from Gorham, Stephen Longfellow Jr., formerly a resident of Falmouth and now a gentleman farmer, and Judge William Gorham, one of the few state office-holders to support separation. Of crucial importance were Thomas B. Wait and Benjamin Titcomb who devoted their newspaper, the *Falmouth Gazette*, later renamed the *Cumberland Gazette*, to the cause of statehood. A separate state of Maine would enable the founders to satisfy their political ambitions in a state of their own without the competition for office from the likes of a Hancock, a Bowdoin, or an Adams.[45] Furthermore, statehood would enhance the importance of southwestern Maine and particularly of Falmouth (Portland) itself, the logical site for the capital of the new state. As early as 5 February 1785, the *Falmouth Gazette* pointed up the connection between statehood and Falmouth with an acrostic that said it all:

> From th' Ashes of the old, a *Town* appears,
> And Phoenix like, her plumy head she rears;
> Long may she flourish; be from war secure;
> Made rich by commerce and agriculture;
> O're all her foes triumphant; be content
> Under our happy form of government;
> Till (what no doubt will be her prosp'rous fate)
> Herself's the mistress of a rising STATE.[46]

The genteel Falmouth/Portland advocates of statehood for Maine promoted their cause in terms that were respectful and rational. Although the creation of a new state out of an existing one might be construed as a revolutionary act, it was important to disguise this fact by making the process of separation as conservative as possible. In some respects, separation was like the Revolution itself; radicals who threatened the traditional social and economic order were not welcome.

Formal arguments for separation from Massachusetts were certainly moderate and rational in content. Letters printed in the newspaper, convention resolutions, and handbills changed but little over time. Proponents appealed to historic rights of statehood, to natural law, and to the analogy between the colonies and Britain. On less ideological grounds they pointed out that Maine, geographically isolated from Massachusetts, had its own interests to pursue. Remote from the seat of government in Boston, Mainers could not take an active part in political and judicial matters there. By contrast, statehood would mean a smaller, less expensive, and more democratic government for all Maine citizens. Finally, the new state of Maine would acquire representation in the national government helping to offset the preponderance of influence exercised by the South.[47]

To rally support for their cause, the Portland separationists waged a vigorous newspaper campaign, held several state conventions, and even submitted a petition for separation to the Massachusetts General Court. But to their dismay, separationists discovered that other coastal communities in Maine—even Portland itself—were divided over any scheme that might jeopardize valuable economic ties with Massachusetts and with Boston in particular.

On the other hand, the concept of statehood did win support from the least desirable segment of Maine's population, the turbulent backcountry, whose self-appointed spokesman was none other than Samuel Thompson. After the war, thousands of settlers, many of them war veterans principally from Massachusetts, sought land in Maine. About 56,000 people resided in Maine in 1784; only six years later that number had expanded to over 96,000, and by 1800, Maine's population surpassed 150,000.[48] But the postwar scramble for land also included speculators who used their political connections with the Massachusetts government to profit from the demand. The old Pejepscot and Kennebec Proprietors were revived after the war and reasserted their claims to great tracts of Maine along the Androscoggin and Kennebec river valleys. In addition, a new landed elite evolved from the Revolution as individuals, such as former generals Peleg Wadsworth and Benjamin Lincoln, acquired thousands of acres in central Maine. Their holdings, however, were dwarfed by the millions of acres Henry Knox obtained farther Downeast. Conflict was inevitable; new settlers occupied whatever tracts appealed to them in the belief that it had been king's land won by the war for the common benefit of all. Too frequently, however, they discovered they had squatted on land claimed by absentee landowners whose agents threatened them with legal action and forcible removal if they did not secure a proper deed. Tensions over land titles, debts, and taxes during a postwar depression made Maine's backcountry a very volatile region.[49]

Discontented, restless backcountry farmers saw in statehood for Maine their own vision of a small, simple, less expensive government responsive to their needs in contrast to the government of Massachusetts with its unholy alliance with the Great Proprietors. But these were just the sort of allies the genteel, conservative Portland-based initiators of separation needed the least. Maine's backcountry carried the whiff of radicalism and violence against legally constituted authority.

Events in western Massachusetts made backcountry support for Maine statehood all the more suspect. Rumblings of social and economic discontent had pervaded western Massachusetts ever since the end of the war. The postwar depression heightened complaints about excessive taxes, arbitrary and expensive courts, the scarcity of money, and an expensive government located in far-off Boston. Popular discontent led to conventions, protests, riots, and eventually an armed uprising named after one of its leaders, Daniel Shays. Although the state militia quickly put an end to Shays's Rebellion in the winter of 1787, the uprising made a major negative impact on the movement for Maine statehood. Shays's Rebellion did not extend to Maine's backcountry; nonetheless, it was impossible for Maine's restless, angry subsistence farmers to escape the charge of Shaysism leveled by nervous absentee landowners and the Great Proprietors. As Maine's backcountry people were drawn into the movement for separation, they brought such accusations with them . . . and the additional one of disunion.[50]

Hard on the heels of Shays's Rebellion came the Federal Constitutional Convention in Philadelphia, and then respective state ratifying conventions. Although the Massachusetts state convention ratified the Federal Constitution in February 1788, it did so by only nineteen votes and over the vigorous opposition of delegates representing the western rural towns, the seat of Shays's Rebellion, joined by those from back-country Maine. Leading the opposition was none other than Maine's own, Samuel Thompson, notorious for his role as mob leader during the Revolution and as an outspoken advocate of statehood for Maine.

By the time of the ratifying convention in early 1788, Thompson had gained a certain aura of respectability as a successful businessman, entrepreneur, and elected representative to the Massachusetts legislature. But he had not mellowed; several times in convention debates he had to be called to order for the violence of his rhetoric. Thompson's denunciation of the new Federal Constitution stands today as classic anti-federalism : the framers had exceeded their authority; they had created a centralized government at the expense of the states and bestowed despotic power on fallible men unrestrained by a bill of rights; the ratifying process was flawed, and in addition, the new constitution legitimized the institution of slavery.[51] On losing the vote to reject such a constitution, Thompson talked wildly of traveling to the western counties of the state to rekindle the spirit of rebellion against so dangerous a frame of government.[52] It was only talk, but the damage was done.

To Massachusetts Federalists and those opposed to statehood for Maine, it was easy to blur all distinctions among anti-Federalists, Shaysites, and proponents of Maine's statehood into one mass of disunionists who would dismember the national union by rejecting the new constitution, dismember orderly, civil society by advocating domestic rebellion, and dismember the state by separating Maine from Massachusetts. Despite the moderation of the original Falmouth/Portland promoters, the separation movement had been discredited and tarred with the brush of every kind of radicalism. It died at what proved to be the last of the Portland statehood conventions in 1789. Attendance had been dwindling at previous meetings until at this final one only three delegates arrived. They elected one of their number to be chairman, a second to be secretary, and then when there was no one to second the motion made by the third to adjourn, the first phase of the Portland-based movement for statehood collapsed—and with it collapsed Portland's dreams to be the capital of a rising state.[53]

The movement for statehood would revive, subside, and revive again under new leadership beyond the confines of Portland. It reached fruition in 1820 under the aegis of modern party politics and a national crisis over slavery that enabled Maine to separate peaceably from Massachusetts and to enter the union preserving the balance between free states and slave. Portland then momentarily enjoyed enhanced status as capital of the new state, but only until 1832. Maine's backcountry and Downeast towns once more denied Portland's claims to political leadership by removing the capital to Augusta, a more accessible and democratic location for the towns of the interior. In the long contest between Maine's metropolis and its hinterland, the metropolis lost out once again. And the tug of war still continues as Maine's populous, prosperous, and polished entrepot, Portland, continues to contend with modern-day Samuel Thompsons and their followers from the interior and from "the county"—where the difference is more than the dialect.

Notes

The author wishes to express his gratitude to Charles P. M. Outwin for comments and information in preparation for this essay. Especially valuable, Outwin, "An Index of Political Figures, of All Persuasions, involved in events preceding or attendant upon the destruction of Falmouth in Casco Bay, 1765–1775" (unpublished paper, 2004).

   1. There are numerous accounts of the burning of Falmouth. For published primary sources, see documents from Jacob Bailey, Daniel Tucker, the log of the *Canceaux*, and Mowat's report to Vice Admiral Samuel Graves in *Naval Documents of the American Revolution*, ed. William B. Clark, *et al.*, 10 vols. (Washington, D.C.: Government Printing Office, 1964–1996), 2: 500–02, 513–16, hereafter cited as *NDAR*. See also *Henry Mowat: Voyage of the Canceaux*, ed., Andrew J. Wahll (Bowie, Md.: Heritage Books, 2003), 310–20. See also "Letter from Rev. Jacob Bailey in 1775, Describing the Destruction of Falmouth, Maine," *Collections of the Maine Historical Society*, 1st ser., 5 (1857): 441–50, hereafter cited as *CMEHS*. A somewhat more patriotic account is "A Short Acco't of the Destruction of the Town of Falmouth," 23 April 1782, *Documentary History of the State of Maine*, ed. James P. Baxter (Portland, Maine: Lefavor-Tower, 1914), 20: 406–08, hereafter cited as *Doc. Hist. ME*. For the most complete modern account, see David Yerxa, "Admiral Samuel Graves and the Falmouth Affair: A Case Study in British Imperial Pacification, 1775" (M.A. thesis, University of Maine at Orono, 1974), usefully abridged in Yerxa, *The Burning of Falmouth, 1775: A Case Study in British Imperial Pacification* (Portland: Maine Historical Society, 1975).

   2. "Letter from Rev. Jacob Bailey," *CMEHS*, 1st ser., 5(1857): 449.

   3. Falmouth Town Records, 10, 14 Oct. 1765, microfilm of typescript copy, Maine State Archives, hereafter cited as MESA; *Journals of the Rev. Thomas Smith, and the Rev. Samuel Deane . . . ,* ed. William Willis (Portland, Maine:

Joseph S. Bailey, 1849), 1, 15 Jan. 1766, 316–17, n.5; 8 Jan. 1766, 207, hereafter cited as *Smith and Deane Journals*; *New-Hampshire Gazette*, 31 Jan. 1766; *Boston Gazette*, 3 Feb. 1766, hereafter cited as *NHG* and *BG*; William Willis, *History of Portland, 1632–1864* (Portland, Maine: Bailey and Noyes, 1865, reprinted Somersworth, N.H., and Portland, Maine: New Hampshire Publishing Co. and Maine Historical Society, 1972), 481–82.

4. *Smith and Deane Journals*, 16 May 20, 1766, 209; Willis, *Portland*, 482–83, n.3.

5. *Smith and Deane Journals*, 7 Aug. 1766, 319–20n; Francis Waldo to Surveyor General, Falmouth, 11 Aug. 1766, *Doc. Hist. Me.*, 14: 8–9; *NHG*, 22 Aug. 1766; Willis, *Portland*, 484; Hiller B. Zobel, *The Boston Massacre* (New York: W.W. Norton, 1970), 50–51.

6. *Smith and Deane Journals*, 10 Sept. 1765, 206; *Bennet v. Bryant*, Records of the Cumberland County Court of General Sessions, October 1765; Records of the Cumberland County Court of Common Pleas, October 1771, 1772, Maine State Archives, Augusta, Maine; Records of the Superior Court for Cumberland and Lincoln County, Minute Books and File Papers, 1771–1772, Suffolk County Court House, Boston, Mass.; William Tyng, Sheriff of Cumberland, to Gov. Francis Bernard, Falmouth, 11 Aug. 1768, *Doc. Hist. ME*, 14:84.

7. Falmouth Town Records, 21 Sept., 4 Dec. 1768, MES; *BG*, 18 June, 9 July 1770; *NHG*, 13 July 1770; *Smith and Deane Journals*, 24 April 1770, 218, 26 June 1770, 328.

8. Memorial of Arthur Savage, 27 Nov. 1771, *Doc. Hist. ME*, 14: 143–47; Willis, *Portland*, 489–91, n.3.

9. Sworn Testimony of Arthur Savage, Boston, 27 Nov. 1771; Proceedings of the Council Regarding the Riot at Falmouth, 27 Nov. 1771, *Doc. Hist.ME.*, 14:147–49.

10. *Brightman v. Veazie*, Records of the Cumberland County Court of Common Pleas, vol. 2: April 1768–Oct. 1772, April Term, pp. 494–96, MESA.

11. Magistrates of Cumberland County to Gage, Falmouth, 20 Feb. 1775, *Province in Rebellion*, ed. L. Kinvin Wroth (Cambridge, Mass.: Harvard University Press, 1975), doc. #728: 2036–2037; Vice Admiral Samuel Graves to Philip Stephens, Boston, 11 April 1775, *NDAR*, 1:176–77. Court Martial of Lieutenant William Hunter and Master Maltis Lucullus Ryal, 27 Feb. 1775, Wahll, ed., *Henry Mowat: Voyage of the Canceaux*, 257–58.

12. Falmouth Town Records, 3 Feb. 1774, MESA; *NHG*, 4 March 1774.

13. Reprinted *NHG*, 18 Feb. 1774.

14. Reprinted *NHG*, 13 March 1774.

15. *BG*, 21 Aug. 1775; Willis, *Portland*, 499, 515.

16. William D. Williamson, *A History of the State of Maine . . .*, 2 vols. (Hallowell, Maine: Glazier, Masters, 1832; Reprinted Freeport, Maine: Cumberland Press, n.d.), 2:412; *NHG*, 24 June 1774; *Smith and Deane Journals*, 14, [29], 30 June 1774, 225.

17. Enoch Freeman's Almanac, 1774, 241–43, Portland Public Library, Portland, Maine.

18. Cumberland County Resolves and the Declaration of William Tyng, *American Archives . . .* , ed. Peter Force, 4th ser., 6 vols. (Washington, D.C.: M. St. Clair Clarke and Peter Force, 1837–1853), 1:798–99, hereafter cited as *Am. Arch; Smith and Dean Journals*, 21 Sept. 1774, 225, 335; Willis, *Portland*, 894–95.

19. *Am. Arch*, 4th ser., 1:798–801.

20. Gorham Town Records, 31 August 1774, MESA.

21. Minutes of the Falmouth Committee of Inspection, 2–3 March 1775, Willis, *Portland*, 895–96; *Smith and Dean Journals*, 12 April 1775, 226; Some of the Principal Inhabitants to Lieutenant Henry Mowat, Falmouth, 2 May 1775, and Lieutenant Henry Mowat to Vice Admiral Samuel Graves, Falmouth, 4 May 1775, and Log Entry, 11 May 1775 in Wahll, ed., *Henry Mowat: Voyage of the Canceaux*, 263–64, 266.

22. Minutes of the Falmouth Committee of Correspondence, 3 March 1775, *Am. Arch.*, 4th ser., 2:313.

23. Cumberland County Convention, 9 March 1775, *Ibid.*, 4th ser., 2:92.

24. Extract of a Letter from the Chairman of the Committee of Inspection at Falmouth to Samuel Freeman, Falmouth, 12 April, *Ibid.*, 4th ser., 2:318.

25. *Smith and Deane Journals*, 21 April 1775, 336; 25, 29 April 1775, 227.

26. Rev. John Wiswall to Mr. Hind, Secretary to the Society for the Propagation of the Gospel, Boston, 30 May 1775, Wiswall Papers, Maine Historical Society, Portland, ME, hereafter cited as MEHS.

27. Nathan Goold, "Falmouth Neck in the Revolution," *CPMEHS*. 2nd ser., 8 (1897), 93.

28. Deposition of Rev. John Wiswall, Mowat Papers, MEHS; Letter from Falmouth to a Gentleman in Watertown, 11 May 1775, *Am. Arch.*, 4th ser., 2:552–53.

29. Enoch Freeman to Samuel Freeman, Falmouth, 10 May 1775, *Am. Arch.*, 4th ser., 2:550–51; Willis, *Portland*, 511 n.2.

30. Letter from Falmouth to a Gentleman in Watertown, 11 May 1775, *Am. Arch.*, 4th ser., 2:553–54.

31. Williamson, *Maine*, 2:427.

32. Letter from Falmouth to a Gentleman in Watertown, 11 May 1775, *Am. Arch.*, 4th ser., 2:555.

33. Vice Admiral Samuel Graves to Lieutenant Henry Mowat, Boston, 6 Oct. 1775, *NDAR*, 2:324–26; see also relevant documents in Wahll, ed., *Henry Mowat: The Voyage of the Canceaux*, 296, 311–25; Yerxa, *The Burning of Falmouth*, 119–27.

34. Lieutenant Henry Mowat to Vice Admiral Samuel Graves, Canceaux, Casco Bay, 19 Oct. 1775, *NDAR*, 2:513–16.

35. Lieutenant Henry Mowatt, R.N., to the People of Falmouth, Canceaux, Casco Bay, 16 Oct. 1775, *Ibid.*, 2:471.

36. Lieutenant Henry Mowat, R.N., to Vice Admiral Samuel Graves, Canceaux, Casco Bay, 19 Oct. 1775, *Ibid.*, 2:513–16.

37. Compare *Ibid.* with Letter from Jacob Bailey in 1775 Describing the Destruction of Falmouth, Maine, *CMEHS*, 1st ser., 5 (1857): 441–50.

38. Willis, *Portland*, 900–902.

39. The exact population of Falmouth on the Neck is impossible to determine precisely and so is the percentage of refugees. At this time the town of Falmouth included several communities on the mainland, such as Cape Elizabeth, Stroudwater, Purpoodock, and Back Cove as well as the settlement on the Neck, and population figures were given collectively for Falmouth as a whole. Willis, *Portland*, 373, 438, 521, estimates the population on the Neck in 1764 to be about 1,260, one-third of the town's entire population. Given a decade of growth and prosperity, as well as the increasing number of transient laborers, apprentices, and seamen, the population could easily have reached 2,000 or even 2,500 by the time of the Revolution. Willis estimates an average of six members per family, so if 160 families were rendered destitute by the bombardment, about one thousand persons were homeless, and this again does not account for renters and transients who lived wherever they could. Thus, on the basis of these estimates, 40 to 50 percent of the population on the Neck became refugees. These figures do not include those who left the burned-out town voluntarily to seek safety and/or a livelihood elsewhere. In personal correspondence with this author, Charles P. M. Outwin, a specialist in Portland's early history, disputes Willis's figures as far too conservative both in the total population living on the Neck, the number of persons per family, and, correspondingly, the depopulation of the Neck that followed the burning.

40. Jedediah Preble to John Waite, Boston, 5 March 1777, Willis Papers, Autograph Letters, MEHS; Reports from pro and anti-Thompson conventions to the General Court, 17 Sept., 21 Oct. 1779, *Doc. Hist. ME*, 17:143–46, 401–02.

41. Willis, *Portland*, 550, 553 n.1, 562; *Smith and Deane Journals*, 10, 12 April, 1 Aug. 1784, 252–53.

42. William D. Barry and John Holverson, "The Revolutionary McLellans: A Bicentennial Project of the Portland Museum of Art" (Portland, Maine: Portland Museum of Art, 1977), chaps. 1–2, on file at MEHS.

43. Willis, *Portland*, suggests some postwar trading difficulties by the exclusion of American vessels from British ports in the West Indies, 557. For example, Willis's figures show a decline in the arrival of vessels at Falmouth between 1785–1786 (588–89), and notes that no ship was owned in Portland as late as 1787 (560). These were difficult years for the United States as a whole as it recovered from the war and the need to adjust its commerce as an independent nation outside the British empire.

44. Willis, *Portland*, 579–82.

45. Ronald F. Banks, *Maine Becomes a State* (Somersworth, N.H. and Portland, Maine: New Hampshire Publishing Co. and Maine Historical Society, 1973), 12–13; see also notes, 209–13.

46. *Falmouth Gazette*, 5 Feb. 1785. Hereafter cited as *FG*.

47. *FG*, 4, 11, 18 June; 9, 30 July; 6, 13 Aug.; 5 Nov. 1785; 23 March 1786; *Cumberland Gazette*, 11 May, 28 Sept. 1786. Banks, *Maine Becomes a State*, 13–17.

48. Banks, *Maine Becomes a State*, 5.

49. Gordon E. Kershaw, *The Kennebeck Proprietors* (Somersworth, N.H. and Portland, Maine: New Hampshire Publishing Co. and Maine Historical Society, 1975), chap. 13; Alan Taylor, *Liberty Men and Great Proprietors* (Chapel Hill, N.C.: University of North Carolina Press, 1990) is especially valuable.

50. James Leamon, "In Shays's Shadow: Separation and Ratification of the Constitution in Maine," *In Debt to Shays: The Bicentennial of an Agrarian Revolution*, ed. Robert A. Gross (Charlottesville, Va.: University of Virginia Press, 1993), 281–96.

51. Jonathan Elliot, ed., *The Debates in the Several State Conventions on the Adoption of the Federal Constitution*, 2d. ed., revised, 5 vols. (1888, Reprinted New York: Burt Franklin, 1968), 2:15–16, 33–35, 61, 80, 96, 107, 140.

52. Leamon, "In Shays's Shadow," 282.

53. Banks, *Maine Becomes a State*, 24.

4

Longfellow's Portland

Charles Calhoun

In 1807, the year of Longfellow's birth, an enterprising sea captain decided it would be more prudent to seek his livelihood on land than on the waves. Lemuel Moody erected an observation tower, eighty-two feet high and well ballasted with granite, on the slope of Munjoy Hill at the eastern end of the Portland peninsula. He spent most of the rest of his days looking from the top of it, through a splendid English telescope, at what the searoads and the weather might bring. A quirk of topography gave Captain Moody a much better view of the Atlantic than was possible from the inner harbor. In his maritime world, time literally was money: to know as soon as possible which vessel was approaching, and what cargo it might hold, was a tremendous advantage to the merchants at dockside. These merchants had financed Moody's tower and stocked it with their various signal flags, as colorfully heraldic in their way as any knight's escutcheon.[1]

To break his solitary watch, Captain Moody allowed visitors up the steps of his observatory—visitors as distinguished as President Monroe in 1824, as everyday as his friends and neighbors. To survey for the first time from its cupola the harbor and hills must have been a thrilling moment in the life of every Portland boy. Sensitive, alert, eager to learn, young Longfellow was able to assemble from such vantage points that rich stock of maritime images that he would draw upon, thirty, forty years later, in building his reputation as the most popular poet in the English-speaking world.[2]

The tower still stands, newly repainted red; the view itself remains unchanged in its essentials. Casco Bay is a maze of islands and ledges, the heart of the city still perches on two sides of the long ridge of the peninsula, and on the western horizon rise the White Mountains of New Hampshire (a view less distinct than in Longfellow's day, thanks to the Midwest's gift of industrial pollutants). The open fields of Longfellow's youth are now densely built over, and the malodorous Back

Figure 4-1. Portland Observatory (1807), from a stereoview by Marquis F. King, c. 1875. Courtesy of the Maine Historic Preservation Commission.

Cove has been civilized, but Deering's oaks still shed their acorns, and the Portland Head Light celebrated in one of Longfellow's poems still guides vessels into the harbor.

Longfellow was born on 27 February 1807, in a now-vanished house at the corner of Fore and Hancock streets temporarily occupied by his parents, Stephen and Zilpah, and belonging to his uncle. Among his earliest impressions of the world must have been the squeal of the herring gulls and the rich, rotten smells of low tide: the house was separated only by a small beach from the harbor. He remained there a few months, but a tang of salt air pervades much of his poetry (the last poem of his long career in 1882 praised the bells of the harbor of San Blas, and the posthumously published collection *In the Harbor* included a short lyric, "The City and the Sea," surely inspired by his perceptions of Portland).

It was an inauspicious year in which to be born. Jefferson's mis-guided effort to keep the United States neutral in the global struggle between Britain and Napoleonic France had damaged the commerce of New England. The Reverend Samuel Deane's journal for 1807 lists twenty-four ruined merchants, including Longfellow's uncle. He adds: "These were among the principal merchants of the town, and largely engaged in navigation, whose occupation and means of success were suddenly blasted by the non-intercourse act of 1806, followed by the embargo law of 1807, which laid up the numerous and valuable vessels of our merchants to perish in the docks."[3] A soup kitchen was estab-lished in the market square to feed the indigent. The War of 1812 would bring further disruptions.

Yet it says something about the commercial vigor of Portland that it sprang back so quickly in Longfellow's youth. Its location helped: an ice-free, well-sheltered harbor near the mouths of two rivers connect-ing it to a rapidly developing back-country. From the forests came oak, pine, beech, ash, and elm to be sent to timber-hungry Europe and the West Indies; from the farms, pork, beef, cheese, soap, candles, butter, for the West Indies (paid for with an ocean of molasses, converted into either sugar or rum).[4] Portland-based ships conducted a brisk coastal trade with other New England ports and carried Southern cotton to European mills. Still part of Massachusetts, the District of Maine was growing increasingly independent-minded, and there were those who thought its leading city might soon rival Boston as chief entrepot of northern New England.

In mid-life Henry Longfellow became Henry *Wadsworth* Longfel-low, joining many other New Englanders in attaching a distinguished maternal family name as a kind of patent of gentility. There was cer-tainly no name more distinguished in the District: Henry's grand-father Peleg Wadsworth had been a valiant Revolutionary War leader on the Downeast front and then a six-term Federalist congressman and successful merchant-farmer. In 1785–1786, General Wadsworth had built the first brick house in Portland, conveniently situated on the main road into town and a few steps from the town market; from an appendage of the house he sold the produce of his estate at Hiram and some of the cargo—sugar, china, fancy goods—in which he had invested on the vessels unloading just down the hill. (Fore Street was in Longfellow's youth the waterfront.) The general had raised eleven children in the house; Henry was to share it with his own parents, three brothers, four sisters, a maiden aunt, and various servants. (The deceptive calm of today's house museums, including Longfellow's boyhood home, is in striking contrast to how densely they were originally inhabited.)

Henry's father Stephen was the fourth Longfellow by that name in New England, and there would be two others after him. The family, if not quite as dashing as the Wadsworths, nonetheless had produced a series of public-minded lawyers and schoolmasters. If never as rich as Portland merchant-princes like the McClellans, the Longfellows were well-established members of the local elite, in a society in which such distinctions were just beginning to be effaced by Jacksonian democracy. Henry grew up in a small, self-contained circle of lawyers and judges; his first marriage was to the daughter of the local Judge of Probate, and his hapless brother Stephen Jr. made an unhappy union with the daughter of the distinguished jurist-diplomat, Judge Preble. By Henry's youth the house on Congress Street was looking somewhat old-fashioned. A chimney fire in 1815 gave his father an occasion for adding a third story, bringing the "Old Original," as the family affectionately called their home, closer to the Federal architectural ideal.

Though modest by Boston standards, the neighboring buildings embodied the values of the ruling elite in the Maine of the Early Republic. The most urgent task for this post-Revolutionary generation was to establish order on the still unruly frontier. Within a few minutes' walk of the Longfellow house stood First Parish Church (in 1825 an imposing neoclassical stone structure replaced the wooden colonial meeting-house), the Court House and jail, and (after 1820) the State House, where the legislature sat until the capital was moved to Augusta in 1832. On the other side of Congress Street the Market Square formed the commercial heart of the town, and Portland Academy, where Henry prepared for college, completed this small acropolis.

In later life, at least in public, Longfellow bathed the Portland of his youth in glowing colors, most famously in "My Lost Youth," his ode to the city of his birth and his elegy for *le temps perdu*. In fact, he grew up in troubled times. His father, a loyal Federalist long after that party had self-destructed, was caught in the battles over statehood (which he championed in the 1790s but opposed in 1819) and in the larger struggle for power between the coastal elite and increasingly self-assertive back-country farmers. Religion offered no refuge: the Longfellow family's liberal Unitarianism was under attack throughout the poet's youth from trinitarian Congregationalists as well as from the evangelical "unwashed." Stephen Longfellow senior served one undistinguished term as a Federalist congressman in 1824–1825 and was given the honor of welcoming Lafayette to Portland, but he succumbed in early middle age to a combination of chronic ill health and a failure of self-confidence. His son's extraordinarily successful career as a poet builds on two foundations: his parents' cheerful Unitarianism, with its faith in human possibility and its rejection of Calvinist gloom, and his father's staunch Federalism, with its adulation of the nation's founders and its neurotic anxiety about the future of the Republic.

Henry's middle name was also a direct link with what aleady seemed a more heroic age: Henry Wadsworth was his mother's elder brother, who had sacrificed himself in a daring exploit in Tripoli harbor during the war against the Barbary pirates. Young Henry himself had at least a glimpse of naval adventure, growing up in Portland during the nation's second war with Great Britain.

Captain Moody atop his observatory seems to have been the first to see the puffs of smoke. The proximity of the British fleet at Halifax, the questionable loyalty of many Mainers Downeast, and folk memory of Mowatt's raid in 1775 led many Portlanders during 1812–1815 to expect a British attack from the sea at any moment. (They were to be saved by the District of Maine's strategic unimportance.) In response to reports from fishermen that the British brig H.M.S. *Boxer* was approaching Portland harbor in the fall of 1813, the U.S.S. *Enterprise* set out in pursuit. The two ships engaged in a brief battle on 5 September, off Monhegan Island, and the *Enterprise* quickly disabled the enemy vessel. The young British captain, Samuel Blyth, was killed in the first round of fire; his American adversary, William Burrows, was mortally wounded soon after but lived long enough to receive the *Boxer*'s surrender.[5] Some thirty years later, Longfellow would write:

> I remember the sea-fight far away,
>> How it thundered o'er the tide!
> And the dead captains, as they lay
> In their graves, o'erlooking the tranquil bay
>> Where they in battle died.

This passage in "My Lost Youth" is pure poetic license: the battle took place in the Gulf of Maine some forty miles from Portland, far beyond earshot. But Captain Moody was first to report that the *Enterprise* was bringing the *Boxer* back as a prize, and six-year-old Henry would have witnessed the elaborate funeral honors accorded the two captains before their burial in Eastern Cemetery, not far from his own namesake's cenotaph.

During an 1846 visit back to Portland, Longfellow remembered another incident in that anxious time. In 1814, the British once again were blockading the harbor. The local authorities decided to erect a battery at the easternmost point of Munjoy Hill and exhorted every citizen, rich or poor, young or old, to pitch in. As Longfellow noted in his journal for 27 July:

Then took a long walk alone round Munjoy, and down to the Old Fort Lawrence, which as a boy of seven I helped build by rolling stones down the hill. I lay down in one of the embrasures for the cannon, and listened to the lashing, lulling, rippling sound of the sea just at my feet. It was a beautiful afternoon, and the harbor was full of white sails coming and departing. Meditated a poem on the Old Fort.[6]

He never wrote the poem, but "My Lost Youth" evokes "the bulwarks by the shore, And the fort upon the hill."

Perhaps under his mother's influence—and despite a period in the student militia at Bowdoin—Longfellow exhibited throughout his adult life a strong sense of pacifism, which only the Civil War would persuade him to abandon. It is worth speculating whether anxiety among Portlanders at the prospect of an imminent British attack during 1812–1815 made a strong enough impression on a young boy from age five to eight to persuade him of the horrors of war.

Another line in his Portland ode piques one's curiosity: he remembers "Spanish sailors with bearded lips." Given the extent of Portland's trade with Cuba and the West Indies, these mariners were surely Hispanic without necessarily being Iberian. The multiracial, multiethnic population of early nineteenth-century maritime Portland has been overlooked in most accounts, but recent scholarship has begun the difficult process of recovering this lost history. (See the essays by Maureen Elgersman Lee and David Carey in this volume.) A contract for an indentured servant named Sambo survives in General Wadsworth's business papers, and the newly married Longfellows had a black domestic when they set up house in Brunswick in 1831. His Bowdoin graduating class in 1825 had included John Brown Russwurm, who was to become a leading black editor and colonizationist. Longfellow's most "radical" work as a poet—his seven *Poems on Slavery* published in 1842—suggest a sympathy for African Americans that may have origins in his youth. (Did the creator of Hiawatha know any Native Americans in his Portland years? A century of frontier wars in colonial Maine had not totally destroyed the aboriginal Wabanaki, but the survivors had been reduced to a marginal status. Evidence of Longfellow's early interest in their history is limited to some juvenalia, including two poems that commemorated the "massacre" of white settlers at Lovell's Pond.)

The young Longfellow had spent holidays at his grandfathers' farms at Hiram and Gorham (both of which survive today), but it was only with his departure for Bowdoin College, some twenty-five miles away in Brunswick, that he experienced his first real separation from Portland and his family. Even this was relative: he entered college the same year as his older brother Stephen, and Bowdoin in the 1820s was, socially and politically, an extension of his Portland circle. The college had been chartered in 1794, and opened in 1802, as an attempt by the "great and the good" of coastal Maine and the lower Kennebec valley to replicate Harvard on the banks of the Androscoggin. Bowdoin came close enough for local needs, although the infant institution soon found itself mired in denominational and political controversy.[7] In hindsight, it was a mistake not to have established the college in Portland—Bramhall's Hill, at the western end of the peninsula, would have been an admirable site—for the city lacked, until the expansion of the University of Southern Maine in the 1980s, the stimulus of an ambitious institution of higher learning. A Portland-based Bowdoin might have developed into a small university, somewhat on the Dartmouth model, with a medical school and a law faculty.

But Brunswick was chosen, partly for geopolitical reasons, partly because of an enduring American conviction that students would be exposed to fewer vices in rural settings than in seaports. During Longfellow's three years in residence at Bowdoin, he returned home as the college calendar allowed; his opportunity to go abroad to study languages during 1825–1829 marked a sharper break with the world of his youth. He taught modern languages at Bowdoin from 1829 to 1835, then made another long European trip (during which his first wife died) before taking up his duties as a Harvard professor in 1836.

Longfellow was truly filial and strove to keep up with his family in Portland, whether through frequent correspondence, their rare visits to Cambridge, or his annual trips to Maine. His parents' worsening health through the 1830s and '40s and his brother Stephen's gradual decline into alcoholism and depression made these visits something other than holidays. Longfellow's own despair over his unsuccessful courtship of Frances Appleton from 1836 until she finally accepted him in 1843 added to the tensions. A poem like "The Rainy Day" ("written in the old home in Portland" in 1841—by family tradition, in the back parlor overlooking the garden) catches the mood: its bouncy final stanza, after ten lines of gloom, is a kind of therapeutic whistling in the dark.

Longfellow's occasional journal entries about visits to Portland through the 1840s and 50s illuminate his relationship with the city of his memory as well as chronicle its actual physical changes. The tone is nostalgic, often melancholy, brightened with occasional sharp observations of the local scene.

In a sketch written in Portland as early as 1837, for example, he has his fictional persona sitting in the branches of a dead oak, "the favorite retreat of his boyhood," reflecting on how in his own soul "dark, serious melancholy thoughts were springing up to take the place of the glad, green vison of his boyhood." The next year, however, he declares: "Portland looks dull enough. I think I shall grow lazy here."[8]

In his youth in the early 1820s Longfellow had been exposed to a circle of very promising Portland writers, including Seba Smith, the inventor of American vernacular humor, and his wife Elizabeth Oakes Smith, and John Neal, the multitalented lawyer, novelist, and art critic. Yet the city had not been able to sustain their literary careers. "Call on John Neal, who seems to be head over ears in business," Longfellow noted in 1838. "Literature he seems to have given up:—exchanged for granite quarries and house buildings. Thus does the soul become duller."[9] The other Portland figure whom Longfellow never failed to seek out was the family's learned minister, Ichabod Nichols, of First Parish Church. "Dr. Nichols in the morning, with material enough in his sermon to make six."[10]

Longfellow's journals are rarely very self-revealing, but do suggest a gift for social observation. He spent an evening in 1838 at Mrs. Deering's. "Some dozen damsels there; all quiet and well-behaved, with one ranting glad-hearted wild one, all soul, and grace: and Miss Sophia, with little feet like mice." His uncle's house at Gorham provided a contrast: "Life runs riot at the Colonel's, as of old. Fair cousins, grown up from girls to ladies, with a best parlor and a centre-table. But in the common parlor, what a boisterous life among the great boys, just as of old, when we were little boys. Recalled the Past, in talk protracted into midnight."[11]

One factor that might have discouraged more frequent visits was the crudeness of transportation. The Western Mail Stage left Boston at 2:00 A.M. and arrived in Portland at 7:00 P.M. the next day. (A return trip meant leaving Portland at 4:00 A.M., reaching Boston at 8:00 P.M.) A more rapid overnight trip could be made by steamer, but this required trying to sleep in a crowded public cabin ("that pest-house," Longfellow called it in 1840, highly susceptible as he was to catching colds.) Suffering from such "a fearful ague" after spending the night on the boat, he concluded: "Hawthorne's idea of gnomes digging with pic-axes in hollow teeth is a good one!"[12]

By 1843, however, a railroad connected Portland with Boston's Haymarket Terminus. Travel was still not comfortable, given the smoke, dust, and cinders, but it soon required only half a day. By 1846 he was able to travel with Fanny and their children in relative comfort and to introduce them to the pleasures of a coastal vacation.

Strolled down into the dull-looking town with father. Old familiar faces of grocers and shopkeepers, that I knew when a boy. For the most part next [to] no changes in the streets . . . I already feel the effects of the sea-air; stealing over me with its drowsiness and oblivious spell, the song and breath of the Syrens of the sea.[13]

He went to hear an antislavery lecture and hoped it would do some good in a part of the world "where there has been such apathy on the subject of slavery." A trip to Gorham by the Stroudwater Road made him reflect: "How dreamy these environs of Portland always seemed and still seem to me. The rough roads, the gloomy houses, the haunted tin-factory and the patches of woodland which when a little boy I believed infested with robbers."[14]

Later, crossing Tukey's Bridge at the eastern end of the peninsula and visiting Martin's Point on Casco Bay, he was displeased to find that "a huge white hotel has been erected there; and from hence forward all seclusion is banished." But he took the opportunity to introduce his four-year-old son Charley to the sea and to the pleasure of throwing rocks into the water; Charley was to grow into one of the most courageous of American yachtsmen.

Local life that summer had its novelties:

Doctor Merril's house was struck by lightning last evening; the highest room shattered; clapboards bulging out; one window burst to pieces; walls discolored and all the bell-ropes melted and broken. What a ferocious visitor! bursting into the house so unceremoniously, and yet ringing all the bells at once to announce his approach; and away again after shaking hands with the inmates, and dancing wildly on the bell wires. A kind of Robin Good-fellow, with his "Ho! ho! ho!"[15]

At the reading room, he learned that work on the new railroad to Montreal—which was to make Portland the chief port for eastern Canada for some seventy years—had been delayed because the Irish workmen had struck for a raise from $1 to $1.25—they were "all accordingly discharged." Walking later with his father on Munjoy Hill, they discussed a South Carolina newspaper's "long and violent tirade against me for publishing the Anti-Slavery Poems in the cheap edition." Longfellow added: "How impatient they are, the hot Southrons."[16]

That evening he walked with Fanny down Elm Street to Back Cove:

It was a delicious scene. The inverted purple and green shadows of the opposite shore, deepened on one edge into the blacker hues of the woodlands, and fields, and on the other softened into the sweet silvery tints of the water. Four boats hung with idle sails in the midst of the cove . . . On the shore were boys bathing, and playing. Suddenly over our heads we heard the sharp scream of a sea-bird, who threw himself heavily with one broken wing into the water a few rods from land; and struggling vainly to rise again, was caught by the boys in one of the boats. The crowd on the shore welcomed his capture with the delight of young savages, running to and fro and yelling like little fiends. One cried out: "Show him for a sight, and ask a cent apiece!"—And a more gentle boy who ran by us, the young poet of the rising generation probably, said,

"It was a crane
Flew down the lane."

He little dreams that his poem has been recorded. I remember, when I was a boy of his size, as with two companions I dashed through the street on a stick, crying out

"We three
Champions be!"[17]

And hence is published for the first time the earliest verse of the poet whose *Evangeline* the next year would make him world famous.

The Longfellows returned the next summer, staying at the Verandah Hotel—the same one he had objected to, the year before—and continued their exploration of the shores of Casco Bay as part of the vanguard of well-to-do urbanites who were to rusticate themselves to the coast of Maine in decades to come. This solved the problem of imposing on the inhabitants of the "Old Original" for lodging. According to local legend, Henry's sister, the frugal Anne Longfellow Pierce, was the last householder in Portland to have permission to keep a privy, as late as 1901. She had become aware as early as 1843, however, that some improvement in that department was appropriate for big-city visitors. As she wrote to her brother Alexander, who was off surveying the U. S.–Canadian boundary, on the eve of the newlyweds' arrival:

I see no other change in the Old Original Mansion except in one particular, in which perhaps you will rejoice . . . The case "in limine," as the lawyers say, was this—Your newly-inducted & lovely sister Fanny was coming for a visit & what was to be done?—such a dingy, dismal, dark, "dem'd" place as that to pass five minutes in was enough to disgust any one with the Mansion forever—to dig & to build anew, there was no time—so the great artist & your only true refresher was called in, &—- the thing was effectually touched over inside with a coat of a color a cross somewhere between a dirty light slate & a dingy white.[18]

Anne Pierce not only maintained the "Old Original" but proved a sharp observer of the Portland scene for her family, now scattered, from far northern Maine to Cambridge to New Orleans, where her sister Mary Greenleaf spent half the year as a result of her husband James's career as a cotton broker. The exceptionally cold winter of 1848, for example, produced this vignette:

Our beautiful harbor for several days the past week presented the novel & extraordinary scene of hundreds of people walking ad libitum over its surface—belles and beaus walking to the Islands—pedestrian parties to Diamond Cove—no pic-nics that I heard of—hundreds of "merry skaters" coasting in all directions, & in addition to all these every possible variety of equipages . . . Carriages—Cabs—sleighs—lumber-boxes, & sleds crowded with people, driving like mad, from shore to shore, & point to point—stranger than all the rest were the boats put upon runners & sleds, with all sails spread, impelled by the wind as rapidly, if not as usefully, as if in their usual element—altogether presenting a curious & timely scene—while from House, Peaks & Hog Islands, from the Fort, & even Cape Cottage tripping it on foot, to the City, was the great way of communication.[19]

In the late 1840s, the Longfellows were to establish themselves more permanently for the summers at Nahant, on the North Shore of Massachusetts, a resort more convenient to their Cambridge home and more popular with their friends. (It was not until the children were old enough to sail on their own in the 1860s that they discovered Maine locales like Mount Desert Island.) Meanwhile, in Portland Longfellow continued to hear: "Rail-road—rail-road, rail-road! This the theme of every tongue . . . And so I went down by rail-road, talked of rail-roads there, and this afternoon returned home by rail-road. At the ticket-office, whom should I find but my old schoolmaster Bezaleel Cushman. Descended to this from head master of the Portland Academy. Laying pride aside, I should prefer this last place to the first."[20]

His father's final illness in the summer of 1849 brought the family back on the ubiquitous train. "As we sped along, with all the fleetness of steam, I could but feel that perhaps with more rapid flight the great death angel was out-running us, and might reach the house before me." They booked rooms at the United States Hotel, on the north side of Market Square on Congress Street, and began visiting, two or three times a day, the room at home where Stephen lay dying. "This Portland is a beautiful place," admitted Longfellow, "though now so dusty, that walking is a torment, and sitting by the windows we are powdered all over." It was "a very monotonous life, broken only by night-watches by my father's bed. He sleeps for the most part."

Blaming lack of exercise for his "Hamlet-like disgust with everything," Longfellow read Dickens and watched a procession of the Sons of Temperance. (Portland's mayor, Neal Dow, was about to achieve passage of the famous Maine Law of 1851, which put the state at the front of the prohibition movement.) Longfellow found solace elsewhere: "Strolled into Cole's 'Picture Gallery.' Sat on a sofa and the air of Art was wafted about me, and I had a delicious feeling of the old galleries come over me, as I loooked dreamily upon the heads and landscapes."[21] He had in fact done much to encourage Maine artists, including the painter Eastman Johnson and the sculptor Paul Akers. His father grew feebler.

[3 August] This morning, at three o-clock, my father died, very quietly, without pain, a gentle release from a world in which for twenty-seven years he has borne the burden of disease and despondency. In the midst of his career—at the age of forty-five, he was smitten with this disesase which now terminates fatally at the age of seventy-three. Twenty eight years of illness! A life of suffering!

[9 August] Went to Father's office—the dusty—deserted—silent place—where he tolled so day after day—The Ledger showed his reward in page after page of upaid charges! Alas! for a lawyer in a little town!

[25 August] Left Portland by rail-road. On the hill-side saw the [stones] of the grave-yard gleaming white, where from his shroud my poor, old father seemed to wave me a last adieu!

Six years later, in pain from influenza, Longfellow found himself re-visiting in his mind the images of his childhood. "At night, as I lie in bed, and cannot sleep, a poem comes into my mind—a memory of Portland, my native town—the City by the Sea. 'Sieda la terra dove nate fui / Sulla marina'" (*Inferno* V, 97–98. In Longfellow's own translation of Dante: "Sitteth the city, wherein I was born, Upon the sea-shore . . .")

The next day, he noted: "Wrote the poem; and am rather pleased with it; and with the bringing in of the two lines of the old Lapland song; 'A boy's will is the wind's will / And the thoughts of youth are long, long thoughts.'"[22] "My Lost Youth" may have served as his emotional fare-well to Portland, though Longfellow was to return there, usually for no more than one night, at least once a year until 1881. As he had confided to Charles Sumner back in 1849, "Intellectually speaking this is a dull place. It exhausted itself in producing a Willis, and a Neal, and your humble Servant."[23] After the deaths of his mother in 1850 and his aunt Lucia in 1863, his widowed sister Anne Pierce lived alone in the house and depended on his small gifts of money to maintain it. Longfellow had grown to enjoy the company of his younger brother Alexander, who was working for the Coastal Survey. Visits to "Highfield" offered an escape from an increasingly commercial downtown. Alexander's "snug cottage" stood on a hill overlooking the city. Longfellow's own contribution to the scene was a slip from the famous Washington Elm on Cambridge Common, which he sent to Alexander in 1852 and which a later owner embellished with a memorial tablet.[24] Highfield burned to the ground in the early twentieth century, but the house and what it represented to the owner's brother survive in "Changed," written dur-ing an 1858 visit.

From the outskirts of the town,
   Where of old the mile-stone stood.
Now a stranger looking down
I behold the shadowy crown
   Of the dark and haunted wood.

Is it changed, or am I changed?
   Ah! the oaks are fresh and green
But the friends with whom I ranged
Through their thickets are estranged
   By the years that intervene.

Bright as ever flows the sea
   Bright as ever shines the sun
But alas they seem to me
Not the sun that used to be,
   Not the tides that used to run.

The elegiac tone grows stronger in his journal entries about Portland. Visiting in 1860, he writes: "This has become for me a land of ghosts and shadows. Within two years people have grown so much older! and so many have departed, it seems like a new town with new people!" His college friend William Pitt Fessenden seemed "buried in politics." John Neal was "a good deal tempered down, but with fire enough still."[25]

Anne's letters provided a lively chronicle of Portland life. The telegraph office was across Market Square from her house; crowds thronged there day and night in April 1861 as news of Fort Sumter came in. (Earlier that spring, a promising young actor named John Wilkes Booth had performed Shakespeare at Deering Hall, on another side of the square.) On 10 April, Anne wrote: "Our City is all alive—Union flags are flying in every part of the town . . ." By 28 April there were "some five hundred soldiers almost within stones throw of us, quartered in companies. & marched to & fro to their meals, & to ch[urch] to day." Anne described how the women of Portland supported the Union cause: "Our committee of ladies have been very efficient, & as elsewhere, we have all been at work for the last three days—in that time we have accomplished 1600 flannel shirts—800 towels—ditto pocket hdkfs. ditto neck ties, ditto bags with buttons . . ."

Anne prepared bandages under a surgeon's instruction: "with such work in hand one cannot help realising the evil days upon which we have fallen—while on the other hand occupation does much to help me keep quiet." Senator Fessenden's son William was getting up a company in which Longfellow's nephew Harry was the first to enlist— "but it assumed a different character from what was expected & intended, & filling up with Irish & rowdies, he was induced to take his name off."26

A little more than a year after the Union victory, the family home came within a few blocks of being destroyed in the great fire of 1866; Anne proved resourceful in staying there and taking in the disposed.

My drawing room was turned into an architect's office first—then in the aft. I took in Miss Hall with the dry goods she had saved & put Will upstairs. Edie [Longfellow's daughter Edith] would have been in ecstacies over the activity of the shop life wh. lasted till Sat . . .—My porch had the remains of a lawyers office—my bedroom tin boxes of valuable papers. The front entry a big trunk of clothing sent for the sufferers, & the table & chair piled up with assorrted garments. Edie would revel in all the stir & novelty of things in the old quiet house—the coming of applicants, & the trying on of garments—I am sure I did right not to run away in such a time of need, as in this way I can be of aid to the homeless & suffering—Every room in the house c[oul]d have been let twenty times over.27

Lost in grief after his wife Fanny's death by fire in 1861, Longfellow did find rare moments of peace in these familar Portland surroundings. He wrote to George Washington Greene in 1879: "I am here on my annual visit to the old house, inhaling health with every breath of sea-air . . . I am as 'idle as a painted ship upon a painted ocean.' I only sit here at this upper window, and see the people go by, and commit to memory the signs on the opposite side of the street."28 He may or may not have known that he himself had become one of the sights of the town. Edward Ellwell's 1876 guidebook, *Portland and Vicinity,* advises visitors, "No longer ago than last autumn, any one walking down Congress street, after breakfast, might have seen him seated at the window, reading the morning paper."29

Upon Longfellow's death in 1882, the citizens of Portland, the Maine Historical Society, and the Governing Boards of Bowdoin College staged elaborate ceremonial tributes. By 1886, Portland had raised enough money to place Frank Simmons's neoclassical bronze of the seated, bearded poet on a granite plinth at what became Longfellow Square, where State Street crosses Congress. (A similar statue by the same hand was erected in Washington, D.C., at another Longfellow

Square.) Longfellow left his imprint on the fabric of his native city in other ways, too—a Longfellow School, a Longfellow Arboretum, a Longfellow sonnet competition in the schools, even a Longfellow ale. But it was Anne Longellow Pierce's decision to leave the family home to the Maine Historical Society upon her death in 1901 that guaranteed that Portland would not forget its most famous son. The Wadsworth-Longfellow House, recently restored to its 1850s decor, reflecting Anne's long tenure there, is a major tourist attraction downtown. Like the poet's other home in Cambridge, now owned and operated as a house-museum by the National Park Service, the Portland house—and its docents—have kept Longfellow's name and family story in circulation, however dim his reputation has grown in academe. But one Longfellow house in Portland was enough! The house in which the poet was born survived in what had become an industrial neighborhood until 1954 and was run as a museum by a local eccentric. Few tears were shed at its destruction, in an age when Portland had yet to discover the merits of historical preservation.

"My Lost Youth" remains one of the better known poems of the American nineteenth century, thanks to anthologies. But Portland and its environs also make an appearance in other Longfellow poems—directly, in "The Songo River" and "The Lighthouse"; by inference, in "The Building of the Ship" and "The Ropewalk," and possibly "Keramos." And the city's maritime influence is surely felt in every Longfellow poem that evokes that "breath of the merciful, merciless sea."

Notes

1. John K. Moulton, *Captain Moody and His Observatory* (Falmouth, Maine: Mount Joy Publishing, 2000), 17–43.

2. On the decline of the poet's reputation in the twentieth century, see my *Longfellow: A Rediscovered Life* (Boston: Beacon Press, 2004), 250–62.

Because he is so rarely taught in college and university English departments, there is a dearth of contemporary scholarly comment on Longfellow's work. Newton Arvin's *Longfellow: His Life and Work* (Boston: Little, Brown, 1962) remains the most comprehensive study of the poetry; Andrew Hilen's six volumes of the correspondence (Cambridge: Harvard University Press, 1966–1982) would be more useful if they had a subject index. *Longfellow: Poems and Other Writings* (New York: The Library of America, 2000) includes a detailed chronology of his life.

There are a few signs of scholarly renewal of interest, especially from an American Studies perspective. See, for example, Alan Trachtenberg's *Shades of Hiawatha: Staging Indians, Making Americans 1880–1930* (New York: Hill and Wang, 2004). And there is growing awareness of the multicultural Longfellow. Kirsten Silva Gruesz's *Ambassadors of Culture: The Transamerican Origins of Latino Writing* (Princeton, N.J.: Princeton University Press, 2002) examines the impact of Evangeline on Hispanic writers; Christoph Irmscher sees the poet/translator as a trans-Atlantic cultural force in his *Longfellow Redux* (Urbana: University of Illinois Press, 2005).

3. *Journals of the Rev. Thomas Smith and the Rev. Samuel Deane,* William Willis, ed. (Portland, Maine: Joseph S. Bailey, 1849), 388.

4. [James Gay}, *Description of Portland in the United States, in a Letter from an English Gentleman in America to His Friend in Shropshire* (Shrewsbury: C. Hulbert, 1817), Reprinted 1937 by Walter Goodwin Davis, 3.

5. William Goold, *Portland in the Past with Historical Notes of Old Falmouth* (Bowie, Md.: Heritage Books, 1997 Reprint of 1886 ed.), 483–91.

6. Journals of Henry Wadsworth Longfellow, Houghton Library MsAm 1340, Harvard University, 27 July 1846.

7. On this controversy, see my *A Small College in Maine: Two Hundred Years of Bowdoin* (Brunswick, Maine: Bowdoin College Press, 1993), 71–99.

8. Journals, 6 Aug. 1837; 7 April 1838.

9. Journal, 7 April 1838.

10. Journal, 8 April 1838.

11. Journal, 9 April, 10 April 1838.

12. Journal, 16 April 1838.

13. Journal, 25 July 1846.

14. Journal, 28 July 1846.

15. Journal, 31 July 1846.

16. Journal, 1 Aug. 1846.

17. Journal, 25 July 1846.

18. Anne Longfellow Pierce to Alexander W. Longfellow, 13 Sept. 1843, Anne Pierce Papers, Longfellow National Historic Site, Cambridge, Mass.

19. Anne Longfellow Pierce to Mary Longfellow Greenleaf, 6 Feb. 1844, Anne Pierce Papers, LNHS.

20. Journal, 26 Jan., 29 Jan. 1847.

21. Journal, 27 July 1849.

22. Journal, 29 March, 30 March 1855.

23. *Letters of Henry Wadsworth Longfellow,* vol 3, Andrew Hilen, ed. (Cambridge, Mass.: Belknap Press, 1972), letter 1046, 209.

24. George Thornton Edwards, "Highfields," *Pine Tree Magazine* 7:1 (February 1907), 28–31.

25. Journal, 27 Aug. 1860.

26. Anne Longfellow Pierce to H. W. Longfellow, Pierce Papers bMS Am 1340.2, Houghton Library, Harvard University, 10 April, 28 April 1861.

27. Anne Pierce Papers [1866].

28. *The Letters of Henry Wadsworth Longfellow,* vol. 6 (1982), letter 4478.

29. Edward H. Elwell, *Portland and Vicinity* (Portland: Loring, Short, and Harmon, 1876), 56.

Comunidad Escondida

Latin American Influences in Nineteenth- and Twentieth-Century Portland

David Carey Jr.

In the early morning of 12 September 2002, a van packed with fifteen migrant workers—ten Hondurans and five Guatemalans—was traveling along a remote lumber road in northern Maine when it veered off a bridge into the Allagash Wilderness Waterway; only one man survived. The most fatal traffic accident in Maine's history served as a stark reminder that despite being the whitest state in the nation (people of color make up only 3.1 percent of the population), Maine is home to Latin Americans (and other ethnic groups) who make valuable contributions to Maine's economy, society, and culture. But do they feel at home in Portland? How do people who are largely invisible develop a sense of place?

The Latino community in Portland is small and disparate. Yet its presence is evident in places like Tu Casa, a Salvadoran restaurant; La Bodega Latina, a grocery store that specializes in tropical fruits and Hispanic cuisine; Lourdes International Beauty Salon; and Catholic and Protestant churches that provide Spanish services. Although many face racism and discrimination, increasing numbers of Latino families are settling in Portland. In turn, a nascent interest in Latin America continues to grow among Portland Anglos, who enjoy Latin American music at the Center for Cultural Exchange, pursue trade opportunities in Mexico, sell Latin American textiles in their stores, and study in the Dominican Republic, Cuba, Guatemala, and Chile. Despite a tendency to view this phenomenon as recent, economic and social relations between Portland and Latin America, especially the Caribbean, have a rich historical tradition.[1]

   The history of Latin Americans in Portland and Portland's relationship with Latin America in the nineteenth and twentieth centuries not only sheds light on the plight and contributions of a small yet influential group of immigrants; it also helps to locate Portland in the broader context of the Atlantic world. This analysis situates Portland as a place in two ways. First, trade with Latin America elucidates Portland's place in the international community. For much of the nineteenth century, Portland was a major entrepot of international commerce. At a time when Cuba was the United States' third-largest trading partner, Portland was one of the most important ports in this exchange and Maine-made ships were among the most common vessels trafficking in the West Indies. Ships loaded with lumber, bricks, and ice set sail for Caribbean islands and returned with sugar, molasses, rum, and goods to stock local grocery stores. The wealth generated in this trade affected Portland's physical environment, from landfill-extended wharves to large homes that remain central to Portland's identity. The Portland bricks that dot the streets of Trinidad, Cuba, are symbolic of the intricate relations between Portland and Latin America.

   Second, people were an important, if less voluminous, part of this exchange. Latin Americans' experiences and influences helped to create Portland. Nineteenth-century Portland's diversity was captured in Henry Wadsworth Longfellow's famous line, "I remember the black wharves and the slips / And the sea-tides tossing free / And Spanish sailors with bearded lips." As Longfellow knew, not all Hispanic residents and visitors came via trade or for employment. For example, wealthy Cubans sent their children to Southern Maine to study or summer. Some Latin Americans decided to make Portland their homes. Twentieth-century migrations reflect this past and also reveal new phenomena, such as political exile. Despite this history, efficacious representation of Hispanics has been elusive and Latino participation in Portland's past has been silenced.[2]

   In addition to the Caribbean denizens who settled in Portland, some Portlanders decided to establish their homes (and businesses) in the West Indies. A number of Portland citizens were drawn to Latin America and especially to Cuba for love, business, health, or fame. Others went to foment revolution or defend U.S. interests in the region.

   Understanding Portland as a place is contingent upon understanding it both locally and globally. An exploration of Portland's Latin American connections is useful in two ways. First, Latin Americans bring diverse histories, ethnicities, languages, and perspectives to the community and although not as visible as other groups, they are part of the social construction of Portland. Historical and contemporary perspectives of how Hispanics have thrived, survived, and suffered in Portland adds another layer to the city's mosaic. Second, Portland's place in the Atlantic world was to a large extent the product of nineteenth-century West India trade, but shortly after the Civil War, Portland's position as a major port declined. Even though some commerce shifted to South America in the 1880s, the city slowly became more isolated and provincial. Nonetheless, the foundations for cultural, social, and economic exchange had been laid. By recuperating historical connections and emphasizing contemporary realities, I intend to reveal the precedents of and potential for symbiotic relations between these distinct peoples and regions today are revealed.

West India Trade

Economic ties between the West Indies and New England extended back into the colonial period, and Maine merchants were an important part of this trade. By the mid-1600s, for example, Thomas Cutts was living in Barbados arranging trade for his brothers who sent fish and lumber in exchange for cargoes from the West Indies. Colonists throughout New England came to depend on the staples imported from the West Indies, not the least of which was rum. However, after the independence of their thirteen North American colonies in 1783, the British parliament barred U.S. vessels from their Caribbean colonies, even while English fleets enjoyed access to U.S. ports. Intent on rectifying this imbalance, in 1785 a group of Falmouth residents instructed their representative, Joseph Noyes, to oblige England to open its Caribbean ports "to invite our trade." They insisted, "This is a matter of great moment and concern to us in this part of the state, whose principal staple is lumber."[3] Maine's extensive river network and multitudinous sawmills gave it an advantage in the lumber trade. Two years after the aforementioned meeting, seventy-three of the eighty-nine ships that were cleared from Portland sailed to the West Indies. Because of political machinations and diplomatic rifts on both sides of the Atlantic, Great Britain did not completely and finally clear U.S. vessels for direct trade until 1849. Since West India trade was so important to Maine's economy, Portland newspapers followed the negotiations between the United States and England closely and merchants petitioned Congress for dispensations to facilitate commerce. Despite obstacles, trade between Portland and the West Indies persisted during the early national period (often with the aid of bribes). At times, the number of ships heading south exceeded the demand. Some vessels arrived in the Caribbean only to find an over-abundance of lumber and a scarcity of molasses or sugar with which to fill their boats for the trip home.[4]

With good reason, Portlanders long advocated increased trade with the West Indies; their labor and livelihood depended on it. An 1832 editorial in *Eastern Argus*, the Democratic Party newspaper, lauded the West India Trade "by which constant and profitable employment is afforded to a large class of the community."[5] The shipbuilding industry was booming, but coopers, candle makers, bakers (of ships' biscuits) also profited from the traffic. Moreover, since the 1824 molasses tax placed a duty of ten cents on every gallon of imported molasses, Caribbean rum was cheaper than what could be produced domestically. But after the tax was repealed, distilling spirits at home yielded greater profits. Consequently, at one time Portland boasted seven distilleries.[6] Not everyone hailed this economic development, however. Neal Dow, the mayor of Portland in 1850 who was known as the "Napoleon of Temperance," recalled:

Portland was the fountainhead of the liquor traffic in Maine. The nearest important point in the district to the West Indies, a great part of its relatively large commercial business was with those islands, and depended in great measure upon liquor. Portland's wharves groaned beneath the burden of West India rum awaiting distribution into all contiguous territory by country teams, and to many smaller eastern ports by coasting vessels. Her distilleries were busy converting West India molasses into New England rum, to be in turn similarly distributed by Portland traders.[7]

In large part because of "demon rum's" association with domestic violence, the West India trade precipitated one of Maine's most powerful social campaigns: the women's temperance movement.

Since it was producing 130,000 pounds of sugar annually by the late 1780s and harvesting significant amounts of coffee, Haiti was one of the first colonies to attract the attention of Portland's sea captains and merchants. It was France's richest possession and the wealthiest colony in the Caribbean, yet the blood required to produce sugar abated its sweetness:

during the 1780s, plantation owners worked 30,000 African slaves to death each year. Because the slave trade ensured these workers were replaced, Africans made up more that 90 percent of Haiti's population. In response to the horrors of slavery and inspired by France's revolution two years earlier, in 1791 African slaves led Latin America's first independence movement. Portland Captain William McLellan Sr. arrived shortly after its inception. When Haitian soldiers took possession of McLellan's ship and cargo of lumber worth about $7,000, he did not resist but asked to meet with the rebels' leader, Toussaint L'Ouverture (1743–1803). McLellan impressed his host with a sea letter from President George Washington and negotiated not only his freedom but also the exchange of his lumber for sugar and coffee, which resulted in a profit of over $80,000. McLellan's was one of the last lucrative voyages from Haiti, however, since the new nation struggled to rebuild its economy after years of fighting and turmoil and its international pariah status that continued even after Jean Jacques Dessalines declared its independence on 1 January 1804.[8]

Haiti's economic decline benefited Cuban planters and merchants; the Spanish colony's share of the sugar trade increased significantly in the nineteenth century: whereas only 150 U.S. ships arrived in Cuba in 1796, their numbers increased to 1,882 in 1852. Even during the island's coffee boom between the 1820s and 1840s, sugar was the key to Cuba's wealth, and its expansion eventually consumed coffee farmers' land and resources. By the late 1820s, Cuba had become the world's largest sugar producer and most of it was going to the United States and England. Concurrently, Maine supplied Cuban planters with salted fish to feed their slaves, and Portland was Maine's fish export center. By selling the food that sustained them and consuming what they produced, Maine's major port became a primary beneficiary of Cuban slaves' labor.[9] Maine's historical relationship with slavery is complex; its collaboration with Cuban slavery contradicts its stance against domestic slavery. Portland entrepreneurs who feasted on Cuban sugar stood in stark contrast to Maine's Abolitionist movement and the state's contribution of troops to fight the South in the Civil War. Paradoxically, Portlanders were structurally involved in slavery abroad, yet they were intolerant of it on their soil. This cognitive dissonance reveals moral standards that were malleable in the face of profits and comfort. Unlike their association with Cuba, Mainers received little direct benefit from slavery in the southern United States.

Lumber, bricks, and ice helped to establish Portland as an international entrepot. In part, the invigoration of Portland's seaport was the result of its position as a rail and river depot that received lumber from other parts of Maine, New Hampshire, and Canada. Incoming ships could unload their cargoes onto the railroad, the Cumberland and Oxford Canal, or other various riverine systems that extended into northern New England for extensive distribution. Although the Caribbean islands were one of the preferred partners because of their proximity and their supply of sugar, molasses, rum, and other goods, Portlanders enjoyed traveling to and trading in other parts of Latin America. The amount of traffic in Portland's harbor in the early nineteenth century was considerable.[10] Yet because even Portland vessels generally returned to Boston, New York, or Bath to unload their goods, other northern ports eclipsed Portland's volume. It was not until the 1850s that Portland became the largest and busiest port in Maine. The *Boston Commercial Bulletin* noted, "In their [Bath's] desire to maintain their superiority in this line [shipbuilding] they have neglected a comparatively smaller but more profitable business, while Portland with more sagacity has fostered a trade which has been vastly profitable; and in which a few years since she was not far in advance of Bath. We refer to the West India trade."[11]

It was also during this period that Portland surpassed Boston as one of the main entrepots of sugar and molasses in the United States. Thanks to the near monopoly that Portland merchants had developed with Cuba, in 1853 the city was importing nearly three times as much sugar and molasses as Boston. Portland Sugar Works alone was processing about two hundred hogsheads of molasses a day, much of which was destined for New Hampshire, Massachusetts, and other parts of Maine via rail and boat. One Portland writer noted, "We can but rejoice in the prosperity of our beautiful city, although we can see that a good deal of this prosperity is at the expense of Boston. But still there is room enough for both and no occasion for envious and jealous feelings to prevail between the two cities."[12] Portland's trade continued to expand and focus on Cuba in the 1850s and 1860s. Between 1856 and 1861 only 17 of the 1,040 lumber cargoes from Portland went to any other place than Cuba, and from 1862 to 1864 about 1,000 vessels a year traveled from Maine ports to Cuba.[13] The *Portland Board of Trade Journal* claimed, "Portland had the largest trade with the West Indies, of any port on the Atlantic coast."[14]

One of Portland's most affluent patrons, John Bundy Brown (1805–1881), earned much of his fortune by processing West Indian sugar and molasses. In 1845, Brown and the Boston firm Greely and Guild built Portland's first sugar refinery, only the third in the country. Greely and Guild subsequently abandoned the endeavor, but Brown persevered and expanded the enterprise. By 1855 the Portland Sugar House was employing between 150 and 200 workers in its warehouses, wharves, and refinery, and earning half a million dollars annually. The main refinery's eight stories loomed over Portland's waterfront and processed more then 30,000 hogsheads of molasses a year. In 1856 it was recognized as "one of the chief objects of business interest in our city, both from the magnitude of the buildings comprised under the name, and the extent of works carried on within."[15] Ten years later it employed nearly a thousand people. Because of the voracious demand from Brown's enterprise and two other major sugar refineries in Portland, by 1860 nearly 20 percent of the nation's molasses (more than any other U.S. city) passed through Portland. Even though Brown rebuilt his refinery after it was engulfed by the 1866 fire, the flames were a harbinger of Portland's economic fate, and in 1869 Brown succumbed to competition farther south and closed his Sugar House. Yet the profits from the sugar company allowed Brown to pursue other investment opportunities and become a patron of the arts, opening in his home what was essentially Portland's first art museum.[16]

For some Portland natives, the lure of profits and adventure in the Caribbean were irresistible. One local historian opines, "Regardless of what was to be a Maine boy's occupation or profession, an indispensable part of his upbringing was a voyage or two in the West India trade."[17] One such boy inspired generations of others. As a child, the Reverend Elijah Kellogg (1813–1901) had such a penchant for setting sail on Portland's merchant vessels that his family "indentured" him to country relatives to tame his love for the sea. Although he remained landlocked, he later found an outlet for his passion by becoming a writer of nearly thirty children's books, some of which were set in the Caribbean.[18] Even though Kellogg's writing was prone to moralizing, equivocal historical commentary, and prejudice, his stories enticed Portland's youth to visit places like Cuba, Haiti, Martinique, Jamaica. And for those who did not feel compelled to travel to the Caribbean, Kellogg's books exposed them to life beyond Portland.

Although Portland vessels serviced most of the Caribbean islands, merchants and sea captains developed a special affinity for Cuba. Indeed, the island was Portland's primary connection to Latin America from the 1820s to the 1860s. Because sales were all but guaranteed, Portland merchants offered "liberal advances" on consignments of merchandise from Cuba. In turn, Cubans increasingly demanded the best of Maine's lumber (much of the port city of Matanzas was literally built with New England lumber) as well as boxes and casks for sugar, and hogsheads barrels for molasses.[19] Not all Cubans were in accordance with this trade, however. José de Arango, a planter and treasurer of Havana (1799–1800), considered this trade "shameful" because Cuban forests were "given to the flames or remaining in useless abundance while we empty our pockets for the foreigners benefit."[20] Increasing profits tended to muffle critiques such as Arango's. In light of constant commercial traffic, one Cuban entrepreneur informed readers of Portland's *Daily Courier* that the Matanzas Star Coffee House offered clean rooms, ample meals, and the "choicest wines, cordials, and liquors" to "vessels and visitors."[21] Economic interdependence encouraged mutual awareness, if not close personal relations, between Cubans and Portlanders.

From an Iberian perspective, the trade between Cuba and Portland was significant enough to warrant the establishment of a "Consul for her Catholic Majesty of Spain" in Portland. Since Spanish consuls often cultivated close relations with Portland's business community, it was not unusual for them to board with local merchants or elites. In 1858, a Portland lawyer named Thomas Deblois, whose grandfather was a rich, respected merchant, served as a consular agent to Spain and housed Consul Hipolito de Uriarte. Similarly, Enrique Ainz, who served as consul intermittently from 1863 to 1888, stayed with Thomas Asencio, a Cuban merchant who lived in Portland. When Spanish nationals were traveling or unavailable, the crown entrusted local merchants to represent it. By 1866, Asencio was named the acting consul. His company received a favorable credit rating in *Bradstreet's Book of Commercial Reports of the Bankers, Merchants, Manufacturers* and must have enjoyed lucrative profits, since Asencio was among Portland's highest taxpayers during the Civil War. His son, Enrique, who was a student at the time, later went into business with his father.[22] The Asencios's success manifests the capacity of wealthy Cubans to adapt to Portland and contribute to its prosperity. For prosperous Cubans, life in Portland may not have been much different from that in Havana, Matanzas, or Trinidad.

In turn, some Portlanders decided to make their homes in Cuba. At age nineteen, Horatio Fox (1815–1902) sailed for Trinidad and liked it so much he decided to establish his business and family there. In 1846, he married a Cuban named Mercedes Zerubi, and they had fifteen children together, all of whom were born in Cuba. Horatio owned a sugar plantation and became a successful merchant. Because of his extensive knowledge of the island, several U.S. presidents asked him to serve as the consul of Cuba. Following in his footsteps, his son Carlos was appointed vice consul at Santiago de Cuba. During Cuba's first major struggle for independence, the Ten Years' War (1868–1878), the plantation was burned and the family fled. When Horatio returned to Portland he joined two other local men at Eaton, Safford, and Fox and their firm enjoyed considerable profits by shipping large quantities of West India sugar and molasses to Portland, New York, Philadelphia. Some of his sons, including Carlos, who married Nellie Smith of Portland in 1878, and Horacio Bruno who worked for the Spanish-American Iron Company in Darguin, Cuba, returned to Cuba after the war. Other Fox children, like his daughter Rosa, decided to make their homes in Portland.[23] In many ways, the Fox family embodied the intimate economic and personal ties between Cuba and Portland.

Expanding Tastes, Profits, and Health

Although sugar and molasses dominated the imports and lumber filled most ships departing from Portland, other commodities traveled between the West Indies and Maine's major port. Dried codfish, salmon, herring, pickled fish, alewives, beans, potatoes, parsnips, onions, grain, soap, tallow candles, fowl, oxen, horses, sheep, swine, small boats, and even house frames ready to put up all headed south from Maine ports. In return coffee, cocoa, chocolate, indigo, cotton, Jamaica Rum, and spices such as nutmeg, cloves, cinnamon, allspice, and ginger stocked the shelves of Portland grocery stores advertising fresh shipments of West India goods. Although grocery stores tended to carry only nonperishable goods from the West Indies, often ships' crews returned with boxes of fresh fruit, such as oranges, for personal consumption. And at least one Hispanic owned a local fruit store in the city. Portlanders also developed a special affinity for Cuban cigars and often Hispanics manufactured, imported, and sold them. In fact, one Portland Hispanic was so confident in the quality of his tobacco that he offered a money-back guarantee to any dissatisfied client.[24]

Maine had yet another natural resource that proved to be marketable in Latin America. The first cargo of ice from Maine destined for the West Indies left Bath in 1815. Three years later Arthur McLellan's brig *William Smith* nearly capsized in the Gulf Stream with a load of ice. The ice trade soon burgeoned; an 1822 announcement in the *Maine Gazette* sought vessels immediately willing to take cargoes of 140–180 tons of ice to Havana. Because of the extensive lumber trade, at times it was difficult to obtain ships to transport ice. Even though Maine's ice trade did not culminate until the 1870s when such cities as New York, Washington, Baltimore, and Philadelphia consumed tons of supplies, Latin America continued to be a reliable customer. When Clark & Chapin of the Consolidated Ice Company in Bowdoinham opened an office in Portland in the late nineteenth century, they shipped cargoes of ice to Cuba, Panama, and cities farther south along the Eastern coast of South America. By the 1890s schooners were heading south with ice loads of up to 1,800 tons. But shortly thereafter, the electrically powered refrigerator made the "frozen water" trade obsolete.[25]

Since the hazards of West India trade and travel included diseases—yellow fever, malaria, cholera—some physicians specialized in tropical medicine. Sailors contracted and spread deadly pathogens wherever they landed.[26] In an effort to address these problems, one Portland doctor, who was "well acquainted with *tropical diseases*" because he had practiced medicine in the West Indies for "three or four years," furnished "*Sea Medicine Chests* at the shortest notice and well adapted to tropical climates."[27] Conversely, some Portland residents traveled to the Caribbean hoping to improve their health. When the twenty-nine-year-old principal of Portland High School fell ill in 1831, he traveled to Puerto Rico "for the purpose of trying the effect of a West India climate."[28]

In addition to the impact on public health, trade between the Caribbean and Portland forever altered the city's physical environment. West India profits encouraged the establishment of the Portland Bank in 1799 and the Maine Bank in 1802. Likewise, increasing business led to expanded and improved facilities. To this end, Long, Union, and Commercial wharves were extended into the harbor on landfill and shortly thereafter they supported stores, warehouses, and distilleries. A number of Portland's finest homes, such as the McLellan House built by merchant, banker, and grocer Hugh McLellan (1758–1823), also originate from this era. As another lasting testament to this trade, a group of West

India merchants were responsible for constructing the observation tower atop Munjoy Hill in 1807.[29] By changing Portland's urban landscape, slavery and profits from the West India trade transformed how people experienced and saw their city; the international flow of resources influenced Portland's identity as a place.

Cosmopolitan Portland (and Global Citizens)

A less tangible but no less important effect of the West India Trade was the way in which it encouraged (even demanded of) Portlanders to recognize themselves as global citizens and resist isolationist tendencies. Advertisements, editorials, and articles from local newspapers reveal an interest in world affairs and effort to understand foreign peoples and nations. One journalist referred to Portlanders as "a great people in their intercourse with the world," and praised President Andrew Jackson's administration for its efforts to resume trade with the British West Indies because "by pursuing this policy he has caused the American character to be held in respect by the nations of the old world."[30] Since it was essential for their trade, captains (and presumably some of the crew) learned how to speak Spanish. Advertisements encouraged locals to take Spanish and French lessons—"the universal languages of our day."[31] Some Portlanders (among whom the most noteworthy was Longfellow) were especially interested in Spanish. They hoped to develop a community that "speaks Spanish with ease," and establish a library of Spanish literature and a reading room that would have Spanish newspapers from "other parts of America."[32] Interestingly, these local bibliophiles understood "America" to denote the hemisphere (much the way most Latin Americans used and continue to use the term)—an indication that at least some nineteenth-century Portlanders were more cosmopolitan and more aware than subsequent generations, who appropriated the word "America" to refer solely to the United States.

Thanks in large part to the West India trade, the Caribbean islands and especially Cuba caught the interest of many Mainers. Those who traveled to and lived in Latin America shared their experiences with family, friends, and neighbors. One Portland woman who lived in Trinidad, Cuba, in 1847 described Cubans as "kind and friendly."[33] Portland's newspapers and magazines ran articles about travel to the Caribbean and life on the islands. Since "a trip to Cuba cannot fail to be one of unusual interest," in 1852 *The Eclectic*, a local literary paper, encouraged residents to attend a panoramic art exhibit of the island in Portland. The editors warned, "Those who fail to visit it will certainly regret that they did not embrace the opportunity to get an insight of Cuban scenery, and Cuban life."[34]

Art was another medium by which Mainers learned of Latin America. Members of Portland's burgeoning artist community often traveled to the West Indies and Latin America, and a number of them such as William Frederick Chadwick (1828–18??) and Franklin Stanwood (1852–1888) painted their impressions. Chadwick's painting *Harvesting Sugar, Cuba* (1873) reveals intimate knowledge of the island and its economy that do not belie his family background. His father, Samuel, was a successful merchant, and at one time the Chadwick family employed a Cuban groom to care for their horses. As a merchant, William Chadwick lived in Matanzas from 1870 to 1876.[35] Stanwood's experience in Latin America came through extensive voyages to the Caribbean and farther south around Cape Horn. He returned to settle in Portland and open a studio there, but his first oil painting, *View on the Pampas of Peru* (1873), was inspired by his travels in South America.[36] In some cases, Portland's artists were commissioned by Latin American patrons. For example, the Portland carver Edward Souther Griffin (1834–1928) sculpted a crucifix for a cathedral in Cuba. Many nineteenth-century artists owed the pursuit of their profession to the West India trade since it contributed to the fortunes of some of Portland's most generous art patrons, such as John Bundy Brown and Asa Clapp (1762–1848). Moreover, the Spanish consul and vice consul (Enrique Ainz and Alberto C. de Ramsault, respectively) were charter members of the Portland Society of Art when it was founded in 1882 and Cuban-born Antoine Dorticos became a life member in 1887[37] (Figure 5-1).

These influences infused and informed a more worldly vision and pride among Portland denizens and made their city a more hospitable environment for Hispanics. Maine's welcome mat was not a foregone conclusion for people of color or other immigrant groups, however. Blacks faced great challenges in Portland (as Maureen Elgersman Lee adeptly illustrates in this volume). An influx of Irish in the mid-nineteenth century sparked a nativist reaction that ostracized, disenfranchised, and even physically attacked the newcomers because Mainers believed Irish immigrants posed a threat to their jobs and Protestant traditions.[38] In contrast, even though Latin Americans were also Catholic,

Figure 5-1. Three Chadwick brothers and a Cuban horse groom, c. 1850. The information with the photograph is emblematic of the invisibility of working class Latin Americans in Portland; the groom is identified only as a native of Cuba. Collections of Maine Historical Society.

the West India trade buttressed their presence, and their modest numbers posed no threat to religious hegemony or the job market.

Portland's close ties with Cuba encouraged nineteenth-century Cubans to settle in the port, but other Latin Americans also lived in the city. The 1850 census reveals thirty-three Portland residents who hailed from Latin American nations and colonies as diverse as Ecuador, Argentina, Guyana, Jamaica, and Martinique. A number of Hispanics sought to make Portland their home by applying for citizenship. Local cemeteries reveal that some, such as the Mexican Cosmo de Sanchez who died in 1848, ended their lives in Portland.[39]

Class Connections

In a more systematic social relationship with Mainers, elite Cuban families sent their children to study in Portland. Others sent their children to summer in southern Maine to avoid Cuba's intense heat and humidity and, more importantly, the height of malaria and yellow fever season on the island. Concatenating commercial and scholastic ties benefited both Portlanders and Cubans financially. In some cases, ships' captains developed close relations with families in Cuba and offered to arrange schooling for their children in southern Maine. Subsequently, Cuban students (who predominantly came from elite families) often returned to their homeland after having made acquaintances with Portland merchants. A number of Cuban graduates from North Yarmouth Academy (NYA), located about ten miles north of Portland, became merchants and even consuls in Cuba. In turn, connections with such Cubans expedited the work of Portland captains and merchants. Without an agent in Caribbean ports, it was difficult to unload one's commodities and fill the ship for the return voyage. Portland merchants clearly understood the value of these relationships. One successful merchant, Samuel Chadwick, sent his son William to NYA in 1847 where he studied with a number of Cubans. The investment paid off: William worked as a merchant in Portland from 1855 to 1870 and in Matanzas from 1870 to 1876. Economic interdependence was also evident in the symbiotic careers of Mary Lancaster Tompson, who owned a private school in Portland that taught pupils "from the best families in the City," and her cousin, Captain Thomas Libby, who traded in the West Indies. Miss Tompson's school had a number of Hispanic students in the 1850s and 1860s.[40]

Westbrook Seminary, a secondary and preparatory school located in present-day Portland, was especially popular among Cubans, the overwhelming majority of whom were male. Portland natives benefited from this exposure; one 1895 graduate named Frederick Thompson (1876–1923) "engaged in industrial development work in Cuba for four years."[41] Likewise, Cubans enhanced their professional lives and developed close personal relations, as this 1898 Westbrook Seminary publication indicates:

Francisco Avello, our Cuban friend, who was a student at the Seminary last year, has returned to his home in Cienfuegos, to engage in a business career for which his work here was preparation. Before leaving America he came down from Boston to spend a few days with Seminary friends. To an on-looker it seemed doubtful if Francisco could tear himself from old friends, from those of Hersey [dormitory] especially, in time to make use of his passage engaged for Cuba. We learn that he was in time, and is now safe in Free Cuba. Prosperity to him![42]

Interestingly, the use of America to denote the United States stands in sharp contrast to some earlier nineteenth-century Portlanders who understood America to include Latin America—an indication that over those seventy-five years Portland may have become less cosmopolitan and worldly. The writer's reference to "Free Cuba" also reveals the sentiments of Portlanders who supported the U.S. invasion of Cuba in 1898, a hotly contested issue in the city and across the nation.

Often schools served as nodes of acculturation. In the 1850s and 1860s some members of the Gutierez family took classes in Miss Tompson's Private School. An early class photograph reveals the faces of Ramon and Juan Gutierez, who enrolled in 1851 and 1861, respectively, but years later the captions under the same photographs read Ramon and Juan Gardiner. Assimilation and name changing were common among immigrant groups in the nineteenth century; Latin Americans were no exception. The 1850 census lists a number of Cubans with non-traditional Cuban names living in Portland, such as John Smith and Jeanette Springer. Unfortunately, it is difficult to ascertain under what circumstances these individuals changed their names, or even if they did so at all. For example, Antoine Dorticos (1848–1906), who came from a French family in Cuba, went by the name Antonio while at Westbrook Seminary but then changed his name back to Antoine after he graduated, perhaps because he taught French.[43] Since names are a fundamental and public aspect of one's identity, these opaque glimpses into the past reveal Latin Americans' diverse levels of acculturation, which in turn sheds light onto how they experienced Portland as a place.

It was probably his financial ties to Portland (as well as growing unrest in his homeland) that inspired the wealthy Cuban planter Piedro Dorticos to send his son Antoine to finish his studies in Maine in 1866. Antoine settled in Portland where he taught French and married Sarah Bates with whom he had two sons, Philip and Carlos. Even though he never secured enough work to dedicate himself to it fulltime, Dorticos's passion was architecture. He built a number of cottages, which received positive reviews in trade journals, the most notable of which were on the Casco Bay Islands. He regularly camped on Cushing Island and in 1876 became the first Portlander to rent a room (in a private home) on Peaks Island. By 1885, Dorticos had designed and built his first cottage on Great Diamond Island, and purchased land on Great Chebeague Island on which he constructed a cottage for his family. Although the twenty-one cottages that remain are a testament to his considerable talent, perhaps his most influential and enduring contribution was in envisioning and developing the Casco Bay Islands as a summer tourist destination.[44]

At least one other Hispanic shared Dorticos' vision for the Casco Bay Islands. At the age of sixteen, Ernesto Ponce (1844-?) learned how to make cigars and eventually opened his own cigar manufacturing business in Cuba. After ten years of success, he moved to Portland and established a cigar manufacturing business on Exchange Street, the heart of the commercial district, where he sold the highest quality cigars and pipes at the lowest prices in town with "no humbug about it."[45] His considerable profits from this endeavor provided the capital for other pursuits so that he became a real estate and mortgage broker. Ponce purchased ten acres of land on Long Island and in 1876, he opened the Granite Spring Hotel, which boasted accommodations for two hundred people, nine cottages, Casino Theater, bowling alley, pool rooms, Ponce's Landing wharf, and "good roads, bathing, fishing."[46] The hotel was open from June to September and many believed that the Granite Spring waters had curative powers. One contemporary noted, "While Ponce de Leon went to Florida in quest of the fountain of youth and found malaria. [*sic*] Ponce of Exchange Street went to Long Island in quest of the fountain of health and found the Granite Spring."[47] He encouraged people to "Come to Long Island, where you can enjoy the ocean and country combined, and only thirty minutes' ride from the city of Portland."[48] Moreover, by hiring Hispanics to work for him, Ponce contributed to their burgeoning population on Long Island.[49] Today, Ponce Street on Munjoy Hill stands as the sole reminder of the role he played in what became a crucial part of Portland's economy. A number of other Latin Americans, such as Thomas Asencio, who made their homes in Portland during the nineteenth century enjoyed success and wielded considerable influence.

For most immigrants, Latin America's racial hierarchies were further inscribed in Maine's major port. Lighter-skinned immigrants were more likely to attend school, work in white-collar positions, and enjoy entrepreneurial opportunities, than were their black counterparts who tended to be employed as manual laborers. The photograph of a black Cuban groom in Figure 5-1 is one example of this correlation. Likewise, at eight years old, Alfonzo Gumersinda must have been one of the youngest Cuban girls who worked as a domestic servant in Portland; the 1880 census identifies her as black. The same census provides an interesting contrast between a twenty-five-year-old black mariner from the West Indies and a twenty-six-year-old white Cuban clerk, both married women from Maine who fit their racial categories.[50] The dichotomous and absolute distinctions in the United States must have surprised Latin Americans who were accustomed to identifying race on a continuum, but in both regions the social construction of racial categories favored whites.

Legal and Other Challenges

For some Latin Americans, success, comfort, and even acceptance were elusive in Portland. After establishing himself in commercial trade and opening a wholesale and retail store in Portland, Isidoro Ojeda had to leave town less than a year after his arrival because the cold climate did not agree with his Cuban wife. Some Hispanic mariners were arrested for deserting their ships. Indeed, many of the Latin Americans who fell into the clutches of Portland's judicial system were involved in West India trade. To cite one example, after years of carrying an outstanding debt, a Cuban merchant was arrested when he returned to Portland in 1873.[51]

In some cases, civil actions were brought against West India merchants. In 1836, the administrators of Samuel Winter's estate sued a Cuban merchant named Joseph Vargas because Vargas sought to claim ownership of a molasses cargo in Portland for which he was never paid. Whether Vargas had prior knowledge and experience in the U.S. legal system is unclear, but if not he quickly learned its intricacies: the Maine Supreme Court ruled in his favor.[52] Vargas's victory is evidence that he, and presumably other Cuban merchants, had the cultural knowledge to challenge U.S. citizens in court and the wherewithal to pay legal advisers. They knew enough about the justice system to use it to their advantage, another reason why schooling in Maine might have been beneficial. In turn, the brazen debtor merchant from Cuba and sailors who deserted indicate that some ignored the legal ramifications of their actions, or at least were willing to take their chances. Legal records further elucidate the disparate experiences of elite and working-class Hispanics in the United States and the transnational nature of their lives.

The legal systems of Latin America also ensnared citizens of Portland, especially those affected by slavery. In 1855, Jane Dunnloo appealed to the citizens of Portland to help her raise one hundred dollars to bail her husband out of a Cuban prison, where he was serving a ten-year sentence for "secreting a slave on board a vessel for escape."[53] Even as the city's prosperity was linked to slave societies, slavery offended the sensibilities of many Portlanders. The aforementioned Portland woman who was living in Trinidad, Cuba, in 1847 praised the natural beauty of her surroundings but mourned "that slavery's galling chain is felt throughout the island." She shuddered at "the shrieks of the slaves, which you hear constantly . . . being nearly all the time at the whipping post," and confessed, "surely I had no idea what it was to hold fellow creatures in bondage, till I lived amongst it."[54] Although Portland was the home to an influential antislavery society, some of its residents sought to earn a profit from the enslavement of Africans. In an attempt to transport eight hundred slaves from Congo to Cuba on his ship *Erie*, Nathaniel Gordon (1826–1862), who was born in Portland to a well-established seafaring family, was apprehended, brought to New York, and convicted of piracy. When President Abraham Lincoln refused to commute his sentence, Gordon became the only person the U.S. government ever executed for slaving.[55]

The cases of Dunnloo and Gordon reveal how distinctly and intricately intertwined Portlanders were with West India trade and people. While some were trying to end slavery and assist those trapped in its evil grip, others were supplying Africans to feed slave societies' voracious appetite for workers. Perhaps, as Dunnloo's case implies, some Portlanders were naïve about their structural involvement in slavery or they chose to ignore it. Dunnloo attempted to hide a Cuban slave at the same time his trade perpetuated slavery. So even if he was successful at freeing that particular slave, his profession was contingent upon the maintenance of Cuban slavery, and therefore by spiriting off one individual he was merely necessitating the importation of another. For those directly involved in the West India trade—merchants, captains, sailors, sugar refinery and grocery storeowners and workers—their livelihood depended on the enslavement of Africans in places like Haiti (until 1791) and Cuba (until 1886). In addition, consumers of sugar, molasses, rum, and other West India goods buttressed that inhumane system; others, including artists, were supported by it.[56] That so many Portlanders reaped some benefit from trade with Cuba is a testament to slavery's reach. Despite fomenting an antislavery movement and creating a cosmopolitan city that welcomed some people, particularly Hispanics, even while it discriminated against others, Portlanders' economic activities helped to sustain slavery in the Caribbean.

Shifting Trade and Interests

Portland's sweet prosperity peaked in 1868, when nearly 60,000 hogs-heads of molasses, and 10,555 hogsheads and 16,800 boxes of sugar ar-rived in its port, but the seeds of its decline had already been germinat-ing. Prohibition in Maine, which lasted from 1851 to 1856, and the 1866 conflagration, which consumed much of Portland, temporarily dis-rupted the city's economy. Yet a subsequent confluence of factors were even more detrimental. By the late nineteenth century, improved sugar technology in the southern United States, cheaper lumber in the British provinces, the shift from sugar boxes to bags, and competition from foreign vessels (particularly those from Canada's Maritime Provinces) and steamships redirected much of the coastal trade. Consequently, Portland's dominance of the West India trade waned. In contrast to the nearly one thousand vessels a year that cleared Maine's ports for Cuba in the early 1860s, by 1887 only twenty-two boats left Maine with cargoes destined for the island. Concurrently, sugar production in Cuba was al-ready in decline by 1867, but the last three years of the Ten Years' War (1868–1878) had taken their toll on the island's monoculture and was a harbinger of Cuba's sugar crisis in the 1880s.[57] These vicissitudes did not eliminate trade with Latin America, however; nor did they eclipse Port-landers' connections with Cuba.

After the Civil War, Maine's lumber trade shifted to Argentina and, to a lesser extent, Uruguay, and peaked in the late 1880s when vessels leav-ing Portland carried over thirty million feet of lumber to South Amer-ica annually. By 1875, both Argentina and Uruguay had a consul in Port-land. Ten years later 73 percent of the spruce lumber transported to Rio de La Plata left from Portland. Granted, much of the lumber came from Canada via the Grand Trunk Railroad, but Portland enjoyed both prof-its and increased employment. The Messgrs. R. Lewis company of Port-land built vessels exclusively for these voyages and quickly came to dom-inate the trade. Unfortunately, Argentina's financial crisis in the early 1890s devastated Portland's lumber trade. Because of depressed prices and decreased demand, in 1894 one journalist opined, "There is the bluest outlook for the lumber business that there has been for years."[58] For a short time in the early 1900s, trade improved and ships returned from ports like Buenos Aires and Montevideo with cattle hides, hair, and bones. Although they unloaded many of their hides in Boston for the surrounding shoe mills, some continued on to Portland to feed the tanning and shoe industry in southern Maine. In 1905, the increased ship traffic reminded locals of "the good old times when this port was doing the bulk of the West India trade and the harbor was crowded with square rigged vessels."[59] By 1911, however, the South American lumber trade had shifted to Boston and Canada, prompting one observer to note in 1915, "not a cargo of lumber has been shipped from here [Portland] to South America for several years."[60] Shipments of West India molasses occasionally arrived in Portland and the city's coal fleet intermittently transported goods to the Caribbean in 1915. Moreover, the Brazilian Railway Company, which owned about half of Brazil's railroad track (5,000 miles) in 1914, had an office in Portland. Yet financial ties with Latin America had all but disappeared by the second decade of the twentieth century.[61]

In addition to the South American trade at the turn of the century, Portlanders were also connected to Latin America through political developments. When José Martí initiated Cuba's second war for independence in 1895, a lively debate ensued among Portland's citizens and in local newspapers about the role of the United States. Appalled by U.S. colonial expansion in Cuba, Thomas Brackett Reed, a native of Portland, resigned in protest from the U.S. House of Representatives on 4 September 1899.[62] But some Mainers had long been trying to annex Cuba, a cause that had more than a few Cuban advocates—at least prior to the U.S. Civil War. Perhaps the most colorful of these characters was John Thrasher (1817–1879). Born in Portland to a Cuban mother, he moved to Cuba with his parents at age sixteen and quickly allied himself with the revolutionaries. He became the editor of the anti-Spanish newspaper *El Faro Industrial de la Havana* and used it to spread revolutionary propaganda. In 1851, Spanish authorities arrested him and exiled him to New Orleans the following year.[63]

These debates and actors notwithstanding, the event that precipitated U.S. intervention in Cuba was the explosion of the U.S.S. *Maine* battleship in Havana's harbor on 15 February 1898—a tragedy that resulted in President William McKinley's declaration of war against Spain. Because the Cuban revolutionaries had all but defeated the Spanish forces by that point, the U.S. Navy quickly controlled the island. But instead of recognizing Cuba's independence, the federal government established a protectorate and thwarted Cuba's social revolution. A number of Portlanders participated in the war and subsequent U.S. occupation, including the Cuban American Carlos Dorticos, son of Antoine

Dorticos. In October 1900, one young soldier in Cuba wrote that although "the Cubans have a [great] deal to be thankful for owing to the aid of the American Government," many Cubans, "say that the Americans are 'Muchos Marlo' [*sic;* very bad] and turn up their noses when we pass by."[64] Despite his dismay at such anti-U.S. behavior, this Portlander believed that some Cubans were more sympathetic than they let on, and in some cases perhaps he was right. Until 1911 when Washington ordered that the U.S.S. *Maine* remains be removed, a group of Cubans made a yearly pilgrimage to the spot of the explosion—marked by the mast—and laid flowers and flags in memory of the victims of the accident. One Cuban attempted in vain to convince authorities to erect a monument there to commemorate the U.S.S. *Maine* and its ensigns.[65]

While few other events in Latin America captured Portlanders' attention like Cuba's war for independence and the explosion of the U.S.S. *Maine*, local newspapers followed uprisings in places as varied as the Dominican Republic and Uruguay.[66] Nonetheless, as the twentieth century progressed, Portland and its residents became more parochial, in part because of the city's decreasing share of international trade and the isolationist effects of World War I.

Education, Labor, and Exile in the Twentieth Century

Just as the sources for the nineteenth-century study of Latin Americans in Portland favors elite white men to the detriment of such groups as the working class, women, and people of color, twentieth-century sources provide similar challenges. Maine's importance and position in the Atlantic world plummeted in the twentieth century; thus sources are scarce in comparison to the eighteenth and nineteenth centuries. Although the challenges are not insurmountable and the researcher's efforts are sure to be fruitful, a detailed discussion of twentieth-century Latin American relations is beyond the scope of this essay. Consequently, the following analysis of Latin Americans in Portland during the twentieth century intends to frame a history yet to be told and suggest directions for future research. The decline in trade notwithstanding, Portland was never devoid of Latin American and Caribbean influences in the twentieth century. And since the 1990s these connections experienced a revival that in some ways mirrors the nineteenth century. According to the U.S. census, the number of Hispanics living in Portland nearly tripled between 1980 and 2000, from 355 to 974, and almost assuredly these numbers are lower than in reality.[67] At the same time, trade between Latin America and Portland also increased. Portland is reasserting itself in the Atlantic economy, albeit to a lesser degree than in the nineteenth century, and (re)positioning itself as a place that attracts Hispanics.

Despite a trend toward a less cosmopolitan city, Portland continued to appeal to West Indians in the early twentieth century. Westbrook Seminary remained the educational institution of choice for many Cubans into the first two decades of the century. As a sophomore, Ricardo "Dick" Geronimo Valladares from Manicaragua, Cuba, was the youngest member of the Westbrook basketball team, which won the state championship in 1904. He also played on the football team. Valladares must have been a ubiquitous figure on campus; photographs of him in his dormitory room, the chemistry lab, and on athletic teams appear in the Westbrook Seminary Catalogues throughout his tenure and thereafter. Although Valladares had a handful of Cuban classmates and his brothers Angel Maximo and Juan enrolled in 1907 and 1920, respectively, none made the lasting impression he had made; the chemistry lab photograph was recycled in subsequent years and appeared in the catalog as late as the 1920s. The school also recognized him as one of its most important "patrons." Like his nickname, the photograph of his room reveals how Valladares assimilated with the local culture (the decor resembles that of a typical Westbrook student at the time) (Figure 5–2). Though his nationality distinguished him, his socioeconomic status and race were similar to that of most of his classmates.[68] Since most Cuban students who studied in Portland came from prosperous families, they shared a class-consciousness with the city's affluent population—an association that must have helped to bridge national, cultural, and linguistic differences.

Relations between Portland and Latin America remained quiet for much of the century until the Mariel Boatlift in September 1980. When President Jimmy Carter criticized Fidel Castro for refusing to allow asylum seekers to leave Cuba, Castro authorized a mass exodus of over 125,000 Cubans to the United States; about one hundred of them arrived in Maine. Since some of the refugees were allegedly prison and mental hospital inmates, these Cubans had trouble finding sponsors. In response, the Portland Refugee Resettlement Program opened a house to provide temporary shelter and social services to refugees. Despite these efforts, more than half of Portland's Cuban émigrés quickly migrated

A STUDENT'S ROOM IN GODDARD HALL.

Figure 5-2. Ricardo "Dick" Valladares in a dorm room at Westbrook Seminary, c. 1904. Westbrook College History Collection, Abplanalp Library, Westbrook College Campus, University of New England, Portland, Maine.

south in search of warmer climates and Spanish-speaking populations. Those who stayed found work and in some cases married women from Portland, but racism was a constant threat. To avoid problems, one refugee said he taught himself to run from the taunts and challenges of local residents. Nonetheless, many were appreciative of the opportunity to live in Portland.[69]

During the 1980s a number of Guatemalans and Salvadorans also came to Portland in search of political asylum from the civil wars in their nations. To compound the deleterious conditions that often precipitated their emigration, the transition to Portland was difficult for many Hispanics. One Puerto Rican woman recalled her arrival in the late 1980s: "People kept asking me what tribe I was from. One woman assumed I was an illegal alien. I told her, 'Honey, I've been American since the late nineteenth century.'"[70] Despite a handful of professionals, most Latin Americans in Portland share long arduous hours of manual labor for low wages. For those from the Caribbean and coastal areas of Latin America, Portland's relationship to the ocean and penchant for seafood have eased their transition, and for some it is their source of livelihood. Many work in the seafood processing plants in South Portland cracking sea urchins and peeling shrimp. Others work in factories, restaurants, cleaning companies; some are domestic servants.[71] The range of experiences and backgrounds intimate diverse identities. Despite their absence from the historiography of Maine and their invisibility in Portland, Latin Americans have been and continue to be an important part of the city's economic and social life.

Overcoming Racism

The 11 September 2001 attacks on the United States had a profound effect on Portland's Hispanics. The incidence of hate crimes increased immediately following the attacks, but one study of Portland found that even two years after the attacks many Latin Americans were experiencing higher levels of anxiety than in the weeks and months after 11 September. Even though hate crimes had decreased, trepidation among Hispanics emanated from the increased scrutiny of government officials associated with homeland security. Many admitted that they would not report crimes and discrimination because they feared the local police would deport them, even if they were documented residents.[72] Tragically, Hispanics' fears were realized on the weekend of 25 January 2004 when U.S. Border Patrol agents raided Latino and Somali businesses, a homeless shelter, and factories that employed people of color. Federal agents arrested ten people for inadequate documentation, but harassed many more, most of whom were U.S. citizens or documented immigrants. Even when one Puerto Rican man showed agents his voting card and explained to them that only U.S. citizens had the right to vote, they continued to detain him. In the aftermath, businesses suffered because many Latin Americans refused to go to work or even leave their homes for fear they would be accosted. As one couple noted, "[The border patrol sweeps] affected all of us because we are all immigrants. Even though our papers are in order, it hurt us."[73] In response,

Hispanic and other community leaders organized meetings and a march, which city officials and other Portlanders supported with their presence.[74] As a testament to the resilience of the Latino community, less than a month after the sweeps a packed crowd turned out to celebrate the Dominican Republic's Independence Day at Portland's Center for Cultural Exchange.

Hispanics face discrimination at work, social service agencies, banks, and in public. Some complain that angry Anglos call them "spics" and tell them to learn English or go back where they came from; others note they cannot walk around local department stores without being followed.[75] But as the Reverend Virginia Marie Rincon notes, "Networking is powerful: when you hear that a store does not treat you right then people don't go to that store anymore."[76] Some Hispanics associate discrimination with the language barrier. A woman from the Dominican Republic who has lived in Portland for five years asserts, "There is discrimination. Many of us are professionals with degrees. We have gone to school, but we don't speak English so people treat us poorly. But we are not illiterate."[77] While children quickly pick up English (and, to the chagrin of some parents, often neglect Spanish), adults struggle with language acquisition. A Salvadoran women who has lived in Portland for eleven years reveals, "The hard thing about being an immigrant is that you have to take classes and work at same time; you also have to be learning about language and culture here."[78]

Discrimination is both a product and facilitator of the invisibility of the Latino community in Portland. As the Reverend Rincon observes, "You don't see Latinos. We are invisible. But some don't want to be visible for two reasons. They are afraid of discrimination and they are here to work not bother people, so they keep a low profile."[79] And, undocumented workers "don't want to be seen."[80] Yet invisibility silences the contributions that Latin Americans make to Portland's economic, social, and cultural life. If, as Rev. Rincon suggests, a silver lining to the 2004 border patrol sweeps emerged, it was that Latino leaders and their communities became more public and united.[81]

Remarkably, even while acknowledging discrimination, many Hispanics refuse to become embittered and often hail the opportunities, environment, and people in Portland. For example, one Salvadoran businessman who was living in a homeless shelter because his inability to speak English impeded his quest to find work, observed: "I am grateful. No country is so democratic as this one, and no country would offer so much help."[82] Similarly, Juan Gonzalez, a Portland business owner from the Dominican Republic, said, "I'm raising my family here, I'm proud to be here and I don't want that stuff that happened [the sweeps] to change the perception that Maine is welcoming to immigrants."[83] Many Latino families moved to Portland because it had a lower crime rate, better school system and job opportunities, and more tranquil life-style than their previous residences.[84]

Not surprisingly, Portland as a place appeals to Hispanics for many of the same reasons it appeals to Anglos. Even with continuing prejudice and discrimination, in many respects Portland is tolerant and proactive. On 2 June 2003, the city passed an ordinance prohibiting police and other city officials from making gratuitous immigration status inquiries—an action that simultaneously pointed to the problem of racial profiling and Portland's willingness to address it. By reaching out to working-class Hispanics, some Anglos have surpassed their nineteenth-century forebears who sought to make Portland a welcoming place primarily for Latin American elites. Although in part this tolerance is born from an economic need for immigrants, most Latino advocates are concerned with institutionalizing equal rights. The growing Latino community and its members' ability to use formal and informal means to secure their rights, combined with progressive elements in the city and increasing acceptance of diversity, has made Portland a place that many Hispanics call home.

Diversity and Erratic Unity

Despite their diversity, Latin Americans share a desire to preserve certain aspects of their cultures. For this reason, a number of venues and events intermittently unite them. Hispanic members of Sacred Heart congregation proudly refer to their church as the United Nations because, they say, "we Latinos are united, it doesn't matter what country or what race . . . we also welcome other religions."[85] Nonetheless, in part because Latin Americans subscribe to other faiths such as Episcopalian and Seventh Day Adventist, fiestas—weddings, birthdays, holidays—and funerals have a greater capacity than religions to bring disparate parts of the community together. A group of men have also formed a soccer team. Social events and retaining language and traditional foods help Hispanics maintain their heritage.[86]

But even this heritage defies concise characterization beyond a shared history of European colonization. Distinctions based on class, ethnicity, gender, nationality, and even language abound, which makes maintaining a united Latino front difficult, except in times of crisis. Close friendships between Salvadorans and Mexicans at Sacred Heart Church belie the tensions between these two groups in Portland that have erupted over competition for jobs. National differences often distinguish community members. Blanca Santiago explains, "A Salvadoran woman said to me that Puerto Rico doesn't have its own flag, so I pulled it up on computer and showed it to her. But then she said, 'Well, you Puerto Ricans are just like Americans, you get all the benefits, you grew up speaking English.' It is like people in Maine saying Portland is like Boston, it is not really part of Maine. 'Real' Latin Americans say Puerto Rico is not like Latin America; it is part of U.S."[87] Latinos who do not speak Spanish often find it difficult to fit in. Differences do not necessarily result in dissension, however. As one Dominican woman explains, "We don't go to the *pupuseria* [Salvadoran restaurant] because it is not our kind of food. There is a difference you know. But I have heard it is a great place for Latinos to get food and to hang out."[88]

Latino businesses in the city almost invariably seek to meet the demand for Latin American goods and services and in so doing they have created the infrastructure of a Latin American community here in Portland. As Juan Gonzalez says, "I want to make my own environment similar to what I had at home."[89] Gonzalez opened his store in 1998 because Portland did not offer the products he was accustomed to eating. Moreover, since his store, La Bodega Latina, is located just a few blocks from a bus station, it is the first stop for many Hispanics arriving in Maine. Gonzalez helps recent immigrants to find work. He proudly refers to his store as the "unofficial Hispanic Embassy of Maine."[90] Latino businesses and community organizations form an effective economic and social network for Portland's Hispanics. In turn, some Portland businesses rely on Latin America products for their success. These economic ties are a microcosm of Maine's resurging financial relationship with Latin America. They recall nineteenth-century trade with the West Indies; between 1998 and 2002 Maine exports to the Caribbean and Central America increased 56 percent, from 18.8 million to 29.4 million dollars.[91]

Caribbean nations and people played a critical role in establishing Portland as one of the Atlantic world's most important ports in the nineteenth century. As Portland became a global city, many of its citizens and residents enjoyed transnational identities. In addition to the captains and sailors who frequently traveled between Portland and Latin America, Cubans studied in Portland and Portlanders established their homes and businesses in the West Indies. Because the West India trade permeated so many facets of daily life in Portland, the city proudly recognized itself as an international entrepot and second home to many Hispanics. The city was less forthcoming about addressing its structural relationship with Caribbean slavery and the benefits it derived from that system, however. In turn, Latin Americans helped to create Portland and its environs with their visions, entrepreneurial spirit, and labor. And Cuban alumni of Westbrook Seminary continue to loom large in that institution's historical memory. But the shift of the West India trade away from Portland and the city's increasing isolation made it less inviting for many Latin Americans. Their broadening impact, economic contributions, and population in the late twentieth century did little to break the opacity of Latinos' presence. Racial epithets, harassment, and profiling were a consistent affront against Portland Hispanics. Ironically, to a certain degree the 2004 U.S. Border Patrol sweeps brought the Latino population out of obscurity. The widespread infringements upon their rights by a federal agency precipitated a united, well-coordinated response from many of Portland's ethnic leaders and groups, support from progressive city officials, and an increased awareness of them on the part of the broader community.

The historical silencing of Latin American and Caribbean influences in Portland obscures both the local Latino community and an understanding of Portland as a global city. Historically, Latin America helped to make Portland an international port, and today Hispanics contribute to creating a cosmopolitan city. Certainly many Latin Americans came to Portland in response to global forces like the West India trade in the nineteenth century and the economic crises and civil wars of the twentieth century, but these vicissitudes also affected Portland's position in the Atlantic world. Latin Americans were not passive victims to these trends; in some ways their actions shaped them. For example, by contributing to two national economies, Salvadorans and Mexicans who send *remesas* (remittances) back to their families embody globalization and the intimate relations between their nations and Portland. They are truly transnational participants in a global economy. Likewise, following in the tradition of Dorticos and Ponce, by establishing their businesses, Hispanics like Gonzalez and Lourdes Carpenter (the owner of Lourdes International Hair Salon) have contributed to the economic development of Portland and helped to create an infrastructure that makes the city more welcoming to Latino and other ethnic groups. Both the ways in which people experience Portland as a place and Portland's place in history can be attributed, in part, to trade with Latin America and the influence of local Hispanics during the nineteenth and twentieth centuries.

Notes

For their contributions to this research and writing, I am indebted to a number of people. I want to thank Joe Conforti for encouraging me to pursue this project and offering sage editorial advice throughout. Oral history informants including Blanca Santiago and the Reverend Virginia Marie Rincon, and others who wish to remain anonymous, provided poignant insights into the lived experience of Latinos in Portland. I conducted the vast majority of my archival research at the Maine Historical Society where Bill Barry generously offered his guidance, insights, and support. Roberta "Bobby" Gray at the Westbrook College History Archives at the University of New England and Linda Stanton at the North Yarmouth Academy Archives also directed me toward relevant documents and photographs. Others who offered fruitful leads were Fred Padula, Douglas Stover, Matt Barker, Larry Glatz, Bill Jordan, John Chesebro, Tad Baker, Earle Shettleworth, Wells Staly-Mays, Beth Stickney, Steve Bloom, John Arrison, Zip Kellogg, Maureen Elgersman Lee, and Eileen Eagan. Finally, Avi Chomsky, Allen Wells, and Bob Gormley offered helpful critiques of earlier drafts of this essay. The invaluable assistance from so many clearly strengthened this article; I am the sole author of its shortcomings.

1. Latin America and the Caribbean or West Indies describe overlapping and distinct geographical, cultural, linguistic, economic, and social regions. These nations and territories are all, at least in part, products of European colonialism. Linguistic diversity includes Spanish, Portuguese, French, Dutch, Creole, English, as well as indigenous and African languages. I use Latino/a to refer to U.S. residents who are either from Latin America or those who identify with their Latin American heritage. For the purposes of U.S. identity politics, the Latino/a category denotes Spanish speakers who share a common history of political and economic victimization. However, because the term is socially constructed, I use the term Latino/a with trepidation, especially since few people from the region would refer to themselves as such, but rather to their national and/or ethnic identity. Hispanic denotes a person from a Spanish speaking nation. I trust the reader will understand the terms Latino/as and Hispanics to describe complex groups of men and women who have some commonalties

and myriad distinctions. Earl Shorris argues, "There are no Latinos, only diverse peoples struggling to remain who they are while becoming someone else. Each of them has a history, which may be forgotten, muddled, misrepresented, misunderstood, but not erased." Earl Shorris, *Latinos: A Biography of the People* (New York: W. W. Norton, 1992), pp. 12–13.

2. Almost invariably, the historiography of Maine ignores the contributions, even the very presence, of Latino/as. In one recent particularly poignant example, Neil Rolde's chapter entitled "Ethnic Maine" makes no mention of Hispanics. See Neil Rolde, *Maine: A Narrative History* (Gardiner, Maine: Tilbury House, 1990), pp. 260–94.

3. *Falmouth Gazette*, 28 May 1785.

4. *Eastern Argus* (henceforth *EA*), 25 Dec. 1806; William Hutchinson Rowe, *The Maritime History of Maine* (Gardiner, Maine: Harpswell Press, 1989), pp. 99–103; William Avery Baker, *A Maritime History of Bath, Maine and the Kennebec River Region,* vol. 1 (Portland: The Anthoensen Press, 1973), pp. 184–85, 205, 221, 222; Wayne M. O'Leary, *Maine Sea Fisheries: The Rise and Fall of a Native Industry, 1830–1890* (Boston: Northeastern University Press, 1996), p. 114. For examples of newspaper coverage of the negotiations between Great Britain and the U.S. see *EA*, 1 April 1828; 1, 5, and 22 Jan.; 12 and 15 Oct. 1830; 15 June, 10 Aug. 1832.

5. *EA*, 15 June 1832.

6. *Falmouth Gazette*, 28 May 1785; *EA*, 1 April 1828, 15 June 1832; "Portland's West India Trade," *Portland Board of Trade Journal,* June 1893, p. 38; Rowe, *The Maritime History of Maine,* pp. 103, 115, 117, 118; Baker, *A Maritime History of Bath*, pp. 219–20, 226, 340, 521; William David Barry, "Bramhall: The Fabled Lost Mansion of J. B. Brown," *Portland Monthly Magazine,* May 1995, p. 13. Just up the coast, Falmouth had a distillery wharf; see Rowe, *The Maritime History of Maine,* p. 115.

7. Neal Dow, *The Reminiscences of Neal Dow: Recollections of Eighty Years* (Portland: The Evening Express Publishing Company, 1898), p. 191. See also William David Barry and Nan Cumming, "Rum, Riot, and Reform: Maine and the History of American Drinking," Exhibition Catalog, 1998, Maine Historical Society Archives (henceforth MHS); and "Anecdotes of Two Odd Characters," Portland Scrapbook, vol. 3, p. 246, MHS Mt p837.11. In 1851, Dow pushed through the nation's first prohibition law.

8. Rowe, *The Maritime History of Maine,* pp. 98, 115; William David Barry and John Holverson, *The Revolutionary McLellans: A Bicentenial Project of the Portland Museum of Art* (Portland: Portland Museum of Art, 1977), p. 35. France did not recognize Haiti's independence until 1825.

9. Louis A. Pérez, Jr,. *Cuba: Between Reform and Revolution* (Oxford, U.K.: Oxford University Press, 1988), pp. 76–85; Hugh Thomas, *Cuba, or the Pursuit of Freedom* (New York: Da Capo Press, 1998), pp. 61, 109, 125–26, 178;

Ralph Lee Woodward, Jr., "Ten Years' War (1868–1878)," in *Encyclopedia of Latin American History and Culture*, vol. 5, Barbara A. Tenenbaum, ed. (New York: Charles Scribner's Sons, 1996), p. 219; O'Leary, *Maine Sea Fisheries*, pp. 116–20.

10. *Portland Inquirer*, 23 Oct. 1849; *Universalist Palladium and Ladies' Amulet*, 5 Jun 1841, MHS; *The Age*, 20 Jan. 1832, p. 1; *EA*, 1 April 1828; *EA*, 10 Aug 1832, p. 2; Charles E. Clark, *Maine: A Bicentennial History* (New York: W.W. Norton, 1977), p. 105; William David Barry, "Franklin Stanwood, Portland Marine Painter," *The Magazine Antiques*, Oct. 1981, pp. 926–30; Rowe, *The Maritime History of Maine*, pp. 102, 116; Randolph Dominic and William David Barry, "Matanzas," *Portland* 5, no. 5 (July–August 1990), pp. 13–15.

11. Baker, *A Maritime History of Bath*, pp. 219–20.

12. "Cuba Trade of Boston and Portland," *Saturday Evening Transcript*, 25 June 1853.

13. "Decline of Cuba Trade," *Portland Board of Trade Journal*, September 1888, p. 160; Rowe, *The Maritime History of Maine*, p. 116.

14. "Portland's West India Trade," *Portland Board of Trade Journal*, June 1893, p. 38.

15. *Portland Directory 1856*, p. 296, MHS Mx P837.1.

16. "Wealthy Men of Portland," *Portland Tribune*, 18 Jan 1845; *Portland Directory* 1856, p. 296, and 1873, p. 318, MHS Mx P837.1; Barry "Bramhall," pp. 13–15; Rowe, *The Maritime History of Maine*, pp. 117–18; Henry Clay Williams, ed., *Biographical Encyclopedia of Maine of the Nineteenth Century* (Boston: Metropolitan Publishing and Engraving, 1885), pp. 207–08; Earle Shettleworth, personal communication.

17. Rowe, *The Maritime History of Maine*, p. 97.

18. Laura Fecych Sprague, ed., *The Mirror of Maine: One Hundred Distinguished Books that Reveal the History of the State and the Life of its People* (Orono: University of Maine Press, 2000), p. 54. Kellogg's books that deal directly with the West Indies include *The Ark of Elm Island* (Boston: Lee and Shephard Publishers, 1897), *The Hardscrabble of Elm Island* (Boston: Lee and Shephard Publishers, 1871); *A Strong Arm and a Mother's Blessing* (Boston: Lee and Shephard, 1880); *The Young Deliverers of Pleasant Cove* (Boston: Lee and Shephard, 1899); and *The Live Oak Boys or The Adventures of Richard Constable Afloat and Ashore* (Boston: Lee and Shephard, 1882).

19. *EA*, 4 July 1856; Dominic and Barry, "Matanzas"; Rowe, *The Maritime History of Maine*, pp. 102, 116.

20. José de Arango, *Jozo, Discurso dirigido al Excmo. Sr. Gobernador y Capitán General, Memorias de la Sociedad Económica de Amigos del País* (1817), pp. 264–73; Thomas, *Cuba*, p. 88.

21. *Daily Courier*, 10 Feb. 1830.

22. Personal communication, Bill Jordan; *Bradstreet's Book of Commercial Reports of the Bankers, Merchants, Manufacturers, and Others in the United States and British Provinces* (N.Y.: J. M. Bradstreet and Son, 1 March 1866); *Portland Directory* for years 1856 to 1889, MHS Mx P837.1.

23. N. M. Fox, *A History of That Part of the Fox Family Descended from Thomas Fox of Cambridge, Mass., with Genealogical Records* (St. Joseph, Mo.: Union Printing Co., 1899), pp. 43–44, 56–57; *Genealogies of Portland Families: A Scrapbook Compiled by Nathan Goold*, 1895 (typed and indexed by Virginia T. Merrill, 1992), MHS MGE P837; Letter from Rosita Carey, daughter of Eben Fox Carey (1891–1964), to Maine Historical Society, 27 Feb. 1995, MHS.

24. Augustine Dockham, *Portland Almanac and Register:* 1860 (Portland: B. Thurston, 1860), p. 44, MHS; *Portland Daily Press* (henceforth *PDP*) 17 October 1870; "Ladies Theatrical Bouquet, Portland Museum," 1 May 1876, MHS; *EA* 25 Dec. 1806; *The American*, 23 April 1842; *Zion's Advocate*, 1 Jan. 1834; *Deering News*, 18 March 1893; Baker, *A Maritime History of Bath*, p. 223; Rowe, *The Maritime History of Maine*, pp. 103, 111C.

25. *Maine Gazette*, 19 April 1822; *EA*, 20 Jan. 1818; *PDP*, 20 May 1889; Gavin Weightman, *The Frozen-Water Trade: A True Story* (New York: Hyperion, 2003), pp. 8–9, 37, 221–23, 226, 228, 236–37, 243–44; Jennie G. Everson, *Tidewater Ice of the Kennebec River* (Freeport, Maine: The Maine State Museum, 1970), pp. 122, 203; Lawrence C. Allin et al., "Creating Maine's Resource Economy, 1783–1861," in *Maine: The Pine Tree State from Prehistory to the Present*, Richard W. Judd, Edwin A. Churchill, and Joel W. Eastman, eds. (Orono: University of Maine Press, 1995), pp. 284–86; Baker, *A Maritime History of Bath*, p. 579.

26. *EA*, 23 Dec. 1803; Baker, *A Maritime History of Bath*, p. 239–40, 389.

27. *EA*, 16 Aug. 1805.

28. *The Age*, 20 Jan. 1832, p. 1. Sadly, after only a few months, James Purinton died there.

29. Rowe, *The Maritime History of Maine*, pp. 103–06; Barry and Holverson, *The Revolutionary McLellans*.

30. *EA*, 15 June 1832.

31. *The Yankee*, 9 July 1823; *PDP*, 18 March 1871; William David Barry, "Portland's Algerines," *Portland Monthly Magazine*, April 1999: 9–11.

32. *The Yankee*, 9 July 1823.

33. Letter to Elizabeth Montfort from Maria, 4 July 1847, MHS collection 14, box 1/6.

34. "Cuban Voyage," *The Eclectic—A Weekly Paper of Literature*, 23 October 1852. See also Sylester B. Beckett, "Leaves from a Journal of a Cruise Among the West India Islands," *Maine Monthly Magazine*, July 1836, pp. 37–45; "Letter VII: A Voyage to Cuba," *Rural Intelligencer: Designed to Make Home Pleasant and*

Happy, 5 Jan. 1856, p. 8; "Letter VIII: A Voyage to Cuba," *Rural Intelligencer*, 12 Jan. 1856, p. 16; "Cuba," *The Phoenix*, March 1903, p. 7–8; "Cuba and the Africans," *The Eclectic*, 11 June 1853.

35. "North Yarmouth Academy Lib 1–2–3." Lib no. 3 July 1914, North Yarmouth Academy Archives (henceforth NYAA); Portland Scrapbook, vol. 1, p. 6, MHS MV p837.4.

36. Barry, "Franklin Stanwood," pp. 926–30. Stanwood also painted at least one canvas while in Buenos Aires, see *Antiques* Aug. 1956, p. 96.

37. "Portland Society of Art" (pamphlet, ca. 1888), MHS, Ms P837p39a; William David Barry, "Edward Souther Griffin: Portland's Finest Ship Carver?" *Down East*, Nov. 1984, p. 112; Barry, "Franklin Stanwood," p. 926.

38. *EA*, 19 September 1826; Rolde, *Maine: A Narrative History*, pp. 260–94.

39. Maine, Cumberland County, 1850 U.S. Census, Population Schedule (Washington, D.C.: National Archives, micropublication M432), roll 252; "Cumberland County Naturalization Index, 1787–1906, Court House, Portland, Maine", passim pp. 12–85, MHS; William B. Jordan Jr., *Burial Records 1717–1962 of the Eastern Cemetery in Portland, Maine* (Heritage Books, 1987), p. 37; Richard R. Wescott, et al., "Reform Movements and Party Reformation, 1820–1861," in *Maine: The Pine Tree State from Prehistory to the Present*, pp. 211–13.

40. "Mary Lancaster Tompson Record of Students and Poetry Notebooks," MHS S-1026 43/9; North Yarmouth Academy Lib. 1–2–3, Lib no. 3 July 1914, NYAA; George C. Groce and David H. Wallace, *The New-York Historical Society's Dictionary of Artists in America, 1564–1860* (New Haven: Yale University Press), p. 117.

41. "Portland Obituary Scrapbook," vol. 4, p. 81, MHS; "Westbrook Seminary and Female College Register and Rank Book" (1878–1905), pp. 76–114, Westbrook College History (Archives) at the Abplanalp Library, Westbrook College Campus (Portland), University of New England [henceforth WCH]; *Catalogue of Westbrook Seminary 1894–1895*, p. 7, WCH.

42. *The Messenger*, Nov. 1898, p. 9, WCH.

43. Mary Lancaster Tompson Record of Students and Poetry Notebooks, MHS S-1026 43/9 (see enclosed article "Children of Prominent Portland Families Attended Miss Tompson's Private School"); Maine, Cumberland County, 1850 U.S. Census, reel 252, p. 27 and reel 250, pp. 280, 349; *Catalogue of the Officers and Students of Westbrook Seminary 1871–72* (Portland: David Tucker, 1872), WCH; *Portland Directory, 1877*, p. 100, MHS Mx P837.1; Thomas, *Cuba*, p. 98; Barry, "Antoine Dorticos."

44. Barry, "Antoine Dorticos"; Stover, *Eminent Mainers*.

45. *PDP*, 17 Oct. 1870. Before opening his shop, Ponce first dedicated a year to learning English.

46. *Casco Bay Directory, 1902–1903* (South Harpswell, Maine: Breeze Publishing Co., 1903) MHS MX P8372; "Ladies Theatrical Bouquet. Portland Musical.

Monday evening May, 1876. Production of Shaughraun," MHS collections; *Biographical Review: This Volume Contains Biographical Sketches of Leading Citizens of Cumberland County, Maine* (Boston: Biographical Review Publishing Co., 1896), p. 251.

47. *Biographical Review*, p. 251.

48. *1908:1909 Resident, Business and Summer Resident Directory for Casco Bay: Maine* (Portland, Maine: Crowley and Lunt, 1908), p. 104, MHS Mx P8372.

49. *The Casco Bay Directory, 1902–1903*, pp. 74–75 (Claudius Isusi); Roberta (Gomez) Ricker, *West by North . . . A Quarter North: Once Upon a Time and Tide in Casco Bay, Maine* (Kearney, Neb.: Morris Publishing, 2003), pp. 39–40.

50. Maine, Cumberland County, 1880 U.S. Census, Population Schedule (Washington, D.C.: National Archives) film T9-0479, p. 167A, 172C; film T9-0478, p. 80B.

51. Lewiston Scrapbook, p. 85, MHS Mt L588; "Cumberland County, Maine Sheriff Records 1795–1957," vol. 3, "Calendar of Prisoners, 1808 March 1 to 1815 February 13," MHS Collection 177; *The Seaside Oracle*, 15 Nov. 1873.

52. John Sheply, *Reports of Cases Argued and Determined in the Supreme Judicial Court of the State of Maine*, vol. 1, Maine Reports, vol. XIII (Hallowell, Maine: Glazier, Masters and Smith, 1838), pp. 93–109, MHS.

53. *Portland Inquirer,* 12 April 1855.

54. Letter to Elizabeth Montfort (Mountfort) from Maria, 4 July 1847, MHS collection 14, box 1/6. Elizabeth Montfort was the recording secretary of Portland's antislavery society.

55. Stover, *Eminent Mainers.*

56. Some contemporary Portlanders explicitly connected rum and slavery. In fact, Steven Simons Foster was attacked for making speeches about it in Portland's churches. Wells Staly Mays, "Demon Rum: U.S. and Cuban Slavery Connections," public lecture, Bowdoin College, 30 March 2004.

57. "Decline of Cuba Trade," *Portland Board of Trade Journal*, Sept. 1880, p. 160; "Portland's West India Trade," *Portland Board of Trade Journal*, June 1893, p. 38; Rowe, *The Maritime History of Maine*, p. 118; Barry, "Bramhall," p. 15; Baker, *A Maritime History of Bath*, p. 510; Rolde, *Maine*, pp. 173–78; Woodward, Jr., "Ten Years' War (1868–1878)," p. 220; Pérez Jr., *Cuba*, pp. 120, 127, 132–34; Thomas, *Cuba*, p. 271.

58. *PDP,* 4 April 1894 (quotation); *PDP,* 29 Oct. 1883, 23 Jan. 1886, 1 Nov. 1887, and 25 Nov. 1891; *EA,* 7 Aug. 1905, 13 Aug. 1909; *Portland Directory* for years 1869–1885, MHS, Mx P837.1.

59. *EA,* 5 Sept. 1905 (quotation); *EA,* 7 Aug. 1905; *Portland Directory* for years 1900 to 1910, MHS, Mx P837.1; David Bushnell, "Argentina: The Nineteenth Century," in *Encyclopedia of Latin American History and Culture*, vol. 1, pp. 151–52; Louis C. Hatch, *Maine: A History* (Somersworth: New Hampshire Publishing

Co., 1974 [1919]), p. 673; Harrie B. Coe, ed., *Maine: Resources, Attractions, and Its People, A History* (New York: The Lewis Historical Publishing Co., 1928), vol. 1, pp. 382–85. As a young woman, Ruth Montgomery traveled to South America a number of times on her father's ship, the *Carey Winslow*. Her photographs document three journeys that took place in 1900, 1901, and 1903, and show workers unloading lumber and bringing on hides on the Parana River, John Chesebro and John Arrison, personal communication.

60. *EA*, 14 July 1915.

61. *EA*, 13 Aug. 1909, 24 July 1911, 10 Aug. 1912, 5 Feb. 1913, 14 &15 July 1915, and 26 Nov. 1915; Todd A. Diacon, *Millenarian Vision, Capitalist Reality: Brazil's Contestado Rebellion, 1912–1916* (Durham: Duke University Press, 1991), pp. 45–46.

62. *EA*, 8 Dec. 1902; American Council of Learned Societies (ed. Dumas Malone), *Dictionary of American Biography* (New York: Charles Scribner's Sons, 1935), vol. 15, pp. 456–59. Local newspapers also reveal a parallel debate in the 1840s when the U.S. invaded Mexico (1846–1848).

63. Herminio Portel Vilá, *Historia de Cuba en sus relaciones con los Estados Unidos y España*, vol. 2 (1853–1878) (Miami: Mnemosyne Publishing Inc., 1969), p. 129; Thomas, *Cuba*, pp. 207–32; *Who Was Who in America: Historical Volume 1607–1896* (Chicago: A. N. Marquis Company, 1967), p. 602; Stover, *Eminent Mainers*. Pérez Jr., *Cuba*, pp. 107, 110–11.

64. *The Racquet* (Portland High School), Nov. 1900, pp. 4–5, MHS MG p837p.2c.

65. Lewiston Scrapbook, pp. 87–88, MHS Mt L588; Barry, "Antoine Dorticos"; Louis A. Pérez Jr., "The Meaning of the *Maine*: Causation and the Historiography of the Spanish-American War," *Pacific Historical Review* 58, no. 3 (Aug. 1989): 293–322; Julian Company Monclus, *De la voladura del Maine a la ruptura de relaciones diplomaticas entre los Estados Unidos y Espana, 1898* (Lleida, 1988); Guillermo G. Calleja Leal, "La voladura del Maine," *Porista de Historia Militar* 39 no. 59 (1990): 163–96.

66. See for example *PDP*, 24 March 1903. By this time, Portland newspapers tended to present Latin American governments as hapless and inept.

67. U.S. Census Bureau, *1980 Census of Population*, vol. 1, Characteristics of the Population (Washington, D.C.: GPO, 1981); U.S. Census Bureau, *2000 Census of Population and Housing*, Summary Population and Housing Characteristics, PHC-1-21, Maine (Washington, D.C.: GPO, 2002). Community leaders argued that Maine's Latino population was grossly undercounted in the 2000 census. Some estimated that between 1,480 and 1,525 Latinos lived in Portland in April 2000. "Hispanics Undercounted, Group Says," *PPH*, 3 April 2001; John Connors, personal communication.

68. *Catalogue of the Officers and Students of Westbrook Seminary* for years 1903–1908, and 1911–1912, WCH; *Westbrook Seminary 1915–1925 Registrar*, WCH.

69. *PPH*, 27 April 1981, 29 August 1983, p. 9; Michael Powelson, "Mariel Boatlift," in *Encyclopedia of Latin American History and Culture*, vol. 3, pp. 523–24.

70. *PPH*, 9 Oct. 1994.

71. Hernan y Marta, 16 Feb. 2004, Portland; Alicia y Eduardo, 3 March 2004, Portland; Blanca Santiago, 18 Dec. 2003, Portland; *PPH*, 29 July 2001; Vanit Sharma, "Fulfilling a Cuban's Dream: The Story of Lellany Castellanos," and Joshua Vachon, "First Impression: The Story of Gustavo Parra and Monire Childs," both in *Maine Images of the U.S.: Essays of the Real World*, Grade 6 Students of the Chase Smith House, eds. (Portland, 2002); *PPH*, 7 Aug. 1974; Scontras, *Time-Line of Selected Highlights of Maine Labor History, 1636–2003*, p. 65.

72. Stephen Wessler, *The Fractured American Dream: The Destructive Impact of U.S. Anti-Terrorism Policy on Muslim, Latino and Other Immigrants and Refugees Two Years After September 11, 2001* (Portland, Maine: Center for the Prevention of Hate Violence, University of Southern Maine, 2003), pp. 25, 32–36.

73. Alicia y Eduardo, 3 March 2004, Portland.

74. *PPH*, 14 Nov. 2003; Meeting called by NAACP, 30 January 2004 (author's observation); *PPH*, 30 Jan. 2004; *Portland Forecaster*, 11 Feb. 2004.

75. *PPH*, 20–23 June 1999; Wessler, *The Fractured American Dream*, pp. 42–44; *Maine Times*, 1 Jan. 2002; Blanca Santiago, 18 Dec. 2003, Portland; Rev. Virginia Marie Rincon, 14 Nov. 2003, Portland; Eduardo, 3 March 2004, Portland; " 'I Have a Dream . . .' A Latino Perspective," panel at University of Southern Maine, Portland, 7 April 2004.

76. Rev. Virginia Marie Rincon, 14 Nov. 2003, Portland.

77. Alicia, 3 March 2004, Portland.

78. Marta, 15 Feb. 2004, Portland (quotation); *PPH*, 7 Oct. 1999; Madlen Moreno, Center for Study of Lives, University of Southern Maine, Transcript Accession #: A96-04-004.

79. Rev. Virginia Marie Rincon, 14 Nov. 2003, Portland.

80. Blanca Santiago, 18 Dec. 2003, Portland.

81. Rev. Virginia Marie Rincon, " 'I Have a Dream."

82. *Maine Times*, 1 Jan. 2002.

83. *Portland Forecaster*, 11 Feb. 2004.

84. Hernan y Marta, 16 Feb. 2004, Portland; Alicia y Eduardo, 3 March 2004, Portland; Rev. Virginia Marie Rincon, 14 Nov. 2003, Portland; *Portland Forecaster*, 11 Feb. 2004.

85. Eduardo, 12 March 2004, Portland.

86. Hernan y Marta, 16 Feb. 2004, Portland; Alicia y Eduardo, 3 March 2004, Portland; Blanca Santiago, 18 Dec. 2003, Portland.

87. Blanca Santiago, 18 Dec. 2003, Portland.

88. Alicia y Eduardo, 12 March 2004, Portland.

89. Juan Gonzalez, "I Have a Dream."

90. *Portland Forecaster*, 11 Feb. 2004; *PPH*, 20 June 1998.

91. *GlobalView: The Newsletter of the Maine International Trade Center*, Feb. 2004, p. 1, and April 2004, p. 12. *Maine Biz: Maine's Business Newspaper*, Nov. 2001; *PPH*, 24 July 2003.

6

Picturing Place

Portland and the Visual Arts

Donna M. Cassidy

> *Portland is the most charming place imaginable—not too small, not too big, full of energy, everybody good looking and such pleasing public behaviour that it is a joy to live here—and since I have a room in one of the old mansions on the grandest street in New England [State Street] I get the full flavour of background here—the houses are simply wonderful huge old mansions—some of them abandoned now by families probably reduced or can't afford to keep them up now and this is one of them—the old McClellan mansion and now a great residence affair and the people that run it typical nice Yankees.*
>
> —Marsden Hartley to Norma Berger, 26 December 1937[1]

These words were penned by the Maine artist Marsden Hartley during a 1937 visit to the city (Figure 6-1). Although Hartley did not paint Portland during this trip, he wrote about it in his essay, "This Country of Maine" (c. 1937–38), which praised New England's shipbuilding and shipping history and the great houses connected to this tradition, including those on High and State Streets in Portland. When he finally painted the city in 1940–41, these old mansions did not serve as his subject matter; rather, he turned to a site identified with Portland for decades by both artists and tourist promoters: Portland Head Light. In *The Lighthouse* (Figure 6-2), Hartley shows a close-up view of the lighthouse, keeper's house, and rockbound coast as seen from the south—a view identical to the one in the postcard of Portland Head Light that he owned.[2] This location was among the most commonly represented scenes associated with the city, depicted by local painters, as in George Hathaway's *Portland Head Light* (1883–90), and by early twentieth-century artists who summered in Maine, as in Edward Hopper's *Portland Head Light* (1927).

Figure 6-1. Photograph, Marsden Hartley in Monument Square in Portland, Maine, circa 1937.
Courtesy of the Maine Historical Preservation Commission.

Figure 6-2. Marsden Hartley, *The Lighthouse,* 1940–1941. Oil on Masonite-type hardboard, 22 × 28½ in. Private collection. Photograph courtesy of Martha Parris and James Reinish, Inc., New York.

Along with tourist images, such art works predisposed Hartley to recognize the coast and Portland Head Light as appropriate subjects when he represented the city. In this case and many others, the visual arts have provided lenses for inhabitants and outsiders alike to see Portland. Over the past three centuries, artists have selected particular sites and people as worthy of framing, creating images and artifacts— from the landscapes of Munjoy Hill to public monuments of local heroes like Henry Wadsworth Longfellow—that have shaped a sense of place. These representations were defined by artistic conventions and changing historical contexts in the city and in the United States more broadly. This essay will explore the power of the visual arts to imagine Portland. In so doing, I will not offer a comprehensive history of art in the city but will focus on two critical subjects—landscape and portraiture—as well as public art and local art institutions to analyze the multiple ways that the visual arts, in picturing Portland, have fashioned an identity for the city.

Framing Portland: From the Panoramic
to the Postmodern Landscape

Perhaps no other type of visual art has defined Portland as a place more than landscape painting. The city's scenery—the Casco Bay islands, the rugged coast, the spacious greenery of its parks—quickly came to dominate artistic representation in Portland's early history, and these sites were framed according to prevailing landscape formulas. The panorama—that is, a complete view of a specific area or locale, one that allows a viewer to see in all directions, to be "all seeing"—was a popular manner of picturing nature in the early republic. Pierre Charles L'Enfant, for example, described the horizontal sweep of the Hudson River and adjacent hills seen from a vantage point above the landscape by combining several sheets of paper in his watercolor panorama, *West Point, New York* (1780s). This work follows a British topographic convention of depicting towns, cities, and countryseats from an elevated position—a convention common in early New England landscapes like Alvan Fisher's *View of Salem from Gallows Hill* (1818) as well.[3] With their horizontal extension and bird's eye perspective, panoramas established a privileged position vis-à-vis nature for the viewer, an appropriate position of power for the emerging middle class as it was transforming untamed nature into urban, commercial centers like Portland. This controlling, imperial gaze also fit the class values and aspirations of the mercantile elite who used nature and its resources for economic gain.

The panoramic mode influenced the way that early Portland was envisioned, favoring one view above others—that from Munjoy Hill, a promontory that rises one hundred and forty feet above Casco Bay at the eastern end of the Portland peninsula. Surveying the harbor islands, waterfront, and landscapes west and north of Portland from atop Munjoy Hill was made easier with the 1807 construction of the eighty-two-foot-high Portland Observatory at the crest of the hill. Lemuel Moody's telescope, which was placed on the lantern deck that crowned the Observatory, allowed for even grander vistas, as Portlander John Neal later wrote: "A charge of fifteen cents is made for the privilege of viewing the harbor and surrounding country, and no person who has made the investment has reason to regret it. There is no point in Maine where the view of sea or land is more delightful."[4] Timothy Dwight, one of the more famous tourists at the Observatory, remarked: "The design of erecting this structure is to descry vessels off at sea. . . . From this elevation there is a noble prospect of the interior, particularly of Mount Washington, rising at the distance of seventy miles, far above all the other mountains in prospect, with a sublimity which mocks description."[5] While Dwight looked westward toward the White Mountains, other viewers gazed downward to Portland harbor.

John Worrall, an English scenery painter who lived in Boston, was one such viewer. He painted the east side of Providence, Rhode Island (1808–12), onto a drop curtain for the Providence Theatre[6] and produced a similar topographic view of Portland's Munjoy Hill in 1820 (present location unknown) as a spectacle for public entertainment. An advertisement in the *Eastern Argus* invited the public to Union Hall to see Worrall's "PANORAMIC VIEW of the Town of Portland, Taken from Mr. Moody's house, near the Observatory—Beginning on the left with the Wharves—the Shipping—embracing all the Public Edifices—Banks, etc., etc."[7] This expansive, all-seeing perspective of the city established what would become one of the distinctive, most frequently painted scenes of Portland well into the nineteenth century—the prospect of Casco Bay and environs from Munjoy Hill. With its vista of the sloping hills and the calm waters of the Fore River and harbor, Charles Codman's *View of Entertainment of the Boston Rifle Rangers by the Portland Rifle Club in Portland Harbor, August 12, 1829* (1830) replicates the view one would have had from the crest of Munjoy Hill, if not the Observatory, while Sylvester Breakmore Beckett's *Martin's Point* (Figure 6-3), done in 1850, shows a vantage point from the top of Munjoy Hill looking north of Portland onto the placid, light-filled bay.

European landscape theorists of the eighteenth century advanced other conventions for framing nature: the Sublime, the Beautiful, and the Picturesque. Epitomized by the biblical landscapes of the seventeenth-century Italian artist Salvatore Rosa, Sublime scenery was characterized by irregular shapes and forms, dramatic lighting, deep precipices and high mountains, a wilderness hostile and threatening to humans. The Beautiful, by contrast, was embodied in the lush, round trees, tranquil lakes, and golden light of Claude Lorrain's seventeenth-century paintings of pastoral views, often neatly framed by trees on each side. The Picturesque sought to reconcile the Sublime and Beautiful, the wild and cultivated. These ways of seeing nature, especially the Picturesque, became part of a new culture of consuming scenery in the early nineteenth century. While British merchants and their families took to walking in the countryside in search of Claudean prospects, their American

Figure 6-3. Sylvester Breakmore Beckett, *Martin's Point,* circa 1850. Oil on panel, 63 × 89 in. Collections of Maine Historical Society.

counterparts sought out the Picturesque, Beautiful, and Sublime in sites near urban centers and in quickly growing tourist destinations like the White Mountains. Appreciating such landscapes, whether from atop the Munjoy Hill Observatory or at public painting exhibitions, became a mark of gentility for the middle and upper classes of Portland, as it did for the elite in other East Coast urban centers and across the Atlantic.[8]

Portland and its environs were mapped out according to these landscape categories, as is evident in Neal's 1874 description of the scenery that could be glimpsed on carriage rides in and around the city. Following the sea shore road northward, from Falmouth to Bath, the traveler could see "pictures at every turn," not the mountains, cataracts, castles, or volcanoes associated with the Sublime, "but the calm tranquil and soothing associations of untroubled country life, with the open sea and the blue heavens to lure you along your way." In sharp distinction, the bridge-road to Cape Elizabeth, south of Portland, led to "'rioting in foam and spray,' along the rugged cliffs that run from Cape-Cottage to the first, or head-light, and thence to the two-lights, and so on to

Prout's Neck, Old-Orchard and Orchard-Beach, where a swift succession of unfinished, rough pictures—or sketches—burst upon you at every stopping place." West of Portland, in Saccarappa, Gorham, or Deering, were "huge trees, and pleasant water-courses, and sunny lakelets, with here and there a primeval wilderness, which might well be mistaken for a park—a nobleman's park perhaps—like that of the Deering-woods."9 The "pictures" that Neal describes—the pastoral (Beautiful) northern coast, the rugged (Sublime) rockbound southern coast with its spraying surf, and the cultivated yet still wild (Picturesque) sections west of Portland—were identical to the scenes of the city painted by earlier nineteenth-century artists.

Charles Codman adopted the Picturesque formula—pools of reflecting water in the composition's center, dramatic lighting, and trees and jagged natural forms framing the scene—in depicting sites in and around Portland. This mode governed his approach to landscapes for one of his major patrons, the shipping tycoon James Deering, for whom he painted many views of his property on Diamond Island and his Portland estate, Deering Oaks.10 In *Untitled (Deering Oaks)* (Figure 6-4), a contrast of light and dark dominates the scene, with the central pond highlighted and the foreground in shadows, suggesting the mystery and wildness associated with the wooded area at this time. Extending from Back Cove nearly to old Falmouth's Fore River, the Deering estate was two hundred and sixty acres of green trees, meadows, and barns, a woodland, tidal waters, rocky ravines, wild oak and walnut trees; neither fenced off nor manicured, it was considered an ideal locale for Portlanders to enjoy a frolic in nature.11 In Codman's painting, nature has been cultivated for human enjoyment, as three figures in the left side of the pond—two women and one man—look out over a small sailboat gliding over the water's surface. Such art works imagined the city as possessing a perfect balance between nature and culture, both a settled landscape and an untamed wilderness.

The Picturesque dominated not only the fine art of painting but other forms of visual culture in nineteenth-century Portland, as can be seen in Sarah Jane Moore, *Memorial Embroidery* (Figure 6-5). Daughter of a prosperous Portland merchant, Moore attended Miss Mary Rea's School in Portland where she learned how to design mourning pictures, a skill considered essential to genteel education for young women at the time. This needlework and painting on satin memorializes Moore's

Figure 6-4. Charles Codman, United States, 1800–1842, *Untitled (Deering Oaks)*, circa 1828. Oil on panel, 19¹³⁄₁₆" × 24". Portland Museum of Art, Maine. Gift of the estate of William P. Beall, 2003.45. Photo by Myersphoto.com.

two siblings. A gravestone, inscribed with the names of the deceased, a river emblematic of passage to the afterlife, and a steepled church were stock elements in mourning pictures. The cemetery scene, with a river and sailboat along with two trees in the foreground, allude to the Eden in the verse on the gravestone but were also common props in pastoral fine art of the time. Moore combines these Claudean conventions with structures that locate the scene in Portland: on the left side of the composition sits the bright red Portland Observatory and surrounding houses on Munjoy Hill, with Portland Head Light positioned on the far right.[12]

The picturesque and pastoral prevailed as ways of representing the city well into the late nineteenth century—in the work of the Brush'uns (or Brushians), for instance. In the 1860s, these amateur and professional artists began painting outdoors in and around Portland following the example of their French Barbizon and Impressionist counterparts. Typically

Figure 6-5. Sarah Jane Moore, *Moore Memorial Embroidery,* 1838. Silk and watercolor. Collections of Maine Historical Society.

they selected sites like Deering Oaks, the Casco Bay islands, Cape Elizabeth (Delano Park in particular), and Stroudwater that had been settled yet still possessed much uncultivated scenery and that recalled a premodern way of life, as in Charles Frederick Kimball's *Twilight at Stroudwater* (Figure 6-6). Absent a smooth, finished academic surface, the foreground brushwork evokes the layering and movement of the marsh grasses, while hazy forms describe the trees and houses in the distance. A marsh and marsh pond sit in the foreground, with houses nestled among the brush and trees in the middle. Like the Barbizon painter Jean François Millet, Kimball selects a transitional time of day—twilight—which sets a contemplative mood, a sense of passing, that fits in well with the associations of this site. A three-hundred-and-twenty-five-acre tract of marshes, wilderness, and woods, Stroudwater was a colonial settlement with

Figure 6-6. Charles Frederick Kimball, United States, 1831–1903, *Twilight at Stroudwater,* 1879. Oil on canvas, 16⅛" × 12¹⁄₁₆". Portland Museum of Art, Maine. Gift of Joseph Maddocks, 1948.14. Photo by Melville D. McLean.

surviving architecture dating before 1800 (the Tate House of 1775, for example). Kimball paints this site at a time when the colonial period was assuming great significance in American culture, when there was nostalgia for this time when it was believed that there was a balance between nature and culture—a balance that went unchecked with modernization in the late nineteenth century by contrast. Kimball's Portland landscapes were often marked with this longing for the past, as in *Old House at Stroudwater* (1880), *Old Mill, Stroudwater* (1883), and *Old Eastern Cemetery* (1885).[13]

At the turn of the century, such pastoral and nostalgic images were common in paintings exhibited at the Portland Society of Art, from Lillian Marie Parker's *Old Canal Bridge (Stroudwater)* (exhibited in 1892) to John T. Wood's *Capisic Pond* (exhibited in 1910).[14] These were middle landscapes, near the domesticated spaces of the city, yet where wild nature was still in abundance. Not far from these locales were the rugged cliffs of Cape Elizabeth and Prouts Neck, " 'rioting in foam and spray,' " "unfinished, rough pictures," as Neal had described them. Codman had

Figure 6-7. Charles Codman, *Shipwreck at Pond Cove, Cape Elizabeth,* circa 1830. Oil on panel. Collections of Maine Historical Society.

not shied away from painting such Sublime scenes. His *Shipwreck at Pond Cove, Cape Elizabeth* (Figure 6-7), for instance, depicts a three-masted schooner dashed against the rocky coast as onlookers gather onshore to try to save the ship, its cargo, and those on board. Two clergymen, Bibles in hand, invoke the Divine to protect the damaged ship and crew. The storm-tossed boat, churning waters, windswept rain, and dark sky serve to remind the viewer of nature's power—the ocean's force, in particular, as an ever-present threat to Portland's maritime culture.

In Codman's painting, nature becomes a vehicle for a lesson in morality, a stage for an otherworldly drama. In the works of Winslow Homer, by contrast, nature is a site for a personal encounter with a secular world of forces detached from any moral center. At first glance, Homer's Prouts Neck paintings appear similar to Codman's earlier ones: they are settings for shipwrecks, destructive storms, crashing waves, and hardy fishermen battling the elements. Yet Homer evolved a distinctive image of the coast, one often absent of human presence and without divine intervention. His study of French Realism—the sketchy manner, seemingly spontaneous compositions of Gustave Courbet and Edouard Manet—left a stamp on his Prouts Neck seascapes of the 1890s. *Weatherbeaten* (Figure 6-8) pictures an elemental battle of natural forces, the pounding surf against the rockbound Maine coast;

Figure 6-8. Winslow Homer, United States, 1836–1910, *Weatherbeaten*, 1894. Oil on canvas, 28½" × 48⅜". Portland Museum of Art, Maine. Bequest of Charles Shipman Payson, 1988.55.1. Photo by Dark Rooms, Inc.

the characteristics of Homer's work—its immediacy, directness, and crusty sea foam—draw the viewer into the drama. Homer's coast became a powerful image of Portland and in the twentieth century the dominant mode of representing the Maine coast for modernists like George Bellows, John Marin, and Marsden Hartley (see Figure 6-2).[15]

Landscape painting in Portland, from Codman's picturesque scenes of Deering Oaks to Homer's sublime displays of Prouts Neck, were invitations to consume the scenery: they contributed to the growth of tourism in the city and region, as they were advertisements of a sort for the islands and coast in and around the city. The Casco Bay islands became leisure destinations early on, as people visited the harbor forts for recreation both before and after the War of 1812. Steamboat service to Diamond Cove on Great Diamond Island, a favorite spot for picnics and sailing excursions, began in 1822, as middle-class urbanites escaped the congestion of the city to relax and recuperate in nature.[16] Painters Charles Codman and George Hathaway, the latter who did illustrations for brochures and guidebooks like *Portland and the Scenic Gems of Casco Bay* (1896) and sold small souvenir views of Casco Bay from his summer studio on Peaks Island, added to the islands' appeal and focused attention on specific sites for tourist consumption. White Head on Cushing

Island became one of these popular attractions for both tourists and artists. Labeled the "Newport of Casco Bay," Cushing drew a more select audience than the other Casco Bay islands, with a smaller boat, the *Admiral,* serving its patrons.[17] It was inviting to Canadians after the Grand Trunk Railroad connected Montreal and Portland in 1853, with the luxury hotel, Ottawa House, providing most of the lodgings for summer vacationers from 1858 to 1917.

Visual artists played an important a role in promoting Cushing Island as they had Diamond Cove earlier in the century. Engravings of Harrison Bird Brown's paintings of the island along with John Calvin Stevens's architectural drawings of his house designs there were published in William M. Sargent's *Historical Sketch, Guide Book, and Prospectus of Cushing's Island* (1886). As Brown's many prints in this book suggest, Cushing Island's geography was infinitely varied: it possessed seashores, caves, "beetling cliffs," an "unceasing roar of waters," headlands, "green glades and fairy-like nooks," "picturesque vistas," and nighttime moonlit scenes. Ten miles of carriage drives and footpaths with seats "at points where particularly fine views will tempt the traveler to linger" guide the visitor around the island. Watching nature, from the drama of ocean storms to the "sublimity and grandeur" of White Head, was part of island leisure and entertainment.[18] With its underwater ledges and rock cliff rising one hundred and fifty feet to face the open ocean, White Head, which John Neal described as "one of the most attractive points along our whole eastern coast,"[19] became the center of painting activity on Cushing Island. In *White Head at Cushing Island* (Figure 6-9), John Bradley Hudson depicts not only this tourist spectacle but the tourist commerce of the Casco Bay islands. He brings the viewer close up to the sublime cliff: the sun creates a bold contrast of light and dark in the sky and on the rocky shore, while the waves churn at the base of the cliff. At the top of White Head stands a group of six tourists, both men and women, enjoying the dramatic view, while a steamboat—one of the many transporting tourists to the island—glides across the calmer waters of the harbor, with sailboats off in the distance.

Boats of varying types figure prominently in Portland paintings, signifying the exchanges within the city and without—its tourist commerce within the harbor and along the New England coast, military exploits, international trade, and even the slave trade—as in Harrison Bird Brown's *Sailing on Casco Bay* (n.d.), Antonio Jacobsen's *The Steamship*

Figure 6-9. John Bradley Hudson, Jr., United States, 1832–1903, *White Head at Cushing Island, Maine,* n.d. Oil on canvas, 24" × 36⅛". Portland Museum of Art, Maine. Museum purchase with gifts from Vassar College alumnae in memory of Janet Hickey Drummond, 1978.194.

"Portland" (1891), Charles Waldron's *Tam O'Shanter* (n.d.), and Franklin Stanwood's *Slave Ship* (c. 1877). Harrison Bird Brown's *View of Forest City Sugar Refinery, Portland, from Across the Fore River* (Figure 6-10) speaks to other exchanges between Portland and the wider world; moreover, it shows the way that industry and commerce were aestheticized or naturalized in Portland art, as it was in New England and American art in general. Brown was supported by wealthy merchants who had made their fortunes in sugar, railroads, and steamships, and John Bundy Brown was one of his major patrons.[20] In 1845 J. B. Brown and the Boston firm Greely & Guild made converting raw West Indies molasses into granulated sugar a profitable enterprise with Portland's first sugar refinery. Brown eventually took over the business himself and, in 1855, his Portland Sugar Company, with an eight-story refinery at Gorham's Corner on Maple Street and warehouses and wharves on the Fore River, helped to transform this Irish neighborhood from a largely residential to an industrial area. In its heyday, Portland Sugar employed one thousand workers and processed five hundred barrels of sugar per day.[21] Other refineries dotted the Fore River at the western end of Commercial

Figure 6-10. Harrison Bird Brown, United States, 1831–1915, *View of the Forest City Sugar Refinery, Portland, from Across the Fore River,* circa 1860. Oil on canvas, 13" × 14⅛". Portland Museum of Art, Maine. Lent by the City of Portland, 2.1977.3. Photo by Bernard C. Meyers.

Street by the 1860s, including the Forest City Sugar Refinery, incorporated in 1863 with a factory two hundred and seventy feet long, fifty feet wide, and five stories high.[22] Commercial Street, which runs along the Fore River below Fore Street and was filled in by the city in 1853, became the center of Portland's import and export business. Railroad tracks for the Atlantic and St. Lawrence (later Grand Trunk) Railroad ran down the center of the street and to the wharves.[23]

View of Forest City Sugar Refinery celebrates the city's commercial district in the late nineteenth century. Harrison Bird Brown shows the Forest City Sugar Refinery, smoke stacks from other factories (Knight & Whidden Plaster Manufactory and Portland Glass Works, for example), wharves, and railway lines from a vantage point across the Fore River.[24] Nature dominates this prospect: the sky, with gradations of blue, pale red, and yellow toward the right, constitutes half of the painting's surface; the lower part of the composition describes the glassy surface of the Fore River, a skiff with three passengers and two boatmen, and the sandy shore on the South Portland side. In a narrow, central band is the working waterfront of Portland's Commercial Street, with its factories, warehouses, trade ships, and railway cars reflected on the river's surface. Brown creates a contrast of dark and light across the painting, with the refinery and its smoke on the left transformed into a golden light at the end of the peninsula on the right. Industry here seems benign, as it did in many contemporary landscapes of New England factory towns. Progress is the theme in such paintings and prints, as the viewer moves through the scene following the improvement of the landscape, often guided by a train speeding toward the brilliant sun, as in Asher B. Durand's *Progress (The Advance of Civilization)* (1853).[25] Similarly, in *View of Forest City Sugar Refinery,* a train travels towards the horizon at the right signaling the export of the factory products to a market beyond and the international economic network of which Portland was part: West Indies molasses is imported and converted into sugar, which, in turn, is sent from the city to a wider market. The realities of this economy—its reliance on slave labor, its imperial underpinnings—are masked by the dazzling visual display created by Brown's artistic hand.

Views of urban, industrial Portland increased in number as new conventions of representation emerged with the advent of art movements like Realism and Impressionism in the late nineteenth and early twentieth centuries. Weary of the staid formula of academic art, the New York Realists painted the modern city, its new architecture and parks, the urban working class, and leisure activities and entertainments, with bold, slap-dash brushstrokes that made the art work seem spontaneous, unstudied, and immediate. These artists, however, couldn't completely shake nineteenth-century aesthetic manners, as they continued to see and paint these new sites as picturesque. Robert Henri depicted the dirty streets of New York as snow covered and neatly composed in *Snow in New York* (1902), while George Bellows portrayed the excavation of Pennsylvania Station dramatically lit by electricity at night and recalling sublime landscapes of the American West in *Excavation at Night* (1908). Night, fog, snow, and rain disguised the less than attractive aspects of the urban environment—and this was true as much of Portland urban scenes as it was of those of New York, as is evident in William Wallace Gilchrist Jr.'s *Congress Square in Winter* (Figure 6-11). In this painting, Congress Square appears without the detailed descriptions that marked earlier city scenes: long sweeping brushstrokes are layered over indistinct street scenes and hazy buildings; the focus is the storm and its atmospheric effects, the visual qualities that typified the Impressionist art that influenced Gilchrist. Through this manner, the artist makes viewers feel as though they are experiencing what it was like to see the square, to even be in the square, during a blinding snow storm. The storm frames the city as aesthetically pleasing, as the physical objects in the scene dissolve to become a series of abstract strokes of color, disconnected from

Figure 6-11. William Wallace Gilchrist, United States, 1879–1926, *Congress Square in Winter,* circa 1915. Oil on canvas, 20" × 26". Portland Museum of Art, Maine. Gift of Dr. Carl and Linda Metzger, 1984.136. Photo by Melville D. McLean.

the urban subject at hand. That this is a nighttime scene was significant as well: electricity brightens Congress Square to create a magical spectacle of the modern city.

The nocturnal cityscape continued to be popular in later twentieth-century paintings of Portland. Robert Solotaire offered a new perspective of the city from the eleventh floor of the Holiday Inn on Spring Street in *View from the Eleventh Floor—Night* (Figure 6-12). This viewpoint—looking down from a tall building onto the urban streets below—had become part of the language of the modern cityscape, from Claude Monet's *Boulevard des Capucines* (1873–74) to Alfred Stieglitz's *From My Window at the Shelton—West* (1931). In a way, Solotaire also reinvents the earlier panoramic tradition here as he uses the perspective from a new skyscraper built in 1973 just as earlier nineteenth-century painters like Worrall had used the prospect from Munjoy Hill and the Observatory. *View from the Eleventh Floor* describes the rooftops of Portland's buildings, the billboards, the Eastland

Figure 6-12. Robert Solotaire, United States, b. 1930, *View from the Eleventh Floor—Night,* Oct. 1978. Oil on Masonite, 24½" × 37⅜". Portland Museum of Art, Maine. Gift of the artist, 1980.160. Photo by Bernard C. Myers.

Hotel, and cars on Forest Avenue through the muted light of dusk. Like nineteenth-century landscape paintings, it shows the relationship between nature and culture, with the foreground geometric order of urban Portland balanced with Back Cove and the mountains in the distance. Despite its focus on modern buildings, Solotaire's work stills locates nature as a presence in Portland—visible in the background just beyond the densely packed structures of the city's center.

View from the Eleventh Floor—Night hints at the diverse places of modern Portland. Similar to Solotaire and unlike early landscape painters who tried to fix Portland's identity and freeze a singular moment or image, many recent artists, shaped by Postmodernism, see Portland as unfixed and ever-changing, with multiple spaces, a place where past and present intersect, as Nathaniel Larrabee, whose painting *White House* (2000) was exhibited in the Portland Museum of Art's 2003 *Biennial,* has commented:

Portland retains a comfortable mix of contemporary urban culture, working industrial seaport, and commercial center. It has preserved enough of its original heritage to provide a sense of continuity in the face of change. Twentieth-century oil tanks are set against earlier era warehouses and contemporary bank office towers; working-class houses are placed against the backdrop of the downtown and city hall buildings. Contrasts of new and old, class and station, artificial and real, all enter into an exciting mosaic. Casco Bay and raw nature are set at the edges, acting as a foil. A T. S. Eliot sense of time past, present, and future pervades the luminous atmosphere.[26]

The 2001 *Back Cove, Heart of Portland* project offered a similar idea of Portland as place. This ecoart collaboration investigated the aesthetic, historic, and ecological significance of this tidal inlet of Casco Bay in three parts: an exhibition of forty contemporary works, biological specimens, and reproductions of historic plans, maps, and photographs; temporary public art by University of Southern Maine and Maine College of Art students installed along the inlet, Baxter Boulevard, and Bedford Street; and sculptor Tracey Cockrell's blue Plexiglas and metal audio boxes placed along what was the original 1781 shoreline. The project recognized the site as it changed over time, from being a dump for tanneries and tile factories and a residential sewage run off during the nineteenth century to its redesign by Olmsted, Olmsted & Eliot at the turn of the century: Back Cove as "simultaneously a tidal marsh, a hidden dump, an historical landmark, and a changing cultural construction."[27]

That Back Cove was the focus of such a project speaks to the historical importance and continuing value of this site and the natural environment to Portland's art and identity. Framed by earlier landscape painters, Back Cove—its coastal location, its visibility in the prospect from Munjoy Hill and the Holiday Inn (see Figures 6-3 and 6-12)—became one of the distinctive landscapes of the city. It was at the center of the turn-of-the-century park system designed Olmsted, Olmsted and Eliot and advocated by Mayor James Phinney Baxter.[28] Like many urban park plans of the time, the Portland one placed a high value on the preservation of natural spots within urban spaces—a value advocated by recent historic preservation and urban conservation organizations in the city, like Portland Trails (organized in 1991). The contemporary concern to preserve the wildness and the elemental within the urban environment, to balance nature and culture, is very much the result of the powerful and prevalent landscape tradition in paintings of the city over the past two centuries which established nature—

the coast, the harbor, the urban woodlands—as essential to Portland's identity as a livable city.

Portraiture: Changing Faces

In the epigraph, Marsden Hartley characterizes the people of Portland as "good looking," with "pleasing public behaviour," "typical nice Yankees." The genteel Anglo that he identifies as the Portland type corresponds to the many early portraits of the city's leading citizens. In the eighteenth century, the elite of Falmouth commissioned prominent regional artists like Robert Feke, Joseph Badger, and John Singleton Copley to paint their portraits just as their Boston counterparts did. All along the New England coast, from Rhode Island to southern Maine, portraits were displayed in the houses of the merchant class, serving as one marker among many artifacts—from stylish mansions to fashionable furniture—that communicated to guests the high social position and character of the sitters. The Falmouth portrait patrons were typically attired in fashionable dress, posed with control and grace, and surrounded with luxury, consumer goods that viewers would associate with character, prestige, and power, as in John Singleton Copley's *Sarah Erving Waldo* (Figure 6-13). Born in Boston, Erving married Colonel Samuel Waldo, son of Brigadier General Samuel Waldo, in 1762 and lived in Falmouth until 1770. Her lace-edged satin dress and jeweled headpiece speak of her wealth and privileged status, as do her elegantly placed hands. The polished mahogany table shows off Copley's skill as a painter, particularly his expertise at rendering textures—a critically important ability as he was able to appeal to the materialism of his merchant class clients. Copley presents Erving not only with appropriate signs of her class but her gender: she holds a sprig of cherries in her hand as fruits and flowers were common markers of feminine accomplishment well into the nineteenth century.[29]

Fine art portraits remained the domain of Portland's elite and helped to make certain families, like the McLellans, stand for the city. *Portrait of Captain Joseph McLellan, Jr.,* painted in Amsterdam and attributed to Johann Baptist Hirschmann (Figure 6-14), pictures the son of the founder of the McLellan shipping firm, who had an adventurous career as a privateer and traveled frequently to Europe and the West Indies. McLellan appears in this pastel portrait as a respectable sea captain, with

Figure 6-13. John Singleton Copley, *Sarah Erving Waldo,* circa 1765. Oil, 50 × 40 in. Photograph courtesy Peabody Essex Museum, Salem, Massachusetts. Gift of Mr. and Mrs. Charles Edward Cotting. Photograph by Jeffrey Dykes.

Figure 6-14. Attributed to Johann Baptist Hirshmann, *Captain Joseph McLellan, Jr. (1762–1844)*, 1789. Pastel on paper, 12" × 9¼". Portland Museum of Art, Maine. Museum purchase with support from the Margaret H. Jewell Fund, 1976.55.

his spyglass in hand, map on table, and ship visible out the window signifying his trading business; seated in an upholstered chair, he wears a lace jabot, patterned vest, and blue velvet jacket with silver buttons that indicate his wealth as a merchant. The artist uses a compositional type that harkens back to earlier New England portraits of shipping merchants, such as John Smibert's *Peter Faneuil* (c. 1742), and establishes maritime industry as part of the McLellan family identity—and that of Portland by association.

In the nineteenth century, itinerant portrait painters like Royall Brewster Smith and John Brewster Jr. depicted upper-class Portlanders in a style more two-dimensional, yet still employed the signs of class and gender typical of earlier works. The emergence of these itinerant artists brought about a change in portrait making in the United States and in Portland: it made portraits available to a wider audience, especially to the middle class. A native of Rehoboth, Massachusetts, Susanna Paine transformed her training in watercolor at a local female academy into a portrait painting business, launching her career from Portland in 1826 (where she remained active until 1831). An advertisement for her Free Street studio in Portland listed the cost of an oil portrait as eight dollars and a crayon one as four.[30] Paine's skill is evident in *Portrait of Mrs. J. H. Corbett* (Figure 6-15): executed during a visit to Lisbon Falls when she was staying in Portland, it presents the sitter with emblems of her social status and feminine accomplishments—her black dress with lace and pink ribbon, white feather head piece, gold earrings, matching brooch, rings, thimble on her finger, and a display of her sewing accoutrements (spools of thread, scissors, and a pin cushion) on a table.

Esther Weeks, seated in the center of the daguerreotype portrait of her family, is dressed much like Mrs. Corbett (Figure 6-16). Developed in 1839, the daguerreotype was considered a democratic medium, making portraits for only a few dollars available in cities across the country, including Portland.[31] The Weeks portrait communicates the family's place as respectable and financially successful citizens of the city. Father, mother, and adult son sit frontally against a plain background with the effect of highlighting their elaborate attire: the father and son are dressed in suits, ties, and satin vests, while the mother, in the center, wears a satin dress with cinched waist, lace collar and cuffs, and a brooch pinned on the collar. John Weeks was a carpenter who lived on Portland's Munjoy Hill. In the late nineteenth and twentieth centuries, daguerreotypes and later studio photograph portraits allowed working-class Portlanders

Figure 6-15. Susan Paine, United States, 1792–1862, *Portrait of Mrs. J. H. Corbett,* 1831. Oil on panel, 26¹⁵⁄₁₆" × 24¹⁵⁄₁₆". Portland Museum of Art, Maine. Gift of Elizabeth B. Noyce, 1996.59.22. Photo by Melville D. McLean.

Figure 6-16. Anon., *John and Esther Weeks with Their Son William H. Weeks*, n.d. Daguerreotype. Collections of Maine Historical Society.

(like the Weeks family) and new immigrants to become part of the city's represented class. In these images, the sitters, at times, speak of their ethnic identity. *Two Chinese Men in Costume* (Figure 6-17), one man identified as Hop Ling, was done at the Portland studio of Charles W. Hearn. In this photograph, the sitters appear in traditional Chinese attire and surrounded by objects like the small screen on the mantle, peacock feathers, and animal skin rug that mark their country of origin and late nineteenth-century Western views of the exotic Orient.

Working-class Portlanders became more visible in twentieth-century visual culture as the fine arts embraced modern life as subject matter. In World War II America, for instance, women workers in overalls populated advertisements, posters, films, and magazines, as evidence of the growing number of women in industrial jobs who replaced the men who had gone to war.[32] Norman Rockwell's *Rosie the Riveter* (the cover of the *Saturday Evening Post*, 29 May 1943), the most widely circulated of

Figure 6-17. Charles Hearn Studio, *Two Chinese Men in Costume,* circa 1890. Photograph. Collections of Maine Historical Society.

these images, had her Portland counterpart in the South Portland ship-yard workers pictured in Mildred Burrage's charcoal drawings. Com-pleted on 1 July 1943, a few months after *Rosie*'s appearance, *Tacker—Waiting—N.E.S.C. (Female Welder Smoking)* (Figure 6-18) describes a female welder in trousers and hard hat seated on a bench and framed by steel beams. Employing the realism common in 1930s art, Burrage se-lects a casual moment as the worker takes a cigarette break. Sitting with an expressionless face and rumpled jacket, the welder appears more like the women in Dorothea Lange's photographs of the Richmond, Califor-nia, shipyard workers (1942) than the heroic, muscular *Rosie*.

Burrage's charcoal portraits allowed the artist a sense of immediacy in approaching her subject—a directness that became essential to the tradi-tion of documentary photography in the twentieth century. Since 1973, the Salt Center for Documentary Studies has worked to record economic and demographic changes and continuities in Maine, including the city of Portland, through photographs and oral histories. Focused on ordi-nary people and everyday life at the end of the twentieth century, Salt photographs of Portland record a diverse modern city, populated by var-ied ethnic groups and immigrants, and men and women across the eco-nomic and cultural spectrum: the cast of characters in these works show the changing faces of the people of Portland, as in the photograph of Cong Ba Nguyen, a Vietnamese African American refugee (Figure 6-19). Such images represent a very different picture of Portlanders than had the visual record of pre-photographic, premodern Portland, and chal-lenge Hartley's construct of Portlanders as typical Yankees.

Memory, Place, and Public Art

Most portraits are intended as private works of art, usually for the dis-play in an individual's home and directed toward members of the sitter's family and class. Some, however, move out of the private into the public sphere, as was the case with Franklin Simmons's *Henry Wads-worth Longfellow* (1888) in Portland (Figure 6-20). The Longfellow Statue Association began raising funds from schoolchildren in 1885 to support the construction of a sculptural memorial to the poet; just three years later, the statue was completed and set up in its present loca-tion at the corner of State and Congress streets. Honorable Charles F. Libby, president of the Longfellow Statue Association, had these words

Figure 6-18. Mildred Burrage, United States, 1890–1983, *Tacker-Waiting-N.E.S.C. (Female Welder Smoking)*, 1943. Charcoal on laid paper. Portland Museum of Art, Maine. Gift of the artist, 1981.411. Photo by Benjamin Magro.

Figure 6-19. Valerie Haynes (Salt Alumna, Spring 2002), *Cong Ba Nguyen.*Courtesy of the Salt Archives, The Salt Institute for Documentary Studies, Portland, Maine.

Figure 6-20. Postcard, Franklin Simmons, *Soldiers and Sailors Monument (Our Lady of Victories)*, 1888–1891, and *Henry Wordsworth Longfellow*, 1888. Courtesy of the Maine Historical Preservation Commission.

to say at the dedication in 1888 (just six years after the poet's death): "We have called to our aid the sculptor's art to perpetuate in enduring bronze the physical aspects of the man, the dignity and charm of his person. But this is not the full meaning of our act; it is the life of the poet rather than his fame or achievements, great as they were, which we would emphasize to-day. We would have this statue stand as a monument to individual worth, a tribute to noble living."[33] Simmons's sculpture suggests the poet's nobility through pose and position. Like figures in most public sculptures of the time, Longfellow is placed on a pedestal above the viewer to indicate his elevated stature. While absent accompanying allegorical figures, he possesses the calm and poise of Simmons's neoclassical figures: he sits gazing into the distance with one leg in advance of the other, his right arm resting on the chair arm, and his cape draping his lap and legs in imitation of the garb that adorned Simmons's ancient heroes and heroines like *Penelope* (c. 1880).

In addition to its primary role of commemorating an individual, the Longfellow monument served functions typical of late-nineteenth-century American public sculpture—to beautify urban spaces and to create a collective memory and civic identity. Located at what was then

State Street Square, Simmons's sculpture added to the aesthetic appeal of the city streets as tree-lined avenues radiated from it. It also helped to define Portland as an artistic and literary center—a marker in bronze of efforts by Portlanders like John Neal and Ann S. Stephens to cultivate a taste for the arts in the city. This work was moreover the first of a long line of public commemorative sculptures in Portland that emphasized heroic, male (largely) endeavors as integral to the city's identity—Simmons's *Soldiers and Sailors Monument* (*Our Lady of Victories* [1888–91]) (see Figure 6-20) in honor of Portland's Civil War veterans and dead; Edward S. Griffin's *Portland Firemen's Monument* (1898); Burn C. Miller's *Thomas Reed Statue* (1910) dedicated to a Portlander who became the Speaker of the U.S. House of Representatives; the *Lillian M. N. Stevens Memorial Fountain* ("*The Little Water Girl*" [1917]) honoring the Portland native who was president of the Women's Christian Temperance Union; Theo Alice Ruggles Kitson's *Spanish War Veterans Memorial* (1924) in Deering Oaks Park; and Victor Kahill's *Maine Lobsterman*, originally exhibited at the 1939 World's Fair and set up in Portland in 1977.[34]

Like Kahill's sculpture, 1930s public art became important in creating local, regional, and national identity less through exceptional heroic figures and more through the common person and landscape. Franklin Delano Roosevelt's New Deal established an art for the people that rejected elitist modernist art that had become disconnected from ordinary citizens. One New Deal art program that advanced this popular art was the Treasury Department's Section of Painting and Sculpture (later called the Section of Fine Arts), which commissioned art for federal buildings and over a thousand post offices between 1934 and 1943. Section murals in New England—as well as across the nation—focused on the themes of history and productive work to create positive images aimed at reconstructing identity and stability amid the economic collapse of the Depression.[35] In the commissions and executions of these murals, the definition of place and control over the representation of history did not go uncontested, as many battles took place over what constituted community identity, including one over Elizabeth Tracy's *Bathers* (1941) for the Kennebunkport, Maine, post office.[36]

In 1944, the people of Kennebunkport wanted to replace their mural of buxom female beach bathers and raised enough money to commission a mural from Gordon Grant, an artist well known along the East Coast for his seascapes.[37] Views of the coast (absent the beach bathers) appeared in the post office murals in Portland and South Portland and without the attendant controversy of the Kennebunkport commission. Henry Mattson was selected to execute the murals for the new Portland post office (built 1933–34), as Treasury officials deemed Mattson, who had a landscape on display in the White House, unlikely to cause controversy. Attracted to the ocean's "elemental aspect, its weight, its awesome depth, the powerful action of its waters," Mattson, who summered in Rockport, Massachusetts, painted the pounding surf along the coast and storm-swept open ocean more than any other subject.[38] It was the ocean and coast that served as the subject for Mattson's Portland murals. Executed in Woodstock, New York, in 1936, the two canvases—*The Sea*, mounted on the north wall, and *The Rocky Coast of Maine*, on the south—were shipped to Portland in 1937 to be installed in the post office (Figure 6-21).[39] These seascapes were viewed as compatible with regional identity, as one reporter in the *Portland Sunday Telegram* stated: "[Mattson] was commissioned to do the Portland Post Office murals because his work, especially his marines [seascapes], have been in sympathy with the Maine 'theme.'"[40] While Mattson's paintings do not represent a specific locale but rather what Mattson called the "rocky surf-slammed coast of Maine, anywhere,"[41] *The Sea* nonetheless resembles the coast near Portland as pictured in Homer's Prouts Neck paintings (see Figure 6-8). The connection between Mattson's work and Homer's would have been fitting at this moment, as 1936 was the centennial of Homer's birth, marked by exhibitions at the Whitney Museum of American Art, Knoedler's Galleries and Macbeth Gallery in New York, and one at Homer's Prouts Neck studio; reviews of these exhibitions stressed Homer's status as a Maine artist and his Prouts Neck paintings as the best of his career.[42]

Homer's Maine (Portland) coast, with its force and danger, informed Alzira Peirce's *Shipwreck at Night* (Figure 6-22), the mural for the South Portland post office. Peirce, unlike Mattson, was a Maine artist who also did a mural for the Ellsworth, Maine, Post Office—*Ellsworth Lumber Port* (1938), which depicted a massive wharf, sailors, and merchants at the height of the town's trade and shipbuilding in the nineteenth century.[43] Peirce's interest in regional history influenced her South Portland Post Office mural as well. *Shipwreck at Night* represents one of Casco Bay's most tragic disasters—the wreck of the *Bohemian*, a boat from Liverpool, off the coast at Cape Elizabeth (Broad Cove) on the evening of 22 February 1864. The vessel was carrying 218 passengers, many Irish

Figure 6-21. Henry Mattson, *The Sea*, 1937. Oil on canvas. U.S. Post Office, Portland, Main. Photograph by Gina Platt.

immigrants; forty-two of those on board died. Residents of the community cared for the survivors and buried unclaimed bodies in South Portland's Calvary Cemetery. This story, as painted by Peirce, reminded viewers of the saga of immigrants to the city as much as it celebrated the humanity of town residents. Like Mattson's mural, it refers to earlier art images of the region—to works like Codman's *Shipwreck at Pond Cove* (see Figure 6-7) and Homer's *The Wreck* (1896).

Re-engaging the larger public in the visual arts and its relation to place has become critical for many recent artists in the context of the late-twentieth-century critique of modernism and concern about the loss of local traditions and concurrent rise of standardized strip malls and national chain stores. In 2000, the Portland City Council adopted an ordinance authorizing the Public Art Program (PAP) which provided .5 percent of the city's annual Capital Improvement Project budget for the restoration or acquisition of permanent public art.[44] While the PAP initially focused on restoring city-owned public sculptures, it

Figure 6-22. Alzira Peirce, *Shipwreck at Night,* 1939. Oil on canvas. U.S. Post Office, South Portland, Maine. Photograph courtesy of Portland Press Herald.

has turned to commissioning new works of public art that fit four categories defined in the PAP's 2002 Annual Plan: art works of remembrance; expressive art works whose primary function is aesthetic; functional art works; and community-based art works that involve collaborations between artists and members of the city's diverse communities. The Portland Art Committee (PAC) aims to create a balance among these four public art types and has commissioned works in each category: the Robert B. Ganley Plaza Marker (commemorating a city manager, and located in City Hall Plaza); the Old Port Sculpture (Boothby Square) Project; the Monument Square Project (a new artist-designed information kiosk); and the Armenian Kar in Bayside.

Given its goal to connect art to local traditions and history, the PAP seeks to advance a civic identity that is inclusive by commissioning "contemporary pieces that reflect the new diversity and cosmopolitan spirit of Portland" and that recognize not only visible political and cultural leaders but the many communities and ethnic groups that contributed to the city's past and shape Portland's present. The Armenian Kar (Figure 6-23), the first project completed under the category of community-based projects, fulfills these aims. Dedicated in July 2003 and designed through collaboration between PAC staff and the Portland Armenian Club, the monument, located on Congress Street across from the façade of the Cathedral of the Immaculate Conception, is a granite slab referring to the ancient Armenian tradition of carved stone markers; written text engraved on the stone relates the history of Armenian people, their immigration to Portland, and community in Bayside. The form

Figure 6-23. The Armenian Kar, 2002. Bayside, Portland, Maine. Photograph by author.

of the monument also speaks to contemporary public sculpture—the Vietnam Memorial in Washington, D.C., and the Jack Kerouac Memorial in Lowell, Massachusetts, for instance—that rely on simple stone markers and inscribed words to create public spaces of remembrance.

The sense of place is critical to other PAP projects, both planned and completed. Boothby Square, located on two grass islands on Fore Street in Portland's Old Port, is the site of the first public art work commissioned under the category of expressive art. Boston artist Shauna Gillies-Smith, who has been awarded the commission, will echo the form of the Fore River by creating undulating waves of grass and stainless steel in the tucked away park, once on the waterfront.[45] Alice Spencer, an artist who lives in Portland and chairs the PAC, sees the ability to create a unique sense of place a critical function of public art: "Our cities have become places of conformity, where there isn't the kind of individuality that most cities used to have. Public art restores that sense of place. You will always know where you are when you visit Boothby

Square after this piece goes into it."[46] The unique qualities of Portland as a city play a role not only in this expressive piece in Boothby Square but in the new bus shelter on the corner of Congress and Center streets in Monument Square, which opened in December 2004 and was designed by Seattle artists Laura Haddad and Tom Drugan. Their kiosk speaks to the coastal location and maritime heritage of the city in abstract ways: the curved roof evokes a segmented lobster tail or seashell; the cast-iron lower walls suggest barnacles; and the angled windows reflect light in imitation of the shimmering surface of the ocean.[47] These two new public art projects define the distinctiveness of the city in its coastal location and maritime culture, just as 1930s public murals and nineteenth-century landscape painting did.

Institutionalizing the Art of Place

Art is available to the public not only in the open spaces of the city streets but in public art institutions—museums, galleries, schools. The patronage and public display of the visual arts were considered essential to Portland's success and identity as a city early in its history. One 1835 article in *Portland Magazine* stated the reasons—both aesthetic and economic—for Portlanders to support the arts. The citizen who does not patronize art and literature has "but half furnished his house, and has omitted that portion which tells best for the taste and intellect of the possessor." Paintings are also "disposable property, which increases in beauty and value as it increases in age, and which will become saleable like other marketable commodities, as the taste and refinement which gives value to these things improve in our country."[48] At the time of this essay's publication, art exhibitions in Portland took place in artists' studios, storefronts, and public halls, and under the auspices of the Maine Charitable Mechanic Association. It was nearly another fifty years before the Portland Society of Art was founded (1882). The Society's goals were "to encourage a knowledge and love of art, through the exhibition of art works and lectures upon art subjects; the acquisition of an art library and works of art, such as paintings, statuary and engravings; and the establishment of an art school and museum."[49] It proceeded to sponsor an art school and regular exhibitions, which were initially held at the "Club House," designed by John Calvin Stevens and located behind the Portland Public Library on Con-

gress Street. At a time when major American cities were building pala-
tial structures to house art collections, as in the cases of the Museum of
Fine Arts in Boston and the Metropolitan Museum of Art in New York,
Portland was without a permanent structure for member exhibitions
or permanent displays. A commentator writing in the brochure for the
1905 Portland Society of Art exhibition lamented: "Think of it! A city
of 50,000 claiming to be a city of culture and refinement, and in its
borders only one small room in which pictures can be properly shown
. . . Portland is big enough and rich enough to have a Museum of Art,
and it has citizens who could by a combination of effort easily bring
such an institution into existence . . . [A museum would provide] an
Art gallery which would enable our own people to see and study
worthy examples, and also prove a great attraction for our many summer visitors."[50] The first permanent home for the Portland Society of
Art was the McLellan House (1801), donated in 1908 by Margaret Mussey Sweat, who in her will provided for the establishment of an art museum and directives to build a new gallery as well. Following her
wishes, the L. D. M. (Lorenzo de Medici) Sweat Memorial Gallery was
added to the McLellan House in 1911.[51]

While the Portland Society of Art was grounded in local interests and
concerned with advancing local artists, it was hardly provincial. The Society made every effort to bring the work of Boston and New York artists to the city to educate Portland artists, patrons, and citizens. Early exhibition records (1882–1925) show diverse subjects (still lifes, portraits,
landscapes, including both local sites and scenes of the Canadian maritime coast, Brittany, Normandy, and the Netherlands) and an array of
styles (Childe Hassam's Impressionism, John Twachtman's Tonalism,
and Albert Bierstadt's grand landscape manner, for example). From 1882
to 1910 numerous local artists exhibited paintings of Portland views—
Peaks Island, Cushing Island, Portland Head Light, and Diamond
Cove—but, by the early 'teens, as Maine became a popular destination
for New York artists, exhibitions broadened to include more artists and
paintings not properly defined as "local" but regional—the work of
Charles Woodbury, Russell Cheney, George Bellows, and the Boston
School painters, for instance.

This shift away from exclusive local interest is institutionalized in the
present incarnation of the Portland Society of Art—the Portland Museum of Art. The galleries and buildings of the Museum in its form
since the 2002 restoration of the McLellan House and Sweat Galleries

map out different spaces and times of art in Portland: the McLellan House itself is a display of Federal architecture; the rooms in the Sweat Galleries locate Portland painting and decorative arts within the larger history of American art; and the Charles Shipman Payson Building focuses on short-term exhibitions and present-day art. These spaces define the mission of the Museum as an educational institution dedicated to the history of regional art and to the support of contemporary artists of Portland and Maine. Recent exhibitions on Charles Codman and Charles Frederick Kimball, along with the Winslow Homer Gallery and Palladian Gallery in the new American art installation, demonstrate the Museum's dedication to studying the art history of Portland. In recent years, the Portland Museum of Art has shown a renewed commitment to contemporary artists with its Biennial exhibitions. Daniel E. O'Leary, current museum director, has stated: "The continuing vitality of Maine's creative communities is the impetus behind the *1998 Portland Museum of Art Biennial,* the first in what will become a tradition of stimulating exhibitions of contemporary art. The goal of the *Biennial* is to present an enlightening cross-section of the best work produced during the past two years by artists who have spent all or part of their time in Maine . . . What emerges is a view of Maine as a creative touchstone for a local, regional, and national community of artists."[52] The Biennials have included few works by Portland artists or of Portland subjects but rather by artists across the state who are engaged in a diverse media and approaches to art; they have established a connection between a Portland art institution and artists/art movements outside the state and region, just as the Portland Society of Art exhibitions evolved in the early twentieth century to include local, regional, and national artists.

The Portland Museum of Art's position between history and the contemporary, between past and present, is embodied in the physical structure of its most recent building. The Charles Shipman Payson Building, designed by Henry N. Cobb of I. M. Pei and Partners and opened to the public in 1983, is both modern and traditional, similar to late-twentieth-century museum buildings across the United States but grounded in local vernacular architecture (Figure 6-24).[53] While the Payson Building's clean, geometric surfaces and large glass windows draw from modern architectural practices, it also possesses materials—brick, granite, pine—common in Maine and in the warehouses and commercial buildings of the Old Port and the Federal mansions along High and State streets near the Museum. The architect planned the building as an extension of the McLellan House and the Sweat Galleries: the red brick, round arches, and granite lintels of the façade speak the language of nineteenth-century neoclassical architecture in Portland and the Museum's earlier structures. Moving through the galleries in the Payson Building, visitors are brought in touch with the city's past. They can look out porthole-like windows onto the rooftops and down to the Fore River just as the original owners of the McLellan House would have gazed out from their second-story Palladian window to inspect their ships docked on the river wharves. Staircase landings, cylindrical in form and with floor to ceiling windows, frame views of High Street, with its brick houses and sidewalks. This architectural feature, along with octagonal clerestories that bring natural light into the galleries, refer to the viewing decks of the region's lighthouses—not least of which is the octagonal Portland Observatory.

Nearly visible from the Payson Building's windows is the Museum of African Culture (formerly called the Museum of African Tribal Art), founded in 1998 to "educate others about the lives and beliefs of Sub-Saharan African people, to interpret and preserve a unique collection of African art and artifacts, and to enrich the communities of Maine and beyond through the celebration of diversity."[54] Co-founded by Oscar Mokeme and Arthur Aleshire, this two-room museum is the only one in New England dedicated exclusively to Sub-Saharan African tribal arts. For Mokeme, the Museum's collection of fifteen thousand objects, which includes carved masks, textiles, and bronze figures from Ethiopia, Zaire, Zimbabwe, Nigeria, and West Africa, "preserve the religious and cultural legacy of Africa that is fast disappearing in a globalized world." Evidence of the diversity of Portland, the Museum helps new immigrants from Somalia and the Sudan maintain connections with their homeland and its cultural traditions as well as teach Mainers about African art and culture.[55]

The Museum of African Culture redefines how we see local art; at the same time, it reminds us that Portland and Portland art have been historically linked to locales far beyond Casco Bay. Local painters and sculptors were part of national and international art networks as they exhibited in Boston and New York and traveled to Europe for art education; one of the most highly recognized Portland artists, Franklin Simmons, spent much of his career in his studio in Rome. As David Carey points out in his essay, Portland artists William Frederick Chadwick and Franklin Stanwood produced landscapes based on their travels to the

Figure 6-24. Portland Museum of Art, Charles Shipman Payson Building. Designed by Henry N. Cobb. Photo by Brian Vanden Brink.

West Indies and Latin America, and Cuban-born artist Antoine Dorticos became a life member of the Portland Society of Art in 1887. Art and artifacts from locales connected to Portland's international trade were, at least on one occasion, displayed in the city. Charles Codman had a "museum of curiosities" in his Portland studio, which consisted of "African spears, clubs, idols, elephants' tusks, and other articles, presented by Mr. [Thomas R.] Hayes, who . . . made several voyages to the coast [of Africa]. These articles were afterwards transferred to the old Portland museum in 'Haymarket Row,' and finally destroyed by fire."56

The place of these international connections in Portland art has taken on new significance in recent years with the exhibition program at the Institute of Contemporary Art at the Maine College of Art. Once associated with the Portland Society of Art (and the Portland Museum of Art), the ICA at MECA defines its mission as presenting "leading-edge exhibitions and public programs that showcase new perspectives and new trends in contemporary art." In the past decade, it has brought the Portland art scene, MECA's art students and faculty, and local artists into a wider global culture, as in the exhibitions of photographs by Iké Udé, a Nigerian-born artist working in New York, and the installations of Wenda Gu, a Chinese artist working in Brooklyn.57 As Mark H. C. Bessire, former ICA director, has explained, "Only recently have Western art institutions begun to recognize and display [the art of so-called marginalized countries like South Africa, Brazil, and Cuba] once thought of as merely of regional interest. The global economy, international media, and the Internet, which break down cultural and national boundaries, have also contributed to the globalization of art."58 While the ICA does not ignore Portland or Maine artists, it redefines the local and regional, in exhibitions like *Quiet in the Land: Everyday Life, Contemporary Art and the Shakers* (a collaboration of contemporary artists and Shakers); *Steel Walls/Waterlines* (1999) (Rez Williams's paintings offering new ways of seeing the fishing boat and culture of the region); and *William Pope.L: The Friendliest Black Artist in America* (2002) (the objects, street performances, and installations of a Maine artist who deconstructs assumptions about blackness and whiteness). Local art is defined beyond the usual frames—beyond easel painting, lighthouses, and picturesque coastal scenes, outside the commercial culture, and linked to art worlds beyond the Maine border.

Institutions like the ICA, Portland Museum of Art, and the Museum of African Culture, along with public art, portraits, and landscape painting, have defined—and continue to define—Portland's identity, its current values and its historical legacy. The Portland that has been created through these art objects and institutions is a Portland that possesses multiple identities. Established by elite Yankees who inhabited early portraits, it was (and is) a city populated by diverse immigrant groups and classes who appear in portrait photographs and are commemorated in public murals and monuments in the twentieth and twenty-first centuries. Following ever-changing artistic styles and theories, artists have reimagined the city over time although certain Portlands appear again and again. One of these is the Portland grounded in its natural environment and geography—as represented in Codman's Deering Oaks, Beckett's harbor from Munjoy Hill, Homer's Prouts Neck, and the more recent Boothby Square project. Even as

Portland was represented in such works as a premodern paradise where nature dominates, images of the city were engaged in advancing modernization—tourism, industry, and commerce. Portland art cannot be understood separate from these larger social contexts. The globalization that defines early twenty-first-century culture is already having an impact on the visual arts in Portland, with the establishing of a city-run public art project designed to preserve local distinctiveness and a new art exhibition program at the ICA that connects the city with the regional cultures around the world. It remains to be seen how Portland as place will be re-fashioned in this new context and how a new balance will be achieved between the contemporary and historical, the modern and traditional, in Portland art.

Notes

I would like to thank Matthew Deschaine and Duncan Dwyer, my research assistants; Caroline Eyler, Patricia Finn, Polly Kauffman, and Jan Piribeck of the University of Southern Maine; Aimée Bessire and Cindy Foley of Maine College of Art; Christine Albert, William D. Barry, Holly Hurd-Forsyth, John Mayer, and Stephanie Philbrick of the Maine Historical Society; Earle G. Shettleworth Jr. of the Maine Historic Preservation Commission; Oscar Mokeme of the Museum of African Culture; Alice Spencer, chair of the Portland Public Art Committee; Kirsten Hammerstrom of the Rhode Island Historical Society; and Michael K. Fortunato, postmaster of the U.S. Post Office, Portland, Maine. I extend my special gratitude to Jessica Nicoll, chief curator at the Portland Museum of Art, for her time and invaluable assistance with this project.

1. Marsden Hartley Papers, Yale Collection of American Literature, Beinecke Rare Book and Manuscript Library, Yale University.

2. Elizabeth Mankin Kornhauser, ed., *Marsden Hartley* (Hartford, Conn.: Wadsworth Atheneum Museum of Art, and New Haven: Yale University Press, 2003), 324.

3. Edward J. Nygren, *Views and Visions: American Landscape before 1830* (Washington, D.C.: Corcoran Gallery of Art, 1986), 112.

4. John Neal, *Portland Illustrated* (Portland: W. S. Jones, 1874), 68.

5. Timothy Dwight, *Travels in New England and New York* (1821), vol. 2, Barbara Miller Solomon, ed. (Cambridge, Mass.: Belknap Press of Harvard University Press, 1969), 142.

6. Frank H. Goodyear, Jr., *American Paintings in the Rhode Island Historical Society* (Providence: Rhode Island Historical Society, 1974), 36–37.

7. *Eastern Argus,* 8 August 1820. This article and others from early nineteenth-century Portland newspapers have been transcribed in "Artists at Portland, Maine 1784–1835," compiled for the Portland Museum of Art by William David Barry, 1976.

8. Dona Brown, *Inventing New England: Regional Tourism in the Nineteenth Century* (Washington, D.C.: Smithsonian Institution Press, 1996), 41–74.

9. Neal, *Portland Illustrated,* 88.

10. See Jessica Nicoll, *Charles Codman: The Landscape of Art and Culture in Nineteenth-Century Maine* (Portland, Maine: Portland Museum of Art, 2002), and Jessica Skwire, *A Treasured Heritage: The Art and History of Great Diamond Island* (Portland, Maine: Portland Museum of Art, 1997).

11. Herbert Adams, "Deering Oaks," in Theo H. B. M. Holtwijk and Earle G. Shettleworth Jr., eds., *Bold Vision: The Development of the Parks of Portland, Maine* (West Kennebunk, Maine: Phoenix Publishing, 1999), 75–78.

12. Betty Ring, *Girlhood Embroidery: American Samplers and Pictorial Needlework,* vol. 1 (New York: Knopf, 1993), 261.

13. Elaine Ward Casazza, *The Brushians* (Limington, Maine: privately published, 1996) and Earle G. Shettleworth Jr., *Charles Frederick Kimball 1831–1903: Painting Portland's Legacy* (Portland, Maine: Portland Museum of Art, 2003).

14. *Twenty-First Exhibition,* Portland Society of Art, December 1892, and *Spring Exhibition,* Portland Society of Art, 13–25 April 1910.

15. Bruce Robertson, *Reckoning with Winslow Homer: His Late Paintings and Their Influence* (Cleveland: Cleveland Museum of Art, and Bloomington: Indiana University Press, 1990), 50.

16. See Skwire, *A Treasured Heritage: The Art and History of Great Diamond Island.*

17. John K. Moulton, *An Informal History of Four Islands: Cushing, House, Little Diamond, Great Diamond* (Yarmouth, Maine: privately published, 1991), 5–21.

18. William S. Sargent, *An Historical Sketch, Guide Book, and Prospectus of Cushing's Island* (New York: American Photo-Engraving Company, 1886), 64–66.

19. Neal, *Portland Illustrated,* 55–56.

20. *Fifty-Eight Maine Paintings 1820–1920: Selections from the Collection of Mr. and Mrs. Walter M. Jeffords, Jr.* (Portland, Maine: Portland Museum of Art, 20 May–10 June 1976), 7.

21. "John Bundy Brown," in *Biographical Encyclopedia of Maine of the Nineteenth Century* (Boston, 1885), 207–08, Harrison Bird Brown file, Portland Museum of Art.

22. "Brown," in *Biographical Encyclopedia of Maine,* 207–08, and George F. Bacon, *Portland: Its Representative Business Men and Its Points of Interest* (Newark, N.J.: Glenwood Publishing, 1891), both in Brown file, Portland Museum of Art. On the Forest City Sugar Refinery, see Neal, *Portland Illustrated,*

46; *Portland Business Directory and Business Man's Guide* (Portland: B. Thurston and Co., 1868); and *Portland Directory and Reference Book, with a Business Directory Attached* (Portland: B. Thurston and Co., 1879), 357.

23. Martin Dibner, ed., *Portland* (Portland, Maine: Greater Portland Landmarks, 1986), 37.

24. *Portland Atlas* (1871) and *Portland, Maine* (New York: Sanborn Map and Publishing Co., 1877), plate 11.

25. Angela Miller, *The Empire of the Eye: Landscape Representation and American Cultural Politics, 1825–1875* (Ithaca, N.Y., and London: Cornell University Press, 1993), 137–65.

26. *2003 Portland Museum of Art Biennial* (Portland, Maine: Portland Museum of Art, 2003), 44.

27. Carolyn Eyler, *Back Cove, Heart of Portland* (Portland, Maine: Area Gallery, University of Southern Maine, 10 May–12 October 2001).

28. Eleanor G. Ames, "Back Cove and Baxter Boulevard," in Holtwijk and Shettleworth, eds., *Bold Vision*, 94–106.

29. Carrie Rebora, et al., *John Singleton Copley in America* (New York: Metropolitan Museum of Art, distributed by New York: Harry N. Abrams, 1995).

30. *Portland Advertiser,* 12 January 1827, quoted in Susanna Paine entry, *Portland Reflections* (Portland, Maine: Portland Museum of Art, 1977), n.p. Also see Susanna Paine, *Roses and Thorns, or Recollections of an Artist* (Providence, R.I.: B. T. Albro, Printer, 1854).

31. John Monroe, "Introduction: The Polished Silver Plate," in *First Light: The Dawn of Photography in Maine* (Portland: Maine Historical Society, 1999), 4–5, 7–8.

32. Melissa Dabakis, "Gendered Labor: Norman Rockwell's *Rosie the Riveter* and the Discourse of Wartime Womanhood," in Barbara Melosh, ed., *Gender and American History Since 1890* (London and New York: Routledge, 1993), 182–203.

33. Quoted in Henry S. Burrage, "Franklin Simmons, Sculptor," in *Maine Historical Memorials* (Augusta: State of Maine, 1922), 128.

34. Nova Seals, "New England and the Sea: Representations of Maritime Identity and Heritage" (M.A. thesis, University of Southern Maine, 2004), 20–26, and Earle G. Shettleworth Jr., "Introduction," in William B. Jordan Jr., *Our Lady of Victories: A History of the Portland Soldiers and Sailors Monument* (Portland, Maine: Greater Portland Landmarks, 1998), 4–5.

35. Marlene Park and Gerald E. Markowitz, *Democratic Vistas: Post Offices and Public Art in the New Deal* (Philadelphia: Temple University Press, 1984).

36. Karal Ann Marling, *Wall-to-Wall America: A Cultural History of Post-Office Murals in the Great Depression* (Minneapolis: University of Minnesota Press, 1982), 272–82.

37. Permission from the federal government was not given to replace Tracy's mural with Grant's; see Marling, *Wall-to-Wall America,* 281.

38. Henry Mattson, quoted in Ernest W. Watson, *Twenty Painters and How They Work* (New York: Watson-Guptill, 1950), 82.

39. Herbert Adams, "Man Behind the Murals," *Portland Monthly Magazine* (September 1999), 25, and Park and Markowitz, *Democratic Vistas,* 212.

40. "Portland Postoffice Murals, Placed Saturday, Are Typical Maine Scenes," *Portland Sunday Telegram,* 7 November 1937, p. D20.

41. "Portland Postoffice Murals," p. D20.

42. Donna M. Cassidy, *Marsden Hartley: Race, Region, and Nation* (Hanover, N.H.: University Press of New England, 2005), 58–60, 65, and "Homer at Home," *Art Digest* 10 (July 1936): 29.

43. Also see Waldo Peirce's *Woodmen in the Woods of Maine* (1937), for the Westbrook Post Office, now in the Portland Museum of Art.

44. For information on the Portland Public Art Program, see Public Art Program, Planning Division, City of Portland, and its web site: *www.ci.portland.me.us/planning/publart.htm.*

45. See Bob Keyes, "Public Art: Money Well Spent?," *Maine Sunday Telegram,* 22 February 2004, pp. A1, A9, and "Is It Waves or Fountains at Boothby Square?" *Portland Press Herald,* 29 October 2003, pp. B1, B12.

46. Keyes, "Public Art: Money Well Spent?," pp. A1, A9.

47. Bob Keyes, "City to Unveil Square's 'Jewel Box,'" *Portland Press Herald,* 1 June 2004, pp. B1, B8, and "Bus Stop Seen as Landmark for City," *Portland Press Herald,* 3 December 2004, pp. B1, B6.

48. Ann S. Stephens, "Paintings and Painters," *Portland Magazine* 2 (1835): 253–55.

49. Portland Society of Art By-laws, 1884. This and all sources below on the Portland Society of Art are from the PSA files, Portland Museum of Art.

50. *Loan Exhibition,* Portland Society of Art, March 1905, p. 7.

51. *Thirty-Sixth Exhibition of Oils and Watercolors,* Portland Society of Art, L. D. M. Sweat Memorial Art Museum, Portland Maine, 24 April–13 May 1911, pp. 6, 10.

52. Daniel E. O'Leary, "Introduction," in *1998 Portland Museum of Art Biennial* (Portland, Maine: Portland Museum of Art, 1998), 3.

53. *In Celebration of the opening of the Charles Shipman Payson Building of the Portland Museum of Art, designed by Henry Nichols Cobb, I. M. Pei and Partners. Opened to the public 14 May 1983* (Portland, Maine: Portland Museum of Art, 1983). Also see Christine Temin, "To Portland and Beyond: 3 Maine Museums Offer New Wings, Works, and Wonders," *Boston Sunday Globe,* 19 August 1999, p. N6.

54. The Museum of African Tribal Art, mission statement.

55. The Museum of African Tribal Art, Educational Outreach package. Also see Pat Davidson Reef, "The Museum of Tribal Art," *Lewiston Sun Journal,* 30 April 1999, p. 7.

56. W. G., "Mr. Cox's African Trade: Supplementary," *Portland Daily Press,* Thursday, 9 March 1871.

57. Mark H. C. Bessire and Lauri Firstenberg, eds., *Beyond Decorum: The Photography of Iké Udé* (Cambridge, Mass.: MIT Press, 2000) and Mark H. C. Bessire, ed., *Wenda Gu: From Middle Kingdon to Biological Millennium* (Cambridge, Mass.: MIT Press, 2004).

58. Mark H. C. Bessire in "New Voices," *Art New England* (June/July 1999) 28.

7

Writing Portland

Literature and the Production of Place

Kent C. Ryden

As the essays in this collection amply demonstrate, Portland considered as a distinctive place has been constructed from a wide variety of elements: historical patterns and events, the presence of different social groups and their attendant cultures, art, architecture, and so on. That is, Portland is its people, their collective life, and the physical and visual world in which they have played out that life. But places are also made of words; part of what constitutes them is the stories that the people in a place tell themselves about themselves.[1] Many of these stories are oral, the informal narratives that Portlanders tell both old friends and newcomers about the personal events of their own lives in the city and the shared events that make up the high points in the collective understanding of local history. Oral narratives are ephemeral, though; written narratives are more lasting and provide a more permanent record of how Portlanders have understood the meanings of their city and conceived of their place in it. The literature of Portland grows out of writers' experience in Portland, the things they have done and heard there, and thus gives us a sense of the insider's view of the place, the sort of view that is rarely available to tourists visiting the Old Port or driving by on Interstate 95 on their way Downeast.

To think about "creating Portland," then, is to think about how the city has been built through words. At the same time, that phrase can take on another meaning if we see its first word as an adjective rather than as a verb: that is, Portland is a place that creates, a city that has had a lively if not voluminous or nationally renowned history of literary production. It is true that much of the literature that has been produced *in* Portland has not necessarily been *about* Portland, but those works have nonetheless given the city a certain cultural stamp, an identity which adds the production of books to the production of art and ships and seafood as an element of what has characterized the place over time. It is also true that writing and reading have always tended to be rather elite activities, so that Portland's literary aspect may not necessarily reflect the cultural and imaginative life of the city as a whole. Still, Portland's writers—or writers in any place, for that matter—strive for accuracy, getting down on paper the city's life and landscape as best they can, rendering place with fidelity to both their own memories and experiences and those of the local audience among which they hope to find an appreciative and approving readership. And even when writers have not focused on creating Portland in their works, Portland has created them as authors, so that their very lives and careers can be understood as expressions of place as well. This is a context in which we can understand Portland's distinctive literary history, a history that in turn frames the ways the city has been rendered in the pages of local authors.

Portland's print culture could not even begin until the arrival of the first printing press in 1785. Owned and operated by Thomas B. Wait of Boston and his Portland partner Benjamin Titcomb Jr., the first books that it produced were *The Universal Spelling Book* and Daniel George's *Almanac;* Wait and Titcomb also began publishing the city's first newspaper, the *Falmouth Gazette and Weekly Advertiser,* on 1 January 1785.[2] For many years thereafter, local literary production was characterized by works that were anything but local in focus, a state that was true of American print culture in general until well into the nineteenth century; as much printed matter was imported, "the literary" was still defined in terms of British models, American literary nationalism had not yet emerged as a cultural priority, and the reading of fiction was seen as an elitist and vaguely decadent activity. In 1801, for example, a total of eleven imprints came off Portland presses exclusive of newspapers: three orations, three almanacs, an ordination sermon, a treatise on double-entry bookkeeping, a pamphlet on cavalry exercises, the minutes of the Bowdoinham Baptists Association, and a broadside on the regulation of the mails. By 1811, a single printer, John McKown, printed twelve works: three sermons, editions of books on theology by Jonathan Edwards and Noah Webster, an edition of Asa Lyman's *The American Reader,* a religious magazine and two other religious works (one by Jonathan Witherspoon), the minutes of a Baptist association, an act to incorporate a society, and a miscellany by Eliza S. True "calculated to amuse the minds of youth without corrupting their morals."[3] During the years 1851 to 1853, only 223 imprints were published in Portland by a total of twenty-one printers and publishers, with most of those imprints being textbooks, minutes, reports, catalogs, laws and statutes, and proceedings of various societies. Two books of description and travel (neither local in focus) were produced during those years, along with two books of English poetry, one prose work, and no works of fiction.[4] For many years, then, while a steady supply of printed matter did emerge from Portland presses, the stream was little more than a thin trickle, and while Portlanders could stay well up to date on religious and political issues and plan their lives according to the strictures of almanacs, as people of their time they encountered little if anything that told them stories about who they were as residents of a distinctive and particular place.

While much of what was available to be read in early Portland spoke of other places (if of any place at all), newspapers and local histories have described and assessed the city much more thoroughly. Since the arrival of that first printing press, Portland has had a lively newspaper scene. From 1785 to 1835, a total of sixteen newspapers were published in Portland, some of them lasting less than a year, others remaining active for decades (such as the *Eastern Argus,* founded in 1803 and published continuously until 1921).[5] Even on the eve of the Civil War, Portland supported eleven newspapers, two dailies and nine weeklies; through consolidations and closings, the city was down to three papers by the 1920s, and supports only the *Portland Press Herald/Maine Sunday Telegram* today (as well as, in recent years, varying numbers of "alternative" weeklies). Newspapers in the nineteenth century tended to be intensely political, overtly and fiercely supporting particular parties and candidates and often being founded expressly to promote certain causes such as temperance and abolition.[6] Each one would therefore have constructed Portland in its own way, presenting the city through a particular ideological slant, making some elements of local life stand out more prominently than others through the stories that editors chose to include and exclude. A newspaper is a kind of lens or filter, letting certain aspects of Portland through into the reader's attention while leaving others out, refracting urban life so as to bring some parts of the city into sharp focus while others remain obscure, telling Portland stories about itself on a daily or weekly basis. For many years, however, those stories tended to be idiosyncratic and few: an early- to mid-nineteenth century paper was generally only four pages long, with many of its columns taken up by advertisements, and most news stories were statewide, national, or international in focus, often borrowed from other newspapers elsewhere through a vigorous process of exchange; no Portland papers employed reporters until the 1860s, and local items were included at the whim of (and collected and written by) the editor/publisher. The modern newspaper, with its daily section of local news, is a twentieth-century creation.

According to the *Portland City Guide* produced in 1940 by the Federal Writers' Program, "A small group of local historians have prepared valuable volumes on the city's early history," including Thomas Smith, Samuel Deane, Samuel Freeman, William Willis, Nathan Goold, and Augustus F. Moulton.[7] Local historians build places through words by the very nature of their work, choosing from among the many facts and events that have left written and material traces and weaving them together into a coherent interpretive story. True, many nineteenth-century histories often tended to be compendious more than selective, stuffed full of everything the historian could find rather than whittled down to a taut and coherent narrative or bundle of narratives; the result is often not a construction of place so much as an enormous warehouse of potential materials for such a construction. William Willis's *History of Portland* is a case in point. This book was first published in two volumes in 1831 and 1833 and then issued in a revised, enlarged, single-volume edition in 1865; the Maine Historical Society published a facsimile volume of this 928-page second edition in 1972. While each of Willis's chapters tends to have a specific focus, be it on religion, politics, or economic activity, the summary in the table of contents of his final chapter gives a sense of his eclectic and comprehensive approach: it covers "Miscellanies, Cumberland and Oxford canal, bridges, promenades, sugar-house, steamships, Board of trade, manufactures, academy and schools, library, Atheneum, authors, charitable societies, cemeteries, epidemics, change of government to a city, taxes, deaths and marriages, immigrants, population and character of the inhabitants, customs of the people at different periods, amusements, theatre, conclusion."[8] Willis's Portland is a dense and complex place, seemingly the sum total of everything that ever happened there; his approach does not take on the storytelling function that we associate with more conventionally "literary" fictional and nonfictional genres.

Portland has been a prominent site of literary production at times throughout its history, although the renown of its writers has tended to be local instead of regional or national, or locked in the past instead of carried forward into the present. Still, in their day figures like John Neal and Seba Smith, two of the writers whose names have still lasted to a degree in local literary tradition, were very well known as novelists or writers of literary sketches. The literary scholar Lawrence Buell offers one glimpse at the early nature of literary Portland, which was a productive place even if it never attained the stature of a Boston or a New York. In his compendious regional literary history *New England Literary Culture: From Revolution through Renaissance,* Buell ranks Portland with other towns like Hartford, New Haven, Litchfield, and Providence as a literary center in the years following national independence, noting that "By the second decade of the [nineteenth] century, it had a lively theater; two Congregational ministers of some literary note; two rival newspapers receptive to local literary talent . . . ; and a knot of young professionals who liked to write," including journalist-humorist Smith, novelist Neal, attorney Nathaniel Deering, and other writers whose names, unfortunately, likely mean nothing to modern Portland readers: Elizabeth Oakes Smith, Ann Stephens, Isaac McLellan, Joseph Holt Ingraham. By the 1820s and 30s, the city hosted several literary outlets as well, Neal's weekly newspaper the *Yankee* and Stephens's *Portland Magazine* being prominent among them. As was noted in the introduction to this book, Portland's active community of writers made a significant contribution to New England literature in the early nineteenth century, one that ranked the city near the cultural centers of Massachusetts in its literary production and impact. However, after the mid-1830s, most of the writers mentioned above had either moved to other cities or stopped writing. In the end, notes Buell, "it became increasingly clear that Portland would be remembered in literary history as little more than a point of origin."[9] And in addition to Portland's growing obscurity as a literary center, the writers who lived there did not often write about their home city, casting their attention and imagination into other, seemingly more fertile, fields, accomplishing in their works the same movement away from the provinces that they would later achieve by their changes of residence.

In an article surveying Maine fiction prior to 1840, Donald A. Sears concentrates on three prominent elements of and contributors to Portland's early literary scene: Neal; Sally Sayward Barrell Keating Wood, "Maine's first novelist," known as Madame Wood for her social prominence and aristocratic mien; and local writers of tales and sketches.[10] In Sears's analysis, Maine fiction in the early republic is

significant primarily insofar as it amounts to an American manifestation of English genres and models. Wood's novels, such as *Julia, and the
Illuminated Baron* (1800) and *Amelia: or, the Influence of Virtue* (1802)
are highly derivative of the gothic and sentimental fiction that would
have been available to the author (including works such as *Ormond,* by
the American Gothic novelist Charles Brockden Brown). The eccentric
Neal, whose novels tended to grow out of his wide-ranging personal
and philosophical opinions (his novel, *Keep Cool* [1817], for example,
"had been written to discourage duelling"), was something of a literary
nationalist, but he too dabbled in the gothic and in European romanticism. Moreover, even when he included New England settings in his fictional works, Portland (or local life and conditions in general) received
little if any of his attention. Perhaps his best-known novel, *Rachel Dyer*
(1828), remains in Sears's estimation "readable today . . . for the vivid,
dramatic recreations of the [witch] trial scenes at Salem." Even a novel
with the ostensibly locally derived title, *The Down-Easters* (1833), is
largely "a gothic novel conveying Godwinian ethics," although the
book's first half "is a sociological study in Yankee characteristics, man-
nerisms, and folkways. As such it is penetrating, accurate, and amus-
ing," and looks forward to Seba Smith's Yankee sketches about Major
Jack Downing of Downingville (to be discussed below).[11]

While his fiction looked beyond the city for its subject matter, Neal
made his biggest local mark in 1874 with his guidebook *Portland Illustrated,* a work that not only introduces the reader to the city's landmarks
and luminaries but also celebrates its unique advantages. "That Portland has never had justice, nor indeed, anything like justice done to her,
begins to be felt and acknowledged by pleasure-seekers and the great
business-world," he announces. "Her capabilities, advantages and resources are found to be absolutely surprising, when carefully investigated; so that, in giving an account of them, one can hardly avoid the
appearance of great exaggeration."[12] Undaunted, Neal moves onto offer
as complete a sketch of Portland life, culture, economy, institutions, and
social notables as he can, framing them all in a tone of praise and admiration: Portland is not simply a neglected city, but a rich and vital place
on a variety of levels.

Neal's nonfiction, then, considers Portland as a distinctive place
much more directly and deliberately than does his fiction, a generic distinction which seems true of Portland writers as a whole over time.
Sears does note that, by the 1830s, writers like Smith, Nathaniel Deering,

Ann Stephens, and Longfellow were "discovering the rich literary lode of their local scene"; however, their "local" tales tended to be set in fictionalized versions of smaller towns in Portland's hinterlands (Fryeburg for Stephens, Brunswick for Longfellow), and "these were no early local colorists; each writer exploited the Yankee resources in his own way and for his own purposes: Deering, for humor; Smith, for political satire; Stephens, for background to sentimental plots; Longfellow, as a point of departure for a tale á la Richter."[13] Portland fiction writers' dependence on existing, imported conventions and genres and their use of local scenes as a convenient means to larger, seemingly more important thematic ends precluded them from considering and getting down in words the distinctive experiences and shared narratives that made their burgeoning city into a singular New England place. The materials for such a consideration were all around them, but, looked at through the lens of literary convention and the marketplace, those materials remained invisible.

The 1940 *Portland City Guide* continues the roster of Portland literary talent down into the first four decades of the twentieth century, suggesting the continued liveliness of the local literary scene, its localized rather than regional or national scope, and its ongoing tendency to focus on scenes outside the city itself. From the perspective of 2005, most of the authors mentioned in the *Guide* are obscure, and their works are long out of print and in most cases not even available in libraries or held only in special collections, no longer circulating among readers in a local literary discourse. "Since the turn of the 20th [*sic*] century," the guide notes, "many writers of varying brilliance have flashed across the literary horizon of the city," but the *Guide*'s metaphor is more meaningful than its authors may have intended: flashing lights on the horizon, be they from fireworks or from meteors, do not provide lasting illumination.[14] Names such as Harrison Jewell Holt, Florence Brooks Whitehouse, Maurice Gardner, and Frances Wright Turner—not to mention the other thirty Portland writers active from 1900 to 1940 that the *Guide* covers—likely mean nothing today to any Portlanders other than specialists, antiquarians, and aficionados of local history and culture.

A conventional approach to literary history, then, gives the impression that Portland has hosted a vigorous if not extensive print culture, although the materials it has produced for creating a Portland through literature are somewhat thin. This is not to say that no writers have directly addressed Portland as a place, though; moreover, Portland has also been defined in certain ways through the manner in which it has traditionally functioned in Maine literature as a whole. In each of these cases, certain common themes and assessments occur, providing us with a Portland that is portrayed consistently both from within and without. At the same time, Portland emerges as a kind of contested space, a city whose meanings are argued over by insiders and outsiders in the pages of their books.

One important aspect of Portland's identity as expressed through literature derives from the city's perceived meaning relative to the rest of the state of Maine. As some other essays in this volume indicate, Portland has historically been seen in tension with, if not in opposition to, other areas of the state that have been viewed as embodying a more authentic sense of Maine identity. In a largely rural state, Portland has long been the largest city, the site of economic, political, and cultural power, a place believed to be more decadent and sophisticated than the hard-working, humble small towns of the hinterlands. In fact, "hinterlands" may be an inappropriate term to use in this context, as it implies that Portland is the center from which all other points in Maine are measured. When viewed through the lens of Maine literature, it is often Portland that emerges as the marginal anomaly, a place both geographically and conceptually on the fringes of what is understood to be the "real" Maine. In recent years, Portland (and southern Maine in general) has seen more and more suburban development and in-migration by people from other parts of New England, to the point where it is sometimes only semi-jokingly described as being in the outer ring of Boston suburbs. These trends have only served to exacerbate long-standing suspicions that, seen as a place, Portland is most meaningfully understood as being a sort of "not-Maine," a city where defining elements of state identity do not hold sway, a city that in fact provides a point of contrast by which those things that are seen to be distinctive about Maine are more clearly discerned and understood. And it is in literature that attempts to directly address questions of Maine identity that this concept of Portland as not-Maine is most pointedly enacted.

Broadly speaking, the literature of Maine identity has tended to follow one of two paths, both of them running deliberately through the small towns and rural spaces of the state. One has described the state as idyllic, pastoral, and premodern, removed both physically and culturally from the ills and stresses to be found in the nation's cities and industrial regions; if Maine is a marginal state in its geography and ways of life, that marginality is a virtue. This literary path begins as far back as the "Yankee" sketches of the early nineteenth century, runs through the small-town stories of writers like Harriet Beecher Stowe and Sarah Orne Jewett, and also animates the twentieth-century literature of rural retreat produced by essayists such as Henry Beston and E. B. White. Another prominent trend in Maine literature has also focused on the state's villages and out-of-the-way spaces but has examined them through a more realistic lens, finding in them a grittiness that may contradict the romanticism of other writers but, in a similar way, also contending that these places contain those aspects of Maine life that most accurately and authentically constitute a distinctive state identity. Jewett's sketches of Dunnet Landing in *The Country of the Pointed Firs* contain hints of economic decline and personal tragedy, but this vision of Maine gained its most vigorous expression in the twentieth century in, for example, the "Tilbury Town" poems of Edwin Arlington Robinson and the fiction of novelists like Ruth Moore, Carolyn Chute, and Cathie Pelletier. Significantly, both of these schools of literary thought skirt Portland deliberately, often mentioning it briefly only to dismiss it as distant, possibly corrupt, and ultimately irrelevant, a place that must be passed through in order to get to the "real" Maine. And even if a Maine writer does not address the presence of Portland directly, the city hovers implicitly over the text through its very absence, its understood status as not-Maine helping both writer and reader more clearly grasp how a particular work shapes and claims its definition of what the state of Maine truly is.

In 1830, for example, Seba Smith's fictional creation Major Jack Downing left his Downeast home of Downingville en route to Portland to sell "my load of ax handles, and mother's cheese, and cousin Nabby's bundle of footings," and in his first letter home he helps establish the literary reputation of the city as a place that stands at odds with the small towns of the state, repositories of good solid Yankee virtue and common sense. After spending some time wandering the city streets, he writes that "I've been here now a whole fortnight, and if I could tell you one half I've seen, I guess you'd stare worse than if you'd seen a catamount. I've been to meeting, and to the museum, and to both Legislaters, the one they call the House, and the one they call the Sinnet." The workings of the state legislature, still located in Portland at that point, leave him particularly bemused, as he finds its chambers a place where people engage in "some of the drollest carryins on that you ever heard of," mostly in the form of long-winded and pointless arguments.[15] From the perspective of this early literary Yankee, whatever his simple yet sensible home village is, Portland is not.

Major Jack inaugurated a still-vital trend in Maine literature, one that finds the home of real Mainers to be far beyond the Portland city limits and that contemplates Portland tangentially if at all. E. B. White, the longtime *New Yorker* and *Harper's* essayist who produced dozens of sketches about life in the environs of his adopted coastal home of North Brooklin, offers a particularly clear and emblematic instance of the exclusion of Portland from considerations of the meaning of Maine in a sentimental 1955 essay titled "Home-Coming." The authentic Maine, to him, is characterized by its decidedly non-urban coast: "the Maine man does not have to penetrate in depth to be excited by his coastal run: its flavor steals into his consciousness with the first ragged glimpse of properly textured woodland, the first whiff of punctually drained cove." The essay reflects White's ruminations on driving to North Brooklin from New York, but huge portions of his drive are excised from his (and the reader's) thoughts: he may "cross the Piscataqua and plunge rapidly into Maine at a cost of seventy-five cents in tolls," but our next view through White's windshield comes when, "five hours later, I dip down across the Narramissic and look back at the tiny town of Orland," where "the white spire of its church against the pale-red sky stirs me in away that Chartres never could." This stereotypical New England village scenery looms large in White's view of the state, as do other, deliberately non-urban elements of scenery. Maine is special precisely because of its distance from modernity: "Familiarity is the thing—the sense of belonging. It grants exemption from all evil, all shabbiness. A farmer pauses in the doorway of his barn and he is wearing the right boots. A sheep stands under an apple tree and it wears the right look, and the tree is hung with puckered frozen fruit of the right color."[16] To have stopped in Portland, with its dense urban fabric, its railroads and bustling waterfront, could only have compromised White's defining sense of Maine as a world apart, and thus he stands for other romantic writers who imaginatively excise the city from their understanding of state identity.

Not all Maine writers have worked in this romantic vein, but even contemporary realists have staked a claim for Maine identity that relies, implicitly or explicitly, on contrasting far-flung small towns with the metropolis and making Portland suffer by the comparison. In 1989, novelist Carolyn Chute published an essay called "The Other Maine" which, in its title alone, deliberately locates an authentic state identity in places like her home town of Parsonsfield, which take on meaning pre-cisely because of their difference from places like Portland. She makes a virtue of the often rough circumstances of the rural working class: "My people here in this town have beautiful eyes, beautiful hands—espe-cially the hands—some hands scarred by work, some not . . . What is also wonderful here is our homes," where "Lots of us have assorted use-ful stuff around our yards—tractors, tractor parts, truck tires, wooden skids, plastic industrial pails, rolled up chicken wire, treehouses (the lopsided kind made by kids), old cars, old appliances." She contrasts this scene with the lifestyles embraced by Maine newcomers who are chang-ing the state, particularly its southern precincts, presumably moved by tourism ads: these people are "strangers that look like the ads, living life as it should be, nothing useful piled around their yards, nothing, just the two or three or four glossy cars." Such people, Chute concludes, "are un-touchable, unknowable, artificial, dangerous," and when read in this context, a novel like Chute's 1985 *The Beans of Egypt, Maine* stands as a portrait of the "real" Maine and a defense of the state's small towns against the advancing greater-Portland juggernaut.[17]

Even Maine literature that does not take as its purpose the state-defining mission of a Smith or a White or that lacks the political edge of a Chute often seems to partake of this sense of Portland as not-Maine, of this implicit understanding that writing a good Maine novel requires getting your characters out of the city. Cathie Pelletier's series of comic novels about the extended MacKinnon clan in the far-northern Maine hamlet of Mattagash—*The Funeral Makers, Once Upon a Time on the Banks,* and *The Weight of Winter*—make antic fun of the problems and limitations inherent in living at, literally, the end of the road; but her characters have a sort of tough integrity lacking in those feckless Mac-Kinnons who have relocated to Portland, with their substance abuse, their bumbling adultery, and their hapless inadequacy to local conditions when they return to Mattagash on their infrequent visits. Van Reid's on-going series of "Moosepath League" novels, which combine historical fiction with a lightly comic tone and a picaresque structure, show an in-formed appreciation of the richness of turn-of-the-twentieth-century Portland; to take a representative example, the first book in the series, *Cordelia Underwood* (1998), takes its main characters in its first pages to Portland's Custom House Wharf, which "was a place of steady com-motion in the worst of weather; but on such a day as the 2nd of July, 1896—when the sun was strong enough to warrant a parasol for strolling

ladies, and the sea breeze brisk enough to suggest a shawl—sightseers
and ship spotters, brightly dressed sweethearts and gallant beaus, sailors, shoremen, lads, swags, and lollygaggers made of the great quay a
swarm of movement and sound."[18] After evoking Portland's landscape,
weather, and rich social world, though, Reid soon puts his characters on
the road to meet adventures in such seemingly more interesting or fic-
tionally appropriate places as Freeport, Boothbay Harbor, Damaris-
cotta, and Ellsworth—the kinds of Maine locations, in fact, that figure
prominently today in many tourist itineraries.

While this discussion has taken in only a few Maine writers of the
past and present, they indicate several key strands of a long-standing literary practice in the state: to write as a self-consciously "Maine writer,"
or even to be perceived as such a writer, has consistently meant writing
about places other than Portland. When we think about Portland as a
place constructed through literature, then, we must take into account
literature produced about the state as a whole, and this literature indicates a long-standing interpretation of Portland as a city defined in
terms of what it is not—it is not rural or pastoral, it is not virtuous and
"Yankee" in character, it is above all not representative of Maine. For
better or for worse, it is a place unto itself.

Authors who write from within Portland rather than assessing it
critically from without, on the other hand, have always told a different
story. For these writers, particularly those working in the genres of memoir and fictionalized autobiography, Portland's being a place unto itself is its greatest virtue: it is a complete and sustaining world, one in
which their identities are so deeply rooted that to contemplate the city is
to contemplate themselves. Every person's experience and memories of
Portland will be different, of course, so that the particular components
of an author's sense of place will be as unique and distinctive as the
course of his or her individual life. And yet many writers who focus deliberately on the city and their relationship to it, despite how varied
those portrayals are, consistently highlight one theme: Portland is an
idealized community, as rich and authentic and Maine-like as White's
North Brooklin or Smith's Downingville, not socially or morally different from them in any meaningful way. One could say that these writers
reverse the polarity of the many portrayals of Portland as not-Maine,
turning a negative perception into a positive one. Unlike the works
mentioned above, however, literary representations of Portland do not
bother to define the city through a contrast with other parts of Maine,

to establish its character by virtue of its superiority to a rural periphery lacking in key cultural qualities. Other writers may look askance at Portland, but Portland writers look around themselves and approve of what they see, feeling no need to project their vision any further. Their city, and their lives within that city, provide ample material for their minds and pens to work on.

There is no established canon of literature about Portland; indeed, most writing focused on the city, particularly recent writing, has been published by small presses in Portland or elsewhere in Maine, and its circulation has tended to be quite local and often ephemeral. A book's lack of national or regional renown, however, does not mean that its contents are somehow deficient in their perceptions and portrayals of the city, that if the author were a better wordsmith or a more discerning observer of life the book would have found a more prestigious publisher. In fact, an author's publishing and circulating a book largely within the Portland community is a good indicator of its perceived authenticity and fidelity to local understandings about the city: the work is produced by an insider for other insiders, an exacting set of readers who are highly likely to disapprove if the author gets something wrong or somehow disrupts and jars their own senses of place. While some of the books touched on here may be obscure if not out of print altogether—in contrast to the portrayals of Portland as not-Maine mentioned above, all of which are readily available from high-profile publishers for a national audience eager to consume images of the "real" Maine—they collectively offer a glimpse of Portland seen through local eyes, a view that is appreciative, often affectionate, fine-grained in its detail, and expressive of a rich world of feeling and experience and belonging.

To take one example, John Preston's essays about gay life and issues, many of them drawn from his experiences and observations in his adopted home town of Portland, appeared in many publications in New England and beyond. After his death, some of his short pieces were collected and published under the title *Winter's Light: Reflections of a Yankee Queer*, a book that offers a glimpse of his sense of place as a gay man in this small city. In an essay titled "Portland, Maine: Life's Good Here," he recalls his itinerant life in his college years and beyond, a period during which he lived in a number of large American cities in turn—Chicago, Boston, Philadelphia, New York, Los Angeles, San Francisco—on the assumption that only in these places could a gay man live comfortably and find a sense of community. As he began to question this assumption and to feel the need to live in a smaller and quieter city, he chose to settle in Portland; moreover, as a native of Massachusetts, Preston still felt a bond of identity with New England and wanted to return to a place "where I understood how people thought" and "where I understood their accents."[19] As he settled into the city and became a prominent local voice on gay issues, he found himself buoyed by the strong sense of community that he saw developing, in which gay men and lesbians looked out for each other, read each other's writing, organized and attended lectures, and worked together for political change. This sense of shared life combined with the cultural bond he felt with Portland as a part of New England, he came to realize, was something he could not find in the other places where he had lived; in this case, Portland takes on meaning not by comparison with the rest of Maine but with the rest of the country. When friends ask if Preston is going to return to New York, he replies, "No. Life's good here."[20]

At the same time, Preston's sense of belonging extends beyond his identity as a gay man and embraces the Portland community as a whole. In an essay titled "A New England Chorus," he ruminates again on how his move to Portland amounted to an attempt to regain the lost sense of community that he remembered from his small-town New England childhood. Preston rediscovers this feeling of mutuality, of a shared sense of self and world view, in his neighborhood barbershop, a place he likens to "the finest New England institution, the town meeting. Everyone is a citizen in a barbershop."[21] While Preston's sexuality was no secret, to his friends awaiting haircuts he was just John, a fellow participant in discussions about cars (he buys a Buick instead of a Volvo in deference to their sensibilities), local events, and the vagaries of the Boston Red Sox. When Preston was diagnosed with HIV, his friends at the shop offered their quiet but firm support. In the end, he felt no real difference between himself and them; on the contrary, he embraced a common membership in a social world that both pre-existed him and welcomed him. "This chorus of New England men narrates an important part of my identity, and their collective voice is so strong that I have stopped fighting it. I sink into it. This is the beginning for me. I start here."[22] While Preston's essays do not ignore incidents of homophobia and the rise of AIDS—as a gay man, his felt experience of place contained pain and anger as well as affection—he suggests, in the end, that he has found as good a place to live as possible, a real community in which his New England identity re-roots itself swiftly and firmly.

    While a writer like Preston constructs Portland as a place through the lens of immediate experience, others do so through the haze of retrospect; if Portland is a good place to be an adult, it was an even better place to be a child, as two backward glances from 120 years apart suggest. In 1884, Edward Elwell published *The Boys of Thirty-Five: A Story of a Seaport Town*, a fictionalized memoir of his childhood in a city here rendered as "Landsport." His town "boasted of having the best harbor on the Atlantic coast" and was "a bustling village" engaged busily in the West Indian trade.²³ The book's fourteen chapters recount a series of what a modern reader might think of as Tom Sawyer–style adventures, in which narrator Harry Ingersoll and his neighborhood gang engage in mock battles with boys from other parts of town, gingerly cross the wintertime ice to Peaks Island, celebrate the Fourth of July, get invited aboard a merchant ship, and generally amuse themselves all over town. The book offers a detailed portrait of the Portland peninsula of the early nineteenth century, rendered through the boisterous perspectives and priorities of American boyhood. The world looks and feels different to children than it does to adults, and Elwell's Portland is an Edenic world of friendship and exploration from which adulthood amounts to a fall from grace. In the book's epilogue, Harry is traveling through the California mining country and comes across one of his old playmates, Tim, who grills him on the whereabouts of the old gang and the changes that the city has witnessed. Upon hearing about one change too many, Tim vows never to go back; his sense of place is so firmly fixed in the past that having it challenged by present reality is too painful to contemplate. When he learns that the Observatory is still standing, though, he softens: " 'I'd go back just to see that, and Diamond Cove.' His voice wavered a little, and I thought I saw a tear gathering in his eye, but it disappeared in one of the customary twitches of his countenance."²⁴ It is not unusual for adults to idealize the places of their childhoods, and Elwell links that sense of nostalgia to a realistically rendered past cityscape; his boyhood is a specifically *Portland* boyhood. What a writer like Preston finds in the barbershop, Elwell calls forth from memory, each locating an idealized community in the same (albeit changed) geographical space.
    Elwell was probably better known among the general public for the several editions of his guidebook *Portland and Vicinity* that he published in the 1870s and 1880s; *The Boys of Thirty-Five*, for all its geographical specificity, stands firmly within the genre of what today would be called young adult fiction. There is another genre that constructs

place much more deliberately and directly than fiction, however realistic—indeed, for which place is its very purpose. This is the sort of book that seems easy to find in any small city: the locally published "backward glance" by an amateur author—episodic, impressionistic, aimed at giving readers the flavor of the past, designed to celebrate and certainly not to criticize. Among many examples, a book like Howard C. Reiche Jr.'s 2002 *Closeness: Memories of Mrs. Munjoy's Hill* might be seen as representative in tone, in substance, and in its function as a sort of personal testimony of place. It is difficult to self-consciously address the characteristics of a city or neighborhood when one is immersed in it daily; only with the distance of time or space can a place become an object of contemplation. Looking back on his Depression-era childhood in the working-class neighborhood of Munjoy Hill, Reiche notes that at the time "I didn't think it was different, or special, or that there were a whole bunch of people who lived and fit together quite smoothly. I never analyzed it, or thought about it. I just went along with the flow and lived it. Only when I think back does its uniqueness begin to surface." And here too, the neighborhood's salient characteristic is the way it functioned as a community, a small Maine town within a larger city. "Everyone knew everyone. Neighbors knew what was going on with their neighbors and pitched in when help was needed, knowing their time of need might be just around the corner." Neighbors and local tradesmen functioned as an "extended family" which supervised children and kept them from getting in too much trouble.[25] The facts contained in the author's reminiscences seem less important than the tone, the affective timbre of the remembered neighborhood. Place is felt as much as experienced; its stories carry with them an emotional freight that shapes memory and guides the selection of events from which public constructions of place are built. In a book likely not read by many people who do not have some past or present connection to Munjoy Hill, the shared emotional surface of the neighborhood among those who love it both shapes how it is portrayed and ensures the acceptance of that portrayal.

Place-based memoirs like Reiche's are a staple of small local publishers, and collectively they constitute a literary mosaic of sorts, an assortment of individual visions and experiences that, when the viewer stands back from them, constitute a unified picture, a common sense of what the city has meant to its residents. The individual tiles of that mosaic may vary in shape and color and texture, but all present Portland as a richly sustaining community, and all tend to focus on the unremarkable and everyday rather than the prominent and epochal. Philip Candelmo, in a book called *Shifting Tides: Memoirs of an Ordinary Man*, notes that "In the grand scheme of things, I will leave no enduring legacy to the world at large," and yet "I was able to transform an ordinary life into something that produced more than ordinary results," primarily in the depth of his friendships and the satisfactions of his family life.26 In this memoir, place is defined by people, by the bonds of affection and emotion that give life form and meaning. Similarly, Ann Allen Brahms's *The Key Is Under the Flowerpot* is a story about family as much as about place and self, if the three terms are even distinguishable from one another: in looking back on her life, a life defined by relationships to friends and relatives many of whom are no longer alive, she attempts "to try to capture a small part of a world that no longer exists."27 Neither of these books or the many other books like them are remarkable for their content, but that is precisely the point: they may be uniquely personal narratives, individual attempts to outline the felt experience of place, but they are also universal, instances of the sorts of stories and memories that fill the heads of many other Portlanders. In linking landscape and identity and history and experience and memory, books like these exemplify the everyday understanding of Portland as a meaningful place that city residents see everywhere when they look around themselves.

Portland has served as a setting for fiction as well, of course, even if no one has yet produced anything that might be considered the Great Portland Novel. Such productions range from youth-oriented seaport adventure tales like James Otis's 1909 *The Sarah Jane, Dicky Dalton, Captain: A Story of Tugboating in Portland Harbor* to Phyllis Knight's 1994 lesbian detective novel *Shattered Rhythms: A Lil Ritchie Mystery* and Brent Askari's 1999 slice-of-confused-young-woman's-life novel *Not Ready for Prime Time*. Works like these often simply use the city as a stage set for characters and activities that could just as easily have been located elsewhere, or confirm the presence of the waterfront as a prominent component of Portland's imaginative landscape. Askari's twenty-two-year-old protagonist Justine Nichols, though, makes a comment about Portland that, in one way or another, could stand for anyone who has written about the city as a positive and sustaining place:

I live in Portland, Maine, and I love the place.

I love Portland's red-brick buildings and clapboard houses, the salty smell of the Atlantic blowing through the streets, its mix of being semicosmopolitan and a working port at the same time, and the way the sun ducks below the pines and melts into the ocean . . .

I have an affinity for people who are characters. In elementary school, I was drawn to the kids who were different. Most kids enjoyed doing things in groups, but what I liked was talking to the kid sitting at the far edge of the playground, away from all the slides and swings, the kid who was mumbling to herself, playing with a twig like it was a doll or a rocket ship while all the other kids were playing dodgeball. I wanted to kneel down and ask her what she was saying to her twig, I wanted to know where her rocket ship came from and where it was heading.

Portland is that kid.[28]

While Portland's writers may not share Justine's sense of the city's idiosyncrasy, they would all agree that it is a unique place, well worth listening to. Not all the literature produced in Portland has taken the city as its subject, but when writers have chosen to focus on the ground beneath their feet and the social and cultural world around them, they have amply demonstrated that Portland is indeed a "character"—both an interesting object of contemplation and a central, shaping presence in their books and in their lives.

Notes

1. For more on the concept of the sense of place, particularly insofar as it is expressed and perpetuated by narrative means, see Kent C. Ryden, *Mapping the Invisible Landscape: Folklore, Writing, and the Sense of Place* (Iowa City: University of Iowa Press, 1993).

2. Writer's Program of the Work Projects Administration, *Portland City Guide* (Portland: Forest City Printing Company, 1940), 150, 169.

3. For this and other information on the producers and products of Portland's early print culture (as well as that of other early American towns and cities where printed matter was generated), readers may consult the standard reference works on the subject: Charles Evans, *American Bibliography* (New York: Peter Smith, 1941–1959), and Ralph R. Shaw, *American Bibliography: A Preliminary Checklist for 1801–1819* (New York: Scarecrow Press, 1958–1983).

4. Marie Fischmeister, "Checklist of Portland, Maine, Imprints for the Years 1851–1853" (M.A. Thesis, Catholic University of America, 1966), 104–05.

5. See William B. Jordan, *Index to Portland Newspapers: 1785–1835* (Bowie, Maryland: Heritage Books, 1994).

6. For more on the culture of colonial and nineteenth-century American journalism, see, for example, Charles E. Clark, *The Public Prints: The Newspaper in Anglo-American Culture, 1665–1740* (New York: Oxford University Press, 1994); William Huntzicker, *The Popular Press, 1833–1865* (Westport, Conn.: Greenwood Press, 1999); and David Paul Nord, *Communities of Journalism : A History of American Newspapers and Their Readers* (Urbana: University of Illinois Press, 2001).

7. *Portland City Guide*, 159.

8. William Willis, *The History of Portland* (1865; Reprint, Somersworth, N.H.: New Hampshire Publishing Company, and Portland: Maine Historical Society, 1972), viii.

9. Lawrence Buell, *New England Literary Culture: From Revolution Through Renaissance* (Cambridge, U.K.: Cambridge University Press, 1986), 29–30.

10. Donald A. Sears, "Maine Fiction Before 1840: A Microcosm," *Colby Library Quarterly* 14:3 (1978), 109.

11. Sears, 116–18.

12. John Neal, *Portland Illustrated* (Portland, Maine: W. S. Jones, 1874), 3.

13. Sears, 120–22.

14. *Portland City Guide*, 161.

15. Seba Smith, *The Select Letters of Major Jack Downing* (1834; Reprint, Upper Saddle River, N.J.: Literature House/Gregg Press, 1970), 4, 7.

16. E. B. White, "Home-Coming," in *The Essays of E. B. White* (New York: Harper and Row, 1977), 9.

17. Carolyn Chute, "The Other Maine," in *The Quotable Moose: A Contemporary Maine Reader*, Wesley McNair, ed. (Hanover, N.H.: University Press of New England, 1994), 228–29.

18. Van Reid, *Cordelia Underwood; or, The Marvelous Beginnings of the Moosepath League* (New York: Viking, 1998), 9.

19. John Preston, *Winter's Light: Reflections of a Yankee Queer* (Hanover, N.H.: University Press of New England, 1995), 24.

20. Preston, 30.

21. Preston, 151.

22. Preston, 159.

23. Edward Henry Elwell, *The Boys of Thirty-Five: A Story of a Seaport Town* (Boston: Lee and Shepard, 1884), 9–10.

24. Elwell, 254.

25. Howard C. Reiche Jr., *Closeness: Memories of Mrs. Munjoy's Hill* (Falmouth, Maine: Long Point Press, 2002), 5–7.

26. Philip Candelmo, *Shifting Tides: Memoirs of an Ordinary Man* (Scarborough, Maine: Fiddlehead Publishing, 1998), 228.

27. Ann Allen Brahms, *The Key is Under the Flowerpot* (Portland: Brahms Publishing, 1999), vii.

28. Brent Askari, *Not Ready for Prime Time* (New York: Carroll and Graf, 1999), 8.

8

Working Portland

Women, Class, and Ethnicity in the Nineteenth Century

Eileen Eagan

Shaded by trees in the city's Western Cemetery, a monument to the victims of the Irish Famine of the 1840s marks the burial site of Irish immigrants to nineteenth-century Portland. Near the edge of the cemetery, in the old Catholic Ground, the stone features a classic graphic of the famine: an emaciated woman with two children holding her hands. In a city where public sculpture features prominent men, mostly Yankee, this memorial represents the presence of immigrants and women as part of Portland's past. The monument stands near the tombs and homes of the wealthy Portlanders who employed many of the Irish women as servants.

Portland's history was shaped by its geography—its location on the ocean, near Canada and natural resources. But people have created, and recreated Portland; the nature of the population has helped determine the city's character. In turn, the city has shaped the experience of the people who arrived. Immigrants to Portland shared the problems and promise of those who settled elsewhere. Their lives, however, were, in some ways, different from those of their fellow countrymen and women who settled in San Francisco or Boston, or other places in New England, such as Bangor, Maine.

Coming to Portland

In the nineteenth century, Portland's primarily English population was joined by new groups: first the Irish, Canadians, Portuguese, some

Scandinavians and, later, Italians, Eastern European Jews, Armenians, Greeks, Poles and smaller groups from other nations. African Americans built a community on Munjoy Hill. Portland attracted fewer immigrants in general than Boston, fewer Germans than cities like Buffalo or Milwaukee, and fewer French Canadians than Maine towns like Westbrook or Biddeford. Still, newcomers from overseas (and across the Canadian border) did arrive.

At the time of the Civil War, Portland's largest immigrant group was the Irish. As a result of the famine migration beginning in the late 1840s, the Irish outnumbered other newcomers, by 1860 amounting to two-thirds of the city's foreign-born and 11 percent of the city's total population of about 30,000. By 1900 the first- and second- generation Irish were 15 percent of Portland's population of 50,000.[1] Their history illustrates the ways in which the culture of the immigrants interacted with the local culture, altering their adopted community even as it changed their own lives. In particular, the experience of Irish women shows how cultural ideas about gender can affect, and are changed by, immigrant experience. This is especially true of ideas about work. Portland was built by the labor of immigrants and that work was done by women as well as by men.

Factors that influenced the experience of Irish immigrants in general included the size of the city, number and percentage of Irish immigrants, and nature of the town (or sometimes of rural settlements).[2] Differences among Irish emigrants themselves also mattered. What part of Ireland they came from, when they came, whether they were Catholic or Protestant (or neither), English-speaking or Irish-speaking, or literate in either language—all of these elements help explain variations in the history of American Irish communities.

Although some Irish individuals settled in Maine in the eighteenth and early nineteenth centuries, the largest numbers migrated in response to the "Great Famine" from 1845–50. Those migrants were predominantly Catholic (the earlier Irish migration included Protestants) and poor. There were enough Irish in Portland by 1833 for the building of St. Dominic's—the first Catholic Church in the city—on State Street, slightly west of and above the Irish neighborhood of Gorham's Corner.[3] The building, now the Irish Heritage Center, dominates the view from the harbor of Portland's West End. The church, and its school, became centers of Irish life.

Some Irish came by ship directly to Maine (or Boston); others arrived in Canada and then took the railroad to Maine. Still others came from

Halifax and the Maritime Provinces or traveled down the Chaudiere-Kennebec route from Quebec. They included first-generation Irish and the children of Irish settlers in Canada. Once here, the immigrants settled near the waterfront in an area originally extending from "the east end of Portland at the base of Munjoy Hill to Gorham's Corner in the west end, and along most of the smaller streets intersecting Fore Street."[4] In the second generation, some moved up the hill, west of Gorham's Corner, or north of Congress Street, and eventually west to Libbytown, in the area near Union Station.

One major area of Irish settlement in Portland was Munjoy Hill, on the eastern end of Portland, with the Eastern Promenade and affluent families on top and the waterfront and docks below. The Irish started at the bottom of the Hill. The other major area was Gorham's Corner, toward the center, tending west, and very close to the waterfront and wharfs. Going toward the West End, the land begins to rise again and ends at the Western Promenade, where class and ethnicity defined neighborhoods. That is, the very rich lived in their mansions looking toward the White Mountains; their servants lived with them, generally in the attic, or walked up the gentle rise from Gorham's Corner, and Irish families lived down the hill, and worked on the waterfront.[5]

Of the two areas, the Gorham's Corner area (where Pleasant, Center, Danforth and Fore streets meet) was the most Irish and densely inhabited part of the city.[6] Well into the twentieth century, it remained the place where immigrant Irish settled when they came to Portland. Munjoy Hill was more diverse, with a Yankee community of skilled workers and fisherman, a substantial number of Canadians from the maritime provinces, a variety of nationalities among sailors, and some ethnic communities, including an African American community, centered around first the Abyssinian Church and then Green Memorial.[7] By 1900 Eastern European Jewish and Italian communities had developed, also near places of worship on Munjoy Hill. While the Hill was a mixed area, parts of it were heavily Irish, and in the nineteenth century they were the largest non-English group in the neighborhood.[8]

The custom, still evident in nearby Calvary Cemetery, of identifying on their tombstones the person's county or town in Ireland indicates the importance of continued ties to the homeland and to their local place of origin. The Portland Irish came from a variety of towns and counties in Ireland, but mainly from the west and south. Many of the famine and post-famine migrants emigrated from Galway and Connemara—the

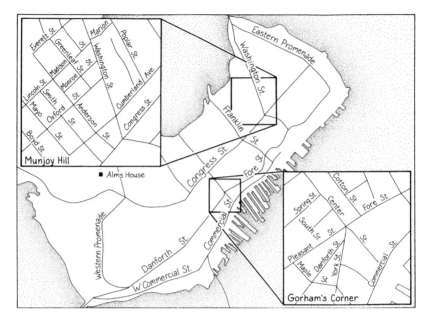

Figure 8-1. This map shows the concentration of Irish residents in Munjoy Hill and Gorham's Corner neighborhoods in 1870. The Alms House, on Portland (now Park) Street near Deering Oaks Park, included many poor, disabled Irish among its inmates.

rocky, impoverished west of Ireland—and were Gaeltacht, that is, speakers of Irish Gaelic as their first and sometimes only language.[9]

Another significant aspect of the western Ireland origins was that the province of Connaught, which included Galway, had a high percentage of single women among its emigrants.[10] Indeed, a distinctive aspect of Irish migration, compared to other groups, was the substantial presence of single women. Mid-nineteenth-century Germany, for example, exported more single men and families. In contrast, over the nineteenth century the numbers of Irish men and women who migrated were about equal and after 1870 more women, mostly single, left Ireland in search of better conditions and new lives.[11] The independence of the single Irish women, and the need to support themselves, shaped their lives and new communities. Portland was no exception.

In the study of immigration, national origins and ethnicity matter, but so does gender. Popular (and sometimes scholarly) history of immigration is often presented as the history of "great or successful (fill in the blank) men." As one historian notes, "Most histories of immigrants in

the United States begin with the experiences of migratory men disguised as genderless humans . . ." New research documents the role of
women in migration and their impact on the life of immigrant communities and the places where they settled. Irish and American ideas about
women played a key part in that experience.[12] This was conspicuously
true of the Irish in nineteenth-century Portland.

The culture and experience they brought with them influenced Irish
women's options in Portland, as in America as a whole. The economic
needs, geography, and attitudes of the people in the communities in
which they settled also affected Irish women's experience. For many of
the Irish, as for other women migrants, their journey was from lives as
"peasant maids to city women";[13] however, some began with internal
migration from the family home in the countryside into domestic employment on an estate. Other women first engaged in domestic labor in
Irish towns (or sometimes in England) and then migrated to North
America (including Canada as well as the United States) and found similar employment. Besides experience in domestic work, Irish women
possessed skills as seamstresses and dressmakers.[14] Other "cultural capital" that women transported to new places included literacy, usually the
ability to speak English, and a degree of optimism and faith in their capacity to improve their lives.[15] In addition, strong family bonds are represented by the practice of chain migration: emigrants sent money back
for another family member's travel to the United States. For example, a
woman who came to Portland and found a job as a domestic would send
money for her sister to join her and often also arrange for a position in
the same or a nearby household.

Some Irish communal values and religious attitudes discouraged
individual ambition or encouraged fatalism in the name of acceptance
of God's will, but those Irish women who chose to migrate demonstrated their willingness to go against those prescriptions, and to
search for liberty, security, love, escape, simple survival or adventure.[16] While they often left home to help their families survive,
women who migrated by themselves challenged Irish fatalism. As one
historian of Irish American women notes, "Although possessed of a
profound religiosity that belittled what people could do for themselves
to alter the course of human events, the Bridgets, Maureens, Norahs
and Marys decided to try just that."[17] In doing so, women, perhaps
even more than men, rejected some and drew on other parts of their
Irish heritage.

While bringing their experiences with them, the emigrants also arrived in large numbers in a context of rapid industrialization and growing regional differences. The period from 1840 to 1900 saw mixed industrial development and societies torn between modernization and traditional economies. In Portland, for example, by 1880 occupations like hostler, and carriage painter, lamp lighter, and fish curer, mixed with telegrapher, traveling salesman and bank teller, blacksmith and boilermaker—men's occupations all. Trade and commerce still created most jobs. The railroad and the docks dominated the labor of Irish men. Among Irish women traditional female jobs like needlework and domestic service prevailed.[18] Still, changing technology affected "women's work" too. Some women by 1880 were "sewing machine operators" and by the end of the century many were telephone operators.[19] In the late nineteenth century department stores and other businesses were offering "white" or actually pink collar jobs to women. Some professions expanded or opened up, teaching, medicine, nursing, and law. In Portland, however, in contrast to cities like Boston, the latter types of employment offered few opportunities to women, and fewer still to Irish women. The majority of employed Irish and Irish American women continued to labor in domestic service, needlework (at home or in shops), and some factory jobs. Portland women did not labor in occupations, such as types of factory work, that in other cities were beginning to be unionized.

Types of Work

Class, ethnicity and residential patterns shaped the geography of Irish women's work in Portland. Two major areas were Munjoy Hill and Gorham's Corner. A third location where Irish women worked was the "downtown" area where some businesses, notably hotels, employed them, and where boarding houses offered women an alternative to living at home or in the homes of their employers and access to jobs outside of the family neighborhood. This type of housing was important because women could rarely afford to live on their own and because cultural prescriptions within the Irish community, and within American society in general, opposed individual women living by themselves. Finally, many Irish domestic workers lived and worked in upper-class neighborhoods such as the West End.

The 1880 census shows, imperfectly but in some detail, the lives of Irish women, and the ways in which their labor was determined by family, neighborhood, and economic opportunity and its limits. The story resembles the patterns of female work in Maine in general and in New England as a whole. The three major areas of non-farm employment for American women between 1880 and 1900 were domestic labor, the needle trades, and factory work. Irish women displayed their own variation, shaped by their choices and opportunities. Despite the stigma attached to being a servant in America, nineteenth-century Irish women, unlike women of other groups, chose domestic work over other kinds of jobs, including factory work.[20]

The widespread image of "Bridget" the Irish maid was based on reality. In the mid-nineteenth century the expansion of an urban middle class and the existence of a pool of available workers fostered a demand for domestic labor in northern cities.[21] The Irish were arriving in large numbers just when there was a call for their labor. Irish women also brought experience with domestic work in Ireland.[22] In Portland, the developing middle and upper classes combined with the growth of a hotel industry to create a demand for domestic servants in private homes and in hotels.

The majority of Irish women in Portland worked in those jobs or other kinds of domestic services.[23] In Maine in general, Irish, and also Canadian, immigrants began to replace "native" household workers.[24] There was a hierarchy among different kinds of household help and an ethnic dimension to those divisions. The best paid domestic employees –nurses, cooks, and housekeepers—were the least likely to be Irish. On the other hand, "nurse girls," young and poorly paid, kitchen workers and laundresses were more likely to be Irish.

In hotel work employment (and pay) was also stratified, and ranged from cooking and housekeeping, to the labor of chambermaids, dishwashers, scrubwomen, and table waiters.[25] Hotel employment and domestic work in general changed over time. At mid-century servants frequently lived where they were employed, in private homes and hotels. By 1900, more domestic workers, including hotel employees, lived at home.[26]

Although before 1900 most Irish women in Portland were employed in domestic service, other Irish immigrants worked in needle trades, as dressmakers, seamstresses, tailoresses, and milliners. These represented different skills, and different pay, with tailoresses generally at the top and seamstresses at the bottom. The occupations also varied in terms of where the labor was performed—at home, in a small shop, or in a factory. The ability to work at home meant that even married women or widows with children could be employed as dressmakers or seamstresses.[27]

Toward the end of the century, clothing making was increasingly factory work, but throughout the nineteenth century "putting-out" work was common. In Maine, as in other parts of New England, this tended to distribute clothing manufacture around small towns and rural areas rather than concentrating it in Portland.[28] The putting-out system also employed Irish women in Portland.

Although Portland did not become a major clothing manufacturing center, by 1900 garment factories on Middle street, not far from Munjoy Hill, employed women and men in gender-defined labor; men did the cutting and pressing and women did the finishing, including details like buttonholes.[29] Some of this work was put out as well, with the male tailors serving as middlemen to distribute it to female seamstresses.[30] Although working at home had certain advantages, it also added more labor to women already burdened by family responsibilities.[31] Such practices also discouraged workers from organizing to demand better wages. Some women worked in tailor shops, but factories were undercutting that business. The 1892 Maine State Labor Report noted the growth of sweatshops, which also took away business from tailoresses and tailors.[32]

Despite these problems, for many Irish women in Portland the needle trades remained a respectable and flexible source of income. Sewing was a skill that women brought with them from Ireland. Women's role in the rural economy there involved such work as spinning, knitting, sewing, and lace making. The mechanization of the textile industry was one factor that undermined women's role in nineteenth-century Ireland and provoked female emigration. Rural Irish women, including those who had been linen makers at home, did not take their skills into the Irish cities; they carried them abroad.[33] In particular, they brought them to cities in the United States.

The third, and generally least popular, area of employment for Irish women in Portland was factory work. A smaller percentage of Irish women worked in factories in nineteenth-century Portland than in domestic work or sewing. In 1880, the women who worked in the city's shoe shops were mainly Yankees, Canadians from the Maritime Provinces, and a small group of French Canadians. At the same time, some Irish women worked canning fish or packing and wrapping in a chewing gum factory. They dominated the "female" jobs—bunching and wrapping—in a match factory.[34] The negative aspect of experience in the match factory—exposure to phosphorus and diseases resulting from it—may have reinforced a preference for domestic labor.

Working in the match factory was by no means the worst possible, lowest status job. That honor probably belonged to rag sorting, a job dominated in Portland (and other cities) by immigrant Irish women. Poorly compensated and often done in dimly lit or badly ventilated places, rag sorting was really the bottom rung of the industrial process. The cloth itself was sorted for use as either paper or "shoddy," a kind of fabric made from used cloth.[35]

Some Irish women worked in the rag sorting department at the Cumberland and Presumpscot Paper mill in neighboring Westbrook, where the Presumpscot River provided waterpower. In Portland, the rag sorting work was done in junk shops, where the pay was less, working conditions generally worse, and a higher percentage of employees were Irish women. In 1900 Portland hosted multiple junk shops on Munjoy Hill, on Commercial Street wharves, and on Fore Street close to Gorham's Corner. For example, in 1900 Bessie Maynard, then seventy years old, a widow, apparently living alone, was working as a rag sorter in a junk shop in Portland. Maynard had been born in Nova Scotia of Irish parents. She could read and write and lived on Cotton Street, near Gorham's Corner and the area of junk shops that offered work to women living nearby.[36]

The Maine State Labor Reports of the 1880s and 1890s provide accounts sympathetic to, if a little distant from, the workers being studied.[37] In 1888 and 1892 the reports paid particular attention to female employees and included surveys and comments of the workers themselves.[38] The authors, middle-class reformers, generally women, were interested in working conditions as well as wages.

The survey of rag sorters in Maine showed that most were Irish or of Irish parentage. Wages were higher in the paper mills but overall about the lowest of all occupations—about three to four dollars a week, or less (compared to, for example, cooks in hotels who might make $3.50 plus board). The workers often had little education or opportunity for advancement to other jobs. The lowest pay reported in 1892 was $1.05 a week, to a fifty-five year old woman who had been at work in the junk shop three years. She had just begun work at age fifty-two and was probably a widow. Born in Ireland, she had four years of schooling but she could read and write English.[39] Another woman who had worked in the junk shop for twenty-five years was making $3.50 a week.[40] Rag sorting was connected with the spread of diseases such as small pox.[41] Like the work in the match factory, rag sorting and rag picking was a public health issue in nineteenth-century Europe and the United States. As in other cases, immigrants and Irish women in particular became victims of and associated with disease.[42]

Despite these hazards, some women had little choice. This was true of employees in the junk shops of Portland, where such businesses were often located close to or in immigrant neighborhoods. The junk shops sometimes offered the only available jobs.[43] At the turn of the twentieth century rag sorting was still a job for poor women and children, in Portland a job for Irish women in particular, laboring and living at the bottom of the barrel.

Work and Neighborhoods

Women's occupations reflected the neighborhoods in which they lived, as well as their education, literacy, marital status, and family situation. Their jobs also depended on economic developments in the city. The absence of an extensive garment industry and the presence of a seaport and fishing and canning industries shaped women's options. So did the geography of neighborhoods.

The Irish women did not work in a vacuum; they lived and labored within communities that were similar and different. By 1880 Gorham's Corner and Munjoy Hill were identifiable neighborhoods. As already noted, Munjoy Hill, which was larger, included people of a variety of ethnic backgrounds and classes. There were no clear-cut, permanent boundaries between groups, and people were mobile within and between neighborhoods (they might move up the Hill). On the other hand, there were distinct areas, especially visible to those who lived there and not always evident to historians looking from the outside.

Churches and their parishes, as well as schools, streets, and businesses could mark a neighborhood.[44] Portland did not have the French/Irish division among Catholics that shaped conflicts and neighborhoods in cities like Lewiston, but in the twentieth century Italian and Polish Catholics built their own churches, at the foot of Munjoy Hill and on Portland's West End, respectively.[45] As long as St. Dominic's was the only Catholic church in Portland, its parishioners had a symbol that tied the Irish together. The building and dedication in 1869 of the Cathedral of the Immaculate Conception gave the Munjoy Hill Irish their own parish and symbol, and perhaps an ecclesiastical edge.[46]

Still, the presence of the church may have been less significant in defining the lives and work of Irish women in the two neighborhoods than the proximity to employers. The main jobs for women in both neighborhoods were domestic work, sewing, and, to a lesser degree, factory work but there were differences depending on access to types of employment.[47] Proximity to a factory sometimes overcame women's inclination toward other employment.

One factory close to Munjoy Hill that employed Irish women was Curtis Chewing Gum. Located near the waterfront, it was within walking distance from Irish areas of Munjoy Hill and Gorham's Corner. In the 1890s women packed the gum for wages of $3.50 a week.[48] Gum wrapping was generally young women's work, done mostly by teenagers, with a considerable turnover.[49] While the work itself wasn't hazardous, some conditions caused concern. Female employees in one gum factory did not have a room to change in or a toilet and they had to go outside the building to a nearby hotel.[50]

By the turn of the century, things had improved, perhaps as a result of state legislation generated by the labor reports, but also because the women in that area had other employment options. Many of the young women left the factory in the summer to take jobs in the tourist industry, "to go to the mountains, work in laundries, or other places employing extra help." The gum company paid a bonus to those who worked every day in a "premium period" of June, July, and August.[51]

Seasonal work offered an option to single Irish women who were not tied to one place. Since they did not have contracts with their employers, who felt free to lay them off seasonally, factory as well as domestic workers could take advantage of the burgeoning tourist industry and take summer jobs in resort areas. In Bar Harbor, for example, the large "cottages" required more employees than the visitors wanted to bring with them; those positions were filled by Maine women (and some men), many Irish.[52] In other ways the seasonal work limited women's incomes and made their occupations seem peripheral. The unsteady nature of female employment was exacerbated by the cycles of depression and economic decline in the nineteenth century.[53]

In the Munjoy Hill area in 1880 a total of 523 women worked in the paid labor force.[54] Of these, 205 were of Irish birth or Irish parentage.

Of the non-Irish, most were born in Maine to Maine parents. A substantial number were of Canadian background, especially from the Maritime Provinces. A smaller number were African American. There was a handful from other countries. For example, there was a Russian Jewish community in the area. None of the women in that group was listed as being employed; most were married. Almost 40 percent of Munjoy Hill's employed women were Irish, well above the percentage of Irish in Portland's population (about 15 percent) and of the population of Munjoy Hill as a whole.

Of the Irish, 40 percent (including servants and laundresses) were in domestic work, 38 percent worked in the needle trades as seamstresses, dressmakers, or tailoresses, 9.7 percent were factory workers, about 3 percent percent were milliners, and another 3 percent (six) were teachers. Of the non-Irish, 30 percent were in domestic work, 33 percent were in needle trades, 9.7 percent were milliners, 15 percent were in factory work and just over 12 percent were teachers. The non-Irish women had a little more diversity of occupation: one was a "sewing machine operator," three were nurses, several worked for printing companies, and one was a clairvoyant. Of all the domestics in both groups, some were live-in servants on the more affluent parts of Munjoy Hill, but most seem to have been living at home and working out, perhaps for several employers.

While most Irish-born women worked as domestics, in the needle trades, or in manufacturing some women did run and occasionally owned small businesses, generally either boarding houses, variety stores, or groceries. These shopkeepers were often widows, married and with few children at home, or sisters working together. Given that few married Irish women were listed in the census as employed, the role of the female shopkeepers was a conspicuous exception. One example was Mary Starkey, who ran a variety store on Washington, a heavily Irish, mixed commercial-residential street on Munjoy Hill.[55] Born in Ireland, she was married to John Starkey, a carriage trimmer. They lived, probably above the shop, with their adopted son and a boarder. The unemployment of her husband, in an occupation that was becoming outmoded, enhanced Mary Starkey's role in producing the family income.

Gorham's Corner included Center, Pleasant, Danforth, and York streets. Center, running from Congress Street down to Commercial and the waterfront, was geographically the main street of that area. It contained a mix of shops on the ground level of the three- or four-story brick buildings and quite densely packed multifamily structures. In

1880, the lower part was almost entirely Irish, many recent immigrants, but the upper area near Congress contained people of various ethnic backgrounds and included a Chinese man who boarded with an Irish family and ran a laundry. Center Street, and Gorham's Corner in general, was an area of longshoremen and their families. Work, for women, was based on access to Commercial Street and the waterfront but also proximity to the upper-class homes on the West End.

Like the women on Munjoy Hill, the Irish women in Gorham's Corner were employed in domestic work, the needle trades, and factory work. Munjoy Hill offered a somewhat wider variety of occupations. In each area there were some shops and factories that employed local women. Generally, the Irish women were concentrated in lower-paid jobs, with few in the developing white-collar employment and strikingly fewer in teaching.

The Portland Star Match factory, on West Commercial Street near Center Street, employed women from the Gorham's Corner area. From about 1870 to 1908 when it was bought by an out-of-state business, the factory employed many young women, often teenagers, mostly Irish, to work bunching and wrapping matches for sale and shipping. In some respects their working conditions were better than in other places; they did have indoor toilets and a changing room. However, handling the matches with the phosphorus tips exposed them to "phossy jaw," a condition that basically ate away at the teeth and jaws. The state's labor agent, Flora Haines, visiting the factory in 1888, described the effects of this exposure.[56] "The forewoman, a very pleasant and sensible young woman, has been in this factory eighteen years," Haines noted. " She did not look well. The whites of her eyes and skin were yellow . . . She told me she had lost but three teeth. On the occasion of the loss of one of these, she was away from her work during *nine months*."

In addition to the phosphorus poisoning, there was also the danger of fires. The company's efforts to alleviate this danger consisted of giving each worker a basin with a wet sponge in which she could dip any matches that happened to catch fire while being handled.[57] A shocked Haines proposed that the girls not be allowed to stay in the room during their lunch hour and that the rooms should be ventilated before work and during the day. "I am sure a good walk to and from work at noon would do much for the employees."[58] Haines also noted that of the thirty-eight women the company employed, twenty-eight were "Irish-Americans" and the rest were "Americans."[59]

Despite the conditions, young women from nearby neighborhoods, especially Gorham's Corner, took jobs at the match factory. Although there was turnover, some woman continued there for many years. In 1892 forty-six women worked at Portland Star Match factory as bunchers, in addition to the forewoman.[60] All but three were of Irish birth of parentage. The forewoman, after twenty-two years, was making $9.00 a week. Most workers were younger, had been there a shorter time, and were making around $6.00 a week.[61] The pay was better than wages for women in some other factories, and for jobs such as rag sorting.[62]

For women in Gorham's Corner, nearby businesses like the match factory and the middle- and upper-class residences on the West End offered employment. In 1880, of twenty-four working women living on Center Street, for example, twelve, or half, were employed in domestic work, five were in the needle trades, and another five in factory work. On an adjacent section of Pleasant Street, five Irish women were domestics, five were in the needle trades, two sisters ran a boarding house, and one young woman worked at the gum factory. Most of the domestic workers lived at home and worked elsewhere.[63] No one in the Gorham's Corner area in 1880 was employed as a teacher.

While it is certain that the married women and widows in Gorham's Corner found ways to bring income into the household, only one widow from Center Street was listed in the census as employed. Jane Neillen had been born in New Brunswick to Irish parents. Fifty years old in 1880, she was the head of household with one daughter at home and was employed as a cook. Her fourteen-year-old daughter, Agnes, also worked as a domestic. On nearby blocks, two married women and one widow were also employed. Ellen Dooley, fifty, born in Ireland, and living with her daughter, son-in-law, and their two children, worked as a domestic. Mary Silva, Irish-born as well, was also employed as a domestic. She was married to a Portuguese fisherman. Neither Mary Silva nor Joseph Silva could read or write. They lived with their three children: two sons who were fishermen and a daughter still in school. On Pleasant Street, Ellen Gibbons reflected another difficulty of life. She and her husband were both born in Ireland. At sixty-eight years she was working as a domestic. Her husband was unemployed and listed in the census's section on illness, as "intemperate." Drinking was just one of a variety of ills that along with on-the-job accidents could leave a working-class family without an income and give women the additional burden of laboring outside the home.

The fact that no women in Gorham's Corner were employed in the public schools is noteworthy. As late as 1900 in New England and elsewhere, teaching was the major professional occupation open to women. Furthermore, in other places, including Boston and New York, Irish women had made substantial inroads into the public schools. By 1870, 26 percent of schoolteachers in New York City were Irish women.[64] In Portland, no Irish Catholic women were employed as public school teachers until two Irish men became members of the school board, the first appointed in 1869 and the second elected in 1880 after the school committee system was changed to allow voting by wards.[65] The creation of Catholic girls' schools and eventually, in 1915, a Catholic women's college that provided teacher training, St. Joseph's, helped second-generation Irish women to move into public as well as parochial classrooms.

Domestic work continued to be a mainstay of employment for Irish women from Gorham's Corner, but by 1900 more labored in the gum and match factories. In 1900 at least nine young women from the area, mostly on Center and Pleasant streets, worked at the match factory.[67] Their average age was about twenty-two. All were living with their families.[68]

Two examples from this group show the relationship among family structure and size, the role of female-headed households, and the importance of adult children's income. Mary Lee, who worked in the match factory, was twenty and single. She was born in Maine of two native Irish parents. Her widowed mother, Johanna, fifty years old, was the head of a household on lower Center Street that included four adult children: Mary, the youngest, Annie, twenty-six, William, twenty-four, an electrician, and Elizabeth, twenty-two, a housekeeper. Another match packer was Nellie McDonough, twenty-five, also born in Maine of Irish parents. She lived with her widowed mother, Hannah, forty, the head of household on Spring Street, a sister, Delia, twenty-three, who probably also worked in the match factory, and four other siblings ranging from eight to twenty-four years of age.[69] Clearly the two oldest daughters' work was crucial in supporting the household. Even households with a father as breadwinner needed the work of children, including daughters, especially when the family was large.[70]

Not all Irish women labored within the boundaries of their neighborhood or lived in the family home. Their presence extended into other parts of the city and into the downtown area. In 1880, they worked and lived in three sorts of places. One was in the homes of the middle and upper class and in their neighborhoods, especially on the West End and Western Promenade, but also on the Eastern Promenade and the top of Munjoy Hill, and the area just north of Congress where lawyers and doctors lived, on Deering Street, for example. Another area was in the hotels downtown, between Munjoy Hill and Gorham's Corner. The third was in institutions of contrasting sorts, including religious communities like the Sisters of Mercy and the Alms House.[71]

Viewed through the lens of domestic servants' eyes, Portland's elite neighborhoods look quite different from the image conveyed by plaques on houses giving the name of the upper-class Anglo-Saxon male owners. On the West End and Western Promenade, for example, there was another world among the servants who worked and lived in the houses of the Drummonds and Paysons.[72] Typically, the servants had one afternoon off a week. For many it was Wednesday, and, in good weather, especially in the summer, the women would walk on the eastern and western promenades. As the stories go, the women were often joined by Irish men, either servants themselves, carriage drivers, for example, or longshoremen, who left the docks and the Irish neighborhoods and entered another domain.[73]

Another world lay down the hill and off the peninsula far from the elite neighborhoods. Rag sorting, if not usually an occupation of choice, was generally preferable to the Alms House. Such dirty, low-wage employment at least offered a degree of independence. For Irish women, and men, arriving at the Alms House was a sign of deep desperation and destitution. Located near what is now Park Street and Deering Oaks Park, the poor farm was the place where the destitute, insane, and sick mingled and worked to justify their care by the indoor relief system of the city. In Portland, as in other cities in the mid- to late nineteenth century, many of the inmates were Irish. Nationally Irish women, especially married women and widows, were well represented among the needy, including those in almshouses.[74]

In June of 1880, when the federal census was taken, seventy-three people were living and working in Portland's Alms House. Thirty-seven were Irish-born including thirteen women ranging in age from twenty-six to eighty-two years. Three of those women were married (in two cases the husband was also in the Alms House), two were widows, and the rest were single. The Alms House served as a public institution for the ill and disabled as well as the poor. One of the Irish women was blind, and two "insane."[75] Some of the "inmates" would be there temporarily, but others would remain until they died. It is unlikely that many people enjoyed life on poor farms, but for those born in Ireland there was a terrible irony in fleeing their homeland, and its workhouses, only to end institutionalized in their new land.[76]

Another type of institution offered women more, and different, opportunities. For women in Ireland and in the United States, Catholic religious orders offered economic as well as religious benefits. At the same time, the nuns provided services that allowed other women to improve their lives.[77] In late-nineteenth-century Portland, the Sisters of Mercy, an Irish order, taught in schools, ran an orphanage, and provided a "safety-net" for poor and working class women. They were also working women themselves, and offered another public face of Irish women in Portland.[78]

In 1880 the Sisters of Mercy had a convent, orphanage, and school on Free Street in downtown Portland, near many businesses but also not far from Gorham's Corner, Munjoy Hill, or the new Cathedral. Of the thirty nuns, seventeen had been born in Ireland and the others had Irish-born parents.[79] Nineteen of the nuns were teachers. The children in the orphanage shared the nuns' ethnic as well as religious background: one was born in Ireland and almost all the rest had Irish parents. On the other hand, of twenty students in the school for the deaf, only one had Irish parents; all the rest were from Maine with parents all born in Maine. It is likely that those students' tuition helped to subsidize the sisters' other work providing services for the Irish community and its families.

The commercial development of Portland lead to the construction of many hotels that offered temporary and long-term residences for travelers and business people. As is still true, the hotel business was staffed by a hierarchy of workers and primarily by immigrants. Irish labor, and especially that of Irish women, supported the proliferation of hotels and expansion of their services. If hotels were "worlds unto themselves" they were also places where Irish women had a strong presence. Employment practices varied among the hotels; some were more willing to give immigrants visible as opposed to backstairs positions. By 1880 they were major employers of domestic workers directly from Ireland or those who had grown up in the Irish neighborhoods of Portland.

Three hotels—Preble House, the Falmouth Hotel, and the United States Hotel—employed about sixty women in positions ranging from chambermaid, laundress, and dishwasher to waiter and head housekeeper. The women's jobs did not include hotel clerks, headwaiters, or firemen. Irish men held some of these jobs. More than 75 percent of the female domestics were Irish, and most of them were Irish-born. The other women were mainly from maritime Canada. All of the female employees lived in the hotel. At the Preble House, of nineteen "servants," with an average age of twenty-five years, fourteen had been born in Ireland and twelve could not read or write English. Responding to the state labor survey, one hotel employee observed, "It is not so bad in Portland as in some places where I have worked."[80]

Portland's commercial life and waterfront activity offered another opportunity to Irish women—running boarding houses. In 1880 Margaret Musgrave, fifty-seven, a widow, owned and managed a sailors' boarding house on Fore Street, not far from the wharves. She lived with her son John, twenty-six, who also managed the boarding house, his wife, Nora, twenty-six, and Mary A. Murray, twenty-two, a domestic servant born in Nova Scotia of Irish parents. Before marrying William Musgrave, a "trader and rumseller," Margaret Barry had migrated from County Cork to Portland in the 1840s and had worked as a domestic.[81] After her husband's death in 1860, Margaret, left with a young son and daughter, opened the rooming house that she would run for the next thirty years. She did well, and in 1871 was one of only two Irish women on the tax lists of the city who had made enough money to pay more than $100 in taxes.

The Next Generation

At the turn of the century downtown hotels and private homes continued to employ large numbers of Irish women, but many no longer required that the domestics board in the hotel or employer's residence. The women could walk to work from home, take a trolley if they could afford it, or live in a boarding house, preferably run by another Irish woman. Still, many Irish women continued to be employed in domestic labor. Some of these were newly arrived immigrants. In 1900, in Portland's fourth ward, which included Gorham's Corner, 42 percent of employed women were in domestic work, and 18 percent in factories. Others were still employed in the needle trades, but increasing numbers worked as waitresses and clerks in stores. Thirty women were teachers, twenty-nine of them Sisters of Mercy. One woman, Elizabeth Walsh, was a public school teacher.[82]

As the second generation of Irish American women began to move into different, sometimes better-paying jobs, they also began to move out of Munjoy Hill and Gorham's Corner into other parts of the city. That process in Portland was slower than in bigger cities like Boston with larger Irish populations. Still, in Portland, as elsewhere, women played a crucial role in Irish social mobility. Family income included that of married women who were employed seasonally in the canning industry on the wharves. By 1900, single Irish American women in Portland became telephone workers, nurses, clerks and saleswomen, some began to own their own shops, and more became teachers. They made economic gains by using education, family networks, and solidarity with other workers in unions. They also used their single status to pursue careers.[83]

In many respects, the experience of Irish and Irish American women in Portland is similar to the experiences of their counterparts elsewhere in the United States and especially in New England. Like those women, and other immigrants, the Portland Irish were confronted by industrial capitalism, developing technology, and by nativism and bigotry.[84] At the same time, the Irish women brought their own culture and assertiveness. Their group identity, defined by their working-class status, nationality, and religion, set some parameters to their lives. Irish and American gender ideology established other boundaries. Despite the women's best efforts, the road to freedom sometimes led to the Alms House. If streets were not paved with gold, many women did find ways to survive and eventually to create new lives. In doing so they drew on, and challenged, old ideas about community and about women's roles and skills.

Notes

1. Michael Connolly, "The Irish Longshoremen of Portland, Maine, 1880–1923" (Ph.D. Dissertation, Boston College, 1988), 42, 106.
2. Although the Irish, especially after 1840, generally settled in urban areas, there were exceptions. See for example, the story of Benedicta, Maine, an Irish Catholic agricultural community created in Aroostook County in 1833, in Edward T. McCarran, "A Brave New World: The Irish Agrarian Community of Benedicta, Maine," in Michael Connolly, ed., *They Change Their Sky: The Irish in Maine* (Orono: University of Maine Press, 2004), 121–37.
3. For the early History of the Irish in Maine and in Portland, see Connolly, ed., *They Change Their Sky,* 41–155, and James Mundy, *Hard Times, Hard Men:*

Maine and the Irish: 1830–1960 (Scarborough, Maine: Harp Publications, 1990). On famine migration in general see Kerby Miller, *Emigrants and Exiles: Ireland and the Irish Exodus to North America* (New York: Oxford University Press, 1985), 291–97.

4. Michael Connolly, "The Irish Longshoremen of Portland, Maine," 115.

5. The classic example is the manager of Portland Star Match factory who lived on upper Danforth and who could look down the bluff at the factory, safely placed against a cliff and well below the owner's home.

6. Parts of Munjoy Hill were densely populated and densely Irish too, as were some streets between Munjoy Hill and Gorham's Corner. A particularly dense and apparently troublesome area in the 1850s was the so-called "Sebastopol Block" near Fore and India streets (at the foot of the Hill). Connolly, "The Irish Longshoremen of Portland," 114. In some ways, the two areas were not so separate—at least initially.

7. See Maureen Elgersman Lee's essay, " 'What They Lack in Numbers': Locating Black Portland, 1870–1930."

8. For two differing views of the extent and nature of ethnic concentration on Munjoy Hill, see Connolly, "The Irish Longshoremen of Portland, Maine," especially pages 114–48, and Hannah Ashley, "Streets, Parks, Yards and Houses: Material Life as an Index to Social History on Munjoy Hill, 1850–1915" (M.A. thesis, University of Southern Maine, 1992).

9. For a discussion of the extent and importance of Irish speaking in Portland, see Kenneth E. Nilsen, " 'The Language that the Strangers Do Not Know': The Galway Gaeltacht of Portland, Maine, in the Twentieth Century," in Michael Connolly, ed. *They Change Their Sky,* 297–339. See also Connolly, ed., "The Irish Longshoremen of Portland, Maine," 44–46.

10. Kerby A. Miller, *Emigrants and Exiles,* 582; Hasia Diner, *Erin's Daughters in America: Irish Immigrant Women in the Nineteenth Century* (Baltimore: Johns Hopkins University Press, 1983), 33–34. On the lives and culture of women in Galway, including education and language, see Maureen Langan-Egan, *Galway Women in the Nineteenth Century* (Dublin: Open Air books, 1999).

11. Diner, *Erin's Daughters,* 30. For discussion of the impact of economic developments in home countries on the nature of women's migration see, Donna Gabaccia, *From the Other Side: Women, Gender and Immigrant Life in the United States, 1820–1990* (Bloomington: Indiana University Press, 1994), 4–26.

12. See Donna Gabaccia, *From the Other Side,* xi. Of course the role of all women (and ideas about gender) shaped the physical as well as economic life of cities. See Sarah Deutsch, *Women and the City: Gender, Space and Power in Boston, 1870–1940* (New York: Oxford University Press, 2000).

13. Harzig, Christine, ed., *Peasant Maids/City Women: From the European Countryside to Urban America* (Ithaca, N.Y.: Cornell University Press, 1997).

14. Deirdre Mageean, "To Be Matched or to Move: Irish Women's Prospects in Munster," in Harzig, ed., *Peasant Maids/City Women*, 86.

15. Janet Nolan notes that as a result of improvement in education in Ireland in the late nineteenth and early twentieth century Irish women emigrants had high literacy rates relative to those who remained and also to women of other emigrant groups. Janet Nolan, *Ourselves Alone: Women's Emigration from Ireland, 1885–1920* (Lexington: University of Kentucky Press, 1989), 69–70. That was also a change from the situation during the famine migration of the 1840s and 1850s.

16. Nolan, *Ourselves Alone*, 27.

17. Diner, *Erin's Daughters*, 29.

18. Connolly, "The Irish Longshoremen of Portland," 121–22.

19. United States Bureau of the Census, 10th Census of the United States, Manuscript Census Schedule, Cumberland County, Portland, Maine, 1880 (hereafter cited as U.S. Census).

20. Diner, *Erin's Daughters*, 74; Mona Hearn, "Life for Domestic Servants in Dublin, 1880–1920," in Maria Luddy and Cliona Murphy, eds., *Women Surviving: Studies in Irish Women's History in the Nineteenth and Twentieth Centuries* (Dublin: Poolbeg, 1989), 148–79; Nolan, *Ourselves Alone*, 78.

21. For a contemporary study see, Lucy Maynard Salmon, *Domestic Service* (New York: Macmillan Company, 1887).

22. Nolan, *Ourselves Alone*, 63–65.

23. See U.S. Census data for 1880 and 1900.

24. *Sixth Annual Bureau of Industrial and Labor Statistics of the State of Maine, 1892* (Augusta: Burleigh and Flint, 1893). Hereafter cited as *Bureau Annual Report*. Pp. 112–22.

25. See, "Tables of Working Women's Returns," ibid., pp. 112–22 for the categories of work of "hotel help" and "family help," their weekly wage and the birthplaces of individuals and their parents. This is a statewide report but certainly includes some Portland returns.

26. See the U.S. Census for 1880 and 1900. In 1880 servants were enumerated at the hotels where they lived. By 1900, a few hotels still had live-in servants but other hotel employees were being counted at home.

27. For a discussion of women in the needle trades in Boston, see Thomas Dublin, *Transforming Women's Work: New England Lives in the Industrial Revolution* (Ithaca, N.Y.: Cornell University Press, 1994), 163–204.

28. Dublin, *Transforming Women's Work*, 34–35. Paul E. Rivard, "Maine Manufactures, 1820–1880," in Richard E. Judd, Edwin A. Churchill, and Joel Eastman, *Maine: The Pine Tree State from Prehistory to Present* (Orono: University of Maine Press, 1995), 323.

29. *Bureau Annual Report*, 1888, pp. 115–16.

30. Rivard, "Maine Manufactures," 323.

31. The labor agent noted in the 1892 report, "While the work done at the homes of our people may add somewhat to the family purse, many a woman is broken down in health from the overexertion and late hours imposed." *Labor Report,* 1888, 32. Note the assumption that the family has another source of income.

32. *Bureau Annual Report,* 1892, 49. "Sales goods, as made under the sweating system, are driving out the tailoresses and small tailors injure the regular trade by selling suits to measure which are sent to sales goods makers, and can be made up by them at a great reduction from the price of regular shop work. Tailors frequently become agents for the tenement house sweating system."

33. Nolan, *Ourselves Alone,* 31, 67. While women in Belfast did work in textile factories, that industry did not take hold in Dublin or other cities in the south and west. For needlework among Irish Women in the United States, see Diner, *Erin's Daughters,* 74–80.

34. 10th U.S. Census, 1880.

35. *Bureau Annual Report,* 1888, 137; 1892, 10.

36. U.S.Census, 1900.

37. For discussion of the state labor reports see Carol Toner, "'Hard Work to Make Ends Meet': Voices of Maine's Working-Class Women in the Late Nineteenth Century," *Maine History* 42 (August 2004): 23–45.

38. In 1888 a "special agent," Mrs. Flora Haynes of Bangor, was responsible for the report on women's work; she visited workplaces across the state and distributed questionnaires to working women and guaranteed confidentiality. *Bureau Sixth Annual Report,* 1892, 6–7, 9–158.

39. The report returns do not say where the junk shops were; however, the narrative of the report states that there were "about sixty women and girls at work in the various junk shops in Portland, sorting over rags." *Bureau Annual Report,* 1892, 42.

40. Ibid., 98–100.

41. In fact, rag sorting has an illness named after it: "rag sorter's (or "wool sorter's) disease," a form of anthrax that could result in skin ulceration and can also lead to pneumonia. Peter Homan, "Working Can Damage Your Health," *Pharmaceutical Journal* 263, no. 7076 (December 1999): 1007; *http://www. Pjonline.com/Editorial/19991218/articles/workingcandam* (accessed May 2004).

42. Judith Walzer Levitt, *Typhoid Mary: Captive to the Public's Health* (Boston: Beacon Press, 1996), 164–66.

43. U.S. Census, 1900.

44. For a study of the identity of people with their parish, see Eileen M. McMahon, *What Parish Are You From? A Chicago Irish Community and Race Relations* (Lexington: University of Kentucky Press, 1995).

45. Histories of parishes, especially memorial issues, can reflect and perhaps exaggerate these identities and rivalries. See *St. Dominic's: 175 Years of Memories, 1822–1997* (Portland, Maine: Smart Marketing, 1997).

46. Edward H. Elwell, *Portland and Vicinity* (1881; Reprinted Portland: Greater Portland Landmarks, 1975), 47–48.

47. The following information and analysis is based on the 1880 United States Census, the manuscript census, for all of three enumeration districts—45, 46, and 47—and part of another—48—included within the Munjoy Hill area and a little downtown, and part of one enumeration district—52—which included the Gorham's Corner area. They focus mainly on one street, Center Street, with the nearest parts of intersecting streets. It is a smaller group. In addition to census data, I have used some information from the Portland city directories (1879 and 1881). These sources are incomplete; then as today census counters don't find everyone.

48. *Bureau Annual Report*, 1892, 39–40. According to the report, the wages were lower and less steady than wages in similar shops in Massachusetts and New York.

49. *Bureau Annual Report*, 1892, 39–40; 142–43. One of anonymous women who responded to the Maine labor committee's inquiry was twenty-four and had worked in a gum factory for ten years. She was born in Maine but her parents were Irish-born; she had attended eight years of school. Two respondents had gone to school for eight and seven years. In reply to the survey's question about why they hadn't gone further in school, all three answered: "own fault."

50. *Bureau Annual Report*, 1888, 72–73, 143–44; 109.

51. *Bureau Annual Report*, 1907, 152–53.

52. Judith S. Goldstein, *Crossing Lines: Histories of Jews and Gentiles in Three Communities* (New York: William Morrow, 1992), 155, 219.

53. For the impact of national and regional economic changes between the Civil War and 1900 see Judd, Churchill, and Eastman, eds., *Maine: The Pine Tree State from Prehistory to Present*, 448–79.

54. The following figures are from the United States manuscript census for 1880, Portland.

55. U.S. Census, 1880.

56. *Bureau Annual Report*, 1888, 139–40.

57. Ibid., 139.

58. Ibid., 140.

59. Ibid., 138.

60. *Bureau Annual Report*, 1892, 102–3.

61. Ibid. The average age of the bunchers was between twenty and twenty-one and the average numbers of years employed at that job was 2.57. However, sixteen had been employed for less that one year. Of those employed for a year or over, the average time was six and a half years. Years of schooling ranged from twelve to one—a girl from New Brunswick who had started work at eight years of age gave as her reason for not continuing school, "poverty." The average schooling was ten years but nearly half had eight or less and eleven had six

or less. Ironically, one girl gave as her reason for not continuing school past six years as, "sickness."

62. Wages in the gum factory were about $3.50 a week.

63. U.S. Census, 1880. The information in this section is from the manuscript census, 1880, enumeration district 52.

64. Dublin, *Transforming Women's Work,* 208. Diner, *Erin's Daughters,* 97.

65. Eileen Eagan and Patricia Finn, "Mutually Single: Irish Women in Portland, Maine, 1875–1945," in Connolly, ed., *They Change Their Sky,* 260.

66. U.S. Census, 1900.

67. U.S. Census, 1900.

68. Two were the daughters of widows who had other children at home. One was the daughter of a widower. Another group of young women who worked at the match factory lived in a boarding house on Beach Street, near the factory.

69. U.S. Census, 1900.

70. U.S. Census, 1900. Two examples of large families are those of Mary Norton and Hannah Feeney. Mary lived with her father Patrick, sixty, a bartender, widower, and the head of the household, and a sister and six brothers ranging in age from twenty to nine, the three youngest at school. Hannah lived with her father Bartley, forty-eight, a longshoreman, her mother Hannah, 49, and seven other children ranging in age from twenty-five to two. The youngest three were in school; the five oldest children were employed.

71. All these examples of locations of working women are found in the fifty-second enumeration district of the 1880 census, which includes Gorham's Corner.

72. Transcript of interview with Barbara Cloutier, 16 April 1984, Victoria Society Oral History Project (Maine Historical Society). Cloutier, whose maiden name was McDermott, emigrated in 1921. Her story is similar to that of Annie Flaherty Concannon who migrated to Portland in 1899 and was hired, through an employment office, by a family who lived on the Western Promenade. "Eire's Home, But Portland Is Not Forgotten," *Portland Press Herald,* 24 January 1952.

73. Connolly, "The Irish Longshoremen of Portland, Maine," 122. See also Nilsen, "'The Language that the Strangers Do Not Know,'" in Connolly, ed., *They Changed Their Sky,* 320–23.

74. Diner, *Erin's Daughters,* 107–8.

75. U.S. Census, 1880. On almshouses in New England, including the one in Portland, see David Wagner, *The Poorhouse: America's Forgotten Institution* (Lanham, Md.: Rowman and Littlefield, 2005).

76. On the British Parliament's passage of the Irish Poor Law of 1838, mandating locally supported workhouses in Ireland during the famine, see Miller, *Emigrants and Exiles,* 282, 284. On the Irish and poverty in Worcester, Massa-

chusetts, in the 1880s, see Timothy Meagher, *Inventing Irish America: Genera-tion, Class, and Ethnic Identity in a New England City, 1880–1928* (Indiana: University of Notre Dame Press, 2001), 51.

77. Diner, *Erin's Daughters*, 130–37.

78. On the role of the Sisters of Mercy in Portland see Eagan and Finn, "From Galway to Gorham's Corner." The orphanage moved to High Street in 1888 and became known as St. Elizabeth's.

79. U.S. Census, 1880. Eleven of the nuns had been born in Maine.

80. *Bureau Annual Report*, 1892, 157.

81. U.S. Census, 1880; "The Western Cemetery Project" (South Portland, Maine: Ancient Order of Hibernians, 2001), 55–56. (A grocer's widow, Bridget Dumphy, was the other Irish woman paying more than one hundred dollars in taxes.)

82. U.S. Census, 1900.

83. Eagan and Finn, "Mutually Single: Irish Women in Portland," 257–75.

84. The story of the Ku Klux Klan's attacks on Catholics in Maine in the 1920s, and on Catholic teachers in particular, suggests that these constraints did not disappear.

9

"What They Lack in Numbers"

Locating Black Portland, 1870–1930

Maureen Elgersman Lee

In July of 1870, barber Charles Eastman lived in Portland with his wife, Harriet, and their five children. A prosperous man, Eastman owned $3,500 in real estate and $1,500 in personal property. The Eastman name remained prominent in Portland for generations; notable among the family members were Harry William and Sadie Louisa Eastman, two of Charles Eastman's grandchildren. Harry Eastman worked as an elevator man at a Congress Street commercial building and Sadie was reportedly a well-known socialite. In addition to attending to work and social obligations, the Eastman siblings also served as the only Maine agents of the *Colored American Magazine,* a monthly publication devoted to African American history, culture, and science. Published by Boston's Colored Co-operative Publishing Company, the *Colored American* had agents across the United States. The magazine's editors considered their monthly something of a necessity for Black Portlanders who, when the twelfth United States census was taken in June of 1900, numbered less than three hundred. The *Colored American* offered its own unique perspective on Blacks in Portland when it wrote in May of 1901, "What they lack in numbers, they fully make up in appreciation."[1]

Historically, Portland has been the Maine city with both the largest overall population and the largest Black population. As such, it has also been the city most documented for its Black history. Previous academic and popular studies have focused on the history of slavery and abolition, the modern civil rights movement, select families and individuals, and the city's Black religious pillars, the Abyssinian and Green Memorial AME Zion churches. The scholarship, however, has yet to produce a detailed profile of Portland's Black community during the formative postbellum years of 1870 to 1930, a sixty-year period during which Black residents actually declined both in number and as a proportion of the city's growing population. Despite their diminished numbers, Blacks in Portland constituted a heterogeneous community that could claim many of the same economic, social, religious, and civic achievements as Blacks in often larger, but comparable, New England cities. The following analysis uses United States census manuscripts, city directories, obituaries, and other public records to locate Portland's Black population during the late nineteenth and early twentieth centuries—not only to gauge its numbers, but to examine how its nativity, labors, daily life, and institutional development defined what it meant to be Black in this southern Maine city.[2]

The People

When the ninth United States census was taken in 1870, the Civil War was over, and Reconstruction was under way in the former Confederacy. While physically removed from the southern states, Maine saw a noticeable increase in its Black population between 1860 and 1870, an increase that has been attributed to the migration of White southerners and their Black slaves-turned-servants and the organized settlement of freedmen in the state. This northward movement enlarged the state's African American population, and raised it from 1,327 in 1860 to 1,606 by 1870. The increase proved temporary, however, and Maine's Black population declined to 1,319 by 1900 and to 1,096 by 1930. As one might expect, the proportion of Blacks in Maine declined as well. In 1870 Blacks comprised 0.3 percent of the state's population, by the turn of the century they accounted for 0.2 percent, and by 1930 they were 0.1 percent of Maine's total population.[3] The 1870 to 1930 Black population contraction was also felt in Portland. In 1870, the 334 Blacks who lived in Portland accounted for 1.1 percent of the city's population. Portland Blacks numbered 291 in 1900, and represented 0.6 percent of the city— virtually half of their 1870 figure. By the time the national census was taken in 1930, the city of Portland recorded more than seventy thousand residents, only 268 or 0.4 percent of whom were African American.[4]

Maine's Black population was neither the largest nor the smallest in New England; it generally remained in the middle third of New England state populations. In 1900, for example, Maine's 1,319 Blacks formed a population larger than in Vermont (826) and New Hampshire (662), but dramatically smaller than in the leading states of Massachusetts (31,974), Connecticut (15,226), and Rhode Island (9,092).[5] However, Black Portland itself was virtually at the bottom of the population scale of comparable New England cities. In 1930, for example, Portland's 268 Blacks were smaller in number than the 361 African Americans in nearby Portsmouth, New Hampshire, and were dramatically outnumbered by the Black communities in Newport, Rhode Island (1,554); New Bedford, Massachusetts (3,631); and New Haven, Connecticut (5,302).[6]

Despite the steady decline in both the number and proportion of Blacks in Portland, the city remained a magnet of Black residency, and much of the state's Black population could be found there. Also, at all times between 1870 and 1930, the proportion of Blacks living in Portland was consistently higher than the proportion of Blacks living across the state. In 1870, the proportion of Blacks in Portland was almost four times that of Blacks in the state. In 1900, Portland Blacks were found in concentration three times the state level, and in 1930, the Black concentration in the city was four times that for Blacks in the state. Stated differently, in 1870 and 1900, more than one out of every five African Americans living in the state of Maine resided in Portland. By 1930, it was almost one out of every four.[7]

Maine's Black population was predominately native born. For example, of the more than 1,300 Blacks living in the state in 1900, 83.5 percent were born in the United States. Most of these African Americans were natives of Maine, and the rest were born primarily in other parts of New England, and in the South and Middle Atlantic regions of the country. A small number of Blacks in Maine were born in the more interior states of Ohio, Tennessee, Kentucky, and Louisiana; very few claimed nativity in the western half of the country.[8]

Maine-born Blacks living in Portland between 1870 and 1930 included steamboat stewardesses Isabella and Emily Baxter. Other Black Mainers included barber Charles Eastman and his family; clothing repairer William Brown; and cook Edward Carter, his wife, Isabella, and their children. Cook Vincent Edward, his wife, Mary, and their son Joseph were all born in Maine as well.[9] Blacks from elsewhere in New England included cook Henry Ball. Born in New Hampshire, Ball lived in Portland with his wife, Sarah, and their three children, all of whom were Maine natives. Barber Franklin Humphreys was from Massachusetts. Seaman Thomas Bailey was from Connecticut, and lived in Portland with his wife, Ellen, and their daughter, Sarah, both of whom were also of Maine birth. Other Blacks born in New England and living in Portland in 1870 included seaman Phillip Manuel of Massachusetts, wife and mother, Annie Ruby of Vermont, barber James Ball of New Hampshire, cook Benjamin Barnett of New Hampshire, and their respective families.[10]

African Americans born in South Atlantic states and who were building lives in Portland were also well represented. Seaman Daniel Bush, barber William Armstrong, clothes cleaner Henry Palmer, and Mary Paris, a wife and mother, were all born in Pennsylvania. Thomas Fisher was a native of New York. William Armstrong's wife, Elizabeth, and steamboat steward John Richardson were both natives of Delaware, while cook Joseph Spencer, laborer John Paris, and retired seaman John Graves were all from Maryland. Virginia had been the birthplace of seaman-turned-barber Corbin Smith, barber Joseph Taylor, and steamboat waiter Charlie Robinson. Mother of two, Eliza Bell, and seaman George Fitzgerald were both natives of Washington, D.C. Those who came to Portland from birthplaces in the Deep South included Floridian carpenter Michael Martin, and Louisiana natives Louis Alexander and Joseph Bennett, both of whom worked on ships or steamers.[11]

Blacks born outside the United States constituted a smaller, but notable, presence in Maine. In 1900, 16.5 percent of Maine's Black residents were foreign born. They were small in number, comprising a mere 0.1 percent of the more than twenty thousand foreign-born Blacks enumerated in the United States that year, and 5 percent of the more than 4,300 foreign-born Blacks living in New England. In Portland, as across the country, most foreign-born Blacks came from two distinct and differing regions—Canada and the Caribbean. Black Canadians living in Portland consistently hailed from the maritime provinces of New Brunswick and Nova Scotia. Natives of New Brunswick included dressmaker Elizabeth Dean and housewife Leanisa Bennett. Blacks living in Portland but born in Nova Scotia included porter Archibald Johnston; his sister, music teacher Henrietta Johnston; and Eliza Love, a wife and mother of four. Other Blacks, like hostler Arthur Willis and elevator operator Hazel Payne, were also born in Canada.[12]

Portland's Caribbean-born population hailed from a variety of British, French, and Spanish island colonies. Though far removed from the geography of the Caribbean basin, Portland's position as a port city and its seafaring relationship with the West Indies were likely factors in facilitating at least some Blacks' relocation to Maine. Seaman John Rose, for example, was born in the British island colony of Jamaica. Also from Jamaica were husband and wife David and Mary Dickson, who, together, would raise a very successful family in Maine. Una Richardson, wife of North Carolina native Edward Richardson, was also from that island; their children would also establish themselves in Portland business and public office over their lifetimes. Seaman George Moulton was born in St. Thomas, while his wife, Anna, was from Bermuda. Henry Thomas, yet another Portland-based seaman, hailed from the French island of Martinique. Cooper John Paris and carpenter Felix Junco were both reportedly born in Cuba. Other Blacks, like day laborer Augustus Holly and Elks Club cook Alfred Martin, were also Caribbean natives.[13]

The relatively few Black nationals in Portland not from Canada or the Caribbean islands generally came from either the Portuguese colony of Cape Verde or from England. Portland's Cape Verdean population was a mere fraction of that of New Bedford, Massachusetts, where Cape Verdeans played a critical role in the region's whaling industry. Chef John Verra was born in Cape Verde in the late 1870s and was probably living in Portland by 1910. Boat steward Domingo Barrows is listed as having been born in Portugal, but it is probable that he also came from the Cape Verdean islands. Seaman Joseph Jones was born in England, as was cook Christopher Trimmingham.[14]

Manuscript census information helps illuminate the international and interstate movement of Blacks, as well as some of the family dynamics introduced by such change. Nova Scotia natives Joseph and Margaret Franklin emigrated from Canada to the United States in 1891. In 1900, they lived in Portland with their six children, who ranged in age from fourteen years to seven months. Joseph, Margaret, and their eldest surviving child, Alice, were still recorded as being Canadian citizens in 1900; the five other Franklin children, all born in Maine, were American citizens. In the case of Black interstate migration where individual or familial movement is not recorded in the census, the nativity of Black Portland's children helps inform Black migration to Maine. Such is the case of the Phinney family, who lived on Munjoy Hill at 200 Congress Street. Falmouth Hotel porter John Phinney was a native of New York, while his wife, Carie, was born in North Carolina. In 1900 the Phinneys had three daughters, three-year-old Marie, one-year-old Hazel, and one-month-old Julia. Both Marie and Hazel Phinney were born in Massachusetts, while infant Julia was born in Maine. This information allows us to place the Phinneys's arrival in Portland sometime between August of 1898 and May of 1900, the birth months of their last two children.[15]

By 1910, Maine's foreign-born Black population had expanded, and accounted for 17.4 percent of all Blacks in the state. Massachusetts was the state with the next largest Black foreign-born population (16.2 percent), while Vermont had the least foreign-born Blacks (2.5 percent) in all of New England.[16] As Maine's largest city and the city with the largest Black population, Portland shared in the diversity of the state's population. It is difficult to say, however, whether distinctions or even tensions developed among Portland Blacks to the degree that they did elsewhere in New England. According to historian Robert Warner, West Indians in New Haven met hostility upon their arrival. They were ridiculed for their foreign and wide-ranging island accents, their different foodways, and their group pride. In New Haven, Blacks from Nevis comprised the largest West Indian immigrant group and established the Nevis Club; those from other parts of the Caribbean formed the Antillean Friendly Association as a means of preserving their identity.[17] While much research needs to be completed, there is evidence that West Indians on Portland's Munjoy Hill used similar means to maintain unity and group identity; they organized social activities and even reportedly established a cricket team that competed in Boston.[18]

The mix of Blacks from the United States, Canada, the Caribbean, Cape Verde, and England gave the Portland community a cultural texture and diversity camouflaged by its position in northern New England and betrayed by its diminutive size. To look exclusively at Black Portland's numbers is to ignore its complexity; to investigate them on their own and in the context of comparable New England cities reveals the population's relative complexity at different historical moments.

Their Labors

The years between 1870 and 1930 brought remarkable changes to the American workplace. Increased industrialization and wide-scale manufacturing shaped the form and the substance of the average workday, and labor unions played increasingly powerful roles in protecting workers' interests. In many cases, however, Black men were refused union membership, a fact that left them out of group-negotiated wages and benefits. This exclusion also pooled them in service-based unskilled and semiskilled labor. As a group, Black women made some notable gains in clerical and manufacturing jobs, but remained relegated to private domestic and public service work. Often overshadowed by technological advances, agrarian economies preserved Black men's and women's positions as some of the nation's most exploited laborers.[19]

In 1870 much of the Portland economy was tied to its place as a port city, and many Black men in the city were an integral part of this labor force. West Indian men, in particular, were employed as seamen. Caribbean natives like Henry Thomas, John Rose, and George Moulton were all seamen. At the same time, native-born Blacks like Louis Alexander of Louisiana, Joseph Bishop of Virginia, and Edward Brown of Maine labored at sea as well. Maryland native John Graves, whom the census recorded as being 105 years old, was retired from what probably had been many years on the ocean. Other men worked on steamers as stewards and waiters; they included Maine native Frederick Stephenson, Delaware native John Richardson, and Virginia native John Robinson.[20]

According to historian Jeffrey Bolster, Black men "turned to the sea to hold families together, acquire property, and attain respectability."[21] In Portland, Black seamen acquired respectable amounts of real and personal property. In 1870, Henry Thomas had $800 in real estate and $500 in personal property. Daniel Bush had $1,000 in personal property, while George Moulton's personal property was valued at $1,100. Steamboat steward John Richardson had $1,000 in real property and $3,000 in personal effects.[22]

In many cases, seamen's wives had the primary occupation of "keeping house." Certainly women with large families or with small children were more likely to remain in the home, but their ability to do so also gave them social respectability at a time when Black women's character was not highly regarded.[23] However, some of Black Portland's women did work on the water, usually on steamship excursions from the city to east coast destinations like Boston and New York. Work at sea also seemed to offer women financial security. Isabella and Emily Baxter both worked as steam stewardesses and probably helped amass the $3,000 in real estate and $1,000 in personal property reported for their household in 1870. Isabella's and Emily's status as single women probably allowed them to take the positions that regularly absented them from the household.[24]

Seafaring, whether oceanic or coastal, took its toll on Black Portland in ways other than the merely inconvenient. In late November 1898 several of Portland's Black men and women were lost forever when the steamer the SS *Portland* went down in a violent storm off the coast of Cape Cod. There were no survivors, and in the days following the disaster, dozens of bodies washed up on the Massachusetts shoreline. The Abyssinian congregation took the tragedy particularly hard. Several of its members died in the sinking and local historians suggest that this blow contributed to the congregation's demise soon thereafter.[25]

African American career seafaring declined in many northern ports by the mid-1850s, and that by the late 1800s seafaring provided less financial support than it had in previous decades. Black sailors who shipped out of their home or adopted ports on a regular basis were replaced by casual workers who sailed for lower wages. Racialized pay scales, hiring practices, and preferences have also been identified as factors that helped end the age of sail for African Americans in New England. In Portland, this occupational shift seems to have been manifested in the relative absence of Black sailors in 1900, as compared to 1870, and in the noticeable increase of Black hotel and railroad porters by 1930. Black men less inclined or less able to make the transition out of ship work may have left Portland for other American port cities, most in the southeastern or Chesapeake regions, where opportunities remained intact.[26]

Those men whose jobs kept them on dry land held diverse positions, whether as proprietors or employees. Maine native Charles F. Eastman was forty-four years old when the 1870 census was taken. He worked on his own accord as a barber at 7 Franklin Street, as did his twenty-two-year-old son, Charles F. Eastman Jr. Charles Eastman's other sons, George and James, also barbered, establishing Eastman Brothers at 365 Fore Street. James and George Ball were also barbershop proprietors, and operated Ball Brothers, a shop at 154 Fore Street. Over the years Black Portland had a variety of other barbers, including William Armstrong, Joseph Taylor, and Luther Manuel.[27] Barbering was often a lucrative occupation in the Black community, as evidenced by Charles Eastman Sr.'s 1870 report of $5,000 in real and personal property. Black barbers, especially those who operated their own shops, were respected as semiskilled workers who provided a coveted service and as proprietors able to work for themselves.[28]

Nationally, the early twentieth century was not an easy time for African American laborers. African American men were generally refused membership in the nation's increasingly powerful labor unions. In

1925, A. Phillip Randolph made history when he organized the Black employees of the Pullman Railroad Company into the Brotherhoood of Sleeping Car Porters and Maids, the nation's first all-Black labor union. It was not until 1937, however, that the Pullman Company fully recognized the Brotherhood.[29]

An examination of Maine's 1930 work force yields some insights into the changing nature of Black men's labors in Portland. For the 363 Black working males aged ten and over, manufacturing and mechanical industries as well as domestic and personal service comprised the largest categories of labor. An identical 27.3 percent of Black men in Maine—more than one-half—laborered in these two types of jobs. Within these labor groups, however, Black men's work was highly concentrated in general labor and servant positions, respectively. Transportation and communication accounted for 18.7 percent of Black males' employment, and agricultural work accounted for 10.2 percent. Other men found work in forestry and fishing (5.0 percent), trade (4.7 percent), public service (3.3 percent), professional service (1.7 percent), clerical positions (1.4 percent). Black men worked across the labor spectrum and they frequently occupied jobs as chauffeurs, truck drivers, janitors, and railroad laborers.[30]

Black men's labor in Portland tended to reflect the general pattern set at the state level. With some exceptions, by 1930 most Black men in the city were service workers in local hotels, private clubs, and commercial buildings, or were general laborers. Arthur Johnston, a husband and father of three young children, was a porter at a local hotel. Emory (also Emery) Dodge, also a porter, worked at the Falmouth Hotel on Middle Street, while David Dickson portered for the North Country Music Company on Congress Street. Various men also worked as cooks and chefs. Widower and father of four children, John Verra was a chef at the Elks Club. Panamanian Lloyd Marshall was a dining car cook. In 1930 Walter Gaskill was an auto mechanic. Arthur Nash and Edward Richardson washed cars.[31]

Portland was home to few Black male professionals or skilled workers. Maryland native James Cornish was pastor of the Gospel Temperance Mission. Cornish would have been an active minister, as the Mission held two Sunday services as well as services or meetings on Saturday and Wednesday evenings. A husband and father of a young son, Joseph Simpson worked as a clerk at George W. Rankin Drugs, conveniently located just a few doors from his family's residence at 99 Congress Street. Daniel Giro Jr. worked as a clerk at the Eastern News Company on Union Street.[32]

While Black men as a group saw their places in the local labor market transformed, Black women moved into the work force in increasing numbers; the work into which they moved, however, was overwhelmingly servile in nature. In 1907 the United States Census Bureau gathered material from the 1900 census and produced a volume of statistics that focused exclusively on American women and work. That collection, *Women and Work,* allows valuable insight into the lives of Black Portland's working women. In 1900, 167 Black females in Maine, sixteen years of age or over, were breadwinners. More than three-quarters of the women were between the ages of sixteen and forty-four, with the single largest group being those women between the ages of twenty-five and thirty-four. Across the state, Black women's labor was heavily concentrated in domestic and personal service, with this type of work constituting at least 80 percent of their work in the state. In 1900, 58.7 percent of Black working women were servants and waitresses, 13.2 percent were laundresses, and 7.8 percent were housekeepers and stewardesses.[33] In that same year, Portland recorded 107 Black females who were sixteen years of age and over. Of these women, thirty-two (29.9 percent) were breadwinners in their families. This proportion was higher than for Portland's native white female population, of whom 23 percent were breadwinners, but slightly lower for foreign-born white females (30.7 percent) and for native white females with one or two foreign-born parents (35.0 percent). If Portland followed the state trends, more than four out of every five of the city's Black female breadwinners were domestic or personal service workers.[34]

The profile of Black women working in Maine did not change dramatically over the next thirty years. In 1930 there were 147 Black females ten years of age and over employed in Maine. Given Black women's limited access to diverse employment, as compared to Black men, it is not surprising that four out of five Black working women in Maine remained in domestic and personal service jobs. The majority of these women were, like their male counterparts, servants. Although the second largest labor category for Black women in Maine was manufacturing and mechanical trades, this category accounted for only 18.4 percent of the Black female work force. Other women held clerical positions (3.5 percent), worked professionally (2.0 percent), or labored in agriculture (0.7 percent). There were no Black women reported in forestry and fishing, transportation and communication, trade, or public service.[35]

Like their male counterparts, few Black women in Portland held professional jobs even when they had the proper training. Black female professionals, therefore, formed a small, elite group. Within this group, teachers were well represented. Henrietta Johnston, a Nova Scotia native and single woman in her early twenties, taught music in Portland in 1900. Llewena Hill became an elementary teacher in the city after her 1921 graduation from Gorham Normal School. In 1930, Marguerite Giro, also single and in her early twenties, was a substitute teacher in the city.[36] However, various African Americans who grew up in Portland and Bangor in the early to mid-1900s have reported that they could not teach in Maine. The state's ban on Black teachers appears to have been more convention than law, a custom mitigated perhaps by local attitudes concerning racial difference and by the needs of educational institutions. It is clear that while some Black women were permitted to teach, Black men's ability to train and work in the field of education was significantly curtailed. Overall, Black women fared better than men in gaining teaching positions, but often, as in Hill's case, only temporarily (Figure 9-1).[37]

There were relatively few Black female health care professionals in Portland. Nettie Smith, wife of then seaman Corbin Smith, was a nurse in the early 1900s, although it is unclear where in the city she worked. When the Portland chapter of the NAACP formed in 1920, two Portland women—Eula H. Milligan and Emmeline Williams—identified their occupations as nursing. It is possible that—but not entirely clear if—these women were Black. It is also unclear if they were formally trained as nurses or worked as personal nurses and attendants in private homes.[38]

Beside the preponderance of domestic and service-related work, one notable trend among Black working women in Portland was the distinct increase in Black female elevator operators by 1930. Helen Franklin was an elevator operator at the Casco Mercantile Trust Company on Middle Street. Hazel Payne (also Paine) boarded with Franklin and was an office building elevator operator. Geneva Lawrence Gaskill, wife of Walter Gaskill, worked at the Eastman Bros. and Bancroft Department store on Congress Street. Other Black females operating elevators in Portland included Irene Dodge and Elena Harris. It seems professional training did not restrict some women from becoming elevator operators. Llewena Hill, the 1921 Gorham Normal School graduate, was no longer teaching in 1930. Having married Oscar Mathews a few years earlier, she was now counted among the growing number of Black female elevator operators in the city.[39]

Figure 9-1. Llewena Hill, as she appears in the 1921 Gorham Normal School yearbook, *Green and White*. She worked briefly as a school teacher before marrying. Hill was also a charter member and officer of the Portland NAACP. University Archives, Special Collections, University of Southern Maine Libraries.

Their Daily Lives

Black men and women's ability to find gainful employment critically defined how and where in the city they would make their homes and raise
their families. For most Black families, this meant living in the city's first
and second wards. In 1870, for example, almost half of Portland's Blacks
lived in the second ward, and four out of every five Blacks lived in either
the first or second ward. By 1900, the majority of Blacks remained concentrated in these two wards, with the first ward now having the highest
Black numbers. By 1930, Ward One remained home to the largest number of Blacks in the city. There was, however, a noticeable shift in Black
Portland's population distribution, as Blacks made their homes within
the vicinity of Brighton Avenue and closer to the Westbrook city line. In
fact, Ward Seven had replaced Ward Two as the division with the
second-largest Black population. Blacks like Llewellyn and Sarah Hill,
Oscar and Llewena Hill Mathews, and Edward and Una Richardson
helped make up the more than 28 percent of Black Portland living in the
seventh ward. For white Portland, the distribution of leading wards was
somewhat different. In 1870, the seventh ward had the largest concentration, with 18.5 percent of Portland's white population living there. The
first ward followed, trailing by less than two percentage points. In 1900,
the seventh and first wards continued to see the highest concentrations
of the city's white residents. By 1930, however, it was the ninth ward that
had the single largest white population, with 18.9 percent of whites living there; the seventh and eighth wards followed with 15.6 percent and
15.4 percent, respectively (Figure 9-2).[40]

   For Black Portland, life centered on and around Ward One's Munjoy
Hill, in the city's East End. African American families like the Gaskills,
Singletons, Loves, Phinneys, Manuels, Johnstons, Dodges, Dicksons
and others made "the Hill" their homes, even as the Black population
was beginning to shift westward. Among the various streets that criss-
crossed Munjoy Hill, Lafayette, Montreal, Merrill, and lower Congress
streets saw particularly high concentrations of Black residency. In 1900,
Arthur and Sarah Willis lived at 39 Lafayette. Up and across the street
lived widow Mary Jones and her household; hotel porter John Phinney
and his growing family; and steamboat waiter Griffin Harris, his wife,
and their four children. Behind the Harris family, lived Luther and Anita
Manuel and their infant daughter, Isabel. By 1930, the Jones, Phinney,

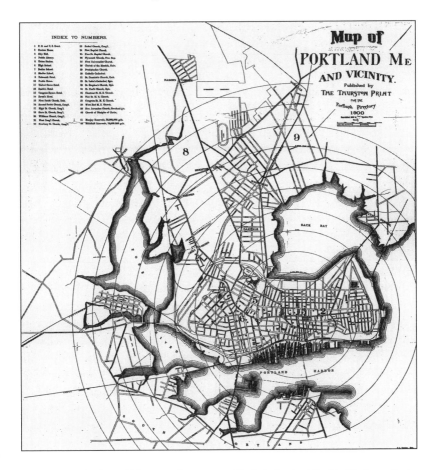

Figure 9-2. Portland Ward Map, 1900. In 1900 most Blacks in Portland lived in Wards 1 and 2; by 1930, most lived in Wards 1 and 7. Collections of Maine Historical Society.

Harris, and Manuel families had left Lafayette, but laundress Lucy Heuston, hotel porter Arthur Johnston and his family, hotel porter Emory Dodge and his wife, Irene, store porter David Dickson and his extended family, and elevator operators Hazel Payne and Helen Franklin all lived on this relatively small street on Munjoy Hill.[41]

Emory and Irene Dodge's daughter, Beverly, grew up on Munjoy Hill, graduated from various local schools, including the North School and Portland High School, and recalls what life was like for her.

[I]t was a wonderful neighborhood, although we probably didn't realize it at the time. But looking back, it was quite nice. Both my mother and father worked, so the neighbors used to watch us. And I used to say we had Irish grandparents because you had to behave no matter what . . . In the summertime, the neighbors used to take me to the beach every day. The Eastern Promenade. We were a very close neighborhood.[42]

Montreal Street was another Munjoy Hill lane that saw Black residency over the years. Steamboat steward John Gaskill and his wife, Charlotte, the Reverend William Singleton and his wife, Charlotte, and steward John Palmer and his wife, Louisa, all lived on Montreal Street. Those who made homes on lower Congress Street included Cecil and Rose Hinds, Joseph and Iris Simpson, Domingo and Bessie Barrows, and Joseph and Margaret Franklin.[43]

Washington Street (now Avenue), located at the foot of Munjoy Hill and running from Congress Street out toward the Falmouth line, was home to many Black families as well. In 1900, cook and St. Thomas native George Rose lived at 103 Washington with his wife and three children. Two doors up the street from the Rose household lived teamster George Johnson, his wife, Sarah, and their two youngest children. Farther up and across Washington Street lived laborer Lewis Johnson and his wife, Susan, in the rear of house number 158; fish curer William Manuel and his wife, Sarah, at house number 164; and carpenter Felix Junco and his wife, Hattie, at house number 204.[44]

The profile of Black Portland's home buying and home renting patterns tended to fall within the state-wide averages for Black residency. African Americans across the state were overwhelmingly urban; as city residents they were also less likely to own their homes than Blacks who lived in rural settings. Of the 292 Black households in Maine in 1900, 27.4 percent were owned (free), 10.96 percent were owned with a mortgage or other encumbrance, 53.4 percent were rented, and 5.1 percent were of unknown status.[45] For Blacks in Maine, one-person and two-person households made up the largest proportion of domestic arrangements. Among home-owning Black families, however, two-person and four-person families were the largest groups. Among tenant families, the largest groups were one-person and two-person families. By 1930, the median size of Black families in Maine was 2.86 members.[46]

In Portland Black home values varied, with examples being found above and below the (Black) Maine median of $2,000 to $2,999. For example,

Rhoda Lawrence, her daughter, Geneva Lawrence Gaskill, and her son-in-law, Walter, all lived at 49 Lafayette Street. Lawrence's large one-and-a-half-story frame dwelling was valued at $1,800. The same was true of the 16a Federal Street home of Baptist clergyman James Cornish and his family. Other homes were valued lower or higher. Chef John Verra's one-and-a-half-story, single-family home was valued in 1930 at $1,000. The two-story frame house at 48 Lafayette, occupied by the Dicksons and the Dodges, was valued considerably higher. At $4,000 it was one of Black Portland's more expensive homes.[47] As urban dwellers, Blacks in Portland were generally less likely to own their homes. Blacks usually paid between $15 and $25 a month or between $180 and $300 a year to rent their homes. Drugstore clerk Joseph Simpson, his wife, Iris, and their young son lived at 99 Congress Street where the rent was $25 a month. Boat steward Domingo Barrows paid the same amount for the 199 Congress Street home where he, his wife, Bessie, and their four children resided. Carrie Harris paid a lower $16 per month to rent her home at 24 Monroe Street. Alonzo Nash's rent was below the market average; he paid $10 dollars per month for his family's Marion Street home.[48]

Their Institutional Development

The years 1870 to 1930 marked significant institutional development by and for Blacks in Portland. As a group, African Americans in the city had already played visible roles in the region's abolitionist and colored convention movements of the mid-nineteenth century. In the twentieth century, they rose to meet the new and different challenges of expanding civil and women's rights. In doing so, they established local branches of national organizations.[49]

African Americans in Portland had a number of churches from which to choose. Many African Americans in the city worshipped at the Abyssinian Church on Newbury Street until it closed around 1917. Blacks also attended the African Methodist Episcopal (AME) Zion Mission, popularly identified in city records as the Mountfort Street Church. Pastored by Munjoy Hill's Rev. William Singleton, the church was later renamed Green Memorial AME Zion church in honor of one of its most dedicated supporters, Union Station porter-turned-bootblack Moses Green.[50] In terms of education, Blacks in Portland attended a variety of elementary schools. Most Blacks attended Portland

High School. As the Black population in Ward Seven grew, an increasing number of African American students would eventually matriculate at Deering High School.[51]

One of Black Portland's greatest achievements was its ability to forge its own organizations, outside the norms of church and school. The most visible was probably the Portland chapter of the National Association for the Advancement of Colored People (NAACP). The NAACP Portland chapter organized in early 1920 and became the state's first official branch when it was chartered later that year. In all, sixty-two names graced the application, significantly exceeding the minimum fifty members required for a NAACP charter. Applicants held a variety of occupations, from maid and matron to housewife and music teacher, from street cleaner and janitor to porter and preacher. Each charter member paid the required application fee of one dollar.[52]

Portland's chapter of the NAACP was chartered shortly after the New Haven and Newport branches were established. Organized in 1917, the New Haven branch reportedly saw sizeable growth and seemingly achieved membership in the hundreds in its early years. Newport's local NAACP chapter was incorporated in 1919, one year before the Portland branch. It, too, had sizeable numbers of people, and its membership, like Portland's, was drawn across the spectrum of nativity, sex, education, and class. Whether because of size, location, or accessibility, the New Haven and Newport chapters were able to draw the attendance of leading NAACP personnel more successfully than Portland. Both the New Haven and Newport chapters, for example, gave audience to NAACP co-founder, *Crisis* editor, and leading intellectual W. E. B. DuBois at least once. Portland founded its NAACP chapter much sooner than neighboring Portsmouth, New Hampshire, which did not establish a branch of the organization until 1958.[53]

The specific impetus for the Portland chapter's creation is unclear from NAACP branch files, but it is clear that it dealt with various local and state issues after the 1920 chartering. One high-profile case followed closely by the NAACP surrounded the May 1921 murder of New Bedford native James Walker, a sailor on the schooner *Mary F. Barnett,* which had docked in Portland. Walker and other Black crewmen on the *Barnett* had reportedly violated an agreement to boycott local vessels, an agreement born of local tensions between seamen and ship owners. According to the *Portland Evening Express,* a group of ten to fifteen men beat several

Charter Members of NAACP Portland Branch, 1920

Name	Occupation	Name	Occupation
Dr. Herndon White	Physician	Mrs. Ella Kent	Housewife
Mr. J. C. Fisher	Bank Messen.	Mrs. Alfred Martin	Housewife
Mr. Edgar Howard	Nurse	Rev. George Simms	Preacher
Mrs. Moses Green	Housewife	Miss Gordia Adams	Domestic
Mrs. Edgar Howard	Housewife	Mrs. L. B. Gaskill	Housewife
Mr. Silas B. Ball	Mail Clerk	Miss Harriette Watson	Maid
Mr. Charles A. Wayman	Porter	Mr. Benjamin Wilson	Chef
Mrs. A. L. Palmer	Housewife	Mrs. Benjamin Wilson	Domestic
Mr. James Linton	Street Cleaner	Mr. Edward Norris	Steward
Mrs. Sarah E. Ruby	Cateress	Mr. J. A. Galloway	Chef
Mr. Cyril Durrant	Butler	Mrs. J. A. Galloway	Housewife
Mr. Troy Rodgers	Porter	Mr. P. O. Hill	Merchant
Mrs. Edward Fubler	Domestic	Mrs. P. O. Hill	Housewife
Mr. James Taylor	Preacher	Miss Florence Hill	Music Teacher
Mrs. James Taylor	Housewife	Mr. Harold Hill	Clerk
Mr. John Moore	Chauffeur	Mrs. John Spaulding	Housewife
Rev. J. S. N. Tross	Preacher	Mrs. Frances Robinson	Cook
Mrs. Herndon White	Stenographer	Miss Maude Robinson	Graduate Nurse
Mr. Moses Green	Station Porter	Mr. Wayne Tillman	Station Porter
Mrs. Joseph Franklin	Domestic	Mrs. Wayne Tillman	Housewife
Mrs. Rhoda Lawrence	Housewife	Mrs. Carrie Lynch	Domestic
Mrs. George Simms	Housewife	Mr. James D. Bridges	Mail Porter
Mr. Percy Morrissette	Cook	Mr. Robert Boston	Porter
Miss Gertrude Franklin	Maid	Miss Eula H. Milligan	Nurse
Mrs. J. F. L. Hill	Matron	Mr. Joseph Franklin	Janitor
Miss Llewena Hill	Student	Mr. Edward Trimmingham	Mechanic
Mr. Walter Richey	Painter	Rev. Otis Cornish	Preacher
Mrs. Belle Jackson	Housewife	Mrs. Otis Cornish	Housewife
Miss Emmeline Williams	Nurse	Mr. John Dumas	Mail Porter
Mr. Clarence Franklin	Baker	Mr. Cornelius Harris	Butler
Mr. John Thompson	Chauffeur	Mr. Alfred Martin	Waiter

Source: Application for Charter of Portland, Maine, Branch of the National Association for the Advancement of Colored People, 1920, NAACP Branch Files: Portland, Maine, 1913–1922, Box 1-G84, Folder 3, Manuscript Division, Library of Congress.

Black sailors onboard. Walker received the worst treatment. His assailants fractured his skull and threw him in the harbor where he drowned. Searchers had to employ grappling hooks to retrieve his body.[54]

The *Portland Evening Express* ran several front-page articles about the Walker case, and NAACP president Joseph Fisher recounted the news to NAACP headquarters in New York City. He advised National Secretary James Weldon Johnson of the case's legal progress:

I saw two of the men Sunday and they told me the story and I told them I would be in the court when they are [arraigned] for a hearing. I also told them that I rep[resent] the N.A.A.C.P. Branch of Portland and would help them if they need it . . . I was in the court this morning and all of the colored victims were glad to see me there. Mr. Johnson[,] I don't think they will need the N.A.A.C.P. to help them. But I think it[']s my duty to report the case to you.[55]

Fisher's letter to Johnson not only illustrates his leadership of the Portland chapter; it also confirms that the local branch did not operate in a vacuum. Blacks were regularly in communication with the NAACP office on Fifth Avenue, with Director of Branches Robert Bagnall, and with National Secretary James Weldon Johnson, one of the most significant African American figures of the day. A graduate of prestigious Atlanta University, James Weldon Johnson, together with his brother, Rosamond, composed the song, "Lift Every Voice and Sing," in 1901. It soon became known as the "Negro National Anthem."[56]

The Portland NAACP's vigilance in the James Walker case complemented the activities of the Bangor chapter, which was chartered in 1921 as only the second such branch in the state. In Bangor, the NAACP opposed a third showing of D. W. Griffith's *Birth of a Nation* and asked the mayor to intervene because of the film's racist content. Neither Bangor's mayor nor its chief of police was able to find any legal premise to support the NAACP's request. Seemingly undeterred, the NAACP leadership approached the theater's manager who, although against offending the city's Black citizens, would not cancel the booking because of its extensive advertising. The Bangor NAACP successfully negotiated to have the film edited. After screening the changes, members appeared satisfied "that the film was considerably cut, since last shown in Bangor, and the most objectionable scene was omitted."[57]

The Ku Klux Klan maintained an extensive Maine presence during the 1920s. The group actively intimidated African American, Jewish, Catholic, and immigrant communities throughout Maine. With chapters across the state and Klan headquarters in Portland, the organization influenced local and state politics. It helped shape Portland city elections in 1923 and the gubernatorial race of 1924.[58] The Portland NAACP was surely aware of the group's presence, and in October of 1922, Bagnall encouraged the Portland branch to make the fight against the Klan "a steady one rather than a spasmodic thing."[59] Bagnall further counseled the chapter to join forces with other powerful groups in Portland:

We would advise that you arrange conferences with the leading Jews and Roman Catholics, also Labor leaders, as the Klan is against all of these, as well as against the Negro, and that you get them to enter actively into the fight. You can obtain very easily the cooperation of the Jewish women clubs and the Knights of Columbus for the Roman Catholic Church.[60]

Unfortunately, surviving NAACP branch files do not shed light on NAACP collaborative activity, nor do they illuminate the nature or success of any anti-Klan activity.

In November of 1922, Portland's NAACP chapter had an election with unprecedented results. It not only chose its first female president, it elected an all-female executive board. Mrs. Thalia Perry of 85 Fore Street was elected president, and outgoing president Arthur Edwards described her as having "intelligence and a great many other good qualities, including tact that is essential in filling this office." Edmonia Green, wife of Moses Green, was chosen vice president; Nellie Martin, wife of former Elks Club cook, Albert Martin, became treasurer; Mrs. Gladys Durrant, wife of butler Cyril Durrant, was secretary; and Miss Llewena Hill, now a Gorham Normal School graduate, was re-elected assistant secretary.[61] It is difficult to tell whether the Portland NAACP's election of an exclusively female executive body signaled its progressiveness or whether it marked a decline in Black men's interest in leadership. The Portland chapter's outgoing president saw the 1922 election results as a sign of promise and the basis for optimism about the upcoming year. Despite the NAACP's accomplishments of its early years, the organization was in decline by the late 1920s, and was inactive during the 1930s. The Portland NAACP would emerge again—in the late 1940s and 1950s—with the same impermanence. The branch began again in 1964, and in 2004 celebrated forty years of continuous activity.[62]

By the late nineteenth century, African American women had become a powerful force in the anti-lynching, women's suffrage, and social reform campaigns. One of the most visible groups, the National Association of Colored Women (NACW) had members like Mary Church Terrell, Ida B. Wells-Barnett, and Mary McCleod Bethune. Few would argue that Black Portland was the center of Black women's club activity in New England, but it was not oblivious to the movement, either. The *Woman's Era*, the monthly newspaper of Josephine St. Pierre Ruffin's Woman's Era Club, alluded to Black women in Maine in the newspaper's inaugural issue of 24 March 1894. In that edition, it justified its entrance into the "already overgrown field" of newspaper publishing and defined itself "as a medium of intercourse and sympathy between the women of all races and conditions: especially true is this, of the educated and refined, among the colored women, members of which class may be found in every state from Maine to Florida."63 Despite the proximity of Boston, the newspaper's home base, to Portland, the activities of specific Black women in Maine appear to be absent from the *Woman's Era's* reporting. In August 1895, for example, Black women's clubs from along the eastern coast met in Boston as part of a National Conference of Colored Women. No Maine women were identified as having attended.64

By the summer of 1905, however, much had changed, and Black women in Portland were visible members and leaders in the Northeastern Federation of Women's Clubs (NFWC). Nettie Smith, a nurse and the wife of barbershop proprietor Corbin Smith, helped open the Northeastern Federation's ninth annual conference, held in Boston that August. By the end of the conference proceedings, Edmonia Green had been elected one of the Federation's six vice presidents to serve under NFWC president Alice W. Wiley. At the Federation's eighteenth annual meeting in the summer of 1914, Portland manicurist Sadie Ruby Sibley, daughter of entrepreneur William W. Ruby, became one of the organization's seven vice presidents under the leadership of New Bedford's Elizabeth C. Carter. In 1915, Sarah Hill, wife of Llewellyn Hill and mother of Llewena Hill, became one of seven vice presidents as the NFWC continued under Carter's leadership.65

In ways similar to that of the Portland NAACP, Black women's travel to various parts of the northeast, their interactions with other club women, and their leadership duties put them in contact with some of the leading Black women in the movement. In 1905, for example, Margaret Murray Washington, wife of Booker T. Washington, addressed the NFWC's Boston convention, where she spoke of the importance of mothers' meetings and related her own success with women in Tuskegee, Alabama. Powerful regional contacts for Black Portland's club women included Roberta J. Dunbar, a rising star in the NFWC, and a future board member of the NACW, under President Mary Talbert and Vice President Hallie Q. Brown.66

While the sixty years between 1870 and 1930 comprise a relatively brief moment in Black Portland's history, they were formative years in which the community's significance was not bound by the limits of its population. Various Blacks living in Portland during this period went on to leave indelible impressions on the city and the region and even exerted influence nationally. The Gaskills remained not only in Portland but on Munjoy Hill for most their lives. After serving the Army during World War I, Walter H. Gaskill became a long-time member of the Merchant Marines. Gaskill married Geneva Lawrence, and when he died in 1966, he lived at 46 Lafayette, in close proximity to his childhood home. John E. Gaskill outlived his older brother Walter by twenty-five years, and lived to be ninety-eight years old. John Gaskill married music teacher Marguerite Giro. During his lifetime, Gaskill spent more than forty-five years working for the Central Maine Power Company and two decades serving as a Portland Harbor safety inspector. Gaskill, a former semi-professional baseball player, had the honor of being inducted into the Maine Baseball Hall of Fame in 1976. Prior to his death, John Gaskill lived at 56 Lafayette Street, a few doors from his brother, Walter.[67]

Edward and Una Williams Richardson's son, Clifford ("Kippy"), was a multiple-term member of the city school committee. A veteran of the United States Army, a proprietor of a successful cleaning business, and a former high school track star, he became one of the most well-known African Americans in the city. Harold Richardson, Clifford's brother, also entered local office and was a member and past chair of the Portland Water Board. Together, Clifford and Harold Richardson helped make the Richardson name well known among Portland's Black and white citizens.[68]

Jamaica natives David and Mary Daly Dickson raised a highly successful family of five children on a modest janitor's salary. To David Dickson's credit were his civic activities, his founding of the Black service organization known as the Community Club, and later, his support of a Portland-based USO chapter for Blacks. Mary Daly Dickson was honored publicly in 1950 when she was named "Maine Mother of the Year." Three of the Dicksons's sons became doctors, another son became a college president, and their only daughter became a Washington, D.C.–based leader in higher education policy and research. All of the Dickson children eventually moved out of Portland and out of Maine.[69]

Emory and Irene Dodge's daughter, Beverly, graduated from Portland's Mercy Hospital School of Nursing and moved to New York where she continued her graduate education, with degrees in the fields of health and education. When she was a senior at Portland High School, Dodge learned that the Washington, D.C., hotel where the rest of her

classmates would lodge during their school trip refused to accommodate her. With much publicity and some intervention from then Maine
Senator Margaret Chase Smith, the capital hotel reversed its decision.
Beverly Dodge traveled to Washington, D.C., stayed at the hotel, and, in
effect, desegregated the public establishment.[70]

Despite its northern New England locale and comparatively small
population, Black Portland was not on the margins of Black life during
the late nineteenth and early twentieth centuries. Members of this
rather diverse population held various jobs, supported historically
Black churches, established a NAACP branch, were active in the Black
women's club movement, and networked with other African Americans of regional and national prominence. Conversely, reports of Black
Portland's activities in the *Woman's Era,* the *Colored American,* and the
New York Age exposed their presence to the serials' respective regional
and national readerships.[71] What Blacks in Portland lacked in numbers, they may have made up in appreciation. It is much clearer, however, that what they lacked in numbers, they fully made up in hard
work and institutional expansion.

Notes

1. In 1870, Charles Eastman's eldest son, Charles, followed in his father's
footsteps and also worked as a barber. Charles Eastman Jr. married Sarah Ange-
lina Parrott; Harry and Sadie Eastman were their children. Charles Eastman Jr.
died in November of 1898. The *Colored American Magazine,* February 1901, 317;
May 1901, 69–70; 1899 Portland City Directory. Photographs of Harry and
Sadie Eastman were featured in the May 1901 issue of the *Colored American,*
pages 53 and 55, respectively. The *Colored American* published from 1900 to
1909. One of its most well-known editors and contributors was Pauline E. Hopkins, who had been born in Portland in 1859, but moved to Boston as a child.
Hopkins acted as the *Colored American*'s literary editor until illness forced her
to cease her relationship with the magazine in late 1904. For writings by Hopkins, see *The Magazine Novels of Pauline Hopkins,* Schomburg Library of
Nineteenth-Century Black Women Writers (Cambridge, U.K.: Oxford University Press), 1990.
2. Various treatments of Blacks in Portland in particular and Maine in general include Randolph Stakeman, "Slavery in Colonial Maine," *Maine Historical
Society Quarterly* 27, no. 2 (Fall 1987): 58–81; "The Black Population of Maine,
1764–1900," *New England Journal of Black Studies,* no. 8 (1989): 17–35; Shoshana

Hoose and Karine Odlin, *Anchor of the Soul*, VHS, 60 min., 1994; Elwood Watson, "William Burney and John Jenkins: A Tale of Maine's Two African-American Mayors," *Maine History*, 40, no. 2 (Summer 2001): 113–25; Bob Greene, *Maine Roots IV: The Manuel/Mathews/Ruby Family* (Family Affair Production, 2003), African American Collection of Maine, Jean Byers Sampson Center for Diversity in Maine, University of Southern Maine Libraries.

3. Stakeman, "Black Population of Maine," 21–22. Maine's Black population rose in subsequent decades, and by 1960 Blacks made up 0.3 percent of the state population, and 0.4 percent by 1990. The figures have been rounded up to the nearest decimal point. United States Bureau of the Census, *Ninth Census of the United States, 1870*, Vol. 1, Population; *Twelfth Census of the United States, 1900*, Vol. 1, Population, Part 1; *Fifteenth Census of the United States, 1930*, Vol. 3, Population, Part 1.

4. *Ninth Census of the United States, 1870*, Vol. 1, Population; *Twelfth Census of the United States, 1900*, Vol. 1, Population, Part 1; *Fifteenth Census of the United States, 1930*, Vol. 3, Population, Part 1.

5. *Twelfth Census of the United States, 1900*, Vol. 1, Population, Part 1.

6. *Fifteenth Census of the United States, 1930*, Vol. 3, Population, Part 1, 2.

7. *Fifteenth Census of the United States, 1930*, Vol. 3, Population, Part 1.

8. United States Bureau of the Census, *Negro Population in the United States, 1790–1915* (New York: Arno Press and the *New York Times*, 1968), 62, 75–79.

9. Ninth Census of the United States, 1870 (manuscript; hereafter "ms"); Twelfth Census of the United States, 1900 (ms).

10. Ninth Census of the United States, 1870 (ms).

11. John Paris was Mary Paris's husband. Ninth Census of the United States, 1870 (ms); Twelfth Census of the United States, 1900 (ms); 1899 Portland City Directory.

12. Ninth Census of the United States, 1870 (ms); Twelfth Census of the United States, 1900 (ms); Fifteenth Census of the United States, 1930 (ms); Bureau of the Census, *Negro Population*, 62.

13. Ninth Census of the United States, 1870 (ms); Twelfth Census of the United States, 1900 (ms); Fifteenth Census of the United States, 1930 (ms).

14. Ninth Census of the United States, 1870 (ms); Twelfth Census of the United States, 1900 (ms); Fifteenth Census of the United States, 1930 (ms); Briton Cooper Busch, "Cape Verdeans in the American Whaling and Sealing Industry, 1850–1900," in *Making a Living: The Work Experience of African Americans in New England,* ed. Robert L. Hall and Michael M. Harvey (Boston: New England Foundation for the Humanities, 1995), 422–42. See also Robert C. Hayden, *African Americans and Cape Verdean-Americans in New Bedford: A History of Community Achievement* (Boston: Select Publications, 1993).

15. Twelfth Census of the United States, 1900 (ms); 1899 Portland City Directory. By 1900 Margaret Franklin had given birth to a total of thirteen children. Of those thirteen children, only six were living in 1900.

16. United States Census Bureau, *Negro Population,* 83.

17. Robert Austin Warner, *New Haven Negroes* (New Haven: Yale University Press, 1940), 192–94.

18. David Carey Jr., Interview with Cecil Hinds, 13 February 2004, Portland, Maine.

19. Jacqueline Jones, *American Work: Four Centuries of Black and White Labor* (New York: W. W. Norton, 1998), 301–36, 463–73; Howard Zinn, *A People's History of the United States 1492–Present,* revised ed. (New York: HarperPerennial, 1995), 247–349; Jacqueline Jones, *Labor of Love, Labor of Sorrow: Black Women, Work, and the Family, from Slavery to the Present* (New York: Vintage Books/Random House, 1995), 110–95.

20. Ninth Census of the United States, 1870 (ms); 1871 Portland City Directory. Some of the men's occupations identified in the 1870 census do not agree with the 1871 directory, indicating that some men may have left their jobs as seamen, that they worked seasonally, or that they worked multiple jobs.

21. W. Jeffrey Bolster, *Black Jacks: African American Seaman in the Age of Sail* (Cambridge, Mass.: Harvard University Press, 1997), 158, 220–23.

22. Ninth Census of the United States, 1870 (ms).

23. Ninth Census of the United States, 1870 (ms). Black women in the late nineteenth and early twentieth centuries were keenly aware that their moral character was under attack. One of the objectives of Black women's club activity was to protect the Black female image. Knowing that they were judged not by the best, but the lowest Black woman, the NACW chose as its motto "Lifting As We Climb." See Paula Giddings, *When and Where I Enter* (New York: Morrow, 1984), 97–99; Dorothy Salem, "National Association of Colored Women," in *Black Women in America: An Historical Encyclopedia,* Vol. 2, ed. Darlene Clark Hine, Elsa Barkley Brown, and Rosalyn Terborg-Penn (Bloomington: Indiana University Press, 1993), 842–51.

24. Ninth Census of the United States, 1870 (ms). The Baxter household was interesting in that it was all women. The head of the household, Abigail, was thirty-eight years old in June of 1870 and her primary occupation was keeping house. Isabella and Emily were twenty-six and twenty-two years old, respectively, and the household's only breadwinners. Sarah, twenty-four; Jeanette, twenty; and Alyada, six; completed the family. The census does not identify the women's exact familial relationships; they may have been sisters, with young Alyada having been one of the women's daughters.

25. Herb Adams, "African-Americans on the Steamship Portland," *Portland Monthly Magazine,* Winterguide, 1999; "The sea gives up one of its ghosts— Legendary steamship Portland located in marine sanctuary off Massachusetts,"

30 August 2002. Available at www.cnn.com/2002/US/historic.shipwreck [Accessed 29 July 2004]; Hoose and Odlin, *Anchor of the Soul.*

26. Bolster, *Black Jacks,* 158, 220–23.

27. Ninth Census of the United States, 1870 (ms); Twelfth Census of the United States, 1900 (ms); 1871 Portland City Directory.

28. Ninth Census of the United States, 1870 (ms).

29. Jones, *American Work,* 328–29.

30. *Fifteenth Census of the United States, 1930,* Vol. 4, Population.

31. Fifteenth Census of the United States, 1930 (ms); 1930 Portland City Directory.

32. Fifteenth Census of the United States, 1930 (ms); 1930 Portland City Directory. The 1930 census and 1930 City Directory report different employers for Daniel Giro. The census reports that he was a clerk for a wholesale broker, while the directory reports that he worked at Eastern News.

33. United States Bureau of the Census, *Statistics of Women at Work. Based on Unpublished Information Derived from the Schedules of the Twelfth Census: 1900* (Washington, D.C.: GPO, 1907), 144–45, 184, 185.

34. Bureau of the Census, *Women at Work,* 146.

35. *Fifteenth Census of the United States, 1930,* Vol. 4, Population.

36. Twelfth Census of the United States, 1900 (ms); Fifteenth Census of the United States, 1930 (ms); *Green and White,* The Yearbook of Gorham Normal School, 1922, University Archives, Special Collections, University of Southern Maine Libraries.

37. For personal testimony of the exclusion of Black teachers in Maine, see Shoshana Hoose and Karine Odlin, *Anchor of the Soul,* 1994, VHS, 60 min.; "Bangor: Many Hundreds Gone," in Randall Kenan, *Walking On Water: African American Lives at the Turn of the Twenty-First Century* (New York: Alfred A. Knopf, 1999).

38. 1907 Portland City Directory; Application for Charter of Portland, Maine Branch of the National Association for the Advancement of Colored People, 1920, NAACP Branch Files: Portland, Maine, 1913–1922, Box 1-G84, Folder 3, Manuscript Division, Library of Congress. A third woman among the Portland NAACP's charter members also was a nurse. Maude Robinson, of 114 Grove Street in Augusta, is listed in the records as a "Grad. Nurse."

39. Fifteenth Census of the United States, 1930 (ms); 1930 Portland City Directory.

40. United States Bureau of the Census, *The Statistics of the Population of the United States . . . Compiled from the Original Returns of the Ninth Census (June 1, 1870)* (Washington, D.C.: GPO, 1872; Reprint, New York: Norman Ross Publishing, Inc., 1990), Vol. 1, Population; *Twelfth Census of the United States (1900),* Vol. 1, Population, Part 1; *Fifteenth Census of the United States (1930),* Vol. 3, Population, Part 1.

41. Twelfth Census of the United States, 1900 (ms); Fifteenth Census of the United States, 1930 (ms); 1899 Portland City Directory; 1930 Portland City Directory.

42. Interview with Beverly Bowens, 31 March 2001, "'Home Is Where I Make It': African American Community and Activism in Greater Portland, Maine," Oral History Project, African American Collection of Maine, Jean Byers Sampson Center for Diversity in Maine, University of Southern Maine Libraries.

43. Twelfth Census of the United States, 1900 (ms); Fifteenth Census of the United States, 1930 (ms); 1923 Portland City Directory.

44. Twelfth Census of the United States, 1900 (ms); 1899 Portland City Directory.

45. *Fifteenth Census of the United States (1930),* Vol. 6, Population: Families; *Twelfth Census of the United States (1900),* Vol. 3, Population, Part II.

46. *Fifteenth Census of the United States (1930),* Vol. 6, Population: Families.

47. Fifteenth Census of the United States, 1930 (ms); Sanborn Fire Insurance Company Maps for Portland, 1896, Microfilm Reel #6.

48. Fifteenth Census of the United States, 1930 (ms).

49. See, for example, Hoose and Odlin, *Anchor of the Soul.*

50. 1899 Portland City Directory; Hoose and Odlin, *Anchor of the Soul.*

51. For more on the history of Portland and Deering high schools, visit the Portland Room, Portland Public Library.

52. NAACP to Edgar B. Howard, 24 July 1920; Application for Charter of Portland, Maine, Branch of the National Association for the Advancement of Colored People, NAACP Branch Files: Portland, Maine, 1913–1922, Box 1-G84, Folder 3, Manuscript Division, Library of Congress.

53. Warner, *New Haven Negroes,* 278–88; Armstead, *Don't Take Me in August,* 105–08, 128; Mark J. Sammons and Valerie Cunningham, *Black Portsmouth: Three Centuries of African-American Heritage* (Hanover, N.H.: University Press of New England, 2004), 141, 181.

54. "Hold Several Men for Sailor's Murder—Man Missing After Battle on Vessel," *Portland Evening Express and Daily Advertiser,* 21 May 1921, 1, 5; "Alleged Slayers in Police Court Today—Continuance Asked Special Grand Jury to Consider Case," 23 May 1921, 1, 20; "Scene of the Saturday Morning Murder," 24 May 1921, 2.

55. Joseph C. Fisher to J. W. Johnson, 23 May 1921, NAACP Branch Files: Portland, Maine, 1913–1922, Box 1-G84, Folder 3, Manuscript Division, Library of Congress.

56. Ironically, "Lift Ev'ry Voice and Sing" was written to commemorate Abraham Lincoln's birthday. Deirdre Mullane, ed., *Crossing the Danger Water: Three Hundred Years of African American Writing* (New York: Anchor/Doubleday, 1993).

57. The Queenie Peters letter does not clarify exactly which scene the Bangor NAACP considered the most objectionable. Secretary NAACP to Queenie Peters, 12 January 1921; Queenie Peters to NAACP National Office, 22 July 1921. NAACP Branch Files: Bangor, Maine, 1920–1927, Box 1-G84, Folder 3, Manuscript Division, Library of Congress.

58. John Syrett, "Principle and Expediency: The Ku Klux Klan and Ralph Owen Brewster in 1924," *Maine History* 39, no. 4 (Winter 2000–01): 215–39; "Klan Makes Issue in Maine Politics," *New York Times*, 10 September 1923, 19; "Klan Wins Victory at Portland Polls," *New York Times*, 11 September 1923, 19; "Dirigo Ku Klux," *New York Times*, 12 September 1923, 18. For the 1925 charter of the Androscoggin County Ku Klux Klan, see the Gerald E. Talbot Collection, African American Collection of Maine, Jean Byers Sampson Center for Diversity in Maine, University of Southern Maine Libraries.

59. Robert W. Bagnall to Edgar B. Howard, 11 October 1922, NAACP Branch Files: Portland, Maine, 1913–1922, Box 1-G84, Folder 3, Manuscript Division, Library of Congress.

60. Bagnall to Howard, 11 October 1922, NAACP Branch Files: Portland, Maine, 1913–1922, Box 1-G84, Folder 3, Manuscript Division, Library of Congress. The city of Bangor and the Bangor chapter of the NAACP also grappled with a KKK presence in the early 1920s.

61. Arthur H. Edwards to Robert W. Bagnall, 18 November 1922, NAACP Branch Files: Portland, Maine, 1912–1922, Box 1-G84, Folder 3, Manuscript Division, Library of Congress. The Portland chapter of the NAACP would eventually recharter in June 1948, only to fall into decline by 1953. It was reactivated and officially rechartered in April 1959, but, again, regressed. In May 1964 the chapter reorganized yet again, and the charter was given in ceremony that September. In 2004 the chapter celebrated its fortieth anniversary. See NAACP Branch Files: Portland, Maine, 1913–1922, Box 1-G84, Folder 3; Portland, Maine, 1947–1953, Group II, Box C75; Portland, Maine, 1956–1965, Group III, Box C55; Selena Ricks, "Cause for Celebration," *Portland Press Herald*, 26 September 2004.

62. Arthur H. Edwards to Robert W. Bagnall, 18 November 1922, NAACP Branch Files: Portland, Maine, 1913–1922, Box I-G84, Folder 3; Portland, Maine, 1947–1953, Group II, Box C75, Manuscript Division, Library of Congress.

63. Editorial, The *Woman's Era*, vol. 1, no. 1 (24 March 1894): 8. Microfilm, Boston Public Library.

64. "List of Delegates to National Conference," The *Woman's Era*, vol. 2, no. 5 (August 1895): 13. Microfilm, Boston Public Library.

65. "Women's Clubs at Boston," *New York Age*, 17 August 1905, 3; "New England Women Meeting This Week," *New York Age*, 23 July 1914, 1; "Women's Federation of Northeast Meet," *New York Age*, 15 July 1915, 5; Obituary of William W. Ruby, 2 March 1906, Post Scrapbook, vol. 5, 139–40, Maine Historical Society,

Portland. Corbin Smith operated a shop at 151 Federal Street. The 1914 Portland City Directory identifies Sadie Sibley as "Mrs." rather "Miss"; she boarded at the Franklin Street home of her parents, Sarah and William W. Ruby. See 1907 Portland City Directory; 1914 Portland City Directory; 1915 Portland City Directory; Twelfth Census of the United States, 1900 (ms).

66. "Women's Clubs at Boston," *New York Age,* 17 August 1905, 3; "National Association of Colored Women's Clubs Holds Interesting Session," *New York Age,* 20 July 1918.

67. Obituary of Walter H. Gaskill, *Portland Press Herald,* 30 April 1966, 2; "John E. Gaskill, longtime CMP employee, baseball standout," *Portland Press Herald,* 5 April 1991.

68. "Clifford A. "Kippy" Richardson, city councilor, ran cleaning business," *Portland Press Herald,* 9 July 1994, Portland Obituary Scrapbook, Box 78, p. 292, Maine Historical Society; Interview with Rupert Richardson, March 2001, "Home Is Where I Make It" Collection, African American Collection of Maine, Jean Byers Sampson Center for Diversity in Maine, University of Southern Maine Libraries. According to his interview in Hoose and Odlin's *Anchor of the Soul,* Harold E. Richardson wanted to attend Gorham Normal School after he graduated from Portland High School. Told that Blacks could not teach in Maine classrooms, Richardson pursued a different career path. For more on Richardson, see the Harold E. Richardson Scrapbook, African American Collection of Maine, Jean Byers Sampson Center for Diversity in Maine, University of Southern Maine Libraries.

69. "David A. Dickson Dies Here at 91," *Portland Press Herald,* 5 May 1979, 2.

70. Interview with Beverly Bowens, "Home Is Where I Make It," African American Collection of Maine, Jean Byers Sampson Center for Diversity in Maine, University of Southern Maine Libraries; "Capital Hotels' Color Line Bars PHS 'Best Citizen,'" *Portland Press Herald,* 20 March 1952, 1; "The Washington Story: Beverly Is Going to Capital With Classmates," *Portland Press Herald,* 23 March 1952.

71. The *Woman's Era* had a distributor in New Brunswick, identified only as Mrs. Whetsel. Whetsel was involved in Black women's club activity and attended the 1895 Boston conference hosted by the Woman's Era Club. See "List of Delegates to National Conference," The *Woman's Era,* August 1895, 13.

10

Creating and Preserving Portland's Urban Landscape, 1885–1925

Earle G. Shettleworth Jr.

The configuration and setting of the Portland peninsula captured the imaginations of residents and visitors alike throughout the nineteenth century. In 1855 world-renowned native son Henry Wadsworth Longfellow began his poem "My Lost Youth" with the words, "Often I think of the beautiful town that is seated by the sea." Local author Edward H. Elwell characterized the city in 1876 as "having the seashore at its feet, the mountains at its back; bay, islands, and inland lakes on either hand."[1] In his 1883 book *Peculiarities of American Cities*, travel writer Willard Glazier observed, "The city is built upon a small peninsula rising out of Casco Bay, to a mean central elevation of more than one hundred feet. The elevation of its site, and the beauty of its scenery and surroundings, are fast attracting the attention of tourists, and drawing to the city hosts of summer visitors."[2]

By the 1880s Portlanders had begun to experience an important change in attitude about their community. In previous decades the thriving mercantile port had developed into a nationally significant cultural center. Led by John Neal, America's first art critic, and John A. Poor, the region's premier railroad entrepreneur, this energetic period boasted numerous writers, musicians, sculptors, and landscape painters. Infused with great self confidence, fascinated with local subjects, and backed by enthusiastic patrons, residents saw their city as an economic and artistic rival of Boston. On some levels they were correct. Superb buildings including the Portland Bank, the Merchants Exchange, and Ruggles Sylvester Morse's mansion were equal to any in the land. Still, though individually distinguished, such structures were not part of any unified city plan.

The loss of 1,500 buildings in Portland's downtown during the Great Fire of 4 July 1866 was a terrible economic blow, but as Neal pointed out in his last writings, it presented opportunities as well. The possibility of a central urban vision, with new brick buildings, a water system, parks, and open spaces, was taken up by a new generation of leaders including architect John Calvin Stevens and political progressive James Phinney Baxter. By the 1880s these leaders began to formulate plans for what Portland could become. In the years that followed they would draw not only on their considerable talents, but on the advice and ideas of nationally known experts such as the Olmsted Brothers. In other words, national developments such as the "City Beautiful Movement" informed the urban vision of Portland's civic leaders, whose legacy remains imprinted on the public landscape.

Many late nineteenth century civic leaders were keenly aware of the advantages of Portland's topography and the need for its protection and enhancement. As land on the peninsula became fully developed in the three decades after the 1866 fire, these leaders undertook to preserve perimeter open spaces and enhance public squares. Prominent among those involved was John Calvin Stevens, whose first involvement with this beautification effort came in 1887 when he entered the competition for the Civil War memorial in Monument Square.[3]

In response to a national trend, Lewiston became the first city in Maine to erect a public Civil War monument, which consisted of a bronze infantryman standing on a granite pedestal. Created by Maine sculptor Franklin Simmons in 1868, this format would be repeated in dozens of towns throughout the state. In October 1873, the Portland Soldiers' and Sailors' Association was formed to build a monument to "the hundreds of Portland's young manhood who had paid the price of Union victory."[4] Indeed, war memories were still vivid to a city that had sent five thousand men to the conflict, fully one-sixth of its population. On 15 November 1873, the *Portland Daily Press* praised the effort by stating, "it is proper that our cities should be adorned with works of art which will not only . . . cherish the recollection of exalted patriotism, but will tend to cultivate a taste for the beautiful and assist in the aesthetic education of the people."

From the start, the Association viewed the public space of Market Square as the most appropriate location for a monument (Figure 10-1). The use of the square for civic purposes dated to 1746 when a block-

Figure 10-1. Market Square, circa 1880, showing the Old City Hall at the right and the dome of the New City Hall in the background. Old City Hall was torn down in 1888 to make way for the Portland Soldiers and Sailors Monument, which now occupies the site. Courtesy of the Maine Historic Preservation Commission.

house had been erected there. On its site in 1825 the town constructed a Federal style Market House from designs by the local architect-builder John Kimball Jr. This building was remodeled into a Greek Revival city hall by Charles Q. Clapp when Portland became Maine's first city in 1832. After the completion of a new city hall in 1862, the future of the old one became the focus of much debate. As John Neal remarked in 1874 in his book *Portland Illustrated:*

There has been a seeming determination lately manifested by our people, to have the old City-Hall, or Town House, out of the way, and a handsome square opened for a soldiers' monument, now under consideration, and a fountain worth having. It cannot be denied that, on the whole, we have no better opening for such an enterprise, nor any portion of the city which could be turned to a better account, for the purpose mentioned.[5]

Logical as those words seemed, it nevertheless took the better part of two decades of raising funds and reviewing proposals to achieve the goal of a Civil War memorial in what would be renamed Monument

Square. The first design came from Franklin Simmons, who suggested a thirty-foot column with symbols of the army and navy at the base and a representational figure of the nation at the top. Simmons was followed by a long line of distinguished competitors, who included sculptor Preston Powers and architects Clarence S. Luce and Henry O. Avery.

Early in 1887 the Association's efforts began to achieve results. On the strength of having raised more than $16,000, the group secured the city's permission to replace Old City Hall with a monument. In February, 1887, the Association issued a national call to architects and sculptors for a design which "should be architectural . . . instead of making the monument a mere pedestal for the display of figures."[6] The competition allowed for the modification of previous proposals as well as the submission of new ones within a sixty-day time period. Optimistic about its fund-raising capability, the committee set $25,000 as the cost of building the winning entry.

As the April deadline approached, the Association received a host of proposals, including resubmissions from the New York architects Clarence Luce and Henry Avery. Locally, John Calvin Stevens entered a design for a sixty-eight-foot granite shaft. A preliminary drawing in one of Stevens's sketch books shows that he initially conceived of a monument with an elaborately stepped base and a short, thick column to serve as the pedestal for a winged figure with two seated figures at its feet. The monument was to be surrounded by approaching steps and stone seats.

By the April submission date, Stevens had refined this concept considerably. From the center of a square open platform with a broad flight of stairs on each side rose a square base for a gracefully tapered column topped by a single classical figure holding a sheathed sword in one hand and an olive branch in the other. The classical style of this design was reflected as well in such details as the laurel wreath on the column and the broad arch with its attenuated keystone that enframed a bas relief on each side of the base.

On 20 April 1887, Stevens described his monument proposal in a transmittal letter to landscape artist Harrison B. Brown, who was serving as chairman of the design committee: "The design submitted by me for the Soldiers' Monument is intended to be entirely of Hallowell Granite. The four panels to be filled with bas-reliefs and inscriptions. The height of the monument from ground to top of figure is 68 feet. The figure 15'0" high. Diameter of shaft 9'0" to be of one block of stone. The cost I can only guess at but should think between $30,000 and $40,000."[7]

The design committee rejected Stevens's proposal along with all of the other submissions. One committee member, architect Francis H. Fassett, then provided the "architectural" concept of a rough stone square monument capped by a pyramidal roof reminiscent of the Mausoleum of Halicarnassus. After winning initial approval, this eclectic design was dropped when the cost was found to be $12,000 more than the budget would allow. Two additional alternatives were examined and rejected, a pedestal and shaft proposed by architect Alexander C. Currier of the Hallowell Granite Company and a scheme advanced by James P. Baxter to convert Old City Hall into a memorial building.

In the spring of 1888, the Association ceased the competition process in favor of having Franklin Simmons undertake the project. The sculptor had been employed since 1885 in creating Portland's Henry Wadsworth Longfellow Monument, a seated figure of the poet on a classical pedestal designed by Francis H. Fassett. Located in Longfellow Square, another of the city's prominent public spaces, the Longfellow Monument was unveiled on 29 September 1888. By that time Simmons was at work for the Association with Richard Morris Hunt of New York to plan a square Doric-inspired pedestal of battered granite similar to the architect's base for the Statue of Liberty. Hunt's pedestal was to be adorned on either side by a group of bronze figures, one representing the army and the other the navy. A fourteen-foot bronze figure of "Our Lady of Victories" would stand atop the base. The cornerstone was laid on Memorial Day, 1889, and the dedication took place on 28 October 1891 (Figure 10-2). After eighteen years of effort and nearly $36,000 in expenditures, Association Chairman General John Marshall Brown could eloquently proclaim, "at last, a fitting monument on the fittest spot, of the fairest city of our land."[8]

Referring to Portland as the "fairest city" was not an idle boast but a widely held belief by citizens and visitors alike that the community was endowed with exceptional natural as well as architectural attributes. Prominent among these features were the eastern and western ends of the three-mile-long peninsula. As the traveler Willard Glazer observed in 1883, "At the northeastern most extremity of the Neck, Munjoy Hill rises to a height of one hundred and sixty-one feet, and commands a beautiful view of the city, bay, adjacent islands and the ocean beyond. At the southwestern extremity is Bramhall's Hill, rising to one hundred and seventy-five feet, and commanding city, bay, forests, fields, villages and mountains."[9]

Figure 10-2. The Portland Soldiers and Sailors Monument, shown in this 1892 photograph of Monument Square, was constructed between 1889 and 1891 with a granite base designed by the noted New York architect Richard Morris Hunt and bronze sculptures made by the Maine-born sculptor Franklin Simmons. Courtesy of the Maine Historic Preservation Commission.

The public benefit of these dramatic vistas was recognized as early as 1828 when Portland acquired twelve acres along the east end of Munjoy Hill. Under the leadership of Mayor Levi Cutter, the city bought a similar tract in 1836–37 at the west end of Bramhall's Hill. This purchase was part of Cutter's plan to create the Eastern and Western promenades. Constructed in 1837, these scenic forty-foot-wide drives were planted with rows of elms.

Three decades later Portland established its first public park as a result of the 1866 fire. Bordered by Congress, Franklin, Federal, and Pearl streets, Lincoln Park had been the site of many crowded wooden structures which the city did not want rebuilt because of the fire hazard they would pose.

Free of buildings, the new rectangular park designed by City Civil Engineer Charles R. Goodall was looked upon as a firebreak, which would help stop future conflagrations from sweeping across the peninsula.

During the twenty-year span of City Civil Engineer William A. Goodwin's administration from 1872 to 1892, Portland made further improvements to the Eastern and Western promenades and established the fifty-acre Deering Oaks Park on the northern perimeter of the peninsula. In August of 1878, Calvert Vaux, the noted New York architect formerly in partnership with Andrew Jackson Downing and Frederick Law Olmsted Sr., spent two days with Goodwin to offer his advice on the improvement of the promenades. Following this visit, Goodwin wrote:

It does not require an expert to show us that from whatever direction we enter either of the Promenades, it begins at nothing noticeable throughout. The outlook is grandly beautiful; the foreground contemptible, the trees few and unsightly, devoted in their early infancy to the attrition of cows and the tethering of goats without compensating allowances thereafter. Such grounds should have an approach commensurate with the value of the outlook.[10]

The following December Goodwin presented a paper to the Fraternity Club entitled "Our Public Grounds," in which he outlined his long-range plans for the promenades. With regard to the Western Promenade, he described the approach as "rougher and more uncouth than any piece of country road you will find within 10 miles of Portland. The Promenade is 2,100 feet in length from Bowdoin Street to Arsenal Street. Upon this there are no improvements except that Mr. (J. B.) Brown has set out and cared for good trees along the sidewalk."[11] Goodwin recommended that the approaches to the promenade, Danforth, Bowdoin, and West streets, be widened, flattened, and planted with a double row of trees. He concluded by saying, "The work can never be wholly finished. But it can be begun in a small way and carried on gradually as the city is able."[12] Using this method, William A. Goodwin accomplished grading, sidewalk and esplanade construction, and tree planting on West Street in 1879. The Prospect Point wall and terrace at the head of Bowdoin Street were installed in 1885, followed in 1888 by the planting of a large ornamental bed with a broad path around it at the head of West Street.

During the 1880s Goodwin's Western Promenade improvements helped to draw attention to the West End as a desirable residential neighborhood. Following J. B. Brown's death in 1881, his estate began to sell house lots on the south side of Bowdoin Street. John Calvin Stevens purchased one in 1884 as the site for the new home that he completed there the following year. Early in 1889 Stevens figured prominently in the planning of a new State House at the head of West Street during Portland's abortive attempt to recapture the capital from Augusta. Thus, it is not surprising to find the architect and his partner later that year proposing a Bramhall Park consisting of a system of walking and carriage paths across the face of the Western Promenade escarpment.

John Calvin Stevens and Albert Winslow Cobb unveiled their proposal in a full-page article that appeared in a December 1889 issue of the *Portland Sunday Telegram* (Figure 10-3). Repeating the approach taken in their recent book, *Examples of American Domestic Architecture,* Stevens provided a pen and ink rendering of the concept while Cobb advanced the argument for it in an accompanying essay. According to Cobb, the urgency for establishing Bramhall Park stemmed from the Maine Central Railroad's having erected Union Station at the north end of St. John Street the year before (Figure 10-4). While he praised the Boston architects Bradley, Winslow, and Wetherell for the "elegance" of their chateauesque building, Cobb expressed concern that a crowded tenement neighborhood of railroad workers was rapidly developing across from the station. Should this growth spread south along St. John Street, which paralleled the Western Promenade, it would destroy the vistas from the promenade. In making this case, Cobb provided a graphic description of the consequences of inaction:

Are we to be so eager to economize that we are willing to see this neighborhood, hitherto a wholesome innocuous wilderness, develop into a tract packed full of houses, stables and out-door privies; a thing with all the worst features of a tenement-district, sending up its stench to corrupt the air which blows to Portland from the west?

Now these last are not sweet words. These are discordant words, breeding discordant thoughts. Yet their discord is nothing as compared with the discordant effect upon any observer with eyes and judgement, who traverses the beautiful streets of western Portland, who crosses the open Western Promenade with the glory of that regal landscape filling his eyes, and who suddenly on reaching the brow of a terrace which for nobility has no superior in our land, is affronted by paltry, puerile, and almost unbelievable exhibition.[13]

Figure 10-3. The Bramhall Park proposed by John Calvin Stevens in 1889 would have linked St. John Street with the Western Promenade by rustic walks and drives. This visionary plan would have provided a landscaped entrance to Portland for those coming from the south by rail. Courtesy of the Maine Historic Preservation Commission.

Albert Winslow Cobb's second reason for Bramhall Park focused on the unsightly view for those entering the city by train. To illustrate this point, the architect turned to Chicago's Lakefront Park as his example:

Everyone who has visited the mighty metropolis at the south end of Lake Michigan remembers the Lake Park, along the borders of which run the tracks of the Illinois Central Railroad. The traveler by train who approaches Chicago by this route is more favorably impressed by this stretch of parkway, with its broad expanse of grassland lined by noble trees, above whose tops appear the roofs and turrets of the fine buildings of Michigan Avenue. The people of Chicago knew what they were about when they graced their growing city with this broad touch of beauty at a telling point.

We may learn many valuable lessons from that great Garden City of the West. We may learn from her to be large and generous in dealing out the land over which our city is to be spread; and as a preliminary experiment in this direction, Portland should be dealt as its gift the land, which, stretching along the railroad between the tracks and the western bluffs, corresponds with the Lake Park of Chicago. It will make the railway entrance to Portland a fit portal to the beauties which lie beyond the brow of the high bluff which even in its raw naturalties so impresses the traveler who first approaches it by rail.[14]

In his final argument for Bramhall Park, Cobb cited the wisdom of Boston in enlarging its common during the 1850s in anticipation of the westward growth of the city. He predicted that Portland would

Figure 10-4. From its completion in 1888 until its demolition in 1961, Union Station stood as a be-loved local landmark at the corner of St. John and Congress streets. Beneath the massive iron train shed of this picturesque French chateau–style station, dozens of Maine Central Railroad trains ar-rived and departed each day for more than seven decades. Bradlee, Winslow and Wetherell of Bos-ton were the architects for this stately building, the fond memories of which still haunt Portland. Courtesy of the Maine Historic Preservation Commission.

experience a similar westerly expansion, placing Union Station and the adjacent park at the center of population. In this respect, Cobb foresaw the turn-of-the-century growth of suburbs made possible by the trolley car and the automobile.

Albert Winslow Cobb ended the *Telegram* article with a detailed de-scription of how the park could be created. His emphasis on economi-cal measures accomplished in gradual steps reflected William A. Goodwin's practical approach to developing Portland's parks. After ac-quiring the land, Cobb called for removing whatever buildings were al-ready there. Next he recommended that Goodwin's project of excavat-ing the knoll at the north end of the promenade be extended southward. This would have the dual result of providing more fill for grading streets and making a level space, "a parade or play ground, like the parade ground on Boston Common."[15] Further improvements should include walks and drives, outlooks and terraces, the planting of trees and shrubbery, and the conversion of a swampy hollow into a pond. In this way, Cobb assured his readers that "the splendor of the view of our Western Promenade is secured, foreground and distance, forever."[16]

Despite Albert Winslow Cobb's persuasive proposal for Bramhall Park and John Calvin Stevens's convincing visualization of it, the idea received little immediate support. Unheeded went the plea from the February 1890 *Board of Trade Journal* that "This is a good and practical scheme and if the bulk of our citizens could fully appreciate what our City is yet to be, they would not sleep another night 'til the needed tract was secured."[17] Yet Stevens's and Cobb's efforts apparently won the admiration of William A. Goodwin, who commissioned the firm in 1890 to design picturesque Shingle Style shelters for the Eastern and Western Promenades.

Stevens had first encountered the concept of shelters and outlooks in 1883 when still a partner with Francis H. Fassett. That spring Fassett accompanied Frederick Law Olmsted Sr., John C. Olmsted, and Charles Eliot on a tour of Cushing's Island in Casco Bay to lay plans for a summer colony there. Just a brief boat ride from Portland, Cushing's was joining Little and Great Diamond islands in being transformed into a seasonal retreat. From an architectural standpoint, the Olmsted report that resulted from the visit recommended "that no house be over two stories in height or thirty feet to the top of the roof and at their lower stories shall be of local stone."[18] Moreover, the cottages should be free of "jig-saw or other extremities and puerile ornaments."[19] This prescription for blending new construction into the landscape was faithfully followed by Stevens, who planned most of Cushing's cottages from 1883 until 1910. The use of local field stone and unpainted shingles was also applied by Stevens to the design of the shelters that Olmsted had sited at scenic points on the island. Built about 1885, the largest of these afforded a spectacular vista of the Cape Elizabeth channel from the height of land at the southwestern corner of Cushing's. This rustic structure consisted of an octagonal fieldstone base with eight stone posts supporting a broad hipped roof.

For the Eastern and Western promenades, Stevens and Cobb provided more formal frame versions of the Cushing's shelter that could double as bandstands. In 1890 the City of Portland acquired a small parcel at the southern end of the Eastern Promenade, which William

Goodwin immediately developed into Fort Allen Park. Goodwin located Stevens's and Cobb's octagonal shelter at the foot of the park's sloping hillside to take full advantage of its excellent harbor views (Figure 10-5). The steep contour of the site necessitated a high shingled base accessed by a flight of seven stairs. Eight square posts with small decorative consoles supported an umbrella-like hipped roof.

Surviving sketches for the Western Promenade shelter indicate that the architects considered two different schemes for the head of West Street. The less formal one shows a rectangular, hip roofed stone structure built into the side of the Promenade bluff. A large stone bench extends from one corner of the building to provide seating for visitors. It is this design that appears in the Stevens rendering for Bramhall Park and relates to a mid-1880s shelter by the architect at George S. Hunt's Cape Elizabeth summer cottage. However, the more formal octagonal scheme was the one constructed in 1890. The even site chosen by Goodwin and his architects resulted in a lower, more easily accessible base than the Fort Allen shelter. Eight wide shingled posts supported a broad hipped roof akin to that on the Cushing's shelter. The Eastern and Western promenade shelters pleased Portland's Commissioners of Cemeteries and Public Grounds, who noted in their report for 1890 that "we are under obligations . . . to Stevens & Cobb, architects, for their valuable assistance in the discharge of duties."[20]

Upon the retirement of William A. Goodwin as city civil engineer in 1892, his mantle as advocate for Portland's parks was assumed by James P. Baxter, the highly successful businessman who had turned his energies to civic improvements and historical pursuits (Figure 10-6). These included the gift of the public library building and the writing of treatises on seventeenth-century Maine exploration and settlement. Between 1893 and 1905 Baxter was elected to six one-year terms as mayor. During his public career, he worked tirelessly to achieve the goal of an expanded park system. He first tackled the problem of the private land on the harbor side of the Eastern Promenade by having a plan made of the area showing the property ownership. With this evidence, he publicized the fact that most of it was in private hands, which surprised many who had assumed that it belonged to the city. The landowners were contacted, and after several months of persistent efforts, a number of them agreed to sell their holdings at terms favorable to Portland. One large piece of land was paid for in small annual installments.

Figure 10-5. When Portland established Fort Allen Park adjacent to the Eastern Promenade in 1890, the city's civil engineer, William A. Goodwin, asked John Calvin Stevens and his partner Albert Winslow Cobb to design this octagonal Shingle Style bandstand, which remains a focal point of the park today. Courtesy of the Maine Historic Preservation Commission.

Under James P. Baxter's leadership, Stevens's and Cobb's Bramhall Park proposal was implemented to the extent that the city acted to protect the Western Promenade's scenic vistas by acquiring its slopes. Again citizens thought that the area already belonged to Portland. In the Council, a measure to purchase the land failed, but the mayor later triumphed by exchanging a piece of city property for it with the Brown Estate.

Not satisfied with enlarging the Eastern and Western promenades as well as Deering Oaks, Baxter decided in 1895 to pursue the concept of a boulevard around Back Cove. Although the idea was not original with him, he became its chief exponent, commissioning the firm of Olmsted, Olmsted, and Eliot to plan a landscaped highway to encircle the cove. Shortly after the landscape architects filed their report in May 1896, Baxter began to negotiate for land and secure funds from the city to purchase it. At this point he was unfairly attacked for trying to buy property and resell it to Portland at a profit. Despite this political accusation, he continued to fight for the boulevard for the balance of his public life. His strong stand on the issue once lost him his seat as mayor. However, he was re-elected, and in his inaugural address of 1904 he reported:

Figure 10-6. James P. Baxter's early success in business allowed him to devote much of his life to civic, scholarly, and philanthropic pursuits. During his six terms as Portland's mayor, Baxter (1831–1921) led the effort to expand the city's open spaces in order to create a park system that would include a boulevard around Back Cove, which now bears his name. Courtesy of the Maine Historic Preservation Commission.

On 24 September 1903, the City Council took the first step toward . . . construction of a boulevard around Back Cove substantially on the lines laid down in the report of Olmsted, Olmsted and Eliot in 1896 . . . A small appropriation made each year will soon complete an attractive driveway, which may be made an important part of our park system and open for improvement an extensive tract of land most desirable for residence.[21]

The last line reflects the practical as well as the aesthetic nature of Baxter's vision. His ideas were carried out with sound economic planning and an eye to making various areas desirable for residential development that would benefit the city in real estate taxes.

In 1905, during his last term as mayor, Baxter published a booklet entitled *The Park System of Portland*, which outlined what progress had been made during his administrations and what remained to be done. Accompanying his text were three folding colored maps made by the Olmsted Brothers. The first illustrated Baxter's plan for a unified park system in which the Western Promenade was linked with Deering Oaks, which in turn was connected to a Back Cove boulevard that ended with a bridge to the Eastern Promenade. The other two maps were devoted to the Eastern and Western Promenades, which were shown as tree-lined drives. Sections of the Eastern Promenade were set aside for such active recreational uses as a baseball field and a children's playground. Baxter cited the need for more playgrounds and suggested small parks within the city at such points as Congress Square, the foot of Center Street, and the junction of York and Pleasant streets. To promote his unfinished agenda, the mayor took Portland's officials to Boston at his own expense to show them how parks, scenic drives, and playgrounds could enhance a city.

John Calvin Stevens's and Albert Winslow Cobb's Bramhall Park proposal and James P. Baxter's vision of a Portland park system both had their origins in the urban park movement which stemmed from Frederick Law Olmsted Sr.'s Central Park in New York City. While the effort to maintain a balance between city life and nature began in the 1850s, comprehensive city planning was an early twentieth-century approach to solving a mounting number of interrelated urban issues. Emerging in the first decade of the century, city planning was defined by Frederick Law Olmsted Jr. as:

The intelligent control and guidance of the entire physical growth and alteration of cities; embracing all the problems of transportation facilities or of recreational facilities, congestion in respect to the means of supplying light, air, water, or anything else essential to the health and happiness of the people, but also in addition to the problems of congestions, each one of the myriad problems involved in making our cities year by year, in their physical arrangement and equipment, healthier, pleasanter and more economic instruments for the use of the people who dwell within them.[22]

In 1912 the need for comprehensive planning in Portland was raised for the first time as the result of a highly controversial two-million-dollar railroad proposal. The eighty-one-year-old James P. Baxter did not enter the debate, but at fifty-eight John Calvin Stevens was in his prime as a local public figure and took an active role in the matter (Figure 10-7). The immediate issue was the 1 April 1912 petition of the Portland Terminal Company to construct a line from the Presumpscot River on the north side of the city to Union Station in order to eliminate the track that ran through the increasingly congested suburban areas along Forest Avenue, a principal artery of the Deering area which had been annexed in 1899. The first leg of the new route from the Presumpscot River to Stroudwater won general acceptance, but the second section involved the construction of twenty-six crossings in newly developed areas of the Deering suburbs. Widespread concern over this aspect of the proposal came from its impact on the residential character of the area and the more than $250,000 cost of the city's share of the crossings. Traditionally welcomed as an instrument of progress since its arrival in the mid-nineteenth century, the railroad was now viewed as a potentially negative force.

Between the 1 April filing of the Portland Terminal Company petition and the 3 May vote on it, the railroad issue dominated the weekly meetings of the mayor and aldermen. The 15 April hearing alone attracted three hundred people. The initial opposition to the proposal came from an unlikely source, the Portland Board of Trade, whose stated objective since its founding in 1853 had been "to encourage and promote in every way possible commercial and industrial progress."[23] Representing the Board, civil engineer Edward C. Jordan affirmed the group's support for the new line from the Presumpscot River to Stroudwater, but urged officials to appoint a commission to study the balance of the project. Jordan stressed that alternative routes must be examined in order to "save many citizens their property and their home locations unimpaired in value and preserve also to the city a large residential district that is rapidly filling up and increasing in value."[24] Here in less than twenty-five years was

Figure 10-7. During a career that spanned from 1873 until 1940, John Calvin Stevens (1855–1940) became Portland's leading architect of his time, planning or remodeling several hundred houses and buildings in the city and the surrounding suburbs and islands. Like James P. Baxter, Stevens was deeply committed to improving Portland through well-designed public buildings and spaces, including city hall and the Sweat Memorial Art Gallery. Courtesy of the Maine Historic Preservation Commission.

fulfillment of Albert Winslow Cobb's prophecy that Union Station would be at the center of Portland rather than on its fringe.

After the 15 April meeting, John Calvin Stevens decided that Portland's architects should become involved in the Portland Terminal Company debate. Thus, on the afternoon of Saturday, 20 April, Stevens, his son John Howard Stevens, and seven of their professional colleagues met to discuss the matter. Joining them was the landscape architect Carl Rust Parker, who had worked with the Olmsted firm before coming to Maine in 1910. While supporting the Board of Trade's call for a study commission, the architects took the issue a step further, concluding that the city should table the entire proposal until it could be examined in the context of Portland's overall future growth. As the *Sunday Press* reported on 21 April 1912:

To this end they will suggest that some expert be retained to go into the matter thoroughly from the city's standpoint, as so far expert advice has been only obtained by the railroad interests. And in case the city itself should not feel like appropriating a sufficient amount to pay for such expert advice, to take immediate steps for the raising of such a fund by subscription. They believe that now is the time when the city should definitely take up the question of a city plan, devised to regulate and promote the best results in its growth. These architects, we understand, stand ready to give their services gratuitously as an advisory board to consult with such an expert should their services be required.

Those points formed the basis for the architects' eloquently worded petition which John Calvin Stevens presented to the mayor and aldermen at their 23 April meeting. Authored by Stevens and signed by those present, the document requested that "steps be taken to bring about a City plan which shall provide for the regulation of the City's future growth in an orderly way with proper provision for the ever increasing traffic and business of the City, and to regulate the division of property so that proposed new streets shall conform to the general plan of development adopted by the City."[25]

As the Bramhall Park proposal of 1889 had evoked Chicago as an example, so Stevens's petition did in 1912, noting that "in Chicago at the present time the railroads are cooperating with the City in its endeavor to rectify some of the mistakes of the haphazard growth of the past."[26] The coupling of a need for a city plan with the example of Chicago could well reflect an awareness on Stevens's part of Daniel H. Burnham and Edward H. Bennett's influential 1909 Plan of Chicago.

By taking a bold stand on the Portland Terminal Company issue, the architects assumed a leadership role. Prior to the 23 April meeting, they had conferred with the Board of Trade, which adopted the points in the architects' petition. That evening before the mayor and aldermen, E. C. Jordan and the Board of Trade President Charles F. Flagg argued for the joint architect-board position. On 26 April the Portland Society of Art, in which Stevens held considerable influence, announced its endorsement for the architects' request "that such an expert be secured and such a plan be made for the benefit of the city."[27] This was followed by a vote of the Civic Club of Portland to appoint a committee to attend future hearings "to safeguard the interests of the city."[28]

Following a lengthy discussion, the mayor and aldermen voted unanimously on 3 May 1912 to deny the Portland Terminal Company petition on the basis that "the railroad was proposing to let the city pay handsomely and to an unknown extent for allowing them to make some improvements in their own line."[29] The argument against the new rail line had been won on the practical Yankee terms of cost. However, it had also given birth to concepts and alliances which would have more far-reaching effects. One of the immediate tangible results was the formation of the Maine Society of Architects on 17 May 1912, with its initial membership composed of those who had signed the April petition. George Burnham was elected as the first president, and John Calvin Stevens headed the committee to prepare a constitution and by-laws. This action represented a major step in professional co-operation, which would lead to the establishment of a permanent American Institute of Architects chapter in 1935. Only twice before had Maine architects been known to work in concert: their issuance of a joint fee schedule in 1888 and their opposition in 1889 to Boston architect John C. Spofford's successful bid to design the west wing of the State House in Augusta.

Portland's hastily assembled coalition of business leaders and architects appeared to have achieved victory over the Portland Terminal Company. On 23 May 1912, the *Portland Daily Press* announced that the railroad "will abandon their route through the populous portion of Deering and run through a section that is now practically open country." In reality, the Terminal Company was regrouping to propose a far more ambitious four-million-dollar improvement plan, which comprised an expansion of Union Station and the establishment of a large freight yard on St. John Street in addition to constructing the track through the suburbs. The company outlined these plans to the Board of

Trade at a meeting on 27 November and filed a new petition with the city shortly thereafter.

The Joint Committee of the Board of Trade, the Retail Merchants Association, the Civic Club, and Maine Society of Architects lost no time in organizing against the proposal. On 30 December the group sponsored a meeting at City Hall which was attended by more than one hundred people, including Mayor Oakley C. Curtis and John Calvin Stevens. The keynote speaker, E. C. Jordan, delivered a long address in which he reiterated his opposition to the plan for the previously stated reasons of negative impact on suburban values and the crossing costs to be borne by the city. To these factors he added the new specter of a freight yard below the Western Promenade: "Picture in your mind the effect upon the area included between their proposed freight yard, engine houses and probable foundry, noisy and smoking on one side and their proposed railroad on the other, resulting in the wreckage of the street system from Longfellow Highlands to Congress Street."[30]

In the month-and-a-half between Jordan's speech and the first reading of the petition by the mayor and aldermen, an increasing chorus of voices rose against the Portland Terminal Company. The freight yard concept was especially abhorrent to several local women, who spoke their minds in letters to the press. Mary S. McCobb asked, "Shall the railroad be permitted to use the land under our Western Promenade for a freight yard, and to build its round-house close to our streets? In other words, is Portland to endure at all hours of the day and night the whistling and shrieking of innumerable locomotives?"[31] Mary Gilman Davis advanced a similar argument from the perspective of the city's sizeable tourist population:

If the Terminal proposition is carried out, what will these visitors see when they go to the Western Promenade to enjoy the far-famed view of the White Mountains, and the beautiful intervening country? They will behold acres upon acres of freight yard, reaching out from St. John Street towards Stroudwater. They will hear the noise of the ever-shifting lines of heavy freight cars, and of the puffing locomotives—but the glory of the grand panorama spread out before them will be hidden by smoke.[32]

On 17 February 1913, the mayor and aldermen held their first hearing on the new petition. After the Terminal Company made its presentation, the mayor called for questions from the aldermen and the public.

Toward the end of a lengthy discussion, Western Promenade resident Charles B. Clarke pressed the railroad's chief engineer Bertrand E. Wheeler to make the dramatic admission that the project freight yard would be the largest in Maine, handling 2,500 cars a day, of which only five hundred would serve Portland businesses. At this point, George E. Fogg, representing the coalition of opposition groups, presented a petition for postponement of the matter until it could be studied by a city plan commission with the assistance of a city plan expert. Fogg noted that this was the approach advocated the previous April by the city's architects. The coalition petition included the signatures of John Calvin Stevens, Edward F. Fassett, Frederick A. Tompson, E. Leander Higgins, and Raymond J. Mayo on behalf of the Maine Society of Architects. The mayor and aldermen responded by tabling the terminal proposal until 10 March.

In the brief interim before the next meeting, John Calvin Stevens took the lead in pursuing the question of a city plan. On 18 February, the day following the first hearing, the architect wrote to Frederick Law Olmsted Jr., asking for his assistance because "I know that you are somewhat familiar with Portland as you were interested in Mr. Baxter's project for a Boulevard around Back Cove."[33] Stevens described the railroad plan as "a radical relocation" which "some of us do not believe is the best thing for the future development of this city."[34] This plan had been countered with a proposal to appoint a city planning commission with the authority to hire an expert to help in preparing a city plan. Stevens looked to Olmsted to be that individual "because of your knowledge of the city I thought you would be better able to understand the situation quickly than any other man, beside realizing that your name and authority would go far with the citizens of Portland when your opinion is expressed."[35] Acknowledging the short time frame, Stevens urged Olmsted to come to Portland to examine the situation in order to report his initial findings at the 10 March meeting. Stevens viewed Olmsted's involvement as "the entering wedge toward the appointment of a City Planning Commission and the study of our city for proper development."[36]

John Calvin Stevens's letter received an immediate reply from John C. Olmsted, who regretted that his brother was in Panama and that he himself was recovering from surgery and could not travel. Olmsted offered the alternative of "a visit by one of our capable assistants, who would subsequently confer with us and then attend the hearing and submit a written report soon after."[37] The cost would be five hundred dollars and traveling expenses. Olmsted remarked that his firm's report "would be worth what it would cost, and perhaps more than a report by a less widely known landscape architect at the same cost," but he cautioned Stevens whether "such a report would be sufficiently weighty in its effect on public opinion to accomplish the desired purpose against the energetic opposition of the railroad people."[38]

Recognizing that "the time was so short," John Calvin Stevens wrote to John C. Olmsted on 28 February to decline his offer to send an assistant.[39] Stevens noted that he was "circulating petitions to the City Government for the appointment of a City Planning Commission, and shall fight out our battle upon that point."[40] He closed with the hope that the Olmsted firm could be engaged in the future for a "proper study of our City."[41]

In preparation for the 10 March hearing, the Joint Committee held a meeting on 8 March, which was attended by one hundred citizens. The discussion focused on the proposition of establishing a city planning commission, which would appoint a city planning expert, and a resolution to that effect was unanimously adopted. The first to speak was John Calvin Stevens, who read a paper by Carl Rust Parker that emphasized how city planning was not confined to creating "the city beautiful," but could solve many practical problems in a systematic way, resulting in both economic and aesthetic improvements. For Portland, he defined the critical issues for study as transportation, traffic in the business district, haphazard suburban development, the park and boulevard system, and public health, water, and housing. Stevens concluded with his own observations on the rapid growth of the city planning movement in the United States. He cited as an example Hartford, where the late John Carrere, architect of Portland's new City Hall, had served as the consulting expert. Stevens supplemented his remarks with a six-page report that reflected his knowledge of planning efforts in Chicago, Seattle, Buffalo, Cincinnati, Toledo, Pittsburgh, and San Francisco.

Stevens was followed by George E. Fogg of the Civic Club, who stated that Portland was faced with several major needs, including a Fore River bridge, a police station, a high school, and harbor facilities. While these appeared to be separate projects, Fogg believed that their successful achievement lay in co-ordinated planning. He noted that planning was being conducted in fifty American and European cities and declared that through its influence "the day of corporate domination is over."[42]

Strengthened by such brave words, Joint Committee supporters turned out in force for the terminal hearing on 10 March. Among them was George Fogg, who presented the mayor and aldermen with an opposition petition bearing 813 signatures. Describing the meeting as "a spirited one, applause being frequent and loud," the *Daily Eastern Argus* observed, "There was probably more wealth represented at the hearing last night than has ever been present at any hearing on any subject in the City of Portland. The railroad people with their two hundred and fifty millions on the one side were offset by the great concourse of prominent men and women of Portland, with all that they represent."[43]

Several speakers repeated objections to the adverse impact on the suburbs and the Western Promenade. E. C. Jordan and attorneys H. M. Verrill and Robert T. Whitehouse advocated that the company relocate its freight operations to the former Rigby Trotting Park in South Portland. Jordan noted that 80 percent of the freight cars were not bound for intown Portland. Verrill cited the example of Cincinnati, where an inner city freight terminal built five years before was then being removed to the outskirts. Chief Engineer Wheeler responded that the railroad viewed construction at Rigby as too costly. He then presented an offer in which the city would pay only $125,000 of the new crossing costs with the railroad assuming the balance.

The three-hour meeting concluded with the terminal question being postponed until 7 April. This gave the opposition approximately another month to pursue its case. On March 12 the Joint Committee appointed Carl Rust Parker to contact his former employer John C. Olmsted to arrange a meeting in Brookline for committee members to brief the landscape architect and ask him to file a report critical of the project. Olmsted replied that the only convincing report would be one based on a site visit and that he was now sufficiently recovered to travel to Portland. That afternoon the Joint Committee authorized Parker to engage Olmsted at a cost of five hundred dollars to visit the city the following week.

Arriving by train on the evening of 16 March, John C. Olmsted met with Carl Rust Parker in his Fidelity Trust Building office the next morning. They were joined by John Calvin Stevens, George Burnham, and H. M. Verrill. After some discussion, the five men were taken by automobile to the Western Promenade, where Olmsted agreed that "the proposed extensive freight yards will greatly damage the view."[44] The party then saw the track route from Stroudwater to Union Station and the Rigby Trotting Park. At mid-afternoon, they went to Verrill's office in order for Olmsted to meet other committee members and share his preliminary observations.

John Olmsted began by asking the group not to publish his remarks at this stage because "they were necessarily based on very superficial knowledge and were therefore purely tentative."[45] He asserted that "Mr. Stevens was quite right in saying that the City ought to postpone granting the petition of the railroad terminal company for the new locations until the whole problem had been carefully studied on behalf of the City by experts in connection with a City Plan to outline the main features of the future physical development of the city."[46] Olmsted then proceeded to affirm the Joint Committee's position that the terminal project "would be very damaging to real estate" in the suburbs and that it would "saddle permanently upon an important part of the city the damaging conditions due to the railroad, its trains, freight yard, round houses, with smoke and noise, damage to view."[47] Olmsted agreed that the Rigby site should be adopted for freight purposes and then launched into a detailed description of alternative track routes. John Calvin Stevens followed by urging that five to six thousand dollars be raised for a city plan, half by the city and the rest by public subscription. H. M. Verrill concluded the proceedings by reporting that he had indications that the railroad might withdraw its petition in the face of the continuing opposition.

While the Joint Committee respected John C. Olmsted's wishes not to publicize his preliminary findings, the members were clearly reinforced in their position by his remarks as they prepared for the 7 April hearing. During this session, their strategy was targeted on the need for a city plan. In response the aldermen gave initial approval to an order to appoint a committee to investigate the formation of a city planning commission. The committee would consist of the mayor and four aldermen, who would consult with the public works commissioner, the park commissioner, and the four organizations represented by the Joint Committee. Because Mayor Curtis was not present, the order was tabled pending his approval of its $2,500 appropriation. This action was greeted enthusiastically by the public and the press. Typical of the praise were the words of a 10 April *Portland Daily Press* editorial: "No more important action than the creation of such a committee has been made by the Portland city government in many years, and the fruit it will bear will justify the action."

Sensing defeat for the second time, the Portland Terminal Company withdrew its petition on 12 April. Company attorney David W. Snow commented bitterly to the press that "the Terminal Company felt that its efforts to improve freight and passenger facilities here were evidently not wanted by the public."[48] Ironically, the company soon heeded the advice of its critics by acquiring Rigby Park for its new freight yard. For the Joint Committee, there lay defeat in victory. With the withdrawal of the Terminal Company petition, Mayor Curtis took the short-term view that the need for city planning was over and vetoed the funds that would have made a study possible. Nearly thirty years would pass before Portland would finally adopt a planning board in 1942. Although John Calvin Stevens had died two years before, his influence lived on in the appointment of his son John Howard Stevens as the board's first chair and his son-in-law Neal W. Allen as one of its first members. The Progressive Era efforts of John Calvin Stevens and his contemporaries to protect the urban landscape they had helped to shape finally bore fruit at the outset of World War II.

During the last decade of his life, John Calvin Stevens joined with his son John Howard Stevens and his grandson John Calvin Stevens II in pursing an ill-fated Depression-era project to transform Back Cove into an elaborate recreational area. Following the initial submission of the Back Cove Recreation Park to Franklin D. Roosevelt's Public Works Administration in 1935, the *Portland Evening Express* called the proposal "a beautiful dream, to be sure, but the dream could easily come true."[49] It was this positive belief in turning dreams into realities that led John Calvin Stevens during a fifty-year period to actively participate in a series of urban landscape initiatives for Portland. A Civil War memorial for the city's major public square, an Olmsted-style green space for the Western Promenade, the defending of that area from railroad development through the concept of comprehensive city planning, a New Deal recreation park for Back Cove—these were his causes. In many cases, these projects proved to be elusive dreams which remained on paper, but Stevens's solutions for attaining them testify to his broad knowledge of the urban trends of a half-century. Imbued with the public-spirited idealism of his times, he expended his talent and his leadership in the pursuit of challenging, often unobtainable goals for the improvement of his city.

Notes

1. Edward H. Elwell, *Portland and Vicinity,* Portland, 1876, 21.
2. Willard Glazier, *Peculiarities of American Cities,* Philadelphia, 1883, 354–355.

3. For additional information on John Calvin Stevens, see: John Calvin Stevens II and Earle G. Shettleworth Jr., John Calvin Stevens Domestic Architecture 1890–1930, Scarborough, 1990. Earle G. Shettleworth Jr., John Calvin Stevens on the Portland Peninsula, Portland, 2003.

4. *Portland Sunday Times,* 15 August 1909.

5. John Neal, *Portland Illustrated,* Portland, 1874, 26.

6. *Portland Daily Press,* 17 February 1887.

7. John Calvin Stevens to Harrison B. Brown, 20 April 1887, Portland Soldier's and Sailor's Association Records, Maine Historical Society.

8. *Portland Daily Press,* 28 October 1891.

9. Willard Glazier, *Peculiarities of American Cities,* Philadelphia, 1883, 355.

10. William A. Goodwin, "Our Public Grounds," Fraternity Club Papers, Maine Historical Society.

11. Ibid.

12. Ibid.

13. *Portland Sunday Telegram,* December, 1889.

14. Ibid.

15. Ibid.

16. Ibid.

17. "Bramhall Park," Board of Trade Journal, Portland, February 1890.

18. Summer Homes. Cushing's Island, Portland Harbor, Coast of Maine, New York, 1883. The Olmsted report to the Trustees of the Cushing's Island Company was published in full in this prospectus.

19. Ibid.

20. Report of Park Commissioners, Portland, 1891, 220.

21. James P. Baxter, "Mayor's Address," Forty-Sixth Annual Report of the City of Portland, Portland, 1905, 28.

22. Susan L. Klaus, "Frederick Law Olmsted Jr., *American National Biography,* New York, 1999, 700–02.

23. William Willis, *The History of Portland,* Portland, 1865, 734.

24. "Railroad Hearing," *Daily Eastern Argus,* 16 April 1912.

25. "Petition to the Honorable Mayor and Board of Alderman, City of Portland, Maine," 23 April 1912, Stevens Collection, Maine Historical Society.

26. Ibid.

27. "Want Expert on City Planning," *Daily Eastern Argus,* 26 April 1912.

28. "The Civic Club," *Daily Eastern Argus,* 29 April 1912.

29. "Petition Turned Down," *Daily Eastern Argus,* 4 May 1912.

30. "Terminal Changes," *Daily Eastern Argus,* 31 December 1912.

31. *Portland Daily Press,* 17 February 1913.

32. "The Terminal Proposition," *Portland Daily Press,* 6 January 1913.

33. John Calvin Stevens to Frederick Law Olmsted Jr., 18 February 1913, Olmsted Papers, Manuscript Division, Library of Congress.

34. Ibid.

35. Ibid.

36. Ibid.

37. John C. Olmsted to John Calvin Stevens, 20 February 1913, Olmsted Papers, Manuscript Division, Library of Congress.

38. Ibid.

39. John Calvin Stevens to John C. Olmsted, 28 February 1913, Olmsted Papers, Manuscript Division, Library of Congress.

40. Ibid.

41. Ibid.

42. "City Planning," *Portland Daily Press,* 10 March 1913.

43. "Dramatic Incident at Terminal Hearing," *Daily Eastern Argus,* 11 March 1913.

44. John C. Olmsted, Notes of Portland Visit, March 1913, Olmsted Papers, Manuscript Division, Library of Congress.

45. Ibid.

46. Ibid.

47. Ibid.

48. "Withdraw Petition," *Portland Daily Press,* 13 April 1913.

49. "The Back Cove Project," *Portland Evening Express,* 13 July 1935.

11

From Declining Seaport
to Liberty City

Portland During Depression and War

Joel W. Eastman

Portland was already in decline before the Great Depression, but when the economic downturn hit, the city struggled to meet the needs of its unemployed. Thus, New Deal programs not only relieved the economic burden but also brought a needed investment in municipal infrastructure. However, it was federal defense spending after the outbreak of war in Europe that ended the depression in Portland and created an economic boom. Shipbuilding, in particular, created well-paying jobs, attracted outsiders, and increased population. Moreover, because Casco Bay became an anchorage for the North Atlantic Fleet and a Naval Station was established, the city benefited economically from the presence of the navy. Portland also became a liberty town for sailors whose spending further boosted the economy even as it created new problems for the city. The influx of shipyard workers and the navy created a huge housing shortage and overwhelmed the city's recreation facilities. Again, the federal government came to the aid of the city by assisting in planning, creating and funding programs to alleviate the impact of defense workers and the naval personnel on the community. The programs of the federal government during the Depression and war had a lasting impact on the city.

The Twenties and Economic Decline

On the eve of the Great Depression the city of Portland appeared to be a conservative, Republican, Anglo-American Protestant community. In

reality, immigration had produced a vigorous Democratic Catholic minority before the Civil War, which had been strengthened by arrivals
from southern and eastern Europe at the turn of the century. Portland's
population grew from 69,272 in 1920 to 70,810 in 1930, a rate well below
the national average. Although native whites made up 54 percent of the
population, the remaining 46 percent of residents included African
Americans, English and French Canadians, Greeks, Irish, Italians, Jews,
Poles, and Scandinavians.[1]

The old Yankee elite was not happy with what it saw as the corrupt
and inefficient city government that resulted from the influence of the
minority Democratic politicians. Building upon the anti-immigrant
prejudices that grew during World War I and the Red Scare, the Portland business community pushed for the creation of an efficient, professional, nonpartisan manager-council government where all council
members would be elected at large. Opponents argued that this change
was supported by the resurgent Ku Klux Klan, whose Maine headquarters was in Portland, because it would eliminate minority representation. After being narrowly defeated in a first referendum, manager-
council government was approved in a second vote and implemented in
December 1923.[2] Former mayor Augustus Moulton argued that city
manager government was accepted "because it was believed that . . . a
board of business directors could act more efficiently."[3]

The first issue the new city government had to deal with was the future of the city as a port. After seventy years of using Portland as its
winter port because of its direct rail connection to Montreal, the Canadian parliament voted in 1923 for tariff policy which would divert
shipping to its own ports of Halifax and St. John. By the next year, the
decline began, and by 1929, Canadian exports and imports disappeared
from Portland's waterfront. The city's leadership had held mixed views
on the future of its port since the turn of the century. Many believed
tourism would be a more attractive focus than cargo handling, but the
majority decided to attempt to maintain Portland's shipping business
by improving its port facilities.[4] The state's voters had approved a bond
issue in 1919 to build a modern pier and warehouse on the waterfront
which was completed in 1923. Portland City Council reached out to the
City of South Portland and created a port authority to attempt to attract
shipping to replace the Canada commerce. The joint effort produced
some short-term results, but the decline of the port continued throughout the 1920s. The port authority blamed the high wages of unionized

longshoremen and truck competition, and the two cities abandoned the port authority in 1939. In 1932, passenger boat service to Boston ended, and in 1941, the last New York coastal freighters ceased operations. Fishing, which had been Portland's first industry, also declined in the 1920s.[5]

The Great Depression

The second issue the manager-council government faced was the Great Depression. Portland's welfare services were directed by the Overseers of the Poor, as they had been for two hundred years. The "outside" poor were given aid in their homes, while the "inside" poor, with no place to live, were cared for at the city farm, home, and hospital on outer Brighton Avenue, where the former city of Deering had lodged its impoverished. The able-bodied residents worked on the farm and in the city home to produce, preserve, and prepare their own food. The first effects of the national economic decline were apparent by 1930 when the number of inside and outside poor increased by 14 percent. The city council chairman pledged that "the most rigid economy shall be practiced,"[6] and City Manager James E. Barlow worried that a tax increase might be required to provide work for the unemployed and relief for the poor. The next year Barlow warned that there was no end in sight to the economic crisis and argued that Portland's efforts compared well to those of other cities and had been accomplished "in an economical manner."[7] The city and the state both attempted to create "work relief" for the outside poor, passing bond issues to fund public improvements and then hiring unemployed citizens to perform as much of the work as possible.

By 1932 rising unemployment and failures of banks and businesses produced a major increase in city expenses and a decline in tax revenue. The salaries of all city employees were cut, and appropriations reduced "to release money for the relief of those in distress." However, the city council found the funds to purchase a tract of land along the Presumpscot River and built a municipal golf course. City leaders argued that the course would be an added attraction for summer visitors, allow citizens who did not belong to golf clubs the opportunity to play, and pay for itself. Unemployed citizens were soon put to work building the golf course, as well as maintaining and improving the city's parks, Baxter Boulevard, and promenades.[8]

In the traditional September election in 1932, Maine chose a Democratic governor and placed Democrats in two of the states' three congressional seats, but Portland Republicans won all of the city's seven state legislative seats. In the presidential election in November, the state voted for Herbert Hoover, and 60 percent of Portland voters also supported him.

The New Deal to the Rescue

Although Franklin D. Roosevelt was elected in November 1932, it was not until March 1933 that he took office, and that year saw the economy decline even further. Residents of Portland saw their incomes plummet by 30 percent. Portland fishermen experienced a 50 percent drop in income, while retail sales and tourism also declined significantly. The city's relief costs jumped by 500 percent, three major Portland banks failed, real estate values plummeted, business payrolls were cut, and local businesses were liquidated.[9] The city's $336,549 in bank deposits were impounded and only $212,114 was recovered six years later. The federal government also supplied $130,000 for work relief on public property, and had begun employing heads of families. The federal government also created a Relief Center for Homeless and Transient Men, which was carried on by the Poor Department and operated with the help of the Salvation Army, to provide meals and lodging.[10]

One of the first actions of newly elected President Franklin D. Roosevelt's New Deal in 1933 was to create the Federal Emergency Relief Administration which made grants to a state, which in turn made the funds available to cities and towns for direct relief. These grants were also used to fund some work relief, and Portland undertook a records survey and a sewing project. In early November 1933, able-bodied Maine residents were transferred from direct relief to work relief projects.[11]

City Manager Barlow announced on 9 April 1934 that the city faced "a grave problem" due to the impoundment of city funds in banks, unpaid taxes, and a deficit in the Poor Department, despite federal aid.[12] The city council authorized $250,000 in bonds to fund work relief on roads and parks "to able-bodied men receiving aid from the city." The next year Barlow claimed that "the old aversion to 'pauper relief' [has] largely disappeared," pointing out that approximately 13 percent of the Portland population "received aid in some form," and that the city had the "highest case load in the history of the Welfare Department."[13]

A more permanent work relief organization, the Works Progress Administration (WPA), finally became operational in late 1935 after some delay. The WPA operated through March 1943, peaking in December 1938 with 10,986 men and women employed in Maine.[14] WPA projects were proposed by the city, mostly for work on its infrastructure, streets, sidewalks, sewers, parks, and recreation areas. In 1936, an average of 1,100 Portland residents was working for the WPA. Needy Portland families also received $9,000-worth of WPA produced clothing and surplus food distributed by the WPA.[15]

In addition, 143 Portland young men were enrolled in the Civilian Conservation Corps. The boys were sent to camps in Maine and New Hampshire where they were fed, clothed, educated, and employed on conservation and park projects. The boys were given spending money, but their salary of $25 per month was sent to their families. The city reported that in selecting Portland candidates for the program, "preference is given to boys who are members of families on relief." In 1937, 95 percent of the 134 Portland boys enrolled came from families on relief or ones that were eligible for relief.[16]

In 1936, the Public Works and Park Departments received $86,875 in WPA funds for engineering, supervision, a portion of the wages of skilled labor, equipment hire, and some materials. Public Works used the labor for grading and sewer reconstruction. The Park Department used workers for grading and improvements at athletic fields, the golf course and the city cemetery, and for pruning and spraying of trees along city streets. The city clerk hired workers for the "copying of ancient records."[17]

The WPA's "Federal One" cultural projects were statewide, but Portland benefited greatly. Maine's Art Project created paintings and murals for two Portland hospitals. The Music Project employed one hundred persons and concentrated its concerts in the cities of Portland and Lewiston, with its bands and choruses based in these municipalities. The Writers' Project produced the first in the American Guide Series to states in 1937, and then created guides to several cities, including Portland.[18] The Public Works Administration funded the construction of buildings for federal, state and local government. Portland was granted 45 percent of the cost of a new boiler house, heating plant and laundry, and additional housing for the nurses at the city home and hospital.[19] Other projects in Portland included a building for the Maine Publicity Bureau and a number of staff residences and dormitories at the U.S. Maritime Commission Hospital at Martin's Point.

Despite the infusion of federal funds the Portland economy improved only slowly, and most citizens remained unenthusiastic about the New Deal. However, in state elections in September 1934, the Democratic governor was re-elected, and Portland Democrats put together a strong slate and won all of the city's legislative seats. In September 1936, Portland narrowly voted for the Democratic governor in the largest turnout in its history (12,514 to 12,419 for the Republican candidate), but the Democrats lost the governor's race, partly due to a financial scandal in the state house. In the presidential election in November, Maine and Vermont were the only two states that did not support Roosevelt, and Portland voters cast 55 percent of their votes for the Republican candidate.[20]

The so-called "Second New Deal" emphasized unions as a way to increase wages and improve working conditions, and unions in Portland needed assistance. In 1935, when the National Industrial Relief Administration was declared unconstitutional, most Portland employers had dropped the forty-hour week and returned to the forty-eight-hour week, throwing some workers out of jobs. Portland union members attempted to organize workers, but faced major obstacles. In 1936, the Maine Supreme Court ruled against union members picketing an open-shop theater in Portland. By 1937, Portland workers had resorted to a number of "sit down" strikes, but in April the city council "authorized" the "police to use every legal means to prevent" occupation of "stores and factories." Unions in the building and construction gained members in Portland in 1937, but this was the one of the few increases in the state.[21]

By the Spring of 1937, Portland's expenditures for relief began to decline. Then, worried about inflation, the New Deal cut back on spending, causing a recession. City Manager Barlow recalled that "at the beginning of the year business conditions had been improving and prospects for the reduction of relief looked encouraging." Then the stock market and business fell off, resulting in a sudden and severe recession. City relief expenditures increased rapidly, even with emergency allocations of WPA money.[22]

In 1937, the WPA employed 740 Portland residents. Most were laborers, but unemployed residents with a variety of skills worked for the WPA. Workers transcribed books and short stories into braille for the Maine Institution for the Blind. Housekeepers assisted families with an ill or absent spouse. Teachers taught classes in music, literacy, sewing and other subjects for adults. Workers in the Federal Surplus Commodity Program served 1,114 Portland families.[23]

In spite of the recession the city council took a bold step in 1937 by purchasing the privately owned Stroudwater Airport in 1937 and turning it into the Portland Municipal Airport. Runways were built and graded with WPA labor, and by 1938, passengers, mail, and express cargo were being shuttled between Portland and Boston and into eastern Maine.[24]

After the recession hit Roosevelt increased spending again, and during 1939 and 1940 the economy improved slowly in Portland. Banking had begun a steady recovery in 1934. Tourism increased after 1935, fully turned around by 1937, dropped as a result of the recession, and then reached a new high in 1941. Retail sales finally returned to pre-Depression levels in 1940, and lobster catches, the most important of the fish species, rebounded as well. However, in that same year the city of Portland spent $341,000 on relief, 9 percent of its budget.[25]

Defense Spending and Recovery

After Germany invaded Poland in September 1939, the Roosevelt administration turned attention from the economy to defense, and Portland benefited significantly. The Fifth Infantry Regiment, which had been garrisoned in the harbor defense forts of Portland since its return from occupation duty in Germany in 1924, was sent to defend the Panama canal, and was immediately replaced by a newly formed anti-aircraft regiment, which spend a year in Portland building itself to full strength. Then in September 1940, the 240th Coast Artillery Regiment, Maine National Guard, was called to active duty to join the regular army Eighth Coast Artillery Regiment in defending Portland Harbor. America's first peacetime draft was used to bring both regiments up to a full strength. During the fall of 1940 and winter of 1941, scores of "mobilization" buildings were constructed by private contractors to house the new recruits, providing employment for hundreds of local workers.

In the spring of 1941, another important decision was made that was to have a major impact on the city. On 15 April, the *Portland Evening Express* reported that the U.S. Navy had "selected Portland as the site of one its patrol bases . . . with the likelihood this City will become one of the principal units in a coast defense system it is expected will be set up soon." The city became the home of a U.S. Naval Station, the headquar-

ters for the Atlantic destroyer fleet, whose assignment was to escort con-
voys to Europe, and an anchorage for the Atlantic Fleet. Major construction was soon underway to build a huge refueling station on Long Island
and to construct facilities to house and train the sailors of the fleet. The
U.S. Naval Station grew to a complement of ninety officers and seven
hundred enlisted men, but thousands of sailors came to the base for
training and recreation.[26]

The army and navy ranked Portland Harbor the most important
port in the continental United States because of its proximity to Europe, and the Corps of Engineers called for bids for construction of a
mammoth modernization of the harbor defenses of Portland. Work
began on a sixteen-inch gun battery, three six–inch batteries, observation towers, and submarine mine facilities, all built of heavily reinforced concrete and carefully camouflaged. In addition, an existing
twelve-inch battery and two six–inch batteries were modernized, and
ten anti-motor torpedo boat batteries, mounting 90mm and 30mm
guns, were constructed, making Portland Harbor one of the most
heavily defended in the country.[27]

It was not federal government aid to cities and towns that ended
the Great Depression, but federal spending on defense. Between 1940
and 1941, defense spending in Maine leaped from $130,000,000 to
$500,000,000, dramatically reduced unemployment, and raised per-
sonal income to record levels.[28] Private enterprise also played a role in
the economic recovery of Portland. In May 1941, Standard Oil of New Jer-
sey revealed that due to the sinking of oil tankers on their way to Canada,
which was at war with Germany, it would build a pipeline from Portland
to Montreal to deliver crude oil to its Canadian subsidiaries. The pipeline
would not only save miles of travel by tankers through waters frequented
by German submarines, but also allow oil to be delivered during the five
winter months when the St. Lawrence River was frozen. The twelve-inch
pipeline was quickly constructed, and the first load of 80,000 barrels arrived in Montreal on 15 November 1941. The pipeline construction provided hundreds of jobs, and its operation soon made Portland one of the
largest oil ports on the east coast of the United States.[29]

However, it was a contract with the British government that
changed the area most dramatically. In the fall of 1940, William S. Newell, President of the Bath Iron Works, a shipyard in the nearby city of
Bath, was awarded a fifty-million dollar contract by the British to

build thirty cargo vessels at a site in South Portland, a project that would bring approximately five thousand well-paying jobs to Greater Portland.[30] The Roosevelt administration had approved the deal to assist Great Britain, which was losing ships to German submarines faster than it could replace them. Five days before Christmas 1940 the *Portland Evening Express* (20 December 1940) cited a rise in real estate values and increased consumer spending as an immediate result of the contract, which the paper hailed as the "greatest gift any generation here has received." The paper concluded that "a long period of prosperity for this section may well be anticipated."[31]

The construction of the shipyard had hardly started when the U.S. Maritime Commission signed a $100,000,000 contract with Newell to construct and operate a second shipyard, near the first, to build Liberty ships—cargo vessels to expand the American merchant marine.[32] As 1,500 workers rushed construction of the first yard to completion, work on the second yard began in March 1941. Three hundred construction workers labored twenty-four hours a day, seven days a week, hauling fill to reclaim a waterfront area in South Portland where the second yard would be built.[33]

William S. Newell, president of both shipyards, which eventually became merged as the New England Shipbuilding Corporation, predicted that employment would rise to 4,150 in April 1941, to 5,600 in December, and to 8,000 to 10,000 by the end of 1942.[34] However, the U.S. Maritime Commission decided to expand the second yard and allocate additional contracts to a total of 236, so that employment was projected to reach 23,000 by January 1943, and it eventually reached 30,000 persons, including 3,700 women, making it the largest manufacturing firm in Maine.[35] The yards turned out thirty ships for the British and 236 Liberty ships, 10 percent of all those built, by the end of the war. The workers at both shipyards took advantage of New Deal legislation to create unions, which worked successfully to keep wages high. Other industrial plants in the area with defense contracts created an additional 15,000 new jobs. A government survey concluded in February 1942 that "The local skilled and semiskilled labor supply has been practically exhausted and hiring is being done from outside the commuting area." Initial hopes were that the majority of workers could be found in Maine, but it soon was obvious that a substantial in-migration would have to occur in order to fill skilled jobs.[36]

Housing Workers

The in-migration of military families and workers had a major impact on the greater Portland area. The city grew from 73,643 in 1940 to 77,634 at the end of the decade. When figures for South Portland and Cape Elizabeth were added, the area grew from 92,596 in 1940 to 102,319 in 1950, a growth rate of 11 percent. Ninety-five percent of the workers migrating to Portland were employed in construction, trade, or manufacturing, and 34 percent at the shipyards. In late 1941, the migrants were able to find jobs without difficulty.[37] Finding housing was another matter.

The influx caused an immediate housing shortage. The shipyards asked the Chamber of Commerce to establish a Homes Registration Bureau to assist new workers in finding housing. In August 1941, the Bureau and local real estate agents reported that new residents who wanted to rent would have great difficulty if they had children or were unwilling to live several miles from work. Applications with the Bureau had doubled in each of the previous two months.[38] The next month the *Portland Evening Express* reported that apartment and tenement rentals were scarce and prices high, and that a building boom was underway. A local hotel had reopened, a New York bank was surveying land for "a gigantic housing project," and Boston interests were also planning a housing development. The average values of building and alteration permits were double those of the previous years.[39]

The fact that Portland and surrounding communities had become boomtowns because of the military and defense industry made them eligible for federal assistance. In September 1941, the Division of Defense Housing submitted a program for private construction to meet the housing needs of defense workers in the Portland area. The agency recommended 275 family dwelling units, to rent for less than $50 or for sale at less than $6,000.[40] On 30 December 1941, a representative of the Division of Defense Housing met with local municipal officials and announced that the office had decided that a defense housing project was necessary to alleviate a serious housing shortage and suggested that Portland and South Portland create a committee to work out the details. The Portland Chamber of Commerce protested and immediately wrote to Congressman James C. Oliver, stating that the Chamber and South Portland City Council wanted to postpone action until the Division of Defense Housing supplied data documenting a need for housing.[41]

The Chamber's complaints reflected the concerns of many area leaders. Most were Republicans who felt that New Deal Democrats were
reckless and extravagant and feared that government war projects might
drastically alter their communities. Growth was already straining municipal budgets, while high shipyard wages were making it difficult to
hire and retain government employees. Most officials assumed that the
shipyards would close after the war, and that no other manufacturing
industry would be attracted to replace them. Thus, any houses built
would deflate real estate values after the war, and damage the tax base.[42]

Congressman Oliver wrote to the Defense Housing coordinator expressing the local concerns, but was informed that a program was already being created by the Federal Housing Authority (FHA). It was
completed on 21 January 1942 and approved early the next month. The
housing proposal concluded that "vacancies have declined rapidly," and
that the "local bulk of vacancies is either substandard or on the market
at a high rent." The FHA concluded that 450 to 500 units would be required, and trailers for temporary use would be authorized to accommodate 10,000 persons.[43]

By February 1943, the FHA reported that three hundred trailers were
occupied and fifty permanent dwelling units completed. One thousand
fifty other dwelling units and 750 dormitory apartments were under
construction, and private enterprise was expected to complete 1,600
dwelling units by February. The Maritime Commission had built several
barracks-type temporary buildings at the shipyard to house workers.
Construction of a new junior high school had begun 22 December in
Portland to alleviate overcrowding by the children of war workers, and
an elementary school had been recommended for South Portland to
handle the influx of new students.[44]

Recreation and Prostitution

The influx of soldiers, shipyard workers, and sailors into greater Portland not only overwhelmed the housing supply, but also swamped the
recreation facilities as well, particularly sailors on liberty. The 65,000-
man Atlantic Fleet was divided among detachments which served for
three weeks patrolling or convoying, and then rested for one week. When
a detachment was in port, the anchorage was full of aircraft carriers, bat-
tleships, cruisers, destroyers, tankers, and supply ships, and approxi-

mately three thousand sailors were given liberty at a time. Some men met their families and went home, but most sought amusement in the city. An article in *Life* magazine in November 1941 reported, "There is not much to do in Portland. There are only two or three dance halls, which are filled to the bursting point by four in the afternoon. Then the Shore Patrol turns away the rest. And there are no girls. About 150 girls followed the Fleet from Newport, but the Portland authorities sent them back. All that is left for sailors to do is to drink beer and walk the streets."[45]

The United Service Organizations (USO) was organized early in 1941, and the Portland branches of the groups associated with the USO quickly took steps to assist servicemen, in particular, the YMCA, National Catholic Community Service, and the Travelers' Aid Society.[46] As with housing, the federal government was ready to respond to the needs for more recreational facilities. George W. Grader, the Portland Field Recreation Representative of the Federal Security Agency, reported in October 1941 that there had been no problem in providing adequate recreation until the arrival of the Navy. At that time a Citizens' Recreation Committee was created and representatives of the Army, Navy, USO, city, and the social agencies were all invited to participate.[47]

The committee decided to establish a large Soldiers' and Sailors' Recreation Center at the Chamber of Commerce building, and small centers at Portland's Masonic Temple, YWCA, Jewish Welfare Center, Boys Club, and several local churches. The National Guard Armory near the waterfront was set up with six hundred cots and blankets for enlisted men on leave, and its gymnasium was made available for recreation; the City Hall auditorium was used for dances for the officers and enlisted men of large ships in port. Grader concluded that the recreational facilities were ready for shore leave over Labor day weekend 1941 and worked well, but he cautioned that the committee had to be on alert, for without warning, large number of sailors could descend on the city when ships came in.[48]

A large percentage of the sailors on liberty and the male shipyard workers on their days off looked for female companionship, and so government officials were very concerned about prostitution and the spread of venereal disease. A study completed by Social Protection Section, Defense Health and Welfare Services, found no commercialized prostitution, no special districts, and no open acceptance of prostitution in Portland, but noted that there had been an increase in "professional clandestine activity." As far as the care and treatment of prostitutes, there were three venereal disease clinics in Portland, but the survey concluded that "local facilities are inadequate to meet the demands resulting from an increase in population."[49] A Social Protection Committee was formed by Portland Council of Social Agencies, to be made a part of the local defense council, and the committee monitored the situation through the war.[50]

What government officials described as the "girl problem" had also increased with the growth in population. A federal report concluded that a "great many transient girls have come" to the area, from instate and out, in search of boyfriends, "attracted by the glamour of a large concentration of men in the armed forces." In an average month twenty-seven females were assigned to the county Probation Department, seventeen for sex offenses; twenty-nine girls came under the jurisdiction of the Children's Service Bureau, ten for sex offenses; and seventeen came to seek help of Travelers' Aid. Local girls, aged fourteen through eighteen years, were identified as a problem, because they were unsupervised, whereas those over eighteen could participate in activities at the USO Center. Only the Portland Police Department had a program for the protection of girls.[51]

Trouble in Port City

In November 1942, the Army and Navy Munitions Board commissioned a national "Survey of Congested War Production Areas." The confidential report was issued on 15 January 1943, and included the Portland, Maine, area. The survey concluded that "the high demand for labor in the shipyards is the most serious problem in the area and has produced most of the other difficulties in community facilities and services." The report identified the major labor problem as high turnover, and blamed part of that on a lack of housing.[52]

Transportation was identified as another concern, and the report recommended additional buses and a suspension of an Office of Price Administration limit on miles driven per month for buses, and more gas and tire allotments for shipyard workers. The survey also found that the original food allotment was not adequate when "large numbers of Naval officers and men arrived in the City on leave without advance notice," causing serious food shortages. Furthermore, the report concluded that "the recreational facilities for the Navy men on leave from sea duty are not adequate."[53]

Although the report was not made public, senators and congressmen were given copies. Senator Ralph O. Brewster of Maine used this survey and other information as the basis for a lengthy report on 8 March 1943, which criticized housing, prostitution, production lags at the shipyards, fire and police protection, and overburdened schools, hospitals, and transportation. Brewster recommended that a federal Portland area director be appointed and that federal funds be used to improve health, safety, and housing. At the same time, the U.S. Army was studying venereal disease in the city and the USO ordered an examination of recreational needs. Finally, a subcommittee of the U.S. House Naval Affairs Committee announced that it would undertake its own investigation of problems in Portland.[54]

Just at the time the city was coming under close scrutiny by Congress, a series of local events occurred that drew more attention to Portland. On 12 March 1943, Captain Harold K. McGuire, of the Portland Police Department, criticized U.S. Navy shore patrolmen for not assisting police who were attempting to break up a fight among sailors in the early morning hours. They "stood around like monkeys while cops battled sailors," said McGuire.[55] Four days later, 1,500 shipyard workers rioted at a Portland theater when a midnight striptease show ended unexpectedly.[56] On 23 March, a "drunken free-for-all brawl" broke out at a waterfront diner, and when police tried to break it up, sailors called a policeman a "draft dodger" and announced that "The Navy was bigger than the police department."[57]

On 25 March, the Navy Commander denied liberty to sailors as a protest against "published articles and inhospitality," and stated that if conditions did not improve, the city would not continue to be a liberty port.[58] James C. Maher, chairman of the Chamber of Commerce, quickly arranged a conference with the navy to attempt to solve the problems.[59] Remarkably, a committee of thirty-one businessmen, professionals, and religious leaders offered its services to resolve the differences with the navy, stating that the city wanted the fleet to stay permanently. In response, the restriction on liberty was lifted, and the navy expressed hope that corrective action would be taken.[60] A conference was held aboard the flagship of the Commander, and an "amicable understanding" reached, by which a city councilor was named as a liaison between the city and the Navy.[61]

Recreation Representative Grader argued that despite recent clashes between navy and local police, the several servicemen's centers were working well and meeting the needs of the military. He concluded that problems arose because of the "Puritanical Blue Law" in Maine, which required midnight closing of bars and cocktail lounges, putting service-men and civilians out on the street after midnight. The local Defense Recreation Committee was trying to arrange to have two snack bars and lounges open from twelve midnight to 5:00 A.M. near Union Station. The navy had leased a bowling alley, roller skating rink, tap room and snack bar in Portland, and would keep it open twenty-four hours per day to help handle the flood of sailors, especially in the early morning hours.[62]

A "Colored" Community Center had been established in Portland after the arrival of the navy in 1941. At first the center was opened to both war workers and servicemen but problems developed, and it was limited to servicemen only. However, the army withdrew African American troops stationed in the area early in 1943, causing a decline in participation of men and junior hostesses. It was agreed to expand civil-ian membership again, and the center seemed to be working well, al-though it did not attract many patrons except when the fleet was in the harbor.[63] Because Portland was affected by both the military presence and war industry, the federal government commissioned the National Recreation Association to study existing recreation facilities and make recommendations for changes, and the report was published in January 1943. This was the first professional assessment of Portland's recrea-tional facilities and first comprehensive long-range plan, and it would prove useful to the city for many years.[64]

Problems Solved

By the fall of 1944, the greater Portland area had adjusted to the impact of the shipyards, the army, and the navy, three and a half years after their arrival. All these defense elements were vital to the war effort. The yards turned out the Liberty ships that carried troops and supplies to all theaters of the war. The army defended the naval anchorage, from which naval vessels left to convoy supplies to Europe and to support the invasions of Normandy and southern France. German submarines sank several vessels in the Gulf of Maine and a navy patrol boat off Cape Elizabeth, all with substantial loss of life.

In August 1945, the war was over and the shipyards, the forts, and the naval station were soon shut down. With the closing of the shipyards large-scale manufacturing ceased in the Portland area. With the closing of the U.S. Naval Station the huge invasions of sailors on liberty ended. The housing projects, however, other than the trailer parks, apartments, and shipyard dormitories, did not close. Large numbers of migrants found permanent work and chose to stay in the Greater Portland area, so that the temporary housing projects were kept open for over a decade after the end of the war until private enterprise could create sufficient housing for the additional families. Even after the temporary projects were closed, the buildings continued to be used for housing. The structures were sold, cut up into individual dwelling units, moved to various communities in greater Portland, and placed on foundations to become a permanent part of the housing supply for the area.

One of the permanent housing projects, Sagamore Village, in Portland, was purchased by the city to become its first public housing complex. The other project, Redbank, in South Portland, was sold to a private firm and continued as rental housing. Temporary army and navy buildings were sold after the war and used as summer residences and permanent housing on many of the islands. Navy buildings from Great Diamond Island were moved by barge to Portland to become the first permanent campus for Portland Junior College. Property owned by the army and navy was declared surplus, and state and local governments were able to purchase it. Maine acquired Little Chebeague Island, Jewell Island, and army land in Cape Elizabeth as state parks, and Fort Preble in South Portland as the home of a technical school. The town of Cape Elizabeth purchased Fort Williams as a park. Fort Levett and Fort McKinley became private summer and year-round condominium associations. Long Island eventually acquired the navy fuel annex as a town center and the underground navy tank farm as a recreation area.

Conclusion

Portland had been challenged and changed by depression and war, but it had survived. As a seaport in decline, it struggled to meet the needs of its citizens when the Great Depression arrived. City leaders made use of New Deal programs to help relieve the economic burden and used its own unemployed to rebuild, upgrade, and add to its municipal infrastructure. With the outbreak of World War II in Europe, federal defense spending ended the Depression in Portland and created an economic boom. Shipbuilding and other well-paying defense jobs attracted local workers and outsiders, increasing the city's population, Moreover, because Casco Bay became an anchorage for the North Atlantic Fleet, Portland benefited economically from the construction of a U.S. Naval Station and the spending of large numbers of sailors on liberty. The influx of shipyard workers and the navy created a shortage of housing and strained recreation facilities. Again, the federal government came to the aid of the city by assisting in planning, creating, and funding programs to alleviate the impact of defense workers and the naval personnel on the community.

The many federal agencies, despite their duplication and bureaucratic delay, had aided the city and suburban communities in identifying and meeting their new responsibilities. After the shipyard closed, defense contracts ended and the army and navy left, Portland slipped into stagnation as it had in the 1920s. The waterfront deteriorated, many of the city's residents moved to the suburbs, and the downtown retail district declined as consumers were attracted to new shopping centers constructed in surrounding communities. Portland's leadership would draw on the city's experience during the depression and World War II to meet this new challenge.

Notes

1. Robert W. Eisenmeyer, *The Dynamics of Growth in the New England Economy* (Middleton, Conn., 1967), 60; Edward F. Dow and Orren C. Hormell, *City Manager Government in Portland, Maine* (Orono: University of Maine Press, 1940), 7–8.

2. Dow and Hormell, *City Manager Government*, 20–21, 22, 24, 26.

3. Augustus F. Moulton, *Portland by the Sea: An Historical Treatise* (Augusta, Maine: Katahdin Publishing Co., 1926), 233–34.

4. Robert H. Babcock, "The Rise and Fall of Portland's Waterfront, 1850–1920," Maine Historical Society *Quarterly* 22 (fall, 1982), 63–98.

5. Robert G. Albion, "The Two Ports of Portland: Portland, Maine," *Ships and the Sea* 4 (1954), 48, 50;Dow and Hormell, *City Manager Government*, 10.

6. City of Portland, Maine, *Seventieth Annual Report for the Fiscal Year 1928, January 1 to December 31 and Annual Reports of the Several Departments* (Portland, 1929), 5, 17.

7. Ibid., *1931*, 5.

8. Ibid., *1932*, 4, 17, 225.

9. Richard H. Condon, "Maine in Depression and War, 1929–1945," *Maine: The Pine Tree State from Prehistory to the Present,* Richard W. Judd, Edwin A. Churchill and Joel W. Eastman, eds. (Orono: University of Maine Press, 1995), 515; Dow and Hormell, *City Manager Government,* 11.

10. *Portland Municipal Activities, 1938* (Portland, 1938), 6, 14–15; *1937,* 46; *1938,* 56.

11. Lawrence Lashbrook, "Work Relief in Maine: The Administration and Programs of the WPA," (Ph.D. dissertation in History, University of Maine at Orono, 1997), 73–74, 76.

12. City of Portland, Maine, *Seventy-sixth Annual Report for the Fiscal Year 1934, January 1 to December 31 and Annual Reports of the Several Departments* (Portland, 1936), 4, 4F.

13. Ibid., *1935,* 9–10.

14. Lashbrook, "Work Relief in Maine," 76, 96.

15. *Portland Municipal Activities, 1936,* 36; *1937,* 45.

16. Ibid.

17. Ibid., *1937,* 87, 92, 93–94.

18. Lashbrook, "Work Relief in Maine," 227, 234–37.

19. *Portland Municipal Activities, 1936,* 36, 94.

20. "Brann Victor by More Than 30,000 Votes," *Portland Evening Express,* 11 September 1934, 1; "Republicans Make Clean Sweep," *Portland Evening Express,* 15 September 1936, 1, 3; "46 States Vote For Roosevelt," *Portland Evening Express,* 4 November 1936, 1, 15.

21. Charles A. Scontras, *Organized Labor in Maine: War, Reaction, Depression, and the Rise of the CIO, 1914–1943* (Orono: Bureau of Labor Education, University of Maine, 2002), 214, 233, 233n34, 240.

22. *Portland Municipal Activities, 1936,* 11; *1937,* 4.

23. Ibid., *1937,* 45, 46, 48, 50; *1938,* 18, 54–55.

24. Ibid., *1938,* 62.

25. Lashbrook, "Work Relief in Maine," 37–38, 40, 66.

26. "Navy Picks Portland Harbor as Key Base," *Portland Evening Express,* 15 April 1941, 1, 14; "Portland Is Crowded with Sailors Back from the Sea," *Life,* 24 November 1941, n.p.; Office of Defense Health and Welfare Services, "Portland Defense Area Report," 16 February 1942, 9.

27. "Supplement to Harbor Defense Project, Harbor Defenses of Portland, Maine," Revised 11 April 1945, RG 407, Adjutant General, File 421, U.S. National Archives, College Park, Md.

28. Lashbrook, "Work Relief in Maine," 44.

29. Albion, "Two Ports of Portland," 44.

30. "Cash Is Available for Ship Contracts," *Portland Evening Express,* 19 December 1940, 1; "Newell Lauded for New Enterprise," *Portland Evening Express,* 20 December 1940, 1.

31. *Portland Evening Express,* 19 December 1940, 1; *Portland Evening Express,* 20 December 1940, 1.

32. "Shipyard Site Transferred to Todd-Bath," *Portland Evening Express,* 26 December 1940, 22; "Portland Defense Area Report," February 16, 1942, 10.

33. "Shipyard Nearing Completion as Work for Pipeline Begins: Construction On Second South Portland Plant Speeded Up on 24-hour Schedule," *Portland Evening Express,* 15 June 1941, 1, 2; "Civilian Defense Portland Industrial Plants Booming with Defense Projects," *Portland Evening Express,* 15 July 1941, 1.

34. "10,000 Jobs Possible in Shipyards: Predict Peak by End of 1942," *Portland Evening Express,* 29 October 1941, 32.

35. "South Portland Shipyard Will Build 10 More Ships," *Portland Evening Express,* 4 February 1942, 3; "Portland Defense Area Report," 16 February 1942, 10.

36. "Portland Defense Area Report," 16 February 1942, 10.

37. Federal Works Agency, "Recent Migration," 15 December 1941, 1, 6.

38. William C. A. Willman, Exec. Sec. Portland Chamber of Commerce, Portland, Maine, to Congressman James C. Oliver, Washington, D.C., 12 January 1942, National Archives, RG 212, Box 44; "Rent Dilemma For Families Critical Here: Newcomers Must Live Miles Away: Demand Redoubles," *Portland Evening Express,* 26 August 1941, 1.

39. "Portland Heading for Building Boom: Projects Under Way to House Families of Workers, Navy Men," *Portland Evening Express,* 2 September 1941, 1, 18.

40. Executive Office of the President, Office for Emergency Management, Division of Defense Housing Coordinator, C. F. Palmer, Coordinator of Defense Housing, Memorandum to the Federal Housing Administrator, Office of Production Management, Subject: "Program for Private Construction No. 2, 1 September 1941 to 1 March 1942, Portland Maine Locality," National Archives, RG 212, Box 44.

41. Willman to Oliver, 12 January 1942, U.S. National Archives, RG 212, Box 44.

42. Agnes E. Meyer, "The War's New Class Struggle: Portland, Maine, Is a Startling Example of a City Resisting Warworkers to Preserve Tottering Prewar Economy," *Washington Post,* 19 December 1943, 2B, 3B, 4B.

43. Executive Office of the President, Office for Emergency Management, Division of Defense Housing Coordinator, Portland, Maine, Locality, Prepared: 21 January 1942, Approved: 3 February 1942, 13, 14.

44. Office of Defense Health and Welfare Services, "Defense Report Supplement," 8 January 1943, 2, 3.

45. "Portland Is Crowded with Sailors Back from the Sea," *Life,* 24 November 1941, n.p.

46. "YMCA Taking Leading Part in Service Welfare Program," *Portland Evening Express,* 27 May 1941, 8; "Travelers Aid Society Has Valuable Part in USO Work," *Portland Evening Express,* 29 May 1941, 5; "Catholics Organize Vital USO Program As Part of Church," *Portland Evening Express,* 13 June 1941, np.

47. George W. Grader, Field Recreation Representative, Portland, Maine, 17 October 1941, to Mark A. McCloskey, Director of Recreation, Social Security Board, Subject: "History to Date of Portland, Maine, Recreation," National Archives, RG 215, Box 122.

48. Grader, "History of Portland Recreation," 17 October 1941; "Portland Defense Area Report," 16 February 1942, 26.

49. "Portland Defense Area Report," 16 February 1942, 27.

50. Ibid., 29, 30; Social Protection Committee of the Portland Council of Social Agencies for Office of Civilian Defense, 1942, "Social Protection Problem in Greater Portland, Me., Defense Area: Portland, Cape Elizabeth, Falmouth, Scarborough, South Portland, Westbrook," National Archives, RG 212, Box 45.

51. "Portland Defense Area Report," 16 February 1942, 29.

52. Andrews and Skidmore and Mazigan-Hyland under the Direction of Robert Moses, "Survey of Congested War Production Areas for the Army and Navy Munitions Board," 15 January 1943, Confidential, National Archives, RG 215, Box 123.

53. Ibid.

54. "Attention Focussed in Washington on City Problems, *Portland Evening Express,* 9 March 1943, 9.

55. "Navy Shore Patrol Rapped by Police," *Portland Evening Express,* 12 March 1943, 1, 14.

56. "Police Rap Theater Conditions," *Portland Evening Express,* 16 March 1943, 1.

57. "Sailors Defy Police in Brawl Along Waterfront," *Portland Evening Express,* 23 March 1943, 1.

58. "Navy Shore Liberty Here Is Abolished," *Portland Evening Express,* 25 March 1943, 1, 10.

59. "Council Will Seek to Iron Differences," *Portland Evening Express,* 25 March 1943, 1.

60. "Quick Solution Of Police-Navy Problem Urged," *Portland Evening Express,* 26 March 1943, 1.

61. "Differences Between Police, City and Navy Cleared Away," *Portland Evening Express,* 37 March 1943, 1.

62. George W. Grader, Field Recreation Representative, Portland, Maine, 7 April 1943, to Office of Administrator, Federal Security Agency, Office of Defense Health and Recreation, attn. Mark A. McCloskey, Director of Recreation, Subject: "Recreation Activity Report,"National Archives, RG 215, Box

122; "Sunday Bowling Banned by Police," *Portland Evening Express,* 11 February 1943, 3.

63. Grader, "Recreation Activity Report," 7 April 1943.

64. Richard Knowland and others, "Green Spaces, Blue Edges: An Open Space and Recreation Plan for the City of Portland" (City of Portland, Planning and Urban Development Department, 1993), 867.

12

Creating a "Gay Mecca"

Lesbians and Gay Men in Late-Twentieth-Century Portland

Howard M. Solomon

On 30 November 1990, the AIDS Project, Maine's largest AIDS service organization, held a testimonial dinner in honor of eighty-eight-year-old Portland society matron Frances W. Peabody. Peabody became an AIDS volunteer in 1985, after her favorite grandson died of the disease. She was a founder of the AIDS Project and an indefatigable support to dozens of Mainers and their families living with the disease. She was profiled in *Newsweek,* honored as one of America's "Daily Points of Light" by President George H. W. Bush, and universally idolized in Maine. "Hurricane Fran," as she became known, was presented to the crowd by her fellow AIDS activist and neighbor, John Preston. Preston's gay activism and reputation as America's "best-known gay writer" made him, like Peabody, a Portland icon.[1] Less well known, however, was the fact that much of Preston's fame, including legendary status for his S&M cult classic, *Mr. Benson,* came from his erotic novels. As America's leading gay pornographer and Portland's quintessential straight grande dame shared the platform with AIDS activists and the political and cultural elite of the city, the gay community's historically marginal status seemed to have disappeared. Two mythic figures from two apparently different worlds had helped create an image of a city that would have been inconceivable a decade before.

The creation of Portland as a gay mecca in the 1980s and 1990s is not simply a part of the broader story of the gay revolution in America, or of the emergence of Portland in the 1970s and 1980s from its long post–World War II depression. It is also about changing conceptions of how a community imagines itself, and the myths that it chooses to believe in.

As one contemporary scholar has persuasively argued, "the concept of a 'homosexual person,' defined by desire and sexual behavior, is a relatively recent historical development," barely a century old.[2] This partially explains why there are so few traces of homosexuality in Maine history before the end of the nineteenth century. The absence of lesbians and gay men from the historical record, however, is also a function of how we ask questions about the past.

Students of lesbian and gay history are interested in much more than simply "outing" forgotten lesbians and gay men. The history of sexuality obliges us to rethink the lives of *all* women and men with a more critical eye, and to recognize that categories such as femininity, masculinity, homosexuality, heterosexuality, gender, and so forth, are themselves historical constructions, constantly shifting and changing—not only in relationship to each other, but to the economic, social, cultural, and political environments, as well. For the researcher interested in the history of sexuality and gender, Maine history is fertile, if largely unexplored, territory.

Silence about sexuality, including same-sex sexuality, was lifting at the end of the nineteenth century. In the 1860s, German intellectuals invented the scientific term "homosexuality" in order to discuss same-sex behavior and identity without all the moral and religious connotations that the term "sodomy" carried. In 1892, the even newer term "heterosexuality" appeared for the first time in a medical journal in the United States.[3] Discussions of heterosexuality and homosexuality proliferated within the medical community and among lay people; the rhetoric of sexologists arguing over categories of "normal" and "abnormal," "healthy" and "pathological" flowed into arguments about politics, colonialism, race, and aesthetics as well.[4] Making such distinctions—broadly speaking, between the authentic and the inauthentic—became an obsession of American culture in the last decade of the nineteenth century and the first decades of the twentieth.

The marketing of Maine as the "Play-Ground of the Nation" was also a phenomenon of this period. In the 1890s, Cornelia "Fly Rod" Crosby traveled throughout the Northeast on behalf of the Maine Central Railroad, appearing at sportsmen's exhibitions and writing about Maine's hunting and fishing wilderness. Crosby was one of America's first professional women athletes. Described in the *New York Daily Times* in 1896 as "an athletic country girl, born in the state of Maine . . . as proud of her $1,000 collection of fishing tackle as most girls are of souvenir spoons or blue and white china,"5 her skills in hunting and fishing—and self-promotion—enabled her to challenge the conventions of gender and succeed in a male universe. Crosby's self-conscious image of authenticity was inseparable from the image of Maine she was helping to create: a vacation paradise unspoiled by the dizzying technological and social changes coursing through America's cities. Well-to-do tourists from New York, Boston, and Philadelphia could "rusticate" in Crosby's Maine, get away from it all and discover their authentic selves.

Bohemians and artists discovered Maine between the turn of the century and World War I. Photos of a summer community on Bailey Island, which attracted people from Philadelphia and Chicago, show same sex couples and drag shows.6 On Monhegan Island, at Ogunquit and Bar Harbor, colonies of bohemians and artists were flourishing. Like Provincetown, Massachusetts, in the 1930s and Fire Island, New York, in the 1940s, these were places to escape the sexual and gender strictures of middle-class America—if only for a few weeks in the summer. Life for gay people in America was like "living in the middle of an uncharted, uninhabited country," as F. O. Mathiessen wrote in 1925.7 And Maine, except for a few pockets of seasonal privilege, was no different.

Mathiessen was Harvard's "most famously homosexual professor" and the most significant literary critic of his generation.8 In 1920, he bought a house in Kittery, and there he and his partner, the painter Russell Cheney, spent their time away from Cambridge. Mathiessen and Cheney lived in Kittery (in the words of one of Mathiessen's students) as if they "had settled abroad in some richly provincial locality," with a small circle of week-end visitors and minimal interaction with the locals.9 The same could be said of the gay men who visited Ogunquit as it developed as a beach resort in the 1950s and 1960s, or lesbian notables like May Sarton or Marguerite Yourcenar, who moved to Maine in the 1960s and 1970s.10 For people "from away," the allure was Maine's beauty and solitude, the fact that it was *not* urbanized or sophisticated. Whether for a two-week holiday or to retire, they did not come to Maine to create a community with other gay people. For native-born gay people, Maine held no promise of a community of like-minded people, either. Marsden Hartley, for example, Maine's most famous artist, spent much of his life away from Maine.11 Edna St. Vincent Millay, who was notably bisexual, left her native Camden for New York as soon as she was out of high school, and never looked back.12

"Coming out"—"the process of homosexual identification as a coming to terms with an 'authentic' self"[13]—became the marker of integrity for lesbians and gay men in America, especially with the "birth of the modern gay rights movement" in the 1969 Stonewall Inn riots in New York City.[14] Coming out described not only a metaphoric journey of leaving the heterosexual "closet"—rejecting invisibility and duplicity for an open identity as a lesbian or gay man—but, often, a geographic journey as well. For many, moving to a city made coming out, and putting down roots, possible.

The nativist, populist prejudice that identifies large cities as places of danger and foreignness is deeply embedded in American culture. Add to this the fact that historians of gay history have had a big city-focus, as opposed to a small-town or rural one, and we can understand why the stereotype that gay life existed only in metropolitan areas is so ingrained.[15] When John Preston arrived in Portland in 1979, ten years after Stonewall, America was finally recognizing that there were indeed gay people outside of New York and San Francisco. Preston described his first impressions of Portland in *Hometowns: Gay Men Write About Where They Belong.*

I got my driver's license in 1961, when I was sixteen. The great activity that year was taking long trips in the family car. The periphery of my courage and my parents' patience was Portland, Maine, a hundred miles and change from our home in Massachusetts . . . It wasn't a very exciting place to go. Back then Portland was a city that had been down so long no one could imagine it would ever make it up again. Congress Street, the main street of the city, was lined with styleless shops centered around an antiquated department store. Ugly plastic facades covered most of the commercial buildings in town that were still used, vain attempts to make the structure appear up-to-date. Portland seemed, really, just a place to pass through. It was where you got the ferries to the resort islands of Casco Bay, perhaps where you changed buses to go farther north to Bar Harbor and the other seaside resorts. Portland, itself, was a destination only for traveling salesmen and teenagers who had no place better to go.[16]

Portland was little different in the early 1970s, when a new gay visibility was beginning to proliferate in big city America. Gay men frequented a couple of bars near the corner of Middle and Exchange Street in the rough-and-tumble Old Port—Tommy's Café and the Crow's Nest, "a bar remembered as 'pretty wild,' which featured a male stripper by the name of Stanley [and attracted] street people, winos and prostitutes"[17]—

or Cremo's, at the corner of High and Spring streets on the edge of the
West End, across from the Greyhound Bus Terminal. The only other evidence of a gay presence in Portland were areas around the bus terminal
and in Deering Oaks Park where men cruised for other men looking for
sex. In 1973, Roland's Tavern, on the corner of Cumberland and Forest
avenues, opened as the first bar in Maine catering to a gay clientele.
Within a few years, there would be two or three others: these bars provided the first gay-identified space in the city. Compared to the rest of
post-Stonewall America, however, Portland was still in "the dark ages,"
in Preston's opinion.[18]

In fact, it was the absence of urbane, gay sophistication that made
Portland so stimulating to Preston in the first place. He moved to Portland in 1979 to get away from the pressures of the New York literary
scene, having earlier set up a community center for gay people in Minneapolis and edited *The Advocate,* the country's premiere gay publication,
in San Francisco. Preston was attracted by Portland's rundown
nineteenth-century architecture, its cheap restaurants, its waterfront, the
Georgian homes on Park Street (where he would live), the wharves, the
winters, and, most of all, the working-class men he found in its gay bars.

At first I took it as a sign of backwardness that none of the gay men here
dressed in the fads of Greenwich Village or Castro Street. Then I got to know
more of the men and I discovered the reason . . . The men I would meet in the
bars in Portland really *were* construction workers. They drove motorcycles because they were cheap transportation, not because they were stylish. They
worked on the waterfront because the pay was good, not because it was sexy . . .
I had worried that my sexual fantasies wouldn't be possible in a small place like
Portland; instead I discovered them being lived daily by all the men with whom
I came in contact.[19]

The Portland of Preston's imagination was an eroticized Portland. It
was also, unlike New York or San Francisco, devoid of class conflict:
being gay here was "like being a member of a big club rather than being
part of an exotic minority group."[20] In Preston's Portland, gay men were
comfortable in enclaves of straight masculinity like Norm's Barber Shop
or the local post office.[21] Portland had a down-home sense of scale, "the
smallest city I could imagine living in."[22] Portland was no-nonsense
New England, a town without illusions: "My modern gay belief in the
big-city-as-Jerusalem wasn't shared by my new peers. The idea that this
was *it,* this was where we were all going to end up, bolstered my vision.

Okay, then, we damned well better make it the best place we could."
More than anyone else, Preston was responsible for recasting Maine's
reputation as an inhospitable place for gay people into an hospitable,
welcoming one. Portland was no longer "just a place to pass through," as
it had seemed to Preston in 1961: it had become the destination itself.

In the 1980s and early 1990s, gay publications throughout the United
States published Preston's "Letters from Maine." From the periphery of
Portland (the term he used to describe his first encounter with the city,
in 1961), he cast a critical eye on life in Reagan-Bush America. He wrote
about AIDS, safe-sex, lesbian-gay relations, violence against gay people
and, always, about life in Maine. A large gay audience "from away" discovered Portland—erotic, authentic, down-home Portland—through
Preston's eyes.

In 1991, a *Maine Sunday Telegram* article profiled Preston as a local
hero. The interviewer made passing reference to Preston having
"cranked out some 20 paramilitary thriller novels under pseudonyms,
which to date have sold nearly 750,000 copies." Nowhere did the article
state what many gay readers already knew—that many of these "paramilitary thriller novels" were pornographic novels, and that Preston was
the author of *Mr. Benson,* an S&M cult classic. Instead, the article presented a Preston that even the most homophobic Portlander might ad-
mire: an "unstoppable" writer of "searching, award-winning and generally unprofitable gay-oriented works," living with AIDS and "quashing
the stereotype of the rootless gay man."[23]

John Preston was Portland's most visible gay advocate in the 1980s.
He helped organize the city's first AIDS organization, spoke at the city's
first gay rights demonstration, became president of the AIDS Project,
and by the early 1990s was enjoying access to the region's political and
social leadership. Indeed, the image of Portland he conjured up for his
gay readers—minimal class animosity, unpretentious sexuality, easy acceptance of gay people by straight people—was inseparable from the
public image that Preston had fashioned for himself.[24]

"Portland as 'their Mecca north of [the] Hub'" was the optimistic
subtitle of a five-part series on "The Gay Life" in the 1980 *Portland Evening Express.* In spite of references to some new gay businesses and a live-
and-let-live attitude on the part of straight Portland, the overall tone of
the series conveyed a less positive story than that in Preston's writing.
The gay Portland described in the articles seemed to consist largely of
apolitical and anonymous men fixated on alcohol and sex, a small band

of lesbian feminists struggling to create public awareness, and a handful of straight state legislators trying to pass a human rights bill on behalf of their closeted constituents. Life in this gay mecca evidently meant staying invisible and avoiding harassment as much as possible. As the owner of Wayne's World, a gay book store, put it, "Gay pride marches are nice, but the fewer people who are bothered by us, the better."[25]

He was probably alluding to the activities of Stan Fortuna, Peter Prizer, Susan Henderson, and a handful of other gay men and lesbians who provided the first signs of post-Stonewall visibility in Portland. They were members of the Maine Gay Task Force (MGTF), which formed in 1974 and operated in loose association with the Gay People's Alliance at the University of Maine Portland/Gorham (later renamed the University of Southern Maine), which formed a year later. MGTF activists believed in high profile, direct action. They forced a local television station to pull a homophobic episode of "Marcus Welby" off the air; they picketed a bar in Ogunquit that refused to allow gay people to dance together; in 1976 they welcomed the Bicentennial Freedom Train to Portland with signs reading "Where are the Gay People? Where are the Indians?" They produced the first statewide gay publication, *MGTF Newsletter,* which eventually grew into the monthly *Mainely Gay.*[26]

The belief that gay communities developed only in urban areas, and that gay culture flowed only from city to countryside, has been a commonplace, especially since Stonewall.[27] The experience of Maine in the 1970s, however, indicates quite the opposite. There were pockets of community organizing throughout rural and small-town Maine that were as vibrant as anything happening in Portland. For example, there was Northern Lambda Nord, in Caribou; Mid-Coast Gay Men and the Susan B. Anthony Club, in Belfast; Down East Gay Alliance, in Bar Harbor; Maine Lesbian Feminists, meeting throughout the state, including Augusta and Skowhegan. Maine's first formal gay organization was in the Bangor-Orono area: the Wilde-Stein Club at the University of Maine, founded in 1973.

The Maine Gay Symposium (later, the Maine Gay and Lesbian Symposium) grew out of a conference in Orono which Wilde-Stein sponsored in 1974. For nearly two decades, Symposium (as it was commonly known) attracted Mainers as well as others from throughout northern New England and the Maritime Provinces to its annual three-day gathering. Meeting at different locations throughout the state, Symposium compensated for its lack of rootedness in a specific place with its commitment to creating a statewide community—if only for three days a year. Symposium provided a conduit through which small town and rural activists connected with Portland-based activists, and energy and ideas flowed in both directions.

By 1979, the group that had started as MGTF was defunct, and, in 1980, *Mainely Gay* folded. A new coterie of activists—many of whom had first met at Symposium—was emerging in Portland. Fred Berger, who owned Our Books, on Pine Street, ran for city council (unsuccessfully) as an "out" gay man in 1981, 1983, and 1986.[28] Lesbian feminists like Diane Elze, who had been active in Wilde-Stein in Orono, and Dale McCormick, who had been an organizer in feminist and labor circles in Iowa City before moving to Maine, both relocated to the Portland area at this time. Health care and social workers, many of them students of Richard Steinman at the University of Southern Maine, became active in the community.

The early 1980s was a key moment for the evolution of a gay community in Portland. Audacity Theater produced "Gay Side Story" and "Queer Wars." *Our Paper,* with a statewide circulation of 4,000, began publishing in 1983, in Portland.[29] Even though Maine's first indigenous case of AIDS was not reported until late 1984, a group of gay men formed the Gay Health Action Committee in 1983 to prepare for the inevitable onslaught—and in so doing learned how to build community.[30] Men and women, native Mainers as well as recent immigrants to Portland, were learning to work together.

Charlie Howard's death was a turning point in the history of gay people in Maine. Howard, a twenty-three-year-old gay man, drowned on 7 July 1984 after three male teenagers beat him up and threw him over a bridge into the Kenduskeag Stream, in downtown Bangor. Howard's murder pushed many gay Mainers out of the closet and into community activism. Grief and outrage led to public demonstrations in Bangor and Portland and catalyzed support for a statewide gay rights law (defeated four times in the state legislature since 1975), and for greater police protection against violence.[31]

On 11 July five hundred gay people and their straight allies gathered for a memorial service in Portland's First Parish Church. The organizers were terrified of being harassed when they left the safety of the church, but they knew that the occasion demanded a public demonstration.[32] The march down Congress Street to Monument Square three blocks away was the first major public demonstration in the history of gay

Portland. Two months later, the Maine Lesbian/Gay Political Alliance (MLGPA) held its first meeting, with Dale McCormick as its leader.

From the beginning, MLGPA struggled with two related challenges: creating a statewide organization in a huge, largely rural state, and resisting the tendency to become too Portland-focused. Many lesbians and gay men who were active in Bangor at the time of Charlie Howard's murder, for example, felt ignored by the early MLGPA leadership, largely focused in the Portland area.[33] MLGPA's first mailing address was a post office box in Yarmouth; then a post office box in Hallowell, five minutes from the State House in Augusta, the symbolic center of the state. In 1996, MLGPA opened a state headquarters for the first time, in Portland—acknowledging, finally, the reality that Portland was the center of Maine's gay population.[34]

Charlie Howard's death and the AIDS crisis were the two forces that created a cohort of leaders, and a sense of community, in Portland. Many of these leaders, like Preston and McCormick, were experienced activists "from away" who had made the Portland area their home; others were longtime Mainers, either Portlanders or transplants to Portland from elsewhere in the state. Unlike the experiences of gay activists in other, usually larger, cities, men and women worked together, the men often honing their organizational skills through AIDS organizations, the women often through feminist groups and MLGPA. In words that paralleled John Preston's idealization of gay Portland, McCormick told readers of the first issue of *Our Paper* in 1983 that theirs was a "much more open, much more integrated" gay community than the "very ingrown, totally separatist" one she had left behind in Iowa City.[35]

In 1987, Barb Wood ran for an at-large seat on the Portland City Council, and won, becoming the first "out" gay person elected to public office in the state of Maine. Wood had moved to Portland from Allentown, Pennsylvania, three years earlier. Through the Gay People's Alliance at USM, then through *Our Paper* and MLGPA, Wood connected with other lesbians and gay men living in her West End neighborhood, and soon became a community activist.[36] Also elected to the council in 1987 was Peter O'Donnell, born and raised on Portland's Munjoy Hill. O'Donnell was instrumental in the city council enacting the state's first local human rights ordinance in 1992. O'Donnell became Portland's first gay mayor; lesbian activist Karen Geraghty was later elected to the position, as well. Gay and lesbian activists in Portland and elsewhere in Maine were finding sexual orientation less and less a barrier to their political careers.[37]

Portland would never have a gay neighborhood on the scale of New York's Greenwich Village, Boston's South End, or San Francisco's Castro District, but by the late 1980s, the West End was the home of a critical mass of gay people. Town houses and single family dwellings could be found for a fraction of what they cost in Boston or New York, and Portland was booming. Bars like Blackstone's, Entre Nous, and the Chart Room were all in the West End. In 1992, the AIDS Project moved from Monument Square to the renovated State Street Theater building, across from the Portland Museum of Art, on Congress Street, downtown Portland's main thoroughfare. Downstairs from the AIDS Project, Drop Me A Line (a gay-owned book and stationery shop) served as an unofficial information center for all things gay in the community. A host of new galleries, restaurants, and shops revitalized this part of the city—now designated as Portland's Art District—including the Maine College of Art, which eventually bought the Porteous Building, the "antiquated department store" that Preston had seen on his first visit to Portland in 1961, and renovated it as its new home.

Barely two hundred people took part in Portland's first Gay Pride parade, on 6 June 1987. Nervous about hecklers along the route, keeping to the sidewalk and waiting patiently for the traffic lights to change, the group walked from Deering Oaks Park, on the edge of the Portland peninsula, to Monument Square. In 1990, activists marched from the front of Blackstone's on Pine Street in the West End, down one lane of Congress Street to Tommy's Park, in the newly boutiqued Old Port neighborhood on Portland's waterfront. By 1995, the parade was forming in front of City Hall, proceeding up both lanes of Congress Street and High Street, and culminating in a picnic and celebration in Deering Oaks Park. The changing route symbolized the evolution of Portland's gay community—from a hesitant, marginalized beginning, to the creation of a gay-friendly neighborhood, and, finally, to the appropriation of city government and the business district, which it now claimed as its own.

Under the leadership of Portland-area native Michael Rossetti, Southern Maine Pride developed into an annual week-long celebration. By the mid-1990s, its parade had become Portland's largest parade, attracting hundreds of marchers and groups from all over the state, and the festival in Deering Oaks Park—whose previous gay identity had been only as a place for anonymous nighttime sex—became the site of Portland's largest minority celebration. At the end of the decade, the dance party at the Maine State Pier became the hottest ticket in town, attracting three thousand people and pouring hundreds of thousands of dollars into the local economy.[38]

Pre-Stonewall notions that gay people should be secretive about their identity, or that bars were the only viable centers for organizing gay community, were still strong in Maine in the late 1980s.[39] In Portland, however, new social, cultural, and service organizations—including Southern Maine Pride—were undermining those assumptions. In a racially homogeneous state, with 96.9 percent of the population considered "white" as compared to 75.1 percent nationally, gay people became Maine's most visible minority in the 1990s.[40]

The Matlovich Society was emblematic of this new visibility. Named after Leonard Matlovich, an Air Force sergeant who fought his discharge for being gay in the mid-1970s, the group was started by Ron McClinton, a South Carolinian who had moved to Portland, and Lois Reckitt, a longtime NOW activist who had helped draft the text of Maine's first human rights bill, in 1975.[41] The group offered programs about gay history, literature, social issues, health, and politics, and regularly attracted up to two hundred people to its twice-monthly meetings in the Portland Public Library. "Matlovich" became a place where many Portland-area men and women discovered their connections to a gay community. In John Preston's words, "Just being together and not hiding . . . allows them to create a vision for their life in this small city."[42]

Preston had used the somewhat ironic "big-city-as-Jerusalem" in discussing the gay Portland he discovered in the late 1970s. Barb Wood described gay Portland as "Utopia" in *Our Paper* in 1985. In a 1993 *Casco Bay Weekly* article, Preston referred to Portland as a "Mecca" for gay men who were seeking AIDS treatment,[43] reviving the term that had been first used in the 1980 newspaper series on gay Portland. These references to holy sites and perfect cities reflected the optimism that many gay people genuinely felt about their city, but they obscured its reality, as well. Anti-gay violence, AIDS, and economic tension *were* facts of life in gay Portland, invocations of Jerusalem and Utopia and Mecca notwithstanding

In the late 1980s, the primary cruising area in Portland for men looking for sex with other men drifted from Deering Oaks Park (known as "Pickle Park") to the Western Promenade, on the edge of the West End.[44] City officials and gay men had long been at odds over cruising and sex in public areas. Gay leaders in the 1970s and 1980s, for example, repeatedly complained that police engaged in entrapment, or failed to protect men from getting beaten up. Public officials, on the other hand, claimed—with some justification—that Portland was becoming a mag-net for men from outside the city looking for anonymous sex.[45] But when cruising shifted from Deering Oaks Park, on the edge of the scruffy Parkside neighborhood, to the increasingly upscale West End, police involvement seemed to take a new, more aggressive tack.[46] Chief of Police Michael Chitwood worked hard to develop a close working re-lationship with gay leaders, but he also cultivated a reputation as a tough big city cop (he had come to Portland from Philadelphia in 1988).[47] In 1993 and 1995, Chitwood ordered his force to track the license plates of men cruising and sent them letters warning them of arrest if the behavior continued. To many gay leaders and civil libertarians, Chit-wood seemed more concerned about protecting property values than protecting gay people.[48]

Anti-gay harassment and relations with the police had long been is-sues of contention within the gay community, but nothing would affect the visibility of the gay community in Portland more dramatically than the AIDS epidemic. In 1983—two years after the first cases were reported nationally,[49] but before any AIDS cases were diagnosed in Maine—a group of Portland-area gay men organized the Gay Health Action Com-mittee, and in 1985 set up a telephone hotline. In 1986 it developed into the AIDS Project. In 1990, with a caseload of 120 clients and facing fed-eral cutbacks of up to 60 percent, the AIDS Project was in a financial and organizational crisis and needed to step beyond its activist roots and establish "financial stability, a full-time staff, and increased sup-port."[50] A fund-raising dinner to honor eighty-eight-year-old Frances W. Peabody would turn the AIDS Project around.

The widow of a wealthy shoe company owner, Peabody had been on the board of directors (and often president) of establishment organiza-tions like the Maine Historical Society, the Portland Museum of Art, the Portland Landmarks Committee, the Colonial Dames of America, and many others. When her grandson died of AIDS, in 1985, she took up the cause of AIDS activism and became a founding member of the AIDS Project. Optimistic, no-nonsense, and direct, Peabody embodied the kind of Yankee tolerance that John Preston celebrated in his "coming home" to Portland. Peabody was a comfort and inspiration to countless people living with AIDS and their families, all the time using her con-nections to raise awareness, and money, in establishment circles.

Mrs. Millard S. Peabody—barely five feet tall, an impeccably coiffed grandmother—soon became transformed into "Hurricane Fran." Even though she hated the nickname, Peabody embraced the attention it brought to AIDS-related causes, and manipulated it brilliantly.[51] She was photographed for "Franny Peabody Wants You" advertisements mimicking World War I recruiting posters; she staffed a kissing booth in a celebrity fundraiser along with police chief Chitwood; she appeared regularly in the Southern Maine Pride parade riding in a vintage convertible, bedecked in a straw hat and her trademark pink feather boa, waving to the adoring crowds. In her own way, Peabody was as much a master of self-promotion as her friend John Preston had been, and everywhere that Franny went, the press was sure to go. Her family name and civic credentials were critical to the mainstreaming of gay issues and AIDS activism in Maine. Like Preston, Peabody helped make gay Portland acceptable to straight society. The testimonial dinner raised over $50,000, brought a host of Portland leaders into the fold, and marked a turning point for the AIDS Project's future.

Reflecting what was taking place in other American gay communities, organizations such as ACT/UP, Queer Nation, and Lesbian Avengers were beginning to challenge the kind of mainstream coalition-building in Portland that had made the Peabody fundraiser such a success. On 7 October 1990, just six weeks before the dinner, ACT/UP protesters angrily confronted Jasper Wyman, head of the anti-gay Christian Civic League, when he tried to march in an AIDS coalition walkathon. Diane Elze was prominent in ACT/UP, and also worked for the AIDS Project as a case manager. She also was a leader of MLGPA—someone who could bridge different parts of the community when differences were seeming more and more intractable. When some of The AIDS Project board members admonished Elze for taking a public role in the ACT/UP demonstration, she wrote that "different strategies do create conflicts and tensions at times, and I hope we can continue to discuss our differences in a respectful manner."[52]

Conflicts and tensions within the gay community became more public in 1992, when Portland's gay rights ordinance was successfully upheld in a hard-fought citizen-initiated referendum to overturn it. Radical lesbian members of the Apex Collective, which began publishing a statewide monthly newspaper, *APEX*, in February 1992, led the criticism. At first glance, disagreement seemed to be about campaign tactics: did the gay leadership of Equal Protection Portland cede too much power to political consultants who were not gay? The issues, however, were much deeper than that: in creating a united front to withstand right-wing assaults on gay rights, were generational, economic, and sexual identity differences within the community glossed over, even silenced? Where did compromise end, and sell-out begin? In an *APEX* article entitled "Too Much Business as Usual," Bee Bell summarized the issues: "We got a homophobic campaign that mentioned the G and L words as little as possible, and aimed to trick people into voting for us out of fealty to abstract concepts—you didn't have to be for queerness, just against 'discrimination.'"53 The conflict in Portland was part of a larger, nationwide, conflict pitting transgressive, queer organizing against mainstream-oriented, equal rights–focused gay politics. The Equal Protection Portland campaign of 1992 began a decade-long, and fundamentally unresolved, debate within the Maine gay community over its internal differences and political priorities.54

The 1992 Portland referendum was followed in 1993 by a referendum in Lewiston that rolled back that city's gay rights ordinance. Statewide referenda on gay rights followed in 1995, 1998, and 2000.55 Maine was a battleground in the nationwide cultural wars of the 1990s, and Maine's gay community took a beating during the seemingly nonstop campaigns.56 Opponents of equal rights exploited the stereotype of "the two Maines"—urban/rural, north/south, rich/poor—and created a new one: gay/straight. One local anti-gay leader, Carolyn Cosby railed about "special rights" and "an invasion of carpetbaggers, homosexual militants . . . coming to Maine to BUY your vote."57 National anti-gay groups demonized "liberal Portland . . . where the gays are concentrated" as opposed to "the rest of the state of Maine—which is shot through with common sense and decency and we're in a race now to see if the rest of the state of Maine can overcome the bad apples in Portland."58 Portland as gay mecca became the right wing's Sodom and Gomorrah.

A coalition of gay and straight organizations called Maine Won't Discriminate (MWD), led by Portland attorney Patricia Peard, opposed Cosby's Concerned Maine Families in a 1995 referendum. MWD prevailed by a margin of 53 percent to 47 percent statewide. In spite of its stunning victory, MWD's middle-class, Portland-based leadership was criticized in some circles for running a calculated and conservative campaign rather than using the referendum as an opportunity to educate Mainers about the diversity within the gay community. Against the background of virulent anti-gay rhetoric from outside the community, accusations of sell-out and accommodation became common currency within, and the failure of the 1998 and 2000 campaigns made things even worse.59 The unrelenting pressure led inevitably to widespread burnout and withdrawal.

The Southern Maine Pride parade was still the most visible manifestation of gay Portland, but the spontaneity and energy of earlier celebrations were no longer present. McClinton, founder of the Matlovich Society, and Preston died in 1992 and 1994, respectively; in 1992, Elze left Maine to attend graduate school; McCormick—increasingly active in statewide politics—was no longer living in the Portland area. In a community torn by the endless referendum campaigns, there were no gay leaders who could build the bridges or command the widespread confidence within Portland as these pioneers had. Many who had been active were withdrawing from community life altogether. Maine Gay Net, an internet forum which began in 1995, provided a cyberspace community for people turned off by what was happening on the ground. *APEX* ceased publishing in 1995; *Community Pride Reporter*, which had begun publication in 1993, closed down in 1999. The Matlovich Society and Symposium both folded in 1999, as well: their "time had run out" as other, more narrowly focused organizations came into being.⁶⁰ Young people (members of Outright, for example) remained prominent in the parade, but many veterans of referenda battles and political disputes within the community were dropping out.

In 1998, at the height of her acclaim, Franny Peabody led the Southern Maine Pride parade as its Grand Marshal. Peabody was a darling of the media as well as universally respected, and so her elevation to secular sainthood was understandable. In fact, however, her public adulation in the late 1990s said as much—if not more—about conflict within the gay community as it said about her. The pressure of the nonstop campaigning was overwhelming, heightening the unresolved differences and conflicts of leadership within the community. In the analysis of sociologist Kimberley Simmons, "The complexity of the issues often seemed insurmountable and tended to get reduced to a more accessible level: power-hungry, hierarchical leaders versus a diffuse and ineffective movement. This artificial split was so-often reproduced, through conversation, media portrayals, and gossip that it took on a life of its own."⁶¹ No wonder there was a leadership vacuum: in the words of one activist, "We eat our leaders."⁶² Selfless and above the fray, Peabody evoked fantasies of a unified and apolitical gay Portland harking back to what John Preston had imagined nearly two decades before. By default much more than design, a nonagenarian straight grandmother had become the embodiment of gay Portland.

Franny Peabody died in 2001, at the age of 98. At a public memorial service in the newly renovated Merrill Auditorium, leaders of the gay community shared the stage with Peabody's children, elected officials, Police Chief Chitwood, and the Maine Gay Men's Chorus—everyone bedecked in pink feather boas. A year later, the AIDS Project became part of a new entity called the Franny Peabody Center. The AIDS Project name ceased to exist, obliterating the origin of AIDS activism in a circle of gay men nearly two decades before.

Portland in the year 2000 had become one of the most gay-friendly cities in the country. According to the 2000 census, Portland has the third-largest concentration of lesbian couples, and the tenth-largest concentration of gay male couples, of any city in the United States.[63] Lesbians and gay men were visible no longer only in the West End or Munjoy Hill. Many lived off the peninsula in single-family dwellings in Portland's North Deering, Stroudwater, and Rosemont neighborhoods; others were creating a vibrant community in the Willard Beach area of South Portland; more and more were moving to suburban settings in Scarborough, Windham, Cape Elizabeth. In addition to Portland, several of its immediate neighbors—South Portland, Long Island, Falmouth, Westbrook—were among the dozen or so municipalities in Maine that had local ordinances protecting people on the basis of sexual orientation.[64] Rainbow flags and pink triangles increasingly shared front yards with kids' bikes and barbecue grills.

The "truly renegade" notion that John Preston had insisted upon when he came to Portland in 1979—"to demonstrate proudly his identity as a gay man, but at the same time to seek—no[,] demand—membership in a hometown community"[65]—is now a reality for thousands of lesbians and gay men who call Portland their home. Three decades after Stonewall, middle-class lifestyle seems to have trumped identity politics.

Portland has become a magnet for America's new "creative class," a term economist Richard Florida used to describe the most influential members of America's changing economy.[66] "Whether they are artists or engineers, musicians or computer scientists, writers or entrepreneurs," members of the creative class "share a common creative ethos that values creativity, individuality, difference and merit."[67] Among metropolitan regions of less than 250,000 people, Portland ranks third nationally on Florida's all-important "Creativity Index."[68] Indeed, the existence of a vibrant gay community is as much a cause, as an effect, of Portland's high ranking among American cities in the postindustrial economy now emerging.[69]

In addition to their "common creative ethos," members of the creative class value authenticity in where they choose to live. In Florida's words, "They equate authentic with being 'real,' as in a place that has real buildings, real people, real history."[70] This kind of authenticity is little different from the unpretentiousness and tolerance that John Preston imagined, and Franny Peabody seemed to embody, in the creation of Portland's gay community.[71]

John Preston and Franny Peabody are no longer icons for representing an idealized gay Portland, and fantasies of Jerusalem, Utopia, and Mecca have been replaced by dollars-and-cents reality. When gay activists in the late 1970s and early 1980s first identified Maine's authenticity as its most valuable attribute, they were echoing the language of Fly Rod Crosby, and others, from nearly a century earlier. Economists and urban planners discussing Portland as a creative economy today are doing so as well—but with a difference. In creating an authentic community, lesbians and gay men have helped shape a new Portland.

Notes

1. Michael Denneny, quoted in: Brad Lemley, "A Gay Writer's Survival Guide," *Maine Sunday Telegram*, 27 October 1991.
2. Leila Rupp, *A Desired Past: A Short History of Same-Sex Love in America* (Chicago: University of Chicago Press, 1999), 8.
3. Jonathan N. Katz, *The Invention of Heterosexuality* (New York: Penguin, 1996), 19–21. Also see: David M. Halperin, *How to Do the History of Homosexuality* (Chicago: University of Chicago Press, 2002).
4. Katz, *Invention of Heterosexuality*, 81–82.
5. Quoted in: Julia A. Hunter and Earle G. Shettleworth Jr., *Fly Rod Crosby: The Woman Who Marketed Maine* (Gardiner, Maine: Tilbury House, 2000), 28. Recalling her appearance at the 1896 New York Sportsmen's Exposition, Crosby said years later: "Yes, sir, Fly Rod with her wild and wooly guides, her speaking acquaintance with the beasts and birds of the great north country, was looked upon as some aborigine! I think many were disappointed because I did not emit a war-whoop every so often. What the men thought, I can't say, but I am positive the women all regarded me as a first-class freak!" Hunter and Shettleworth, *Fly Rod Crosby*, 31.
6. "A Bailey Island Album. Snapshots of Summer." Exhibit of the Pejobscot Historical Society, Brunswick, Maine. 1997.
7. *Rat and the Devil: Journal Letters of F. O. Matthiessen and Russell Cheney*, Louis Hyde, ed. (Hamden, Conn.: Archon Books, 1978), xx.

8. Douglass Shand-Tucci, *The Crimson Letter: Harvard, Homosexuality, and the Shaping of American Culture* (New York: St. Martin's, 2003), 149-50.

9. Mathiessen's "concern with the region . . . was rather like that of an American who has settled abroad in some richly provincial locality. There were, indeed, many things about the way the household was conducted which recalled such life abroad . . . though not on any deliberate and self-conscious basis . . .'" C. L. Barber, in *Rat and the Devil: Journal Letters of F. O. Matthiessen and Russell Cheney,* Louis Hyde, ed. (Hamden, Conn.: Archon Books, 1978), 225.

10. Margot Peters, *May Sarton: A Biography* (New York: Knopf, 1997), 286-88; Josyane Savigneau, *Marguerite Yourcenar: Inventing a Life,* translated by Joan E. Howard (Chicago: University of Chicago Press, 1993), 145, 191-202.

11. "The instability of Hartley's childhood and his sense of repeated abandonment were played out when he matured—Hartley never stayed in one place for more than a year. He often found himself separated from family, lovers, and friends by untimely deaths, but just as often, he severed relationships through his own restlessness. He was always leaving town in hopes of finding a place that was more conducive to his art and life." Jonathan Weinberg, *Speaking for Vice: Homosexuality in the Art of Charles Demuth, Marsden Hartley, and the First American Avant-Garde* (New Haven: Yale University Press, 1993), 121.

12. Nancy Milford, *Savage Beauty: The Life of Edna St. Vincent Millay* (New York: Random House, 2001), 86ff.

13. Arlene Stein, *Sex and Sensibility: Stories of a Lesbian Generation* (Berkeley: University of California Press, 1997), 48.

14. David Carter, *Stonewall: The Riots That Sparked the Gay Revolution* (New York: St. Martin's, 2004).

15. See the essays in Brett Beemyn, ed., *Creating a Place for Ourselves: Lesbian, Gay and Bisexual Community Histories* (New York: Routledge, 1997).

16. "Portland, Maine," in *Hometowns: Gay Men Write About Where They Belong,* edited and with an introduction by John Preston (New York: Penguin, 1991), 321-22.

17. Randolf Dominic, "Only the Beginning," *Greater Portland,* Summer 1982, quoted by William D. Barry, *The AIDS Project: A History* (Portland: The AIDS Project, 1997), 2.

18. Quoted in: Brad Lemley, "A Gay Writer's Survival Guide," *Maine Sunday Telegram,* 27 October 1991.

19. Preston, "Portland, Maine," 326-27.

20. *The Chronicle,* 10-24 August 1983, quoted in Barry, *The AIDS Project,* 12.

21. "A New England Chorus," in: *Winter's Light: Reflections of a Yankee Queer* (Hanover and London: University Press of New England, 1995), 151-63.

22. "Portland, Maine: Life's Good Here," *Winter's Light,* 25.

23. Brad Lemley, "A Gay Writer's Survival Guide," *Maine Sunday Telegram,* 27 October 1991.

24. See Michael Lowenthal's "Introduction" to Preston, *Winter's Light*, xiii–xxi.

25. "The Gay Life: Activism Takes Variety of Forms," *Portland Evening Express*, 13 August 1980.

26. Madeleine Winterfalcon interview with Stan Fortuna and Peter Prizer, 4 June 1999, American and New England Studies, University of Southern Maine.

27. "The center is . . . the place that sets the cultural clock: events originate in the capital, and in the provinces there are only echoes and reflections—everything happens belatedly, unfashionably, and as a lame copy of the metropolitan 'real thing.' Postmodernism reverses this modernist centralism into a dispersal and decentering—not least of the metropolis itself." Paul Delaney, *Vancouver: Representing the Postmodern City* (Vancouver: Arsenal Pulp Press, 1994), quoted in: John Howard, "Place and Movement in Gay American History: A Case from the Post–World War II South," in: *Creating a Place for Ourselves: Lesbian, Gay, and Bisexual Community Histories*, Brett Beemyn, ed. (New York: Routledge, 1997), 222.

28. Our Books served as an unofficial community center for gay men, including the Gay Men's Health Collective.

29. "Right now, we are a Portland-based collective. We are keenly aware of the potential for the paper to have a Portland focus. We are committed to *not* having this happen." Editorial in the first issue of *Our Paper,* September 1983.

30. Albert Nickerson, a founder of the Maine Health Foundation: "It's unfortunate it happened in this way, but AIDS *is* making a community happen." "Responding to AIDS in Maine," *Our Paper,* November 1985.

31. Dwight Cathcart, a friend of Howard and activist in the Bangor gay community, wrote an incisive novel based on the murder (*Ceremonies* [Boston: Calamus Books, 2002]); Edward J. Armstrong recounted the murder through the experience of one of Howard's three assailants (*Penitence: A True Story* [Bangor: Lucy Madden Associates, 1994]). Unfortunately, there is no critical study of Charlie Howard's murder and its impact.

32. Conversation with Robin Lambert, 18 August 2003.

33. Mary Kay Casper, panel discussion, "Charlie Howard Twenty Years Later: How Far Has Maine Come?" University of Southern Maine, 2 April 2004.

34. In 1996 the office was at 142 High Street. In 1997, MLGPA moved to 1 Pleasant Street, sharing space in the new Peace and Justice Center with several other progressive organizations.

35. "Carpenter, Teacher, Writer: An Interview with Dale McCormick," *Our Paper,* vol. 1, no. 1, September 1983.

36. "I ran for City Council to make a statement that gays and lesbians didn't have horns, and could be contributing citizens like anyone else, and I did *not* expect to win." Interview with Barb Wood, 10 June 2004. The election was significant in other ways: for the first time in Portland history, there were five women on the nine-member Council.

37. Susan Farnsworth was the first openly gay person elected to the Maine House of Representatives, in 1988. Dale McCormick became the first openly lesbian state senator in the United States when she was elected to the Maine Senate in 1990. McCormick ran unsuccessfully for Congress in 1996; she subsequently became Treasurer of the State of Maine.

38. *Pocket Guide to the Maine Community*. Portland: Michael Rossetti, publisher, 2002.

39. Roy Cain, "Disclosure and Secrecy among Gay Men in the United States and Canada: A Shift in Views," *Journal of the History of Sexuality*, vol. 2, no. 1 (July 1991), 25–45.

40. United States Census, 2002. In 2000, 3.1 percent of Maine residents were foreign born, compared to 11.1 percent nationally.

41. Author's note: I was a founding Matlovich Society board member, and served as co-chair from 1992 to 1995.

42. Preston, "Portland, Maine: Life's Good Here," 29–30.

43. Preston, "Portland, Maine: Life's Good Here," 25; Wood: "View from My Window," *Our Paper*, June 1985; Preston: "The State of AIDS," *Casco Bay Weekly*, 26 August 1993.

44. "Gays Targeted by Portland Thugs," *Kennebec Journal*, 5 October 1990.

45. Phil Gautreau, "Crackdown in the Oaks," *Our Paper*, vol. 2, no. 7 (March 1985). Undercover police arrested seven men on 4 October 1990 for allegedly engaging in public sex on the Western Prom: only one was a Portland resident, the others from Blue Hill, Kennebunkport, Westbrook, South Portland, and Windham. "Gays Targeted by Portland Thugs," *Kennebec Journal*, 5 October 1990.

46. "Gay Men Turn to Western Prom." *Portland Press Herald*, 5 October 1991.

47. Soon after arriving in Portland, Chitwood won the respect of many gay people when he participated in an AIDS bike race, purportedly the first police chief in the United States to do so. "Chief says he'll lead AIDS bike-a-thon," *Portland Evening Express*, 19 October 1988.

48. "Western Prom 'Cruisers' Get Police Letter," *Portland Press Herald*, 28 November 1995. The article referred to the "genteel neighborhood" and "the graceful houses around the Western Promenade."

49. The literature on the history of AIDS/HIV is extensive: see, for example, Douglas A. Feldman and Julia W. Miller, eds., *The AIDS Crisis : A Documentary History* (Westport, Conn.: Greenwood Press, 1998).

50. TAP Executive Director Marjorie Love, quoted in Barry, *The AIDS Project*, 67.

51. Barry, *The AIDS Project*, 20–21, and *passim;* John Preston, "A Woman of a Certain Age," *Winter's Light: Reflections of a Yankee Queer* (Hanover and London: University Press of New England, 1995), 115–24. According to Bill Barry, Peabody "was always a bit annoyed that she and John Preston were called the 'founders' of TAP when Gary Anderson [a University of Southern

Maine student active in starting the Gay Health Action Committee] and a number of other gay men actually did the ground work." Personal communication, 23 September 2004.

52. Quoted in Barry, *The AIDS Project*, 66. ACT/UP split into two chapters in the early 1990s, ACT/UP Maine and ACT/UP Portland.

53. *APEX*, December 1992. Using the relatively new term "queer" and the acronym "LGBTQA" (lesbian, gay, bisexual, transgender, questioning, allies) was itself a challenge to the established leadership of the community. For an analysis of how these issues played out in the 1993 referendum in Lewiston, see Erica Rand, "The Passionate Activist and the Political Camera," *The Passionate Camera: Photography and Formations of Desire*, edited by Deborah Bright (New York: Routledge, 1998), 366–84.

54. Kimberley Simmons, *Grassroots Goes to the Polls: Citizen Initiative and Social Movements* (Ph.D. dissertation, Department of Sociology, University of Minnesota, 2002), 173–284. For analysis of Maine's citizen-initiated referenda within a national context, see: Bayliss J. Camp, *Direct Legislation, Lobbying and Protest: The Institutional Structuring of Political Tactics* (Ph.D. dissertation, Department of Sociology, Harvard University, 2004).

55. In 1993, after being defeated each legislative session since it was first introduced in 1975, a bill extending human rights protection on the basis of sexual orientation passed both houses of the State Legislature—only to be vetoed by Governor John McKernan. The Legislature passed an anti-discrimination bill again in 1997, which Governor Angus King signed, but it was undone by a specially called statewide referendum in February 1998. The 1998 election was the second of the three statewide referendum campaigns—the first in 1995, the third in 2000. In 1995, a gay and straight coalition called "Maine Won't Discriminate" prevailed in opposing the rollback of rights for gay people. In the referendum campaigns of 1998 and 2000, however, efforts to extend civil rights protection in employment, housing, credit and public accommodations failed.

56. Simmons, *Grassroots Goes to the Polls*, 228–64.

57. Pamphlet: "Stop Special 'Gay Rights" Status" (1995). MLGPA Papers. Lesbian, Gay, Bisexual and Transgendered Collection, Glickman Family Library, University of Southern Maine.

58. Transcript: Bob Knight, Family Research Council, speaking at Christian Civic League meeting, Bethany Baptist Church, Presque Isle, Maine, 21 September 1993. MLGPA Papers. Lesbian, Gay, Bisexual and Transgendered Collection, Glickman Family Library, University of Southern Maine.

59. Simmons, *Grassroots Goes to the Polls*, 228–64.

60. *Casco Bay Weekly*, 2 September 1999.

61. Simmons, *Grassroots Goes to the Polls*, 192.

62. Simmons, *Grassroots Goes to the Polls*, 198.

63. Kelly Bouchard, "Same-Sex Couples Drawn to Portland," *Portland Press Herald*, 14 July 2002.

64. In addition to its municipal ordinance, passed in 1992, Portland established a domestic partner registry in 2001. In 2004, Maine is the only state in New England without a human rights bill protecting people on the basis of sexual orientation.

65. Lowenthal, "Introduction," xix.

66. Richard Florida, *The Rise of the Creative Class* (New York: Basic Books, 2002), 8–12.

67. Florida, *Rise of the Creative Class*, 8.

68. Florida, *Rise of the Creative Class*, 324, 348.

69. Florida, *Rise of the Creative Class*, 255–58.

70. Florida, *Rise of the Creative Class*, 228.

71. This rhetoric of authenticity shows up repeatedly in travel descriptions of Portland. For example: "Portland is at once historic and quixotic, banal and boutique-y. It is tinged by worldly Boston but tangibly Down East. Above all, though, the coastal city of southern Maine is that much-abused adjective: real." The article concludes: "And once again you have the sense of connections that still endure, the linkages in place and time that enrich Portland's historic—and genuine—urbanity." Jane Holtz Kay, "A Rough-Hewn Maine Seaport," *New York Times*, 13 May 1990.

Epilogue

Maine, New England, and American City

Joseph A. Conforti

The gay-lesbian discovery of Portland coincided with the city's renewal from decades of economic decline and population loss. John Preston's disenchantment with life in large urban gay ghettos and his retreat to Portland were part of a larger development beginning in the 1970s that helped revitalize the city—the arrival of "lifestyle refugees." The Vietnam War–era back-to-the-land movement propelled young, often highly educated "drop outs" into rural communities in Maine and northern New England. There was also an urban counterpart to this migration. Small, safe cities with inexpensive real estate such as Portland drew educated and creative people. These migrants shunned the fast pace of large metropolitan areas not for rural life but for cities where life could be lived on a more human scale and where individuals, politicized by the Vietnam War and Watergate, could affect civic life, as Preston did in Portland. Lifestyle refugees benefited from and participated in Portland's rebirth, symbolized by the restoration of the city's Old Port.

In the 1960s, the Old Port claimed distinction as one of Portland's seediest places, a fate that befell once-thriving maritime districts in coastal cities throughout New England. Abandoned and decrepit buildings, once landmarks of Portland's recovery from conflagration a century earlier, seemed destined for demolition. Many were leveled before the Old Port began to show signs that it was not doomed. Cheap rents in the forlorn and disreputable part of the city attracted artists, craftspeople, and small entrepreneurs. They found affordable places to work and live. At the same time, real estate speculators purchased large historic buildings at sharply depressed prices. One prominent speculator recalled that the Old Port was abandoned in the evening and he tried to breathe life into his investment. "One of my tricks was to string electric wire with a bunch of light bulbs through the upper floors of the buildings. I attached a timer to it so the lights would come on in the evening and give the place an inhabited look."[1]

Real estate investors and their new commercial and residential renters helped stem the tide of demolition and urban renewal in the Old Port. By 1970, they had organized into an Old Port Association to challenge the city's redevelopment plans. As the area gradually recovered in the 1970s, the Association advocated for city improvements to the historic maritime district. Sidewalk repairs, street lights, tree plantings, and a new parking garage contributed to the Old Port's renewal. Cumberland County government gave a boost to this new momentum. In the face of protests from rural towns, one of which seceded from the county, officials approved a bond issue for the Cumberland County Civic Center built near the Old Port in 1977.[2] Civic Center events along with the growth of restaurants and bars began to revitalize nightlife, as professionals increasingly filled refurbished office space during the day.

The Old Port's block-by-block turnaround in the 1970s gained steam a decade later. Banks were reluctant to invest in early redevelopment projects, and public funds were devoted to razing the old to encourage new construction. Individual investors sparked the Old Port's renewal. After 1981, new tax incentives spurred the renovation of historic buildings. In response to a deep recession and to the flight of investment capital to the Sunbelt, Congress passed the Economic Recovery Act. The legislation offered developers major tax credits to renovate old structures. One Portland real estate investor summarized the law's significance: "it provided the financial incentive to carry the development of the Old Port beyond the sweat-equity stage."[3]

The economic booms of the mid-1980s and late 1990s accelerated the Old Port's commercial and physical rebirth. When new construction, particularly condominiums, threatened to consume the working waterfront, development was restricted to marine-related activities. Portland has preserved its historic ties to the sea. It is a vital financial, cultural, and medical center for a wide region. The city is a magnet both for tourists and for people seeking social services. We close this volume with a brief assessment of contemporary Portland as a Maine, New England, and American city.

Maine

Portland's historic status as a commercial center and the largest city in a heavily rural state has often generated tensions in Maine. As we have seen, colonial farmers resented the merchants of Falmouth Neck, who were perceived as paying low prices for agricultural products and charging high prices for imported goods. Rural envy and hostility boiled over in 1775 when the Neck's merchants were assailed for tepid support of Patriot resistance to British policies. At one point, militiamen from outlying towns pillaged the homes of wealthy residents on the Neck. When statehood was achieved in 1820, Portland served only temporarily as Maine's capital. Rural agricultural interests helped secure the relocation of the capital to Augusta in central Maine in 1832, embittering Portland's political leaders. Beginning in 1837 and continuing into the early twentieth century, Portlanders initiated unsuccessful attempts to reestablish their thriving entrepot as the state capital. The diminished political clout of what has long been Maine's financial, legal, and cultural center may be measured another way. Especially over the last two generations, Maine's largest city—twice the size of its nearest competitor—has produced only one successful gubernatorial candidate. Portland and its environs do not represent the real Maine to many rural folk north and west of the city; it is an affluent extension of eastern Massachusetts. To some, Portland is Maine's San Francisco, an ultra-liberal bayside city filled with people from away.

Populous Portland's political influence has been neutralized by a north-south divide in which small town and rural interests have often prevailed. One consequence has been a history of inadequate state support for education in Portland and southern Maine. The state's land grant university, which began as the Maine College of Agriculture and Mechanic Arts and welcomed its first students in 1868, was established in remote Orono, 130 miles north of Portland. Ten years later, the state opened a Normal School in Gorham, west of Portland, the only public institution of higher education in southern Maine for three generations.

Westbrook and Portland Junior colleges, private schools founded in 1831 and 1933, respectively, were the principal institutions of higher education in the city until 1957. St. Joseph's College, a very small Sisters of Mercy teacher training school for religious and lay women, also operated in Portland between 1912 and 1956, when it moved to Standish, west of the city. In 1957, the state created a small branch of the University of Maine in Portland, and a law school four years later. The University of Maine at Portland and Gorham State College merged in 1970. Since 1978, the institution has been known as the University of Southern Maine. It has grown significantly over the last twenty-five years, as Portland and neighboring communities have blossomed into a prosperous region with an appealing quality of life.

Yet patterns of state funding—shaped by history, geography, and politics—shortchange higher education in the population center of Maine where most new jobs and the bulk of tax revenues are generated. In recent years, the University of Maine at Orono and the University of Southern Maine have enrolled nearly the same number of students. Despite its growth, the University of Southern Maine continues to receive less than one quarter (23.2 percent) of the state budget for higher education while the northern campus controls half (50.1 percent).[4] This significant discrepancy has persisted since the creation of the University of Maine system in 1968. It cannot be fully explained by the larger number of fulltime students and doctoral programs that the Orono campus claims.

The case for inequities in funding for higher education in Maine, based on history, geography, and politics, gains credibility when it is considered in relationship to public school expenditures. State support for public schools is heavily based on property evaluations, which has fueled protests and campaigns for reform. Cities and towns along the coast and in southern Maine with high property values are considered rich, even if, as in Portland, per capita income statistics and pools of poverty suggest a more complex reality. In 2000, 28 percent of all households in Portland had annual incomes of less than $20,000.[5] Many of these families live in Portland's numerous subsidized apartments. Like other property-rich communities, Portland finances local education through real estate taxes and modest support from the state. Property-poor, mostly rural towns in northern and western Maine rely heavily on state funds.

Portland's status as Maine's major social service center further complicates the city's tax and budget problems. Portland draws homeless adults, substance abusers, troubled teenagers, and disabled people from Maine communities where social welfare programs do not exist. The city's nonprofit infrastructure removes property from the tax rolls. A local option sales tax would help relieve the property-tax burden and

Enrollment

	UMO	USM
Fall 2004	11,358	11,089
Fall 2003	11,222	11,007
Fall 2002	11,135	11,382

budgetary pressure. But a legislature with little sympathy for "rich" Portland will not even consider a local sales tax. It is no exaggeration to say that there persists in the state the spirit of those rural Mainers who expressed hostility toward Falmouth Neck merchants in 1775, later supported the relocation of the state capital from Portland, and opposed the financing of the Cumberland County Civic Center a generation ago.

Of course, for many rural people Portland is not part of the "real" Maine, which always seems to be north of where one stands. In a rural state that is 97 percent white, Portland's contemporary diversity extends the city's historic social and cultural distance from so much of Maine. The 2000 census documented that Portland has Maine's most diverse neighborhood—a consequence, in part, of the city's designation as a refugee resettlement site. A census tract along Munjoy Hill that stretches from Back Cove to Commercial Street contains a population that more resembles America as a whole than Maine: 71 percent white, 12 percent Asian, and 11 percent black.[6]

New England

The post–World War II decades were not kind to Maine or New England. Defense spending propped up the regional economy in the late 1950s and '60s, but we now recognize that the region was in the throes of deindustrialization—an economic transition that was often perceived as decline. New England appeared to be part of the Frost Belt that was being supplanted by the Sunbelt as the engine of American economic growth. The decline of defense spending with the winding down of the Vietnam War and the energy "crisis" of the early 1970s exposed New England's seemingly hollow economic core. No wonder gloom enveloped Portland and investors sought more promising places to bet on the future. Maine's deindustrialization paralleled New England's, with heavy job losses spreading from textile to shoe and eventually to paper manufacturing.

New England had been in the vanguard of America's industrialization. Not surprisingly, a new landscape of deindustrialization first emerged in the region. Though ship construction boomed during World War II, Portland had never been a major manufacturing city. As a distribution center, it had depended heavily on trade in goods that originated in other places. Commercial prosperity and geography endowed Portland with assets that acquired new value in a postindustrial economy: a scenic coastal location, maritime heritage, and distinctive built environment. The Old Port's revival announced the city's transformation into a postindustrial place offering an array of services and venues for consumption, leisure, and the arts.

The Old Port's late-twentieth-century resurgence and new cachet were part of a broader New England cultural complex: the revival of regional sentiment and the rediscovery of authentic built environments in an age of concrete, steel, and aluminum. Derelict, decayed waterfronts now became maritime versions of Fenway Park—intimate, quaint, often quirky odes to regional tradition and identity. Quaintness and heritage emerged as marketable commodities that spurred restoration, sometimes historically informed and often not, all along the New England coast. Natives, newcomers, and tourists returned to the waterfront and rediscovered the region's maritime heritage.

From Portland to Portsmouth, Newburyport to New Bedford, Newport to New London, neglected waterfronts were already astir with change in 1976 when Boston's restored 1826 Quincy Market opened. Its success heartened investors across New England. In Portland and other communities civic leaders and preservationists struggled to avoid the "seaside chic" that overran Boston—the proliferation of upscale restaurants and condominiums that displaced the working waterfront.[7] Providence, Rhode Island, undertook the region's most ambitious waterfront restoration. The long-distressed city, once an entrepot at the head of Narragansett Bay, had to uncover its upper harbor, which had been paved over in the name of progress.

Restored and sometimes gussied-up landscapes of consumption and tourism, New England's old ports resembled outdoor maritime museums—Old Mystic Seaport without an admission charge. Indeed, waterfront renewal was not the only way that New England returned to its maritime roots. The impressive growth of institutions devoted to the interpretation and display of the region's seafaring heritage paralleled the postindustrial revival of places like Portland's Old Port. Mystic Seaport, the New Bedford Whaling Museum, Salem's Peabody Essex Museum, Portsmouth's Strawbery Banke, and the Maine Maritime Museum have all undergone major expansion in recent decades. New, smaller institutions such as the Portland Harbor Museum have emerged. Portland is pursuing plans to build an aquarium on its waterfront. Throughout New England, then, seaside chic has been fueled by preservation, cultural tourism, the marketability of heritage, and a revival of regionalism that has provoked an awareness of the importance of place and a quest for historical authenticity.

American City

To be sure, such developments extend well beyond New England. We need to recall that Baltimore was the first city to revitalize its waterfront in ways that provided a model for Boston's Quincy Market, New York City's South Street Seaport, and Monterey, California's, Cannery Row. For all the talk about globalism, the revival of regional sentiment, the quest for local color and authenticity, the commodification of Americana, and the surge of heritage tourism have spread across the nation. The essays in this volume have attempted to link Portland's development to the larger currents of New England and American history. It seems appropriate to end the book with a few words about contemporary Portland as an American city.

Long a business-dominated, Yankee Republican city, Portland has become a citadel of "blue America." The city is more than reliably Democratic. Its politics—shaped by traditional Democratic constituencies, lifestyle refugees, the gay community, and the presence of a university— gravitate toward the party's progressive wing. In 2002, Portland elected the only Green Party candidate to a state legislature in the country. He was re-elected in 2004. Three members of the Green Party currently hold elected positions on the School Committee.

Portland is one of those postindustrial American places with a well-educated population, rich "human capital," and what has been called a "creative economy." A survey of two hundred American cities, completed by the Miliken Institute of California in 2004, ranked Portland twenty-second in the percentage of adults who have earned bachelor's degrees.[8] A thriving arts community is a key element in the city's creative economy. With the Maine College of Art occupying a former department store in the center of the city, an impressive new art museum for a community its size, and numerous galleries, Portland has effectively promoted the arts as means of economic development. The presence of Maine's major medical center and of a public university, two of Portland's largest employers, has attracted creative professionals and research dollars to the city. The University of Southern Maine's Muskie School of Public Service sponsored twenty-nine million dollars of externally funded research in 2004. Portland's newly established Gulf of Maine Research Institute has drawn scientists and grant money to the city.

Portland has a distinctive history, geography, and built environment, but the contemporary city also has much in common with other small urban American places.[9] Its compact geography, preserved built environment, cultural amenities, and human scale link Portland to such old and stable cities as Portsmouth, New Hampshire; Burlington, Vermont; Charleston, South Carolina; St. Augustine, Florida; and Santa Fe, New Mexico. These historic places have retained their modest size and well-defined character while offering urban amenities that include a vibrant cultural life. As Portland's lifestyle refugees discovered beginning in the 1970s, such historic urban communities of modest size are among America's most attractive, habitable places.

Notes

1. Quoted in John Harr, "Imagine a City Too Good to Be True," *New England Monthly* 2 (March 1985): 38. John McDonald, "Old Port Believers Realize Dreams," in Albert Barnes, ed. *Greater Portland Celebration 350* (Portland: Guy Gannett, 1984), 218–19.

2. Anonymous, "Civic Center Lives up to Dreams," in Barnes, ed. *Greater Portland Celebration 350,* 230.

3. Quoted in Harr, "Imagine a City Too Good to Be True," 39.

4. See *www.maine.gov/education/highered* for enrollment statistics. The office of the Chancellor of the University of Maine System supplied the budgetary percentages.

5. Tux Turkel, "View Clear for New Housing," *Portland Press Herald* (2 April 2002): 1C.

6. John Richardson, "Neighborhood Is Maine's Most Diverse," *Portland Press Herald* (3 April 2001): 1A.

7. For seaside chic and an early discussion of waterfront restoration see Jane Holtz Kay, *Preserving New England* (New York: Pantheon Books, 1986), ch. 3.

8. Edward D. Murphy, "Portland Ranks High in Job Vitality," *Portland Press Herald* (17 Nov. 2004): A1, A10. Richard Florida, *The Rise of the Creative Class* (New York: Basic Books, 2002), 8–9, 339.

9. An anonymous evaluator of the proposal for this book suggested Portland's grouping with other historic midsize cities that are well preserved.

Contributors

Emerson W. Baker is a professor and chair of the History Department of Salem State College. He received his Ph.D. in history from the College of William and Mary. He was the managing editor of *American Beginnings: Exploration, Culture and Cartography in the Land of Norumbega* (University of Nebraska Press, 1995), a History Book Club selection, and co-author (with John Reid) of the award-winning *The New England Knight: Sir William Phips, 1651–1695* (University of Toronto Press, 1998). He has been a consultant and on-camera expert for the PBS series, *Colonial House*. He is a past chair of the Maine Cultural Affairs Council and the Maine Humanities Council, and currently serves as vice-chair of the Maine Historic Preservation Commission.

Charles Calhoun is the author of *Longfellow: A Rediscovered Life* (Beacon Press, 2004), the first biography of the poet in more than forty years. Born in Louisiana, he studied history at the University of Virginia and law at Christ Church, Oxford, where he was a Rhodes Scholar. He has also written *A Small College in Maine: Two Hundred Years of Bowdoin* and a cultural guide to Maine in the Compass American Guide series. He works for the Maine Humanities Council in Portland. In 2000 he had a Research Fellowship from the National Endowment for the Humanities.

David Carey Jr. is an assistant professor of history and women's studies at the University of Southern Maine. He holds a Ph.D. in Latin American studies from Tulane University. His publications include *Our Elders Teach Us: Maya-Kaqchikel Historical Perspectives. Xkib'ij kan qate' qatata'* (University of Alabama Press, 2001), *Ojer taq tzijob'äl kichin ri Kaqchikela' Winaqi'* (A History of the Kaqchikel People) (Q'anilsa Ediciones, 2004), and *Engendering Mayan History: Mayan Women as Agents and Conduits of the Past, 1870–1970* (Routledge, forthcoming).

Donna M. Cassidy is professor of American and New England studies and of art history at the University of Southern Maine. She received her Ph.D. in art history with a specialization in American art from Boston University. Her articles on early twentieth-century American art have appeared in *American Art Journal, Smithsonian Studies in American Art, Winterthur Portfolio,* and numerous anthologies and exhibition catalogs, and she is the author of *Painting the Musical City: Jazz and Cultural Identity in American Art,*

1910–1940 (Smithsonian Institution Press, 1997). She also served as a senior consultant for the art section of *The Encyclopedia of New England Culture* (Yale University Press, 2005) and has a new book, *Marsden Hartley: Race, Region, and Nation* (University Press of New England, 2005).

Joseph A. Conforti is professor of American and New England studies at the University of Southern Maine. He received his Ph.D. in American civilization from Brown University. He is the author of five books on New England: *Beyond the City upon a Hill: New England Saints and Strangers in British North America* (Johns Hopkins University Press, 2005); *Imagining New England: Explorations of Regional Identity from the Pilgrims to the Mid-Twentieth Century* (University of North Carolina Press, 2001); *Jonathan Edwards, Religious Tradition, and American Culture* (University of North Carolina Press, 1995); *Samuel Hopkins and the New Divinity Movement: Calvinism, the Congregational Ministry, and Reform Between the Great Awakenings* (William B. Eerdmans, 1981); and *A History of East Providence, Rhode Island* (Monarch, 1976).

Eileen Eagan is associate professor of history at the University of Southern Maine and also teaches in the Women's Studies Program. She received her Ph.D in history from Temple University. She is the author of *Class, Culture and the Classroom: The Student Peace Movement of the 1930s* (Temple University Press, 1981); "Immortalizing Women: Finding Meaning in Public Sculpture," in Polly Kaufman and Katharine Corbett, eds., *Her Past Around Us: Interpreting Sites for Women's History* (Krieger, 2003), and two articles on Irish women in Portland, Maine, "Mutually Single: Irish Women in Portland, Maine," coauthored with Patricia Finn, in Michael Connolly, ed., *They Change Their Sky: The Irish in Maine* (University of Maine Press, 2004), and "From Galway to Gorham's Corner: Irish Women in Portland, Maine," coauthored with Patricia Finn, in Marli Weiner, ed., *Of Gender and Place: Women in Maine History* (University of Maine Press, forthcoming).

Joel W. Eastman is emeritus professor of history at the University of Southern Maine. He earned his Ph.D. in United States history at the University of Florida. He has published a number of articles and books on state and local history. Most recently he coedited and contributed to *Maine: The Pine Tree State from Prehistory to the Present* (University of Maine, 1996) and prepared two essays for *Bold Vision: The Development of the Portland Park System* (Greater Portland Landmarks, 1999). He wrote the script and was interviewed for the video "Portland Past" (2003) narrated by Charles Osgood.

James S. Leamon is emeritus professor of history at Bates College. He contributed to and coedited, with Charles E. Clark and Karen Bowden, *Maine in the Early Republic: From Revolution to Statehood* (University Press of New England, 1988). He is the author of *Revolution Downeast: The War for American Independence in Maine* (University of Massachusetts Press, 1993), which won the New England Historical Association's annual book award.

Maureen Elgersman Lee is associate professor of history and faculty scholar for the African American Collection of Maine at the University of Southern Maine. She received her doctorate in African and African American studies from Clark Atlanta University. She is the author of *Unyielding Spirits: Black Women and Slavery in Early Canada and Jamaica* (Garland Press, 1999), and is completing *Black Bangor: African Americans in a Maine Community, 1880–1950* (University Press of New England, 2005). She has mounted various exhibits on African Americans in Maine, and has recently directed two oral history projects with African Americans in southern and central Maine under the title "Home Is Where I Make It."

Charles P. M. Outwin is a Ph.D. candidate in American history at the University of Maine in Orono. The working title of his dissertation is "The Merchant City: Falmouth in Casco Bay, Maine, 1760–1786." His monograph, "Securing the Leg Irons: Restriction of Legal Rights for Slaves in Virginia and Maryland, 1625–1791," was published in the Winter 1996 edition of the online journal *The Early America Review*.

Kent C. Ryden is an associate professor in the American and New England studies program at the University of Southern Maine. He received his Ph.D. in American civilization from Brown University. He is the author of *Mapping the Invisible Landscape: Folklore, Writing, and the Sense of Place* (University of Iowa Press, 1993) and *Landscape with Figures: Nature and Culture in New England* (University of Iowa Press, 2001), as well as of many articles and reviews on regional and environmental topics. He is a recipient of the American Studies Association's Ralph Henry Gabriel Prize.

Earle G. Shettleworth Jr. is director of the Maine State Historic Preservation Commission. Educated at Colby College and Boston University, he is the author, coauthor and editor of numerous books on architecture and landscape in Maine. *A Biographical Dictionary of Maine Architects* (Maine State Historic Preservation Commission, 1984); *John Calvin Stevens: Domestic Architecture, 1890–1930* (Harp Publications, 1990); and *The Summer Cottages of Isleboro* (Isleboro Historical Society, 1996) are three of his publications. He has delivered hundreds of lectures on Maine architecture and is considered the leading authority on the subject.

Howard M. Solomon is scholar in residence of the Lesbian, Gay, Bisexual, and Transgendered Collection of the Jean Byers Sampson Center for Diversity in Maine at the University of Southern Maine. He is also adjunct professor of history at USM. Solomon received his Ph.D. from Northwestern University and was on the faculty of Tufts University from 1971 until 2004, when he retired as professor of history, emeritus. He is currently writing a history of lesbian and gay communities in Maine.

Index

Page numbers in *italics* represent illustrations.

Hirschmann, Johann Baptist, 146, 148, 149
Hispanics. *See* Latinos
Historical Sketch, Guide Book, and Prospectus of Cushing's Island (Sargent), 139
Historic preservation movements, xix–xx, 87, 317–18, 322
History of Portland (Willis), 176
HMS *Boxer,* 76–77
HMS *Canceaux,* 31, 56–58
HMS *Gaspee,* 50
HMS *Margaretta,* 59
Holly, Augustus, 222
"Home-Coming" (White), 182
Homer, Winslow, 137–38, 158
Homes. *See* Residential development
Homes Registration Bureau, 283
Hometowns: Gay Men Write About Where They Belong (Preston), 298
Hopper, Edward, 127
Hotel industry, 209–10, 226
House Island, xxv
Housing shortage, WWII era, 283
Howard, Charlie, 302
Hudson, John Bradley, Jr., 139, 140
Humphreys, Franklin, 220
Hunt, Richard Morris, 251
"Hurricane Fran," 295, 306–7
Hutchinson, Thomas, 52

Ice trade, 99
Ilsley, Daniel, 32
Ilsley, Enoch, 32, 47, 52, 63
Immigrants: Armenians, 160–61; artistic depiction, 151, 159; Blacks as, 221–23; and current appeal of Portland, xii; discrimination against immigrants, 101–2; diversity of, xxiv–xxv, 193–94; in eighteenth century, 26; Latino, 91, 97, 101–2, 110–15, 116; professional class, 32; and Protestants vs. Catholics, 101–2; racial hierarchies of, 105–6; and working class neighborhoods, xxi. *See also* Irish immigrants; Latinos
Imperialism of English explorers, 4
Indians. *See* Native Americans
Industrial district, xvi, xvii–xviii, 139–43
Institute of Contemporary Art, 166–67
In the Harbor (Longfellow), 74

"Intolerables" act, 52–53
Irish Heritage Center, 194
Irish immigrants: as business owners, 204, 210, 211; family dynamics of, 207, 216n70; immigration profile, 194–98; and influx of itinerant laborers, xxiv; literacy rates of, 213n15; neighborhood dynamics, xxi, 195, 202–10; and religion, 101, 197; second generation, 210–11; strike by railroad workers, 81; women's role in working class, 197–210
Islands: as art colonies, 297; Bang's Island, 16; Casco Bay, xxiii, 104–5, 138–39; cottage architecture, 104–5, 257; House Island, xxv; as Indian wars refuge, 12; Jewell Island, 289; Little Chebeague Island, 289; Long Island, 105, 281, 289; squatters on, 6–7

Jacobsen, Antonio, 140
Jewell Island, 12, 289
Jewett, Sarah Orne, 181
John and Esther Weeks with Their Son William H. Weeks (anon.), *151*
Johnson, Eastman, 83
Johnson, James Weldon, 235–36
Johnson, Rosamond, 236
Johnston, Archibald, 221
Johnston, Arthur, 226
Johnston, Henrietta, 221, 228
Jones, Ephraim, 32–33
Jones, Joseph, 222
Jones, Sarah (Mrs. T. Bradbury), 34
Jordan, Edward C., 262, 265, 269
Josselyn, Henry, 11
Josselyn, John, 11, 12
Junco, Felix, 222
Junk shops (rag sorting), 201–2

Kahill, Victor, 157
Kellogg, Rev. Elijah, 96
Kennebec Proprietors, 64–65
Kennebunkport, 157–58
Key Is Under the Flowerpot, The (Brahm), 189
Kimball, Charles Frederick, 135–36
Kimball, John, Jr., 249
King, Richard, 36–37
King Philip's War, 12